COMPLETE BOOK OF THE ZODIAC

JONATHAN CAINER

BARNES & NOBLE BOOKS
NEW YORK

To M, with love

Designed by Paul Saunders

Data manipulation by Selwood Systems, Radstock

The Library of Congress has cataloged the earlier edition as follows:

Cainer, Jonathan.
    Complete book of the zodiac / Jonathan Cainer.
       p.   cm.
    Includes index
    ISBN 0-8069-5922-3
    Zodiac. 2. Astrology. I. Cainer, Jonathan. Jonathan Cainer's
    guide to the zodiac. II. Title.
    BF1726.C37 1999
    133.5'2—dc21   99–14065
                                      CIP

10 9 8 7 6 5 4 3 2 1

This edition published in 2005 by Sterling Publishing Co., Inc.
387 Park Avenue South, New York, N.Y. 10016
First published in 1997 in Great Britain by Judy Piatkus (Publishers) Ltd,
5 Windmill Street, London W1P 1HF
© 1997 by Jonathan Cainer

ISBN 0-7607-9528-2

CONTENTS

INTRODUCTION

Welcome. This book is designed to take you on a nice, straight, safe journey through the wild and fascinating jungle of astrological knowledge.

By the time you have finished it, you should have a much greater insight into yourself. You'll know more about what makes you tick, what you're good at, what you're potentially capable of, and how you can move on to shape the kind of future you have always dreamed of. Having read it once, you can go back and use it all over again, as often as you wish, to gain a valuable understanding of the forces which shape the character of your loved ones.

However, even if you have visited this jungle before, don't assume it's safe to go wandering off on your own. You'll find lions and tigers out there in the shape of false assumptions and popular but dangerous misconceptions. You'll also discover some creatures that look pretty scary but are actually so tame that they will eat out of your hand. The tables at the back of this book fall into that category. They look big, dense, and off-putting, but I promise you they are simple to use. You'll be just fine as long as you join the tour at the beginning and stick with me, step by step, chapter by chapter.

We're going to begin with your Sun sign. That's the zodiac sign you've always related to, the one that you read about every time you open a magazine or newspaper. Next, we'll explore your Moon sign and investigate the hidden side of your personality that this powerful cosmic symbol reveals.

Then... well, I won't give you a blow-by-blow account of what's in store. I'll just trust that you're going to follow me systematically and that you're not going to go off and start skipping through the chapters unless I tell you it's safe to do so! In the first chapter, you *can* do a little bit of skipping: you don't have to read about every single sign unless you want to. Simply find your own zodiac sign and then join me again on page 85 for an explanation about how to take a big step in Chapter 2.

Chapter One

THE SECRETS OF YOUR SUN SIGN

THE SECRETS OF YOUR SUN SIGN

Before you go racing ahead to read what I've got to say about your Sun sign, let me ask you two questions:

★ Do you really know what a Sun sign is?
★ Are you 100 percent sure that you know what *your* Sun sign is?

We all read Sun sign predictions every day in the newspaper; they have become an integral part of our popular culture. It doesn't necessarily follow, though, that we all know what they are or what they mean. For example, the dates that appear underneath the name of each sign are only approximate. They vary from one publication to another, as anyone whose birthday falls close to such a date will tell you. In addition, perhaps you've heard one of the following statements:

★ "Scorpios are sex fiends."
★ "Geminis will sell their own grandmother if they think they can make a profit."
★ "Every five minutes, Leos have to look in a mirror."

I'm sorry to say that a lot of what passes for "common astrological knowledge" is actually myth, superstition, invention, or embroidery.

As we work our way through this book, you'll gradually begin to see how these outrageous myths have come about. You'll also come across a full explanation of what a Sun sign is and how it differs from a Moon sign, a rising sign, or for that matter, a "Please Don't Walk on the Grass" sign. You'll discover that in many ways you are definitely *not* typical of your sign, and you'll begin to understand why.

Please feel free now to turn to your zodiac sign, unless you're not sure that you can answer my second question. If that is the case, continue reading this page.

HAVE YOU BEEN TOLD THAT YOU WERE BORN "ON THE CUSP?"

The following does not apply to those born in the middle of any zodiac sign, but it's an all-too-painful problem for anyone born near the end of one sign and the start of another. If you fall into this category, I'm delighted to inform you that you were not born "on the cusp." Nobody ever has been nor ever will be! The "cusp," at least in this sense of the word, is an artificial invention, created to cover up the fact that the zodiac signs don't conveniently click over at midnight on a particular date. Everyone belongs to one zodiac sign and one sign only; no one is a little bit of both. It's just that the actual start and end dates of each sign can vary by quite a few hours, backwards or forwards, from year to year.

The only way to find out for sure which sign you were born under is to look up your birth date in a special table, such as the one on page 259. I know you're anxious to get started, and you probably aren't too interested in taking a detour, but I promise you it's worth the effort, and you won't find the process difficult. So, please turn now to page 258, and I'll wait here till you get back.

OK, now you know your Sun sign for certain. If your trip to page 259 just confirmed what you already thought you knew, there's no problem. But what if it has created a major identity crisis? You always thought you were an X, and it now turns out that you are a Y. Please don't panic. First, read what I've got to say about your new sign. You may find that things suddenly begin to make a lot of sense to you. Still not satisfied? Well, there could be another reason why you've always identified closely with your old sign, even though it now turns out that you don't technically belong to it. It may turn out to be your Moon sign or your Venus sign. Just keep reading the book!

ARIES
March 21 – April 20

*No Aries person will ever let a problem get the better of him for long.
No matter how daunting the task, an Aries will rise to it with enthusiasm, courage, and commitment. The Aries heart is as warm as a
summer's day. The Aries mind is as bright as a beacon. An Aries will
never let a friend suffer or an injustice go unavenged.*

ARIES people don't beat about the bush. Whether or not you
like what they have to say, at least they always say it clearly.
Energetic and impulsive, they reach conclusions swiftly; they are
quick-witted and grasp many facts in a short time.

If you want to know what it's like to be an Arian, imagine owning a Ferrari
sports car. Your vehicle is a waste of power and potential if it's not being
pushed to the limit. The temptation is to speed dangerously and brake suddenly, even on city streets. That's why Arians are often considered impatient.
It's also why they are accused of using sledgehammers to crack nuts. But
when there's a long distance to travel in a hurry, that Ferrari comes into its
own. And when there's an important task to tackle, Arians are unbeatable!
Put Arians under pressure and they'll show inspiring efficiency. If you need
to move a mountain, ask an Arian.

Arians love to be kept busy, and they like their friends to understand this.
An Arian is a powerhouse of restless energy which must be channeled con-
structively if it isn't to become self-destructive. If you are planning a party
for your Arian, make sure it's based on an event. And if you're expecting an
Arian to meet you at a certain time, be sure to provide an urgent reason why
he must be there. Better still, dare him to be on time! If you give an Arian a
chance to take the initiative, you'll never regret it.

HOME

An Arian's home can be cozy, but it is never quiet. Even in the depths of domesticity, an Aries person needs to scale the heights of challenge and stimulation.

Outside your own four walls, you may be able to take orders or to compromise. Inside them, however, you hate playing second fiddle. You need space in which to let off steam and a place where you can be in command. What's important is not where your home is or what it looks like, but who you share it with and how much respect you receive. If that's to your satisfaction, a tent in Timbuktu will bring you as much pleasure as a palace.

Your ideal house number is 10.

CLOTHES

Arians dress as they act, quickly! Usually, they wear whatever is nearest to them in the morning. When they dress up, they pick clothes which have instant impact.

Though you have enough confidence and elegance to shine in almost anything you wear, you don't much care for fancy, ornate items of jewelry or clothing. When you pick things that are plain, simple, and strong, they look great on you. Many people, for example, look uncomfortable in a big hat or unconvincing when dressed in red. You don't. You can wear red as bright as it comes and hats as big as they make them. Should the effect be too overwhelming, you can always tone yourself down or add a touch of softness just by wearing a small floral scarf, hat, or belt.

CARS

As a lively, energetic, ambitious Arian, you naturally want to live life in the fast lane. This is fine if you happen to live near Le Mans but a little frustrating if your normal circuit is a two-lane road. Your driving technique is further influenced by a tendency to treat the accelerator as if it were a bee. All you want to do is stamp on it and grind it into the floor. For some reason, this makes your passengers nervous, or it would, if it weren't for the fact that you rarely have any. They all seem to prefer the bus. In theory, you're the ideal Porsche or Lamborghini driver. In practice, you don't need such extravagant engines.

You're the only person on the planet capable of hitting warp factor 5 in a Ford Escort!

FOOD

If an army marches on its stomach, so must an Arian. Armies and Aries are both ruled by Mars, the power planet. When you're hungry, you just can't operate efficiently!

Mars, which rules your sign, has an affinity with all things hot and spicy. In theory, you're a curry lover, able to take vindaloo as hot as it comes and always happy to experiment with Mexican, Thai, or Indonesian restaurants. If you don't have an asbestos tongue, you probably show your typical Arian food traits at breakfast time. You prefer instant to perked coffee, soft boiled eggs to hard, and carton orange juice to frozen or fresh. Why? Because you can't be bothered to wait those extra few minutes. Unless someone else is doing the cooking, it's a case of the quicker it is to prepare, the better!

MONEY

"Banking establishments are more dangerous than standing armies."

"Money can't buy you friends but you can get a better class of enemy."

Although these remarks were made two hundred years apart, it's not easy to tell that the former comes from Thomas Jefferson and the latter from humorist and ecology campaigner Spike Milligan. Both are pithy, incisive, and somewhat cynical. Both reveal a great deal about the Arian attitude toward wealth. You are under no illusions about material matters. The idea of being wealthy may attract one part of your personality, but it sets off alarm bells elsewhere in your psyche. You *can* make progress, but only if you really set your mind to it. You have to create your own opportunities through hard work and, just as important, by *consistent* effort. This isn't always as easy as you might imagine, because you find yourself continually tempted to change horses in midstream or to make a series of wild, spontaneous decisions to enter new territory. You often decide that you'd rather sacrifice security and wealth for the sake of adventure, creative challenge, and/or job satisfaction. Such choices will leave you poorer in economic terms but richer in spirit. Whether or not you feel able to make certain choices depends on how strong your need is for a regular, conventional source of income.

JUST THE JOB?

Adventurer, brain surgeon, campaign manager, chimney sweep, dermatologist, diamond cutter, firefighter, hairdresser, impresario, ironworker, knife sharpener, optician, physical therapist, politician, publicist, race car driver, satellite dish installer, shepherd, sports person.

Five ways to cash in
★ Put $1 in a jar whenever you lose your temper.
★ Look in more than one store before you buy.
★ Persuade yourself that Bill Gates has upset you, and you must teach him a lesson by earning more than he does.
★ Spend less money on fast foods.
★ Form a partnership with a Virgo. This will drive you crazy, as well as make you rich, but then who says life is fair?

Four ways to branch out
★ Get a job testing sports cars for Ferrari.
★ Buy a bike and pretend you're the new Evel Knievel.
★ Get a stopwatch company to sponsor you in a fast and furious sport.
★ Run the marathon.

LOVE

Arians may get misty-eyed over love, but they're normally very down-to-earth about sex. They are demonstrative and passionate. Arians, despite their forceful nature, are incurable romantics at heart. They can be amazingly soft, tender, or sentimental.

Because your sign traditionally symbolizes new beginnings, you tend to be forever seeking the excitement of a fresh start in your relationships. You love the magical feeling you experience when you are first getting to know someone special, and if you're not careful, you'll allow this addiction to spoil your chances of long-term security. You won't have permanence in your love life until you learn to develop a mature outlook. You have to overcome your inner restlessness, your tendency to imagine that the grass is greener on the other side, and your boredom threshold. One sure way to do this is to keep a degree of tension in your closest relationships. Up to a point at least, you actually like not knowing where you stand with your partner. If nothing else, it keeps you on your toes. Consequently, even if your spouse is naturally loyal and steadfast, you subconsciously seek ways to push him to the limits of his patience. You stir up trouble and then act surprised when the sparks fly.

For this reason, you are probably best suited to someone with an equally strong need for a sparring partner. As long as your loved one also enjoys the occasional battle, power struggle, or confrontation, you can rest comparatively comfortable in a tense arrangement that would have most people desperate for a way out. But if your beloved doesn't enjoy this, you have to find a way to become more placid and predictable without fearing that your love life has grown stagnant. Almost certainly the best way involves building or creating some kind of shared challenge. United against a common enemy, you and your loved one can have all the joy of a relationship which contains the necessary tension without the unnecessary heartache.

A SIDEWAYS LOOK AT YOUR SIGN

★ "Aries people are impulsive, rash, hot-headed, excitable, overbearing bullies who never forget who their enemies are, who hate to compromise, and who refuse to take orders."

★ "Arians are wise, efficient, quick-witted, dynamic, affable people who can get along with anyone. These open-hearted, gregarious, spontaneous people rarely hold a grudge."

The two statements above nicely sum up the glaring difference between the popular myth about your zodiac sign and the stark truth. So... which is which?

I'm sure you already know the answer to that question, but to help me illustrate the point, let me tell you about two rather typical Arians I know. Their names are Robbie and Jane. They have different lives and personalities, but I think you'll soon see what they have in common with each other and with you.

Robbie, who is in his thirties, is a builder. He actually has a degree in philosophy, but he says that having stretched his mind in his youth, he now feels it important to stretch his body. He is good-humored, and his favorite phrase is, "No problem!" Robbie has bright brown eyes above a smiling, generous mouth. The good looks are typically Arian. Most people born under this sign have striking features. The talent for building is also quite typical. Not all Arians build, but they all prefer jobs which give them power over their environment. That magic phrase clinches it. Arians simply hate to be negative.

Jane is a high-flyer in the world of publishing. She's larger than life with an attractive face that radiates compassion, determination, and mischief. You wouldn't know it to look at her, but she's one of the most widely respected people in her field. When you see her at work, you realize how she has managed to work her way up from the very bottom to the absolute top. She is irrepressible and uses up more energy in a day than most people do in a week.

Jane and Robbie are two of the kindest people I know; they'll bend over backwards to help anyone. Neither of them minces words, and both have a deep belief in making the world a better place by working hard and playing fair. Like all Arians, they are almost belligerently optimistic. They don't just look on the bright side, they walk around with portable sun lamps in their pockets. Whenever they come across doom or gloom, they plug those lamps into the nearest socket and let the light shine down mercilessly until the darkness retreats. This usually makes them popular. Just occasionally, though, their zest for life irritates people. Nobody likes to look like a stick in the mud, and some people get annoyed when an Arian comes bounding along with an instant answer to a question these people have been fretting over for so long that they've begun to treat it like a pet. They forget that the Aries person is doing them a favor, and they start to think they have been robbed!

Arians, however, are not easily put off. They know they are right to trust their instincts and resent being told to forget them. They just roll up their sleeves, ignore the objections, and dive straight in. Nine times out of ten, once they've started to prove their point, the other person will follow along, which is one reason why Arians are natural leaders. On the tenth occasion, the other person will start nitpicking jealously. It's then that the Arian gets upset and says something impolite. "Humpf," says the person whom the Arian is trying to help, "aren't you an irritable so-and-so!"

And that's how the bad press starts. Now you know the truth.

TAURUS

April 21 – May 21

*A Taurean's greatest gift is his or her empathy with the natural
world. Taureans cannot help but appreciate the majesty and
magnificence of creation, and so in all they do they try to emulate
the beauty and strength that they see in nature. Taureans are loyal,
consistent, and blessed with a powerful ability to inspire others to
reach new heights.*

TAUREANS are tenacious. They know what they want and don't stop
till they get it. Of course, tenacity without capacity is pointless, but,
fortunately, Taureans are also diligent and discriminating. While
your Taurean friend probably prefers efficiency to excitement, it doesn't
mean that he or she is dull. Nothing but the best will do for Taureans. They
have insatiable appetites, not just for food, but for everything fine and
refined. Elegant eccentricity is a Taurean trademark.

It's not easy to explain why Taureans are so acquisitive and earthy, yet so
creative and ethereal. But it's easy for Taureans to be this way. They don't
see it as a problem, and neither should you. If there's a drawback to being a
bull, it's moodiness. When Taureans aren't plodding slowly but surely
towards a goal, they can be melancholic or morose. These patient people
always need to feel they are getting somewhere.

Taureans gain a vital sense of identity and security from their possessions,
so if you want to give your Taurean friend a real thrill, give him or her something to complete or complement a collection. Taureans also collect experiences. The ideal gift could well be a thoughtfully arranged party or outing
or perhaps a rare chance to experience a very special luxury.

HOME

Even a Taurean with a humble abode will manage to furnish it and decorate it more grandly than a palace. Taureans not only love luxury, they insist on it.

When you're choosing a home, the key question is not so much, "Will it house my family?" as "Will it house the paraphernalia I've been gathering over all these years?" You collect knickknacks faster than a carpenter could put up shelves to display them. It's a shame because, if you could only pare down your possessions, you might fit nicely into a rustic cottage. It wouldn't need roses round the door (with your gardening skill, you could soon grow these), but it would need to have a big garden and a spacious kitchen (see Food).

Your ideal house number is 50. (This always scores in the bull's-eye!)

CLOTHES

Although Taureans know how to dress immaculately, they don't normally like to be too bright or bold. They prefer smart but muted clothes.

On special occasions, some people wear silk, velvet, and lace, materials which tend to make most of us look vulnerable and sensitive. When you wear them, however, you usually look affluent, creative, and confident, especially when you pick them in deep, rich colors. Your ideal accessory ought to be a necklace, cravat, or choker. Taurus rules the throat, and though you may not realize this, your neck has the potential to be one of your most impressive assets. You also often need to pick clothes that flatter your figure (see Food).

CARS

As a sensual, refined Taurean, you like a car with style and elegance. Ideally, you would drive a restored masterpiece from a bygone era: perhaps an early Jaguar or an Austin Cambridge. Only two problems prevent you from following up on this idea: the mpg and the gpm (garage hours per month). Thus, your natural pragmatism reluctantly steers you towards the more reliable and economical car. With these, your choice is likely to be based on driver comfort: the softness of the seats, the visual line of the interior design, and the amount of room in the driver's door for king-sized bags of candy (see Food). Big engines don't particularly excite you because you drive as you live: sedately, gracefully, and, just occasionally when heavy traffic demands it, creatively.

FOOD

Gourmet foods naturally suit the Taurean palate. You like to savor your meals, and you have an insatiable appetite for the finest cuisine.

Taurus is traditionally the sign of the gourmet. Some might argue it is also the sign of the goose. However, in all fairness, though you love to tickle your tastebuds, you can usually stop while you can still see your toes in the shower. Your favorite foods tend to be exotic. Given the opportunity, you'd live on a diet of asparagus, caviar, blueberries, mangoes, and quail's eggs. Every night, you'd eat at a different upscale restaurant, and you'd wash it all down with the most extravagant wine money can buy. And for dessert? It has to be chocolate. For all your refinement, you have a terrible sweet tooth.

MONEY

The successful conduct of an industrial enterprise requires two distinct qualifications: fidelity and zeal.

These wise words come from your fellow Taurean John Stuart Mill, one of the leading economists of the nineteenth century. I quote them partly to illustrate your sign's long history of shrewd financial thinking and partly because the quote includes two key words which capture the essence of a Taurean's innate ability to make money. Whether or not he realized it, when Mill chose those words, "fidelity" and "zeal," he was naming the strongest qualities of your sign.

When you believe in something, you stick with it long after more weak-willed individuals might have given up the ghost. Although this occasionally puts you at a temporary disadvantage (you are not always able or inclined to drop your commitments and pursue a sudden offer), in the long term it is a surefire formula. You have the potential, as part of a strong, successful team, to generate a lot of wealth, to rise in status, to become more secure, and to see difficult projects through to successful conclusions. Your capacity to fulfill this potential, however, tends to hinge almost entirely on your ability to sacrifice, temporarily at least, the desire for greater independence and freedom.

JUST THE JOB?

Actor, antique dealer, architect, art collector, artist, auctioneer, baker, banker, blacksmith, candy maker, carpenter, carpet designer, cattle breeder, chef, dancer, farmer, financier, gardener, jeweler, loan shark, musician, nurse, pianist, sculptor, singer, throat specialist, treasurer, vocal coach, yodeler.

Five ways to cash in
- ★ Stop working to pay for your all-consuming hobby.
- ★ Start making your all-consuming hobby pay its way.
- ★ Stop undervaluing your natural talent.
- ★ Start charging for the advice you dish out so readily, particularly to people who don't deserve it.
- ★ Stop feeling so responsible for improving things for others.

Five ways to branch out
- ★ Become a buyer for a gourmet food store.
- ★ Become an appraiser for Christie's, the auctioneers.
- ★ Become the conductor of the New York Philharmonic Orchestra.
- ★ Become the conductor of the Long Island Railroad. (You like collecting money.)
- ★ Become famous for your natural sex appeal; it's your best asset.

LOVE

Taureans are rather possessive. They cherish the things they own, but sometimes they mistakenly think they own another person.

Ironically, the biggest single obstacle to harmony in your love life is your innate and powerful desire for stability. Because you are so anxious to keep magic alive, you tend to resent anything that seems, even vaguely, to threaten the emotional status quo. For you, it's a case of better the devil you know than the one you don't; and that means the reliable hatchback is often better than the trouble-prone sports car.

Why should this pose a problem? Because the only thing we can all be sure of in this uncertain world is that every situation, every person, and even every partnership will eventually change. As a Taurean, you are first and foremost a consolidator. Your instinct is to preserve and protect, to keep and collect. If your partner is of a more adventurous or experimental disposition, you are probably perpetually nervous. And yet, if your partner is equally conservative in outlook, you run the risk of winding up bored, listless, and unfulfilled in a superficially sublime but secretly stagnant situation.

In order to rescue a relationship which has begun to slide down this slippery slope, you simply need to conquer your fear of the great unknown. All too often, we cause our greatest fears to come true simply by working so very hard to keep them at bay. If you can recognize this, you may be able to see the wisdom in becoming just a little less determined to hang on to all that you so earnestly want to remain the same. Let it go. Tell yourself you hardly care whether your partner leaves you, rejects you, or simply grows apart from you.

For anyone else, this might be a recipe for disaster. For you, however, it's a sure formula for success. Your natural caution will never let you take the policy too far. When the danger signals start flashing red, you'll see them. And then, if you respond, you'll be all the better equipped to take the right sort of remedial action because you haven't used up all your energy panicking as soon as the signals started flickering yellow.

Taureans are terribly sensual. They throw themselves into all forms of physical experience and can't get enough of a good thing! Some people think they're greedy!

A SIDEWAYS LOOK AT YOUR SIGN

To understand the nature of your sign fully, you need to think of it as a place rather than a personality trait. So come with me to the island of Taurus. Hop into my plane, fasten your safety belt, and prepare to visit a land of unrivaled beauty.

On arrival, you'll be invited to remove your shoes. It's a local custom in honor of Taureans, who like to feel the earth beneath their feet. Speaking of local customs, our first stop must be immigration control. The Taurean official will want to know whether you intend to fit in with the island routine, and whether you've brought with you something nice to eat or look at!

Having cleared customs, we can now proceed to our hotel. Taurean hospitality is legendary. As you lie on the softest yet most supportive bed you've ever felt, look at the items provided for your comfort. Notice the gold taps in the bathroom: one for hot water, one for cold, and one for the temperature you like best. That painting on the wall of your room is an original; and, yes, the carpet is indeed a hand woven masterpiece. You've come to the home of all luxury, where, within the confines of a reasonable budget, no expense has been spared.

Don't get too settled, though. First, we're going to the famous Taurean beaches, where the sand is white as snow, the sun is hot, and the sea is blue and creamy. You'll see some fine china later on when we get to the museum. If that surprises you, it's because you're thinking of Taurus as the bull in a china shop. Clumsiness, however, is most definitely not a Taurean trait.

Next we'll go to the craft market. If you wish, you can sample the local goods. You'll find everything from sculpture to scarves and from handwoven baskets to homemade bread. Notice that the air is full of lovely music and that thousands of tantalizing perfumes keep wafting your way. However, I must issue a word of warning before I let you go shopping alone. Please don't hurry. Taureans hate it when people try to do things too quickly. It confuses them and makes them angry. And when you ask the price of any item, please don't haggle. Taureans always mean what they say, especially when talking about money! When you've finished admiring the treasures, we can proceed to the high spot of our trip to see things so precious they are not for sale at any price. These are the items in the Taurean museum. Taureans are the world's greatest collectors. Some collect books, records, film memorabilia, stamps, and paintings; others collect things like ideas, recipes, or techniques for healing.

Since we arrived, the sky has been calm, the climate warm, and the wind light. Now a Taurean storm is brewing. It won't last long, but like the storms which occasionally flash over the temperaments of calm Taurean people, it will be ferocious and sudden. Let's get safely back to the hotel. I know from experience that a bitter wind will soon blow down hailstones the size of golf balls. It's the only drawback to life on the otherwise idyllic paradise of Taurus, just as those occasional dark moods are the only drawback to life with (or as) a Taurean.

After the storm, why not join me for dinner? Whatever your favorite food, you can be sure they know how to cook it to perfection. Taureans all love to eat well, and these are not the only sensual pleasures they like to indulge in!

GEMINI
May 22 – June 22

Every Gemini is a dreamer of dreams and a weaver of visions.
Geminis are the zodiac's perpetual children, refusing, even in old age,
to betray their innocent faith in the possibility of a happier world for
all. It is this deep inner well of simple, trusting enthusiasm which
makes every Gemini such a potentially powerful person.

IF you value your sanity, never try to argue with a Gemini, at least not unless you can handle a conversation that sweeps wildly from one subject to another, speeding up, slowing down, twisting, and turning like an intellectual roller coaster. Geminis love a good debate, caring more for the process of persuasion than for the final outcome. They love to ask questions, and they're never afraid to probe people on subjects which others would diplomatically avoid.

Geminis suffer from intermittent dark moods when they don't want to talk to anyone about anything. These, happily, don't last long, and Geminis are soon ready to communicate again. You can say things to a Gemini which most other people would consider crazy, and you will find yourself being taken seriously. Likewise, you can expect to hear the oddest thoughts and ideas earnestly expressed by your Gemini friend.

Geminis can be exasperating because they prefer thoughts to feelings. They try to rationalize things which can't be rationalized, like love, affection, sorrow, or desire. This sometimes leads to brilliant, original insights, but it can just lead to trouble or misunderstanding, as well.

If you want to ensure that a Gemini has a good birthday, forget the cake and the candles. Give them something or take them somewhere that inspires plenty of exciting and fulfilling conversation!

HOME

A Gemini's home needn't be palatial but it must have plenty of interesting things to look at and fiddle with. Geminis can't stand sitting around being bored.

Your perfect home is probably a wigwam in Wisconsin. A lifestyle in the heart of the Native American community would suit you to a teepee, especially if the tribe were to acknowledge your interest in communication by putting you in charge of smoke signals! Failing that, a house in Georgetown, D.C., would keep you up to date with national news. Wherever you live and whatever sort of abode you have, your favorite room is the front hall. For every Gemini, the heart of a home is the hall table with the mail!

Your ideal house number might be 411 because you always like to feel that you've got everybody's number.

CLOTHES

No matter how smartly a Gemini tries to dress, there's always something out of place or over the top. Subtlety is not a Gemini strong point!

Nobody knows better than a Gemini how to dress to kill. Your wardrobe is not so much a treasure trove as an armory. Each outfit is picked to make a statement, and, as a changeable (dare we even say contrary) Gemini, there are many statements you want to make. Your favorite items are those which adjust to your mood. You go wild when you find a shop that sells reversible jackets or dresses with detachable sleeves. You're also a believer in accessories. You have a special fondness for large, chunky pieces of jewelry, and you have a preference for earrings which most people would be more inclined to display on their mantelpiece!

CARS

As you are an adaptable, versatile, spur-of-the-moment Gemini, your dream vehicle has to be something snappy. In moments of fantasy, you favor a luxury limo, but common sense soon ends that idea. Where would you park it? How would you protect it? And, most crucially, how would you steer it into those enticing little gaps in the traffic that you're so fond of claiming? What you really want is the best of all worlds, an enviable status symbol with a slim body and endless energy. But never mind your ideal partner, we're supposed to be describing your ideal vehicle! This has to be a customized two-seat sports car with an ejector seat for tiresome passengers and a device for shooting nails into the tires of anyone who has the nerve to tailgate you!

FOOD

Variety is the spice of life for every Gemini, and this is especially true when it comes to food.

If you're a truly typical Gemini, food is rarely a big deal for you. You'll happily eat whatever happens to be lying around in the refrigerator, as long as it's quick to cook and easy to digest. What it actually tastes like hardly seems to matter. The only time your mouth really starts to water is when you're offered a tremendous variety of new and unusual food. Your naturally irrepressible Gemini curiosity can't resist trying a tiny little bit of absolutely everything. Smorgasbords, for example, really get you going, and some Geminis have been known to travel miles for the chance to try a new delicacy.

MONEY

"It is enterprise which builds and improves the world's possessions.... If enterprise is afoot, wealth accumulates whatever may be happening to thrift; and if enterprise is asleep, wealth decays, whatever thrift may be doing."

It will, I'm sure, come as no surprise to you to learn that the words above were written by a Gemini. You may be even more gratified to learn that they come from the famous economist John Maynard Keynes. If only you (or he) were in charge of the country's finances, our economic progress would always be a success. Of course, if you were in charge of the national debt, you wouldn't have time to pursue all those other exciting financial possibilities that you're so interested in. And this of course is part of your trouble. You want to have your cake and eat it, too. You try to keep as many fingers in as many pies as you can. To extend the culinary analogy still further, you put far more on your plate than you can ever hope to digest. It's a sense of insecurity that prevents you from putting all your eggs in one basket, and it's got to be overcome. It doesn't matter whether you pick the safe route or the more adventurous one. You'll enjoy a great deal of success and enough economic progress to keep the wolf from the door whatever you do, as long as you don't try to be all things to all people or spread your resources too thinly over too many plans and projects. Specialize and you'll thrive.

JUST THE JOB?

Advertising agent, bicycle maker, bookkeeper, bookseller, broadcaster, broker, bus driver, editor, engineer, journalist, lecturer, linguist, mechanic, messenger, nerve specialist, pollster, porter, post office worker, press baron, telephone salesman, traffic manager, typist, weather forecaster, writer.

Five ways to cash in
★ Charge for any information you offer.
★ Sell a product you really believe in.
★ Stop showing off your knowledge in front of your bosses. It makes them insecure and is costing you a pay raise.
★ Let someone else get the better of you deliberately so that you can lull them into a false sense of security.
★ Spend less time on the phone!

Five ways to branch out
★ Write questions for a quiz show.
★ Compile encyclopedias.
★ Go on stage as "The Amazing Mr./Ms Memory."
★ Become the West Virginia sales rep for a coal company or the Alaskan agent for Acme Freezers!
★ Write speeches for politicians.

LOVE

Romance, in the classic sense, does not appeal to most Geminis. They simply want someone to talk to, and, more importantly, someone who'll listen to them! There's a very low boredom threshold in every Gemini. That's why they tend to shift and change so much; they hate the thought of being stuck in a rut.

Some people believe that it is not possible for Geminis to go through their whole lives with just one romantic partner. They argue that people born under your sign can no more manage monogamy than a disc jockey can cope with silence. The theory is that you simply have to have variety, excitement, distraction, entertainment, and a certain amount of danger in your world.

Up to a point, it's true. You certainly can't stick with the wrong partner. Unlike some who might be inclined to learn to live with an error or miscalculation and to suffer the consequences stoically for years, you value your freedom and your happiness far too highly. But this doesn't mean that you are destined to limp from one unsatisfactory relationship to the next until you grow too old to contemplate trying again. It simply means that, instead of constantly changing partners, you need to think about picking one partner who will keep changing to meet the different requirements of a new day.

As a many-sided personality, you need, naturally enough, a multifaceted companion. You need somebody who will at least accept and adapt to your moods, at best actually relish them. Almost certainly this will involve someone a little eccentric and exceptional. But this ought to be a bonus, and the only real difficulty here is that your ideal mate may well turn out to be every bit as volatile and mercurial as you are! You might be the one who has to do the running to keep up while he or she forges ahead. But this is still far preferable to being stuck in a relationship where the same old arguments keep being trotted out day after day, and the same old bones of contention keep being squabbled over.

So don't let anybody tell you that true love is not attainable or that permanency is impossible. It's merely a matter of thinking about what you're entering into before you enter into it next time, or of thinking now about how you might encourage your existing soulmate to explore ways in which he or she can grow with you.

A SIDEWAYS LOOK AT YOUR SIGN

Geminis are supposed to be terribly talkative, but, of course, this is not always true. There are silent Geminis just as there are shy Leos and pessimistic Pisceans. There aren't many, but they do exist. Even the quiet ones, however, have some noisy thoughts. There's no such thing as a Gemini without a strong opinion.

Normally that opinion is well-informed because all Geminis are insatiably inquisitive. They devour newspapers, magazines, TV programs, and books like hungry wolves. What's more, they aren't fussy about what they learn because they feel it's all useful. Sometimes, though, the Gemini opinion can be very tenuous, deliberately so, for Geminis can see real links between the most unlikely, unrelated things. That's what drives them to keep asking questions, and it's also what drives anyone who wants a straight answer to despair!

You see, Gemini is ruled by Mercury, the mythological messenger of the gods. If you've ever seen a bicycle messenger weave and dodge through rush hour traffic, you'll understand why Geminis, firmly under the influence of Mercury, can be so hard to pin down.

The one thing which every Gemini is convinced of from birth is that no point of view is immune to compromise. In fact, it's probably the only thing a Gemini is ever convinced of, because Geminis can always see at least two sides to every story, and often more.

If that last sentence has caused you to raise an eyebrow, perhaps it's because I told you a little earlier that all Geminis have strong opinions. Well done! You've spotted the first of many contradictions in the Gemini mental makeup. You either love them or hate them for it, but if you want to get along well with Geminis you have to understand that they change their minds more often than some people change their socks. They do have strong opinions, but they treat them as starting points, not finishing lines. After every sentence you hear a Gemini utter, no matter how emphatic it is, feel free to add the words, "Unless, of course, you can persuade me of a better idea." These words are not always spoken, but they are always implied.

Some people say this proves that Geminis are unprincipled, unreliable, or just plain awkward. Geminis insist it proves that they are open-minded and able to adapt. At the risk of delivering a Gemini-style judgement, I must say that both points of view have a bit of truth in them. Geminis spring to life when there's a good dispute or debate going on. They hate to battle but they love to barter, and they'll often play devil's advocate just to see what can be learned from pushing a point too far. All this, of course, gives every Gemini a natural merchant mentality. Not all Geminis wheel and deal for a living, but every Gemini has an eye for a bargain, an endless obsession with a fast buck, and a terrific talent for making offers people can't refuse.

By now you're probably feeling a little hurt. I've painted a rather mercenary picture, but I've told you little about the wonderful, soulful, sensitive qualities of this sign. I won't apologize because what you've just read is fair, as far as it goes, but I will stress that Geminis are also kind, amenable, considerate, and creative people. They are wise and adventurous, fun loving and thoughtful. They're very definitely not stubborn, proud, pessimistic, or cold-hearted.

CANCER

June 23 – July 23

Cancerians are the zodiac's most sensitive souls. They cannot help but empathize with, and feel concern for, their fellow humans. They are never happier than when making someone else happy and never sadder than when they fear they have inadvertently caused hurt. Anyone who has a Cancerian for a friend has little need of anything else in life.

CANCERIANS like to play it safe. They would be dull, unadventurous people were it not for one thing: powerful emotions. When a Cancerian feels a strong attraction to someone or something, all caution flies out the window. It doesn't happen often, but when it does it's dramatic. Consequently, Cancerians spend their lives trying to stabilize after the last big upheaval and before the next one.

In the attempt to be steady and settled, Cancerians can put up with amazing inconveniences and let people take them for granted. But when one of those strong inner urges surfaces, they'll overthrow everything they've worked so hard to build and take breathtaking risks and liberties. They justify it with the hope that their action will lead to equal stability under better circumstances. Usually it does.

It's no use encouraging Cancerians to broaden their horizons while they're putting down roots. And it's no use trying to speak to them about common sense when they're in the throes of passion. Either way, they'd have to ignore you. For, while Cancerians are good at looking after others, they hate to be told what to do!

There is one thing that you can always give Cancerians: reassurance. They suffer from guilt and need to be told that it's all OK. The right word at the right time will always mean more to a Cancerian than any expensive gift.

HOME

You can recognize a Cancerian home as soon as you've walked into it. It's soft, homey, and womblike. Once your visitors get settled in, they never want to leave.

Although Cancer is the sign of the crab, you have no inclination to carry your home on your back. The very idea of living without a fixed abode is enough to make you retreat into your shell! To you, home is the most important place in the whole world, and it has to be made cozy at all costs. You delight in creating a safe haven: a secure, warm, welcoming, comfortable, and friendly place. As long as you know you have a space where you can do this, you don't really care if it's a mansion or a humble hut. Your ideal house number is 69. (No, nothing to do with that! It's just that it happens to be the zodiac symbol for Cancer.)

CLOTHES

Cancerians like clothes that make them feel safe. Even those who dress glamorously will have one regular item which they feel naked without.

Some people choose clothes that will help show off their personality. Cancerians tend to prefer clothes that will mask it. This doesn't mean you pick dowdy items; indeed, you probably have a wardrobe bursting with enviably elegant gowns and outfits. It's just that all of these are designed to disguise the sensitive, slightly vulnerable person you tend to feel you are. Your greatest asset is your eyes. Even without a trace of makeup, these are bursting with more character and color than you realize. If you dress to complement the color and shape of the top half of your face, you'll always look like a million dollars.

CARS

To some people, a car is a sex symbol; to others, it's a status symbol. To a Cancerian, it's a sort of mobile closet. Never mind the size of the engine, you want to know about the size of the glove compartment. Will it hold all your tapes, cosmetics, slippers, sandwiches, and maps? For the maps, frankly, you could use a trailer. The idea of being lost in a strange city terrifies you so much that, in addition to a multitude of maps, you also carry an atlas, just in case you should take a wrong turn. Which brings us to the thorny question of what you notice when driving. Not the car itself, that's for sure. For you, any car will always be just another car, until they invent one with a periscope to give a better view of what the people are up to in the vehicle in front of you!

FOOD

The stomach is ruled by Cancer, which is why Cancerians find a sense of security in eating their favorite foods. This, though, makes it hard for them to follow a diet!

Cancerians are ruled by the Moon, which in turn governs dairy products. In theory, you enjoy milk, cream, butter, cheese, yogurt, and eggs. You're also supposed to have an affinity for melons, mushrooms, and fruit. Whether or not this is true, if you are a truly typical Cancerian, you'd much prefer having a nice meal at a table to eating on your feet. Oddly enough, though you can resist the temptation of instant snacks, you are almost perpetually hungry. Like J.R.R. Tolkien's famous Bilbo the Hobbit, you've always got room for a "little something" to fill up the corners.

MONEY

"The growth of a large business is merely a survival of the fittest..."

"The American Beauty rose can be produced in the splendor and fragrance which brings cheer to its beholder only by sacrificing the early buds which grow up around it."

J.D. Rockefeller, who made these remarks, was a Cancerian and an exceedingly rich one at that. His words sum up a dilemma which all born under your sign must face from time to time. On the one hand, you are aware of your natural ability to make ruthless business and financial decisions. On the other, you resent having to compromise the more sentimental side of your nature in the process. Rather than be constantly torn in this way, many Cancerians back away from their chances to make big money. Others compensate by giving free rein to their mercenary instincts for a while, then generously redistributing the proceeds. Rockefeller was a case in point.

I'm not promising you will be as wealthy as he was, but you will always be able to do pretty well for yourself, provided you have a clear idea about what you want to do with your future. Cancerians often find it hard to believe that an old idea or project has now run its course; they keep wanting to pour time, energy, and hope into an investment even if it continues to fail to live up to its promise. You'll always be able to make more of your potential, provided you can overcome your ingrained resistance to the notion of a radical change of direction.

JUST THE JOB?

Baker, bath-house attendant, builder, caretaker, caterer, cook, dairymaid, fishmonger, glassblower, gynecologist, home economist, kindergarten teacher, hotelier, innkeeper, Jacuzzi maker, laundry person, mushroom grower, mammologist, market gardener, nurse, nutritionist, plumber, sailor, shopkeeper, social worker.

Five ways to cash in
- ★ Respond only to every other charity appeal you get, instead of to all of them.
- ★ Rent an apartment above your local branch of WWF and save the bus fare.
- ★ Entertain a little less lavishly.
- ★ Start charging for wear and tear on your shoulder to those who keep crying on it.
- ★ Stop being frightened of grownups or people whom you see as authority figures.

Five ways to branch out
- ★ Run a home for waifs and strays in a depressed inner city area.
- ★ Run for Congress and eventually become Secretary of the Interior.
- ★ Run a healing center which people will rush to enter.
- ★ Run a bar and become known as the happy host.
- ★ Run away to sea, make your fortune, buy a boat, and open up a floating supermarket.

LOVE

Sensuality is a key word for Cancerians. They have a keen appreciation of touch, taste, and smell, especially in love. In partnerships, Cancerians will go to great lengths to keep the union alive, even if it's unhappy. But if their patience snaps, that's the end.

To be in partnership with a Cancerian is to live on the edge of an emotional volcano, forever waiting for a sign that the dormant beast is about to erupt. It's just as well that most of the time you are sensitive, compassionate, caring, and sharing. If all your lover had to look forward to were those angry outbursts, he or she would have packed up and headed for the safety of sleepier shores long ago.

If you want to make your relationship withstand the test of time, you must learn how to control those intermittent explosions. It's no use being a delightfully charming Dr. Jekyll if this merely causes each rare appearance of Mr. Hyde to be more devastating than the previous one. And it's unfair to expect anyone, including your worst enemy, let alone the person you love more than anyone else in the world, to put up with the kind of anger you are capable of bottling up for ages before letting it out with all the devastating potency of a nuclear weapon.

So we have to ask what it is within you that puts the fear of God into others, even though most of the time you seem to live in total terror of everyone else. The answer to a question is often contained within it, and in the situation we have just identified, it's clear that the cause of the former is the latter! Your trouble is that you swing between too many extremes. You forgive and forget petty transgression after petty transgression. You let the matter of the top of the toothpaste tube ride. You leave the issue of who washes the dishes undiscussed. You give the false impression that you are happy to be taken for granted, left to carry the load, and treated as a simple appendage, and then you hit the roof over a matter so trivial as to make all the aforementioned seem like issues worth debating in Congress!

I hate to say it, but every one of your relationships is in essence a power struggle. You hate to be contradicted, can't stand being criticized, and live in terror of being undermined. You don't want things to be equal; you want to dominate like a dictator. And your poor old partner is supposed to put up with this! So what can you do to make things better? You can find other outlets for your need to be in control. Instead of putting all your energy into the relationship, you should put as little as possible into it, on the grounds that your idea of "less" is inevitably going to be most other people's idea of far more than is necessary.

A SIDEWAYS LOOK AT YOUR SIGN

Anyone who really wants to know about the zodiac sign Cancer needs to think long and hard about a particular four-letter word. To each of us, this word means something different but important. It's a terribly emotive word. In a moment, when I tell you what it is, notice how you react: whether you say "Oh," "Ah," or "Ho hum," you'll reveal a secret about yourself. And that, as much as the word itself, says a lot about the kind of people that Cancerians really are.

You see, in the great zodiac scheme of life, Cancerians are guardians of a fundamental value, and, as such, they are like mirrors, absorbing and reflecting other people's feelings about that value. This makes Cancerians both powerful and vulnerable. But before I say any more, I'd better tell you the word. It is *home*.

But I don't mean that all Cancerians are domesticated, house-proud, cozy creatures. Some are, but most embody the spirit of home in a much broader sense. Home is (or should be) a place where everything is right, where you come from, and where you return to. Home is security; home is safety; home is strength; and, most of all, home is something that goes beyond words and clever arguments.

When you really come home, you don't need to think about where you are. You just sink into the comfort and familiarity of your environment, turn off your defenses, and open up your heart. To you, home is not a place; it's a feeling, a state of mind, a state of perfection, and a state of grace. So the thing that all Cancerians seek is a feeling of being "at home," and the thing that all Cancerians have to offer is a way of making others feel they have arrived at a perfect place.

No matter who you are, where you are, or what you're doing, if you've got a Cancerian nearby, the part of the world you're in will feel just like home. Cancerians can do this for you just by being themselves. They don't always do it as soon as you meet them. But never doubt that they are able to, and don't assume that they will foist their idea of home on you. Cancerians, as I've said, are like mirrors: they are really sensitive and can tune in to the very deepest part of your soul and understand exactly what you need.

Why then, if all that is true, can Cancerians sometimes be so crusty, so difficult to get along with, and so tough? Well, there are two reasons for this, both linked to the fact that Cancer is the sign of the crab. Reason one is that, just as a crab has a hard shell but a soft underbelly, Cancerians protect themselves from their own sensitivity by pretending to be harsh. Only when they feel safe enough to come out of their shell will you discover how sweet they are underneath. Reason two is that crabs live by the sea. They only come out when the tide is out, and the thing that makes the tide go in and out is the Moon. The lives of crabs (and Cancerians) are ruled by the Moon, and, like the Moon, they go through phases. That's why Cancerians sometimes seem to be moody!

LEO

July 24 – August 24

A Leo's greatest gift is his or her natural buoyancy. No matter what misfortune may befall them, Leos always maintain faith in humanity and trust in life's hidden magic. By burning these two inner flames, Leos cannot help but bring light and warmth to the lives of others.

LEOS love to be admired. They can't help it; they're just built that way. The trouble is that they are also headstrong, highly strung, and able to annoy people without meaning to. So while they can easily attract the attention they want, they don't always attract the respect which ought to come with it. This is not helped by the fact that Leos can be strong about wanting their own way and difficult when they don't get it! Other people are like this, too, but Leos don't manage to hide their feelings well. It's the chief Leo failing, but the best Leo asset.

Leos may not be able to mask their less acceptable emotions, but they're equally unable to disguise their nicer ones. A happy Leo radiates enough warmth to defrost a refrigerator! With such a sunny disposition, there's normally much contagious enthusiasm to be enjoyed in a Leo's company. Sadly, though, some people find the Leo equilibrium upsetting. They mistake the self-contained smile for insensitivity. However, Leos feel deeply and care passionately. They know that once they let go of their cheery veneer, they'll unleash an avalanche of uncontrollable emotion. You'll see the truth of this when a Leo gives you a present, for Leos never hold back (feelings or checkbooks) if there's a chance to give. And, when giving to a Leo, neither should you.

HOME

Somehow, the finest things in life always find their way into a Leo's lifestyle. But Leos love to share the best of everything with those they care for.

Leos are famed for their generosity but also for their sense of self-importance. What could suit you better, then, than a country estate complete with antiques, tennis courts, and an indoor swimming pool? It's just the thing to go with your chauffeur (see Cars) and, of course, to entertain your friends in impressive style. Delusions of grandeur? Absolutely! Every healthy Leo needs plenty of those. Your current abode may not fit the bill exactly, but I'd like to bet it's the swankiest place on the street or, more relevantly, that you *think* it is! Leos, basically, see themselves as the Joneses with whom everyone else needs to keep up.

CLOTHES

Without exception, Leos dress as if they were playing a part in a play. Most like to be bright and glamorous; all think about their appearance.

Do you have a glorious mane of hair that flows in ringlets down your back? If not, why not? Are you ashamed of your link to the biggest cat in the jungle? Are you trying to cultivate a more reserved image? A typical Leo's hair is his or her crowning glory. Its shape, texture, and color should dictate the nature of every single item of clothing and accessory. Leos who, for any reason, wear their hair short have a harder job selecting clothes that feel right. They need to pick deliberately ostentatious outfits in order to project their proper power; on the other hand, those with the locks can just let the rest of the look fall into place.

CARS

If you're a truly typical Leo, you're not particularly interested in the question of what kind of car you ought to be driving. The real debate centers around what kind of cap your chauffeur ought to wear. There might also be some concern as to whether your limo needs a fully stocked bar or just a Jacuzzi, but otherwise it's simple. You were born to cruise the streets of Hollywood, issuing orders like, "Just stop here for an hour or so, James." If you haven't yet reached this desirable position in life, don't worry, there's still time. Meanwhile, you can carry on driving, in your typically imperious Leonine fashion, as if you have a divine right of way and a license to ignore everything else on the road!

FOOD

Food, for a Leo, should be spicy, colorful, and expensive. Leos aren't greedy, but they can't resist a tasty delicacy, even if they aren't hungry!

As a Leo, ruled by the Sun, you have a natural affinity for citrus fruit, pomegranates, olives, and indeed, for pretty much anything that needs a hot climate in which to grow. You're fond of heat in your food, too, not necessarily curry or chili, but the sharp, aromatic tang of ginger, peppermint, cinnamon, nutmeg, and mustard. You tend to be more of a nibbler than a muncher, not least because, as a figure-conscious calorie watcher, you don't like to pile too much on your plate. Instead, you secretly graze on snacks throughout the day, then burn them all off with your amazing, nervous energy.

MONEY

"Time ... is the center of the chief difficulty of almost every economic problem."

These words from the classical economist Alfred Marshall sum up all too well the astrological pressure that you, as a Leo, so often seem to face. The fact that their author was born under your sign gives them extra poignancy. Was he, I wonder, writing purely from a professional standpoint? We astrologers often discuss the irony of Leonine finances. We notice that, far too frequently for comfort, you have an opportunity but no time to take it, or you have time on your hands but no way to do anything constructive with it. You often have to struggle to introduce a new idea into your world or to bring about a long-desired change in circumstances. Next time the going becomes rough and variable, you might like to take comfort from another statement by the same erudite Leo financial expert. "A new discovery is seldom fully effective for practical purposes till many minor improvements and subsidiary discoveries have gathered themselves around it."

It's the most natural thing in the world for Leos to find their domestic and personal expenses prone to spiral upwards at the slightest provocation. Unexpected repair bills or travel requirements combined with the desire to maintain rather indulgent habits leave you short of cash. Usually the syndrome unfolds as follows. You are just about to sell your home or pawn your heirlooms, when you have an inspiring revelation: you're worth far more than your current lifestyle is enabling you to earn. You will either get a substantial raise, be offered more lucrative employment elsewhere, or be shown a better, more reliable source of income. The funny thing is that as often as not, the above turns out to be true.

JUST THE JOB?

Actor, athlete, banker, bookmaker, brewer, broker, circus ringmaster or mistress, dancer, entertainer, film director, film star, forester, gambler, goldsmith, heart specialist, jeweler, leisure consultant, matchmaker, mayor, monarch, moneylender, mountaineer, novelty goods salesperson, pop singer,theatre owner, usher.

Five ways to cash in
- ★ Marry a wealthy man or woman.
- ★ Divorce them and marry another one.
- ★ Divorce your second spouse and make the next bimbo or boy toy you want to marry sign a prenuptial agreement.
- ★ Coolly and calmly invite perfect strangers to give you money.
- ★ Let the light that's inside you shine and nature will bring the rest to your feet.

Five ways to branch out
- ★ Lead a revolution in a foreign country and become the new ruler.
- ★ Persuade a television company to let you host your own talk show.
- ★ Start a fashion trend and watch everyone follow your lead.
- ★ Star in a movie.
- ★ Make a hit record. It doesn't matter if you can't sing, just pose.

LOVE

Leos like to have admirers, but they aren't attracted to people who fawn on them. To win a Leo's love, you must first win his or her respect. There's not a person on the planet who is impervious to a Leo's charm, though some fight harder than others to resist it.

As a Leo, you are by nature proud and independent. This poses an intriguing question about the kind of partner you ought to be aiming to live your life with. Should they be (a) someone supportive and admiring who will give you the freedom you need, (b) someone equally independent and strong who will provide the stimulating challenge you seek, (c) someone special who somehow combines both of the above qualities, or (d) none of the above, indeed, nobody at all, because ultimately there is no such thing as an ideal match for a Leo? Though in your darker moments of disillusionment you may be inclined to imagine that (d) is indeed the answer, I can assure you that this is completely untrue, as the bright spark of hope in your heart knows only too well.

The key to comfort and long-lasting success in your love life simply involves learning to recognize that romance, in the classic, heart-stopping, nerve-tingling, pulse-racing sense, is simply not a sustainable phenomenon. Real relationships not only have their ups and downs, their strains and stresses, and their moments of complete and total communication breakdown, they have something potentially far more devastating. They have their periods of emptiness, of shallowness, and of frustrating vagueness. It's at times like these that both partners tend to be most attracted to the idea of separation, divorce, or extramarital dalliance, but it's also at times like these that there is the greatest chance to find depth and empathy. People are never happy to have their partner push them into talking when they don't want to talk, sharing when they don't want to share, or loving when they feel they have nothing to give; but there's not a person in the world who cannot be coaxed or tempted into feeling better if his or her partner is truly prepared to show enough sympathy, support, and understanding.

The trouble is that, understandably, you tend to feel you want to receive all this rather than be obliged to give it. So don't feel obliged to give it, feel inspired. Try a little harder and let that ferocious Leo love of independence be what encourages you to persevere when others might give up, rather than stalk off into the jungle in search of a more superficially appealing mate.

A SIDEWAYS LOOK AT YOUR SIGN

Leos are warm, generous, lively, sweet-natured people with hearts of gold and nerves of steel. They are full of fun, soft as butter, sweet as honey, and sharp as lemons. Leos can take anything the world throws at them—anything, that is, except perhaps advice. Offering advice to a Leo is like offering gloves to a fish. It's just totally pointless.

Leos, you see, hate to admit that something is wrong or that they can't cope. They like to walk tall and show the world that they have endless confidence in themselves. Because of this, they often give the impression of being head-over-heels in love with their own self-image. It's really not fair, though, to call them arrogant or vain. A better, more accurate word would be "proud." A Leo is as lost without dignity as a dentist is without a drill. In fact, if it weren't for their pride and, perhaps, their stubbornness, Leos would be perfect.

Get on the right side of a Leo and you'll have a firm friend for life. Leos are loving and lovable, humorous and human, excitable and exciting. Get on the wrong side of a Leo, however, and you'll live to regret it. When crossed, Leos are more than just stubborn, in the same way that, for example, super glue is more than just glue.

A Leo with a point to prove is rock solid, a living example of determination, willpower, and perseverance. These characteristic qualities are, of course, every bit as good as they are bad. When you need someone to stand up for you, when it's necessary to be steadfast and resolute, or when there's plain speaking to be done, a Leo on your team is the most valuable asset you can have. Leos are loyal, Leos are larger than life, and Leos are also, I'm afraid it must be said, occasionally a little lazy!

Just like the lion in the jungle who sleeps as much as twenty hours out of every twenty-four, the lion in the zodiac likes to go at a gentle pace. When the lion wakes up and emits a ferocious roar, everyone stands at attention. But when the lion is quietly snoozing, everyone just as defiantly (if cautiously) ignores him. So Leos can be stubborn, Leos can be lazy, and, most of all, Leos can be proud. It's no accident that the collective noun for a group of lions is a "pride."

But, when all is said and done, despite these faults, Leos are still wonderful people. Leo is ruled by the brightest star in the sky, the Sun. And potentially, every Leo is a shining star here on earth. There's something very attractive and pleasurable about basking in sunlight, or basking in the warmth of a Leo's company, which pretty much amounts to the same thing. Leos have sunny dispositions, and they carry all the qualities of their personality up-front. They don't bother to hide their character defects, and they don't bother to hide their light. As a result, they shine. And because of that, others are quickly drawn to them. That's why most social circles have a Leo at the center, why so many Leos find themselves surrounded by fans and admirers, and why such an extraordinarily large number of showbiz celebrities are born under the sign of Leo. It's true that Leos have outrageous tempers which flare up suddenly and burn with terrifying ferocity, but these always die down just as quickly. They are never used to express vindictiveness, only spontaneous justified anger.

VIRGO

August 24 – September 23

*Every Virgo has a mission to inform and educate. They rarely
lecture others or insist on loudly putting their point across,
preferring to listen, understand, and then teach by gentle example.
The Virgo spirit is essentially a healing spirit. Virgos want nothing
more (or less) than true physical and emotional well-being
for all their fellow humans.*

VIRGOS have tremendous timing and impeccable insight.
Fortunately for the rest of us, they also have searing self-doubts.
These inhibit them from abusing their talents and make them very reasonable people. Neither passive nor aggressive, Virgos are simply sensible yet
sensual. They want to enjoy life to the fullest, but they know that there are
dangers attached to such hungers. They form elaborate contingency plans
and see the potential repercussions of every move. This may sound staid, but
in Virgoan hands, common sense is not a restrictive force. Unlike those who
shoot first and ask questions later, Virgos ask first and only fire if they know
they've aimed the right weapon at the right target.

Virgos don't see their own lives from such a confident viewpoint; they
couldn't be so well organized if they did. On the inside, Virgos feel intimidated by their own ambitions, but at the same time frustrated by their reticence. It's a dichotomy which can't ever (and should never) be resolved. It's
also the reason why Virgos are attracted to other Virgos. Knowingly or
unknowingly, they seek each other out.

Virgos are sociable, amenable, and helpful people, no matter whom they are
with. They are forgiving, patient, and thoughtful. When they give presents,
they choose them carefully, and when you give to them, you should do the
same.

HOME

Despite all that you have read elsewhere, Virgos are not obsessively tidy; they just like to arrange things in an organized fashion, which is not the same thing.

Virgos are supposed to be tidy. Up to a point it's true, but it doesn't follow that your home is a show house. Your personality is far too warm for the stark, cold lines of an immaculate room, and you have better things to do with your time than be forever putting things in drawers. Instead, you vote for organized chaos. Despite your billions of possessions (you hate to throw anything away), you have a place for absolutely everything. The piles, stacks, and bundles, however, make sense only to you. It all adds to your air of genial eccentricity, as, indeed, does your quirky, inventive, but effective approach to interior design.

Your ideal house number is 60 or 65 (to suit your retiring disposition).

CLOTHES

Virgos never wear any clothes by accident. Even scruffy Virgos will have carefully chosen each item they wear for maximum effect!

Anyone who thinks that Virgo is the sign of purity and that you, therefore, ought to dress in white, clearly knows little about astrology and even less about the price of washing powder. Yours is the fecund sign of the harvest goddess, not the prudish sign of the eternal spinster. If you want to show off your best qualities, choose earth tones: dark greens, russet browns, and clay reds. Pick smartly cut, cleverly designed clothes which give an air of authority, keep accessories simple, and watch your shoes. For some reason, you're prone to looking good from your head to your ankles, after which it all tends to go to pot!

CARS

V is for Virgo and Volvo. You may not actually drive one, but something about the unassuming, safety-conscious image of this particular make suits you perfectly, right down to its traditional link with country life. Another reason why you need a tank of a car is because your critical faculties go into overdrive when you get out on the road. Maybe it's the intoxicating aroma of air freshener mixed with carbon monoxide or the nerve-jangling noise of a grinding gear shift, but, oddly for such a usually reserved person, you can't drive far without muttering things like: "What an idiot!" "Who let him out without a keeper?" or "Get out of the way, you ****!" In a less adequately soundproofed vehicle, there is a horrible chance that other drivers might hear you!

FOOD

Virgos are very fussy about food. What they want to eat depends on the mood they're in; often they'll go to great lengths to get what they want.

Would you like a starter of fennel, walnut, and parsley salad, followed by carrot, celery, and bean stew flavored with dill and caraway? You could eat it with hazelnut pâté on oatcakes and follow up with a perfect tart. Mouthwatering? It ought to be, for every single one of these ingredients is traditionally governed by Mercury, the ruler of your sign. Even the absence of meat on the list is apt because, though not every Virgo turns vegetarian, yours is the sign of dietary discrimination. You take great pleasure in keeping yourself intelligently nourished.

MONEY

"Nothing will ever be attempted if all possible objections must be first overcome."

As the esteemed Dr. Samuel Johnson, the author of these words, was born under your sign, I'm sure you'll understand just what lay behind that remark. Virgos have a magnificent ability to overcome their fears and problems by subjecting them to close analysis. They dissect and probe them so carefully and cleverly as to render them totally impotent. Sadly, they sometimes put their opportunities through the same process, with less encouraging results. You could be a far wealthier person if only you could train yourself to apply just a little less cautious forethought from time to time.

You may well want to dwell on this idea at your leisure. You have long suspected that your skills are being undervalued and your talents underemployed. You may decide that the way to attain greater wealth is to gain specialized knowledge in a vital subject: to study, research, or teach.

Or you may discover that you don't need to learn so much to teach, as to delegate some of the mundane tasks on your plate while you profit from your more specific expertise. One thing's for sure, if you want to make the most of your prospects, you definitely need to overcome your natural reticence and your false assumption that others are better qualified than you are to be successful in commerce. As Dr. Johnson once observed: "Trade could not be managed by those who managed it if it had much difficulty."

JUST THE JOB?

Accountant, administrator, animal trainer, bookkeeper, butler, charity worker, chemist, chicken breeder, civil servant, clothier, dentist, dietician, doctor, editor, grocer, governess, librarian, microbiologist, naturopath, nurse, osteopath, photographer, piano tuner, sanitation inspector, teacher, vet.

Five ways to cash in
★ Team up with someone who is far less logical than yourself.
★ Next time someone asks if you happen to have noticed where they put something, charge them for the answer.
★ Only agree to play Scrabble for cash.
★ Become a rent collector and accept bribes to make you go away.
★ Sell some of those juicy secrets you are keeping.

Five ways to branch out
★ Take a job editing the *Encyclopedia Britannica*. That will certainly challenge your talent.
★ Offer your services to proofread telephone directories.
★ Take a course in computers and set yourself up as a programmer.
★ Open up a lost property office.
★ Visit Italy, after deciding that you'll be the one to straighten out the Leaning Tower of Pisa.

LOVE

Virgos are impervious to flattery. Try to pull the wool over their eyes and they may string you along for amusement, but they'll never fall for it. Virgo is really an introverted sign. Even extroverted Virgos tend to hide behind a façade, a social role, or a staged pretense of one sort or another.

Virgos, so we are led to believe, are about as romantic as a cold bath, as sensitive as a lump of concrete, and as vulnerable as a crocodile. If only it were true. You could leave passion to those who possessed the stomach for its punishing aftereffects and withdraw to the safety of your ivory tower to be alone and untouchable forever. The idea, I'm sure, is appealing. But you and I both know that in truth you yearn to be held, to be touched, to be tenderly kissed, and to be lovingly adored. It may all sound gruesomely sentimental, but though the cynic in your mind groans at the very notion, the poet in your soul simply shudders with desire. All this, naturally enough, makes you a bit of a tough person to partner. How is your beloved supposed to know when you want to be shown respect for your intellect and when you want to be swept off your feet? How can your mate know whether to whisper sweet nothings in your ear or put complicated diagrams in front of your eyes? How indeed? And how are you supposed to know whether you want to spend the rest of your life with a lover who looks good but lacks brainpower or with a sophisticated genius who happens to have the dress sense of a horse?

The answer, in a nutshell, is that you want, need, deserve, and are capable of getting (if you have not gotten already) an intuitive expert, a genuine soulmate, an emotional partner who can read you like a book. The only remaining question is: how are you going to find this emotional miracle? The answer to that one is that you're going to create it. You're going to stop fantasizing about that perfect stranger you vaguely imagine you may one day meet and start working with the material that's already at hand.

Almost certainly it's your existing partner, unless he or she has absolutely definitely proved to be beyond all hope. If so, or if you have no partner, possibly it's a friend or acquaintance with whom you have always felt a certain rapport. With this individual, you're going to explore new horizons of interpersonal understanding. You're going to take courses in communication, if necessary. But you're going to build and keep building until you have a bond of understanding that lasts not just till death do you part, but beyond. For every Virgo, this is not just a dream but a perfectly attainable proposition. All you have to do, besides recognize that you want it, is to work on it.

A SIDEWAYS LOOK AT YOUR SIGN

Virgos are difficult to write about and even harder to predict for because they are so erratic. If you find this surprising, I'm not surprised! Most Virgos present a very stable, sensible face to the world. They like others to think they're completely controlled and consistent. To a degree, it's true. Virgos are undoubtedly loyal, dependable, exceptionally intelligent, good-humored, generous, and compassionate. But if you probe a little deeper, you'll quickly come across the factor that makes every Virgo so impossible, impenetrable, and infuriating. What is this characteristic? Oh, how I wish there were a word in the English language that could sum it up.

When I read about how Virgos are rather dull, neat, and tidy folk who detest controversy and make perfect librarians, I laugh! That kind of description may fit some of the Virgo behavior patterns, but it says nothing about the true Virgo spirit. The true spirit makes Madonna look positively prim. It's a wild, chaotic, sensual spirit hidden behind a cool, calm, careful façade.

This, though, is still only half the story about the "dark side" of Virgo. Here's the other half. Every Virgo is, somehow, in some way, a martyr. Martyrs are people who put up with all sorts of pain, deprive themselves of all sorts of pleasure, and deny themselves all sorts of freedom, just for the satisfaction of feeling that they are "doing the right thing." Virgos are people who do all the above because they're afraid that if they did what they really wanted to do, they might end up "doing the wrong thing." So how do Virgos reconcile this Florence Nightingale syndrome with the self-indulgent qualities I've just mentioned? They don't. They can't. And that's why they are so impenetrable.

If Virgos were extroverted, it might not matter so much. They could display one side in public, the other in private. But most Virgos find little pleasure in showing off. Even those who are prepared to stand in the spotlight never let it shine on their true character. As introverts, Virgos are analytical, perceptive, and thoughtful. They're highly aware of the inconsistencies in their own nature, and, to make matters worse, they're normally highly self-critical about them. So they keep their mouths shut and suffer in silence. And what they mainly suffer from is an endless inner battle between the desire to serve others and the desire to serve their passions.

I want to make a confession. I really like Virgos. Many of the people I love most have been born under this sign. I've nothing but admiration and respect for them. The things I like best about my Virgo friends are, usually, the things they like least about themselves. I like their eccentricities and idiosyncrasies. I like their passions.

But the things I dislike about Virgos are the things they normally think are their finest social assets. I dislike the way they let other people take the credit and the way they humbly accept unjust blame or criticism. However, Virgos have X-ray vision. There is no pretense that a Virgo cannot see through, no social grace that a Virgo will be impressed by. Within seconds of meeting you, a Virgo will have decided exactly what makes you tick. That judgement will be absolutely accurate and potentially devastating. Virgos know that they have the potential to reduce other people to a quivering mass of embarrassment just by expressing a few of their observations, and that makes them feel burdened. If a Virgo has ever "seen through" you, you'll know that it hurts! The truth does.

The irony of all this is that Virgos, if they weren't so cripplingly self-critical, would be the most powerful people on earth. Their infallible perceptions could make them an unstoppable force. The only reason why Virgos don't rule the world is that they're so harsh on themselves.

LIBRA

September 24 – October 23

*As the zodiac's appointed guardian of justice, a Libran's task is
perhaps the most thankless of all: to weigh intellect against intuition
and the need to be fair against the need to be firm. In so doing,
Librans are often obliged to make choices few people can understand.
They bear this cosmic burden with eternal grace and good humor.*

LIBRANS, like chameleons, can fit in almost anywhere with almost any-one. That's why they are accused of being indecisive. They are sensitive to social undercurrents and want to do what's expected of them. This stems from a great need to be accepted. Yet it conflicts with another Libran need, to make a strong impression on their social and phys-ical environment. In a Libran mind, that conflict is reconciled like this: if you want your own way, it's better to inspire cooperation than confrontation.

As a philosophy, it's admirable, but in practice Libra is the sign of the scales. Often Librans swing from one extreme to another in an attempt to find a perfect balance. One day, they'll bend over backwards to accept some-one else's viewpoint; next day, they'll charge forward in a furious effort to impose their own. It's a pattern which is consistently inconsistent. Whether trying to be helpful or trying to take control, Librans are affable and charm-ing. It's impossible to know if they are taking care of you or taking advan-tage of you! But Librans don't see it that way. They always believe that what they are doing is for the greater good.

Librans can make even strangers feel special, but, ironically, if your Libran friend is a true friend, he or she won't feel the need to turn on that charm with you. So, if you want to charm a Libran, do something for them that lets them know it's OK, that you love them just the way they are!

HOME

Librans, being sociable, gregarious characters, usually love to entertain people in their homes. Their homes can be humble, but they are always graceful.

Librans are friendly and fair about most things, but they tend to have highly discriminating artistic tastes. You would far prefer a hovel with the right blend of color to a gaudily painted mansion. You like to live in partnership, but when it comes to decor, you must have the final say. Especially important to you is the look of your bedroom. If it doesn't reflect your aesthetic aspirations, it won't inspire you to sleep or to do anything else!

Your ideal house number is 2 (as in "Tea For Two").

CLOTHES

Librans have excellent taste in almost every area of life, but they sometimes fail to apply the same discriminating eye to their own appearance. Often, to be on the safe side, they will find one successful fashion formula and stick to it like super glue.

Being born under the sign of the balance gives you a natural understanding of the need to wear simple outfits with complex accessories and vice versa. It also allows you enough artistic flair to know when you can get away with breaking fashion's ground rules and take courageous risks which pay off. If you're looking for clothes and colors which show off more of your magical, endearing personality, try light touches: a Dennis the Menace badge on the lapel of a business suit or an arty beret worn at a jaunty angle with a simple jumper. It's in the art of clever combination that the well-dressed Libran excels.

CARS

What's the ideal car for a Libran? The answer, as with so many questions involving the sign of the balance, is: it depends. On Mondays you want a traffic-beating bicycle, on Tuesdays a status-conferring sedan. The antidote to a dull Wednesday must be a quirky VW Beetle, while a busy Thursday usually requires a roomy van. Because Friday is payday and there's never enough in the paycheck, an economical diesel becomes desirable. And for those "anything-could-happen" weekends, the ideal vehicle is probably a Land Rover. In the absence of a car for each day of the week, you tend to buy according to your rapidly changing mood. And this, of course, explains your tendency to misjudge those parking spaces!

FOOD

Librans are fussy about decor. In a restaurant, they notice the tablecloth more than what's on the menu!

Voluptuous Venus, the ruler of your sign, gives you a healthy appetite for life's most sensual pleasures. It also gives you an affinity for fruit, which possibly explains why, though you yearn to be part of a "pear," you drive your close friends bananas and often end up playing gooseberry. Seriously, though, you love sweet and juicy fruits, but you also have a terrible weakness for rich and fattening delicacies, especially candy. To balance this, you are forever embarking on intense, demanding, disciplined diets which you stick to rigidly, come hell or high water, for all of twenty-five minutes.

MONEY

"Wealth is not without its advantages and the case to the contrary, although it has often been made, has never proved widely persuasive."

This carefully worded, tongue-in-cheek remark comes from one of the twentieth century's most widely read (and readable) economists, John Kenneth Galbraith. Impressive though his many qualifications are, I'm sure you'll feel even more fond of the great professor if I tell you he was born under the sign of Libra. So he must know what he is talking about, mustn't he? Actually, that's a trick question. Before you answer it, I suggest you read another of his famous maxims: "One of the best ways of avoiding necessary and even urgent tasks is to seem busily employed on things that are already done."

Does this ring any bells? Various astrological factors suggest that it ought to. Librans detest being given orders. This is partly why you aspire so profoundly to running your own business, or at least your own department of somebody else's business, without anything more than cursory interference from a benign boss or respectful client. The trouble is that life's never like this for any Libran, no matter how successful he or she becomes. You will always be able to earn good money, make solid career progress, and even, up to a point, express your creative ingenuity, but only by accepting that every so often, regrettable though it may be, we all have to become a small cog in a greater machine. Temporarily it will be necessary to subjugate your desire for autonomy, repress your resentment of bureaucracy, control your urge to defy authority, and generally bite a series of bullets. Learn to play your part with as much good grace as you can muster, then bide your time. Eventually, the shots will be yours to call.

JUST THE JOB?

Artist, beautician, bedroom designer, civil rights campaigner, cosmetician, decorator, diplomat, dramatist, dressmaker, fashion designer, florist, golfer, judge, juggler, lawyer, milliner, musician, pianist, poet, politician, public relations consultant, receptionist, salesperson, tailor, union leader, wigmaker.

Five ways to cash in
★ Charm the socks off your bank or loan manager.
★ Put your money where your mouth is.
★ Stop siding with the underdog.
★ Get a job as a Kissogram.
★ Put a penny in a jar each time you change your mind, or maybe ten cents, but then again, perhaps only a penny …

Five ways to branch out
★ Become a color therapist and redesign rainbows.
★ Design a range of haute couture to suit Kermit the Frog.
★ Repaint the ceiling of the Sistine Chapel with a modern design.
★ Save the world.
★ Which came first, the chicken or the egg? Establish the definitive answer.

LOVE

Some people show their temper under stress; Librans simply turn on the charm. A Libran's smile can melt the iciest heart and soften the hardest adversary.

If, as Harold Wilson once said, "A week is a long time in politics," it's a veritable eternity in a Libran's love life! Odd though it may sound, your only chance of getting from here to the end of your life with your current partner, no matter how wonderful (or otherwise) he or she may be, is to forget the idea. Give up. Concentrate instead on just getting from here to the end of the week. And then the next one. As a Libran, you are simply not equipped to plan far into the future. The very thought of what you might be doing twenty years from now is enough to give you a simultaneous attack of the heebie-jeebies, the willies, and the dull ache of depression.

All this is mainly because you consider yourself a highly changeable, reactive individual who at any moment is likely to go off and do something radically different. Maybe you will. But you'll come back to where you were, as sure as eggs are eggs and Librans are Librans. You are far more predictable than you imagine. If something or someone means something to you now, they will continue to mean as much, if not more, to you in the distant future, even if you have wavered and wobbled about the matter all the way from here to there. So if you want to make your love last forever, just relax and stop worrying about it all.

A SIDEWAYS LOOK AT YOUR SIGN

Librans are supposed to be placid, well-balanced, easygoing people. But whenever I read that I either end up in tears of laughter or tears of frustration. Who writes such nonsense? Haven't they seen a Libran in action? I can only say if Librans are wishy-washy, what about Margaret Thatcher? If Librans are unexciting, what about Jackie Collins? If Librans have unimposing personalities, what about Sarah Ferguson?

I'll agree you have to look a little harder through the list of famous Libran males before you come across equally strong characters, but you'd hardly say that John Lennon was an uncontroversial character. And I don't think Oscar Wilde was exactly looking to promote social harmony. No, as far as I can see, there's a real desire in every Libran to create a world which is fair and peaceful; but there's also a very argumentative side to the Libran character which normally lies closer to the surface. Librans are, in fact, magnificently courageous and contemptuous of compromise; they simply disguise it behind a façade of congeniality and charm. Librans instinctively know how to put you at ease and off your guard. They know how to smile and nod, how to lull others into a false sense of security, and how to act as if all they really need in order to be happy is for you to be happy.

It's the ability to play devil's advocate which bestows every Libran with a special kind of creative genius, and yet this is also the thing which gives every Libran a very heavy cross to bear. You see, although we're forever being told that the cosmic scales represent intellect at its most powerful, justice at its most benign, and equality at its most fair, the spirit of Libra is the spirit of the balancing process itself, not of the things that may be weighed in that balance. Libra is the only sign of the zodiac to be symbolized by a machine. Consequently, there's a certain something at the heart of the Libran personality which is a little cold or mechanical. I'm not saying they don't have deep, passionate emotions or that they don't care, cry, laugh, love, and live to the fullest; they most undoubtedly do. But no matter what they are going through, whether it's happy or sad, Librans always follow their thoughts rather than their feelings.

The true spirit of Libra is about as far removed as you can get from basic, earthy, primitive human nature. It's the spirit of intellect's triumph over instinct, logic over emotion. And this is why we get the old chestnut about Librans being indecisive. Decisions are what Librans' lives are all about, but no Libran ever makes any decision lightly. They analyze, weigh all arguments carefully, and while they're in the process of making a decision, swing wildly from one extreme point of view to the other, expressing the virtues and vices of each with great force and enthusiasm. Some decisions take them seconds, others take years; but once they're made, they're made for good.

Sometimes the decision-making process can tire a Libran. Sometimes they'll deliberately let certain things happen so as to avoid having to make a decision about them. Often they'll prefer to be in a position where they have no option, rather than be given a choice between one thing or another. Perhaps it's from this that the "easygoing, placid" description has really come. But in my experience, even when Librans decide to let a decision be made for them, it's only because they have decided that that's the best decision. And one thing I know for sure: woe unto anyone who tries to persuade a Libran to rethink anything once his mind is made up!

SCORPIO

October 24 – November 22

*A Scorpio's mission is to discover the truth and awaken others to it.
Scorpios are thus blessed with sharp minds, sharper instincts, and
still sharper tongues. However, as there can be no truth without
understanding and no understanding without compassion, the
Scorpio personality itself is not, in fact, sharp, but endlessly,
vulnerably soft.*

SCORPIOS are determined and direct. They normally get what they
want, or at least what they think they want at the time. The trouble
is that at the heart of every Scorpio there's an insatiable hunger for an
impossible dream. Enough is never enough, and you had better get used to
this if you want to get along with your Scorpio friend. Happily, that restlessness is the hardest thing to handle in a Scorpio, unless you hate straight
talking. Scorpios aren't afraid of taboos: they find it amazing (or amusing)
that people are squeamish about things like sex, death, toilets, or overdrafts.

Scorpios know that their honesty can be controversial, which is why they
are careful about who they allow to get close to them. This, in turn, is why
Scorpios are sometimes considered unapproachable or secretive. It's also
partly why they are accused of having an obsession with sex. Scorpios are
passionate, and they throw themselves body and soul into every experience.
But it's not just sexual intensity they enjoy. They want the most out of life
and take their pleasures as seriously as their commitments. This is another
reason why they can be guarded in company. Scorpios are in awe of their
own powerful desires and hate to be criticized for them.

You won't win a Scorpio's trust by giving a present; only time and sincerity will allow you to do that. But you might win a smile if you give your
Scorpio friend something which shows you accept and approve of him.

HOME

Scorpios are very particular about the atmosphere of their homes and cannot tolerate an abrasive abode.

Plenty of people have household security systems these days, but only Scorpios have burglar alarms to protect their burglar alarms! It's easier to get into Fort Knox than to get into your home, yet despite all those triple-lock doors, chains, peepholes, and "Beware of the Dog" signs, you still tend to wonder if you ought not to go the whole hog and put a moat and draw-bridge around your property. Some people suspect this is not to protect your possessions at all but to guard the secret of what you do in the privacy of your own four walls.

A Scorpio's ideal house number is probably 37C or 101F because they are so hot-blooded!

CLOTHES

Scorpios know how to dress to kill, but they like to wear outfits with a subtle rather than a dramatic effect.

If all they say about Scorpio is true, where are your split skirts, stiletto heels, and fishnet stockings? Or your gold medallions, tight trousers, and open-necked shirts? Actually, some Scorpios do sometimes wear a toned-down, more elegant version of this attire, but they do so for reasons entirely the opposite of the obvious, not to be seductive, but to hide their natural shy-ness. Most Scorpios, however, are content to wear deliberately quiet, smart, sober clothes which let them fade into the background so that they can emerge from it at a moment of their own choosing.

CARS

Though Ford made a car named after your sign, it's not necessarily the one you want to drive. For one thing, you rarely like to do the obvious. For another, as a lover of privacy and mystery, you really don't want such a reveal-ing announcement permanently plastered on your rear end! Ideally, indeed, your sleek and stylish vehicle should have a two-way mirror for a wind shield so that you can see out but nobody else can see in! As for *how* you drive, well, oddly enough, despite your Scorpionic reputation for passion and drama in other areas, on the road, you tend to be as highly reserved as a ticket to a Broadway sellout.

FOOD

Generally, Scorpios like food with sharp, distinctive flavors. They tend to prefer savory dishes to sweet, and they have discriminating palates.

The test of true Scorpios is not their taste in clothes but their taste for cloves of garlic. If, for example, you like the stuff but think of it as a potent, pungent flavoring, you are only slightly Scorpionic. To fully epitomize your sign, you need to see garlic not as a seasoning but as a vegetable, to be eaten cooked, like cabbage, or, better still, raw like fruit! Other sure signs of a typically Scorpionic palate include a liking for sharp, sour, or bitter foods such as horseradish, capers, pickled onions, watercress, radicchio, and rhubarb.

MONEY

"Money is coined liberty, and so it is ten times dearer to a man who is deprived of freedom. If money is jingling in his pocket, he is half consoled, even though he cannot spend it."

The author of these words, the nineteenth-century Russian novelist Fyodor Dostoevsky, was a Scorpio. The words say a lot about your sign's bittersweet relationship with money. You may have a talent for making it and an even more highly developed talent for spending it, but you have long since learned that what it does to you outweighs what it can do *for* you. Money, or rather worrying about money, robs you of precious peace of mind and distracts you from deeper, more important issues. It doesn't necessarily follow that extra cash solves the problem, nor does the answer lie in living the life of a tightwad. You simply need a way to enjoy the freedom it brings while avoiding the trouble.

To do this, you need not have a trust fund, but have a fund of trust in a higher power. Be neither greedy nor careless, but diligent and sensitive, and your finances will always sort themselves out more than adequately. If you ever want to make a little extra money, resolve to bring out the masterpiece you always knew you had within you. The novel, symphony, sculpture, or movie you produce will ensure a tidy nest egg for your old age, provided you give yourself wholeheartedly to such a project. It may be, however, that for practical reasons you are not free to lock yourself in an attic for the necessary time. If these reasons are purely financial, transcend them. If, however, other commitments prevent you from a fully fledged frenzy of artistic indulgence, just do what you can to employ your imagination profitably in more mundane areas of life.

JUST THE JOB?

Acupuncturist, aircraft designer, claims adjuster, dentist, detective, environmentalist, healer, journalist, lumberjack, pathologist, pest controller, pharmacist, produce gardener, psychiatrist, radio therapist, researcher, satirist, sex therapist, snake charmer, spy, surgeon, tanner, tax specialist, undertaker.

Five ways to cash in
★ Pretend your cash belongs to someone else and treat it accordingly.
★ Refuse to pay any more of the bills which are constantly landing on your doormat.
★ Stop allowing money to intimidate you.
★ Take the advice that you are always so free to give to others.
★ Offer your services to the CIA, at a price, of course.

Five ways to branch out
★ Become a TV fitness guru.
★ Pose for pictures in *Playboy* or *Playgirl*.
★ Find the lost city of Atlantis.
★ Seduce Tom Cruise.
★ Produce "fly on the wall" documentaries.

LOVE

Scorpios are not really sex maniacs. They're just very honest and demonstrative about their urges and feelings. It takes a long time before a Scorpio will put his or her trust in another person. But once that trust is given, it soon becomes unshakable loyalty.

If you have difficulty with the idea of making your current love last forever, I put it to you that this is mainly because you feel that you already have an old love, that the magic and the pain is going to last forever, no matter what you try to do about it. Scorpios are, as you know only too well, the most sensitive people in the zodiac. And sensitive people tend to get their hearts broken very early in life. Once broken, sensitive people's hearts never seem to mend fully. Their hearts harden around the places where the scars lie, and it becomes very difficult for the owners of these hearts to let anyone, no matter how deserving and potentially wonderful, get near enough to let them run the risk of being hurt again.

You may consider yourself to be carrying a torch or nursing a wound, or, perhaps more likely, considering Scorpios' tendency to deny what they don't like to think about, simply feeling rather numb for reasons you don't care to examine further. But whatever it is, it's certainly not very fair to the person you are now with or would like to be with one day, or even to yourself. One way or another, you've got to rid yourself of the ghost of your past, get what happened when you were so much younger out of your system, and give your future the chance it deserves. And if you can do that, bearing in mind all you have learned in the meantime about how to be realistic rather than hopelessly idealistic in love, the chances of your finding that genuine happy-ever-after are a lot greater than you might imagine.

A SIDEWAYS LOOK AT YOUR SIGN

Some star signs I look forward to writing about, while others are more difficult. But there's just one that I dread and will do anything to avoid.

Not that there's anything wrong with Scorpios, you understand, it's just that everyone already thinks that they know all there is to be said about people born under this sign, and most of it isn't good. Explaining the truth, even to a Scorpio, is a major battle. I suppose I should get to the point, but I warn you, the following contains explicit reference to matters of a sexual nature. If you find such frankness offensive, please don't read on.

Scorpios are hot-blooded, sensual people with an endless appetite for physical pleasure. They cannot keep their passions under control and are forever surging with primal lust which must be fulfilled, no matter what the cost. They're jealous, mean, broody characters who never trust anyone. Woe unto you if you ever poke fun at a Scorpio. Scorpios bear a grudge with deep malice, plotting revenge and scheming your downfall. Most mass murderers are Scorpios. So are most child beaters, torturers, prostitutes, drug dealers, and real estate agents!

Aha! Just checking that you were awake. That was a powerful paragraph. But just how far through it did you get before you realized I was joking? If you did believe that summary of the many slanderous lies which are frequently told about those who were born under this noble sign, don't feel too bad. Millions of people all over the world believe it, including a large number of Scorpios themselves.

This probably explains the other great myth about Scorpios: the idea that they are secretive. Many Scorpios feel so ashamed of their sign that they refuse to confess their date of birth in public. It's not surprising, but it's sad, because Scorpios truly have a lot to be proud of. There is, you see, a very big difference between a zodiac sign and a person born under that zodiac sign.

Scorpio (the sign) actually does represent sex, penetration, reproduction, the elimination of bodily waste, death by unnatural causes, and pretty much everything that's unmentionable in polite society. Scorpio (the person), however, does not, just as Aries rules pimples, but not all Arians are spotty, and Pisces rules the feet, but that doesn't give them more than ten toes!

So what's the difference between the sign and the person? Well, what's the difference between the United States, the country, and the people of the United States? While you're chewing that one over, let me ask you two more questions.

First, have you ever seen a full horoscope based on someone's date of birth, the year, time, and place? If so, you'll know that all twelve signs of the zodiac are in everybody's chart. Astrology works on the principle that, no matter what sign we are, we all have the potential to display Leonine pride, Cancerian compassion, Geminian wit, and so on. Secondly, why were you so excited when you read that little warning earlier on? Go on, admit it! You thought you were going to read something spicy, racy, and rude, and you could hardly wait! Well, that's because, no matter what sign you are, that warning struck a chord with the Scorpio side of your nature.

So what is that Scorpio factor? Is it really a lust for titillation? No! Think harder about what the warning implied. It did not mention perversion or even passion. All it contained, in fact, was a promise of honesty. If you found it exciting, it was only because it suggested I might tell you some raw truths about life. And these, in our polite society, are fascinatingly rare.

SAGITTARIUS

November 23 – December 21

The Sagittarian quest is for spiritual enlightenment. In all their travels, adventures, escapades, and fascinations, Sagittarians are seeking only one thing: the elusive bridge of wisdom which links the world of the finite to the world of the infinite. Though many choose to wear the jester's cap, it rests on the head of the zodiac's deepest philosopher.

I F you're free and easy, a Sagittarian is your ideal companion. They're game for anything, full of wild ideas, and normally bold as brass. If you're cautious, though, you can rely on a Sagittarian to unnerve you! Sagittarians are as deep and sensitive below the surface as they are happy-go-lucky above it. They hate convention and prefer to express feelings when they really feel them. A Sagittarian, for example, may shower you with gifts one day out of the blue but totally forget your actual birthday. They won't hold it against you if you do the same. In fact, they'd rather you did that than give some dull or predictable token.

Sagittarians love the spur of the moment and can feel badly trapped by a standing commitment. Their enthusiasm lasts only while there's challenge or novelty. This doesn't make them unreliable, for they will always honor an obligation, but they don't really enjoy being dutiful and are at their happiest when anything can happen.

Sagittarians also have great difficulty saying the word "no." It's an endearing quality based on irrepressible optimism. The closest they'll normally come to a refusal is a sort of hesitant "maybe," which might easily be mistaken for a guarded "yes." If you can learn to read the signs and tell which is which, your life will be easier, and their relationship with you will be much happier.

HOME

Sagittarians will happily live in the strangest places, or failing this, they will try hard to make an ordinary home as odd as possible.

Your home may not be sumptuous, but it is always welcoming, or it would be if only your visitors could ever find a chair to sit on. These and the tables tend to be piled high with items you've been meaning to get around to putting away. Fortunately, your friends make allowances for your lack of domesticity. They know you thrive on adventure and would rather spend your cash on plane tickets than roof repairs. They might, however, appreciate it if you could, one day, invest just a little money in a broom or a vacuum that actually worked!

A Sagittarian's ideal house number is probably 2001, because they never have enough space, and they are always longing for an odyssey!

CLOTHES

Sagittarians are notorious for wearing anything they find at hand, but if there's an occasion worth dressing up for, they can outshine everyone!

You're as likely to find a vegetarian at a slaughterhouse as a Sagittarian at a fashion show. You're hopelessly out of touch with current trends and totally unapologetic about it. This might be fine if you were a timelessly tasteful dresser. But are you? Not at all. Not only do you reject modernity, you snub tradition. You think you have a perfect right to wear denim with tweed, army boots with silks, bright red tops with vivid green skirts, and so on. Worse still, you have the downright temerity to look good in these bizarre combinations, most of the time at least.

CARS

You ought to drive a Colt, a Mustang, or a Cavalier. Why? Because yours is the sign of the centaur: half human, half horse. You don't so much buckle into the driving seat as strap yourself into the saddle, and when you set off, you want plenty of horsepower. Wealthy Sagittarians express this preference, along with a tendency towards incorrigible optimism, by choosing cars capable of speeds which could get a 747 airborne. Poorer ones just wistfully wonder whether they could get a V8 engine by pouring Campbell's vegetable juice into the tank! For these and other reasons too numerous and embarrassing to mention, Sagittarian-driven cars tend to end up at the scrap yard earlier than most.

FOOD

Sagittarians are always hungry. Luckily, they burn up lots of calories with their nervous energy. They also tend to eat their food very quickly.

How tempted are you by leek and asparagus soup followed by chickpeas in spicy tomato sauce on a bed of wild rice with a side dish of roast parsnip? And, for dessert, apricot and almond tart spiced with cinnamon and cloves. Each of the above ingredients is governed by Jupiter, ruler of your sign, so if you're a typical Sagittarian, you don't just fancy that menu, you're already halfway into the kitchen to cook it. If cooking is not a thing you do much of, either you're not a typical Sagittarian or you're a frustrated one. Yours is potentially the sign of the brilliant chef and the great entertainer.

MONEY

"If you can actually count your money then you are not a really rich man."

Thus spake Sagittarian millionaire John Paul Getty in the twentieth century. Though he used the word "man," I'm sure he meant "person," and I hope this little linguistic lapse won't stop Sagittarian females from identifying with the spirit of his statement. For those born under the sign of the centaur, there really is no such thing as "enough." Your motto might as well be: "If a thing's worth doing, it's worth doing to wild excess and then a few times more for good measure."

It's not that you're greedy, just that you're endowed with a hearty appetite. It's not that you're unaware of the need for financial restraint, just that you're helplessly extravagant. It's not even, come to think of it, that you're ambitious in the traditional sense. It's just that you have an insatiable curiosity to see how far you can push your luck. As a Sagittarian you tend, sadly, to spend with all the prudence of a drunken lottery winner, even when your financial picture ought to be giving rise to far more sobering thoughts.

Occasionally you will nobly attempt to discipline yourself in one area, only to spoil matters soon afterwards by blowing all you have saved elsewhere.

This is one reason why your bank balance keeps going up and down like a yo-yo. Another is your propensity to avoid steady sources of income in favor of speculative ventures and dubious get-rich-quick schemes. Happily, your ruling planet, Jupiter, has a kind disposition and usually steps in to inject common sense when your own proves sorely lacking.

JUST THE JOB?

Air steward/stewardess, announcer, attorney, broadcaster, cleric, court officer, engineer, explorer, film director, foreign correspondent, humorist, importer, inventor, jockey, judge, philanthropist, philosopher, preacher, publicist, safari leader, sportsman/woman, travel agent, tour guide, university professor, writer.

Five ways to cash in
  ★ Forget about get-rich-quick schemes.
  ★ In fact, forget about getting rich in general.
  ★ Go off and do something self-sacrificing instead.
  ★ Make sure you get plenty of media publicity for your noble endeavor.
  ★ And there you have it, the best way for you to get rich quick.

Five ways to branch out
  ★ Become energy self-sufficient by building an electricity-generating windmill on your roof.
  ★ Open an exclusive holiday camp on the moon.
  ★ Instill the virtues of monogamy into Jack Nicholson.
  ★ Persuade Jackie Collins to write a book without passionate scenes.
  ★ Save the dodo.

LOVE

When Sagittarians fall in love, the fulfillment and expression of that love is of paramount importance. They find it impossible to play it cool. Loyalty means everything to Sagittarians. They give their whole hearts to people they trust, and they expect similar dedication in return.

If you are having difficulty now, or have had trouble in the past, with making a relationship stand the test of time, it is almost certainly because you have tried too hard. As a Sagittarian, you cannot help but feel overwhelming optimism about everything you ever attempt or dream of. You either don't care at all, or you care so passionately that it drives you crazy. And when, as so often happens, you do care deeply, you find it impossible to turn your emotions on and off like the proverbial tap. All this makes you incorrigible and irrepressible, potentially very successful at getting what you want, but sadly, just occasionally, a bit difficult to live with.

People who are prone to a little more self-doubt, emotional insecurity, or just general pessimism find your faith inspiring but overwhelming. Sometimes they even need a break from your Sagittarian smile simply to find out how to manifest one of their own. The trouble here is that you find it hard to let them go. Swinging in classic centaurian fashion from one extreme to the other, you change from having every confidence in the fact that your relationship can eventually be made to work to having none whatsoever.

Making a partnership last a lifetime is thus, for every Sagittarian, ultimately a matter of learning how to make allowances for the slower speed at which their companion probably needs to operate or for the greater depth in which they feel they need to analyze their feelings. And it may also involve learning how to stand back a little when the occasion demands it, without actually going so far as to storm out of the door in a huff!

A SIDEWAYS LOOK AT YOUR SIGN

Before I begin to tell you about the sign of Sagittarius, I must confess a complete lack of objectivity. While it's the sign I know most about, it's also the sign that puzzles me more than any other. And the reason I must be so courageously, self-defeatingly honest is that I am as much a fearlessly frank Sagittarian as you are!

We Saggies, you see, simply can't resist being up-front, outspoken, and a little outrageous. And while that has a lot to do with what being a Sagittarian is all about, it often leads us into hot water. We end up getting accused of being tactless, effusive, and offensive. We just don't know where to draw the line, or rather we do, but sometimes we just don't care!

Fortunately, despite our many alleged faults and character defects, most people seem to agree that we are wonderfully enthusiastic. They sometimes think that we can be unbearably optimistic, intolerably hopeful, and nauseatingly bright and breezy, but at least they concede that our zest for life rarely fails us, and we're never down for very long.

When I was a kid, I used to have a blow-up Yogi Bear with a weight at the bottom. It was as big as I was, and, no matter how hard you hit it, it would just wobble a bit and then bounce right back to an upright position, ready for more punishment. That, in a nutshell, is the Sagittarian spirit, and it's probably also true that, at a physical level, most Sagittarians have similarly extraordinary recuperative powers.

Contrary to popular belief, however, Sagittarians don't all like sports and horseback riding. What most of them do like is challenge. If you want to get a Sagittarian to do something, tell them it's impossible or, better still, dare them to do it! We Sagittarians like the thrill of pitting our wits (and bodies) against adverse conditions and emerging triumphantly. If we really think we can't do it, we won't try. But by and large the only things that frighten us are rules, regulations, bureaucracies, routines, and people who believe that the point of living is to keep your head down, act normal, and do what the world expects.

Having said all this, though, I mustn't leave you with the impression that Sagittarians are one-dimensional beings who have a good sense of humor and a love of travel and adventure but not much else. I would *like* to leave you with that impression, of course, because it's the picture I want the world to have of me and the image that I suspect you, too, would probably prefer to project. But the reason why we try so hard to come across as unflappable and lighthearted is that inside we are sensitive and thoughtful. We care so much about our fellow humans that it sometimes hurts. We feel deeply, we empathize strongly, and we want to do our best for others. But it can't always be done. Occasionally, pain is a necessary part of human growth. That's the fact that we find hardest to face, and when times are tough or we and those we care for are suffering, it's only our unshakable faith in a happier future that keeps us going despite the problems. We are optimistic and positive because we feel we have to be. We see it as our duty to be court jesters, and the worse the world gets, the broader our painted smiles will be.

We Sagittarians somehow instinctively know that faith creates hope, hope creates inspiration, and inspiration creates magic. And when we apply these principles, they work.

CAPRICORN

December 22 – January 20

Capricorns are the keepers of the cosmic clock. The Capricorn quest is to treasure the history and measure the mystery of the passing hours. A Capricorn, however, doesn't so much seek to take time as to give it. To create opportunity for others by helping them make more of life's most precious, yet limited, resource is every Capricorn's noble wish.

IF you need to get something done, contact a Capricorn. These down-to-earth people tackle every task one step at a time and rarely let anything or anyone intimidate them. Even when they're under extreme pressure, you'll rarely see a Capricorn crumble. On the surface, at least, they're steady and stable, inspiring others to entrust them with responsibility and authority. Beneath the Capricorn crust, however, is a very soft center. Capricorns seethe with hidden hopes and intense emotions. They usually repress these, using them as a driving force to propel them towards ambition. Even so, those emotions are still potentially dangerous. Imagine someone who keeps explosives in a safe deposit box buried in the basement of a bank. Sooner or later, something will detonate the explosives. Capricorns know this, but they still hate to admit their feelings.

You must understand this if you are to be a true friend to a Capricorn. It's easy to get along with them at a superficial level because they're so full of useful information and practical ideas. They've always got something interesting to say, and they're good listeners, too. But at a deeper level, there's another story to be told. Gain a Capricorn's confidence, and they'll gradually share their secret, volatile fears. The very act of admission defuses them. So while your Capricorn might appreciate a handy gadget as a birthday present, what you really should give is a chance to bare his or her soul.

HOME

Capricorns like their homes to be safe places, in every sense of the word.

Some people's homes look like palaces, but are full of items you dare not touch or sofas which look lovely but turn out to be as hard as nails. Yours is low on gloss and glamour but high on comfort and practicality. You'd rather have double glazing than stained glass, you'd rather have one sturdy grandfather clock than a shelf full of fancy china ornaments, and you'd rather hang your clothes on the back of the chair than spend a fortune on bedroom furniture that nobody's ever going to see. Your house is usually the last in the street to have the latest decor, but it's always the first place people head for when they want to relax.

Your ideal house number is 40, to remind you of when life begins for a Capricorn!

CLOTHES

Capricorns dress as they speak. They like functional, practical clothes and have little interest in frills or finery unless it's necessary for a role they want to play.

In the mythology of the zodiac, Capricorn rules the past. Though you're quite capable of carrying off an up-to-the-minute outfit, you feel far more comfortable in something classic, timeless, and universally smart. If it happens to be something your mother might once have worn, so much the better. Indeed, better still if it would have suited your grandmother or even grandfather! I'm not suggesting you ought to wander round town in a bustle or a crinoline, but you might look splendid in culottes, hacking jackets, plus-fours, and similar garb from the early twentieth century onwards.

CARS

You won't thank me for saying this, nor, come to think of it, will your bank account. Nonetheless, your ideal car is probably a BMW, a Mercedes, a Rolls, or a Jaguar. As a Capricorn, you place a lot of importance on precision, efficiency, and reliability. You're also, frankly, not immune to a little bit of status seeking. If you're not already the proud owner of one of the above, it's probably because you feel you can't afford to be. Next time you change cars, however, you might consider a "previously owned" upscale vehicle in preference to a younger model of less repute. Such vehicles, like Capricorns themselves, tend to mature beautifully, if well maintained. They also drive, just as you do, comfortably, satisfyingly, and safely.

FOOD

Capricorns tend to prefer plain, wholesome home cooking. They have cosmopolitan tastes but are unimpressed by fancy cuisine or expensively presented food.

Some might call you unadventurous when it comes to your eating habits. You prefer to see yourself as unpretentious. Wholesome, simple "foods of the earth" are the typically preferred fare of a Capricorn. Let the food faddists keep their complicated cuisines; you'll settle for plain, basic, good old meat and potatoes, bacon and eggs, hot dogs and baked beans. Your attitude towards food, as towards so much in life, boils down to: if you've got a successful formula, why change it?

MONEY

"It is in exchanging the gifts of the Earth that you shall find abundance and be satisfied. Yet, unless the exchange be in love and kindly justice it will lead but some to greed and others to hunger."

If you have just skimmed over the quote above in a hurry to get to the "meat," please read it again. It is the meat. The words were written by a Capricorn, the poet Kahlil Gibran. They come from his beautiful book *The Prophet* and sum up all there is to say about your relationship with money. Forget all thoughts of get-rich-quick schemes or opportunities to make a fast buck in an ethically debatable venture. All you ever need in order to keep the wolf from the door is to start doing more of what you're best at, what you know makes sense, and what you know is fundamentally fair and wholesome.

As a Capricorn you are capable of earning a living in many ways. You are efficient, incisive, organized, and diligent. You are also capable of manifesting great authority. Other people sit up and take notice when you make an emphatic statement. Really, though, you need apply none of the above qualities to your financial enterprises. If you do, you will almost certainly end up in a situation where you may have wealth but you have little satisfaction to show for it. The great secret of success, in the true sense of that word, for every Capricorn is to apply dedication to a project or plan that truly means the world to you. When you're engaged in such an honorable undertaking, money finds its way to you like a salmon finds its way home through the ocean.

JUST THE JOB?

Architect, builder, businessperson, chiropractor, clockmaker, economist, excavator, furniture restorer, gardener, government official, leather worker, manicurist, mining engineer, osteopath, plasterer, prison officer, property developer, restoration worker, sculptor, transportation scheduler, vocational counselor.

Five ways to cash in
★ Next time someone makes you a promise, be certain to get it confirmed in writing.
★ Stick to what you're good at and let the rest look after itself.
★ Stop worrying about everything going wrong. It might never happen.
★ Charge more and apologize less.
★ Eat at cheaper restaurants and bring your own wine.

Five ways to branch out
★ Go to work for a government agency and get it to run efficiently.
★ Convert your car to run on solar power and used teabags.
★ Star in a steamy XXX-rated movie (but don't tell your friends).
★ Have the last word in a conversation.
★ Write how-to manuals.

LOVE

Capricorns have no time for the flowery trappings of romance. But if they really care for you, they'll show it in a genuine, endearing way. If you're not convinced that Capricorns are more sensually responsive and better able to give pleasure than any other sign, take a straw poll among your friends!

For you as a Capricorn, the question is not so much how can you make your love last forever as how can you make your feelings for another person come to life in the first place. Unless you're highly atypical of your sign or are in the company of someone who has a tremendously natural, almost chemical, rapport with you, you tend to hold back a great deal of your heart and even your head. You can play the game of love as well as, if not better than, anyone. You can say all the right words, make all the right gestures, do all the right things. But can you really feel sure that you are doing more than going through the motions? More importantly, can your partner?

You can be certain that if your partner is truly the right person for you, they will have noticed, much earlier in the relationship than you might ever have imagined, what a difficult nut to crack you are. They may have discreetly avoided mentioning it. Or they may, perhaps, have commented, realized there was little they could do about it, and decided to make the most of whatever they could get. But they will have sensed your reticence, and they will (naturally enough) have put up barriers of their own in order to protect themselves. These barriers are probably the only things that stand between you and your partner making it through from here to the day when time stands still. To dismantle them, you do not suddenly have to turn into a fountain of sentimentality. But you do have to acknowledge their existence, communicate your concern about them, and consciously work on ways to ensure that your relationship is based on more than just a routine, a lifestyle, a habit, and a fear of change!

A SIDEWAYS LOOK AT YOUR SIGN

When Capricorns aren't busy calling a spade a spade, the chances are they're using that spade to dig deep and prepare strong foundations for whatever project they happen to be involved in. They don't waste time waiting for things to be perfect before rolling up their sleeves and getting to work. They cope with whatever happens to be in front of them, compensating for what's missing, adapting to what's needed, and inventing new ways to use what they've actually got.

Unlike some do-it-yourselfers in the zodiac, Capricorn do-it-yourselfers normally do quite well. If they're putting up a shelf with the wrong size screws, they'll pop in a couple of extra ones at strategic points of weakness in the wall. If they're advertising an event with a limited budget, they'll pick their words carefully to ensure that those who see the publicity feel obliged to attend and bring their friends! Capricorns are masters or mistresses of the "authority game." Even when they're shaking with terror, anxiety, or despair on the inside, you wouldn't know it to look at them. They have magnificent composure and incredible self-restraint.

So far I've been describing an asset, a characteristic that explains why so many Capricorns rise to positions of great responsibility and power. People sense that they're trustworthy, so they delegate authority to them. This is fine, except that Capricorns are actually sensitive human beings who suffer from emotions like fear, jealousy, or insecurity just as much as the rest of us. So sometimes, just sometimes, the things they do or say are unwise, unfair, or unjust. This is an accusation that could be accurately leveled at anyone in any sign, but the trouble with Capricorns is that everything they say comes out sounding sensible and reasonable, even when it's complete and utter nonsense.

This wouldn't be quite so bad if it only meant that Capricorns occasionally abuse their position of respect by misleading other people. You could say it's not their fault, that it's up to others to see through the façade. However, Capricorns are inscrutable not only to others but also to themselves. They have great difficulty separating what they really feel from what they think they ought to be feeling. They try hard always to do the right thing no matter what the circumstances, and they judge themselves harshly when they discover they've been wrong. Despite the fact that Capricorns are rarely wrong, when they do make an error, they make it in style. They make it with their heart and soul, convinced, at the time of making it, that it can't possibly be an error at all. They find it almost impossible to forgive themselves for their mistakes, and, even worse, they have memories like elephants.

Many people find it easy to treat the past as a mysterious world which belongs to someone else; Capricorns are the zodiac's natural historians. To a Capricorn, yesterday is the unalterable foundation upon which every tomorrow is built. They take the past and themselves very, very seriously. A Capricorn who loses self-confidence finds it very hard to regain it, which is why some people born under the sign fail to reach their deserved position in the order of things. What's more, a disillusioned Capricorn can soon become convinced that he or she "deserves to suffer." When that happens, as it often does, they can spend large chunks of their lives turning down opportunities. Fortunately this doesn't last forever. Eventually, their confidence comes back, and the essential qualities of strength, stamina, and leadership re-emerge.

AQUARIUS

21 January - 19 February

Aquarius may be the sign of the water bearer, but Aquarius is no water sign. Aquarius belongs to air and thus to thought, philosophy, and intellect. Aquarians have plenty of sensitivity and passion, but they believe emotion should be the servant, not the master, of the heart. Thus, Aquarians seek to help us all treasure and cherish the gift of objectivity.

IF you need expert advice, ask an Aquarian. No matter what the subject, you can be sure your Aquarian friend will venture a definitive answer. Nine times out of ten, that answer will be informed and accurate; it's the tenth time you must watch out for! Then, though the comments may be delivered with equal confidence, they'll be perilously wrong. How can you tell? You can't. Aquarians don't consider themselves capable of error, so they give no clues. Only if you try to follow the advice will you find it fallible. If you then go back and confront your Aquarian with the evidence, you may get a humble apology, but you're more likely to get a pompous excuse. So, if you are to get along well with them, you need to have a good sense of humor and a slightly skeptical nature. Aquarians are what they are. They can't be changed, so you must learn to love them for it. It's worth doing, because Aquarian assets far outnumber Aquarian defects.

Aloof, know-it-all and self-important they may be, but they are also generous, considerate, and extraordinary. There's nothing dull or predictable about an Aquarian. They're farsighted idealists, humanitarian philosophers, and open-minded thinkers. Once you've gotten used to their odd ways, you'll find their friendship irresistible and their company addictive.

If you want to give an Aquarian a special treat, remember that they're attracted to unusual ideas, eccentric people, and innovative objects. Show them you recognize their special powers of discrimination. They'll love you for it.

HOME

Aquarians feel most comfortable in a home with a nice garden.

Aquarians are quirky, quarrelsome, and querulous. You hate lines, detest crowds, and love to assert your individuality. You wouldn't want to live anywhere you would consider run-of-the-mill, unless, of course, it was an old, abandoned watermill! That, or a converted railway carriage, would suit you fine. Even if circumstances (financial or otherwise) don't allow this, your home still tends to be a museum of self-expression. It's certainly a tribute to the art of experimentation, for there is something that almost works (but doesn't quite) in every room!

Your ideal house number is probably 911 (for the state of emergency you so often live in!).

CLOTHES

The politest way to describe the Aquarian color sense would be "creatively individualistic."

Although you can be outrageous in many ways, you're surprisingly conventional when it comes to clothes. I would even go so far as to say "restrained," but then, financially at least, that's not quite true. You have expensive taste and a keen eye for quality. You would far rather own a few excellently made suits than an entire wardrobe of discount clothes. On special days and holidays, you'll parade with panache in fashionable, even futuristic outfits, but for everyday wear, you prefer to find one basic formula and stick to it. For many Aquarians, this will involve knitwear. You're fond of natural materials like cotton and leather, but you have a special preference for wool.

CARS

The following dialogue sums up the Aquarian approach to driving.

Judge: "You are accused of going the wrong way on a one-way street. What do you say?"

Aquarian: "I was only going one way."

Judge: "But didn't you see the arrows?"

Aquarian: "Arrows? I didn't even see the Indians!"

Your copy of the driving code contains little footnotes which the printers carelessly neglected to place in the other copies. For example, "Never drive through a red light*" (*unless you feel like it), or "Don't pass on the right*" (*unless you're in a hurry). Only one thing is more idiosyncratic than your driving: your choice of car. It *must* be a make that nobody else has heard of and a model that no repair shop can get parts for because (a) you're fussy and (b) more than anything, you love to be exclusive!

FOOD

Aquarians love to experiment with new recipes and dishes. How these actually taste is of secondary importance to their potential value as a talking point.

If you're a truly typical Aquarian, you adore eating out: Indian one night, Chinese the next, Italian the night after, and French the night after that. The more obscure and eclectic the cuisine the better, because, arguably, you enjoy the discovery of new tastes and textures more than the actual process of eating. Unlike some people, you rarely eat for succor and emotional comfort. Indeed, because you're terribly fussy, you'd almost rather go hungry than settle down to eat a boring meal.

MONEY

"Money is like a sixth sense without which you cannot make a complete use of the other five."

The writer Somerset Maugham, who made the memorable remark above, was an Aquarian, and to me his statement reveals a lot about a very specific Aquarian tendency. Few and far between are the people born under your sign who pursue money for its own sake. As an Aquarian, you may be shrewd, you may be successful, and you may even have expensive tastes, but you are not, unless I am very much mistaken, avaricious. To you, money is indeed a sixth sense. Just as you do not actively seek to develop your intuition, you simply expect it to be there when you need to call on it, so you tend to take financial gain for granted. It comes naturally when you're doing the right thing, just as an inspired idea or a smart hunch might do. Your instincts, of course, are pretty good, and so are your potential money-making abilities. Both, however, work best when you're not really trying, in other words when they appear as a side effect of trying to accomplish another goal altogether.

You must beware, however, of a tendency to let your generosity and compassion get the better of you. These laudable qualities can sometimes place an enormous burden on your resources. Should this prove to be an ongoing problem, change the nature of your charitable activities. See them not as a sideline but as integral to your overall game plan. Explore the possibility of doing professionally an aspect of what you are already doing voluntarily. You'll find an opportunity opens up almost as soon as you're in a frame of mind to see it. You'll also find the general economic trend becomes extremely positive.

JUST THE JOB?

Actor, art dealer, aviator, broadcaster, civil rights campaigner, community organizer, computer consultant, congressperson, counselor, electrician, faith healer, furniture designer, inventor, laser technician, lighting specialist, mechanic, navigator, psychotherapist, recording studio engineer, social worker, telecommunications worker.

Five ways to cash in
- ★ Stop trying to "do it yourself" to save cash. You will only end up having less time on your hands to do the things that matter.
- ★ Swallow your pride and accept other people's suggestions.
- ★ Make friends with a wealthy person who likes helping you.
- ★ Stop trying so hard to keep up with the Joneses.
- ★ Don't throw good money after bad.

Five ways to branch out
- ★ Invent a better mousetrap.
- ★ Teach your skills to others.
- ★ Open a charm school.
- ★ Become a movie critic.
- ★ Become a top-level, high-ranking government adviser.

LOVE

Aquarians can be charming and seductive when romance first blossoms. They know how to use any trick in the book to capture your heart. Aquarians are traditionally reputed to be aloof, detached, and unemotional. If only it were true!

Although Aquarians tend to be supremely confident about what they know, what they believe, and what they want to accomplish, many people born under your sign find this natural sense of certainty tends to desert them when asked to quantify what they actually feel. Because they don't like having to confess to doubt at any level, under any circumstance, they will go to great lengths to disguise their confusion. They will make unconvincingly emphatic statements, or else they will appear as noncommittal as possible, hoping that they can fob off requests for emotional reassurance with the excuse that they never talk about things like that.

You may notice that so far I have deliberately been depersonalizing my suggestions about how to make your love last forever. I have given you the option of assuming that I am describing other people born under your sign, but not you. Ultimately, it's a question of "if the shoe fits." But while you decide whether it does, may I make another potentially confrontational comment in the softest possible terms? The great psychologist Carl Jung was a firm believer in the idea that, when one person finds another irritating or difficult to be with, it's because the second person's faults remind the first person of the things they most dislike about themselves. And now, we really must depart from the realm of the theoretical and impersonal. What I am trying to tell you, gently and discreetly because I know that as an Aquarian you despise and detest the very notion of being offered advice, is this: If you want to get along better with the person you are now with, or ever find yourself with in the future, you must look at what it is about them that you cannot tolerate. And you must ask yourself, not how they might possibly change in time, but how you might. And that's how you'll be able to make your love last forever.

A SIDEWAYS LOOK AT YOUR SIGN

Aquarius is the eleventh sign of the zodiac and lies opposite Leo in the celestial circle. Many people falsely believe that Aquarius is a water sign; this is largely because the symbol of Aquarius is a water bearer, an elegant male or female figure who carries an earthenware vessel. The confusion is compounded by the fact that sometimes artists illustrate Aquarius with a simple picture of water being poured from a jug. That's a shame because central to the symbol of the sign is the figure of a human who has traveled to the fountain of eternal wisdom and is now carrying a precious burden of knowledge and understanding. It is the person, not the jug, which is the focal point of the sign. The content of the jug may be liquid, but because it represents a lofty concept, it more properly belongs to the element "air." This is the same reason that Libra and Gemini are also "air" signs. People born under all these analytical, intellectual air signs tend to "think" their way through life, and they often place more importance on big ideas than on feelings and actions. Aquarius is also a "fixed" sign. There are four fixed signs in the zodiac. The other three are Leo, Scorpio, and Taurus. Although these signs are very different, people born under them tend to be set in their ways. The "fixed air" sign, Aquarius, tends to produce people who use their intelligence at all times but who find it hard to change their minds about anything.

Astrologers believe that every object or idea can be catalogued under one zodiac sign. Here is a list of things ruled by Aquarius: altruism, ankles, aviation, batteries, blood circulation, broadcasting, clubs, colleagues, cooperatives, Cyprus, electricity, exploration, frankincense, friends, gas, hope, humanitarianism, inventions, Iran, January, kinetic energy, legislation, modernization, motors, novelty, opals, organizations, paradoxes, parliaments, pilots, progress, radar, radio, reform, revolution, Russia, salt, sapphires, science, shins, society, spasms, stereos, technology, television, wishful thinking, X-rays.

Aquarians hope for a chance to make themselves useful, especially to others, a world in which everyone is happy and healthy, a glamorous and exciting social life, and a place in history as the person who made a brilliant, unique, and unforgettable contribution to their environment. Aquarians fear public embarrassment, private conflict, emotional blackmail, boredom, repetition, the commonplace, social ostracism, family gatherings, compromises, and financial failure. Aquarians like to be one step ahead, to be different, to argue over fine points, to show people how to do things, to be given an intellectual challenge, and to be generous.

Aquarians are simple souls at heart, though most of them will never admit it. They like to give you the impression that they are complex, mysterious, and confident. That's partly why they are misunderstood, and they don't really mind because it means that the only people who get close to them are those perceptive enough to penetrate the surface.

If you want to learn how to spot an Aquarian on first meeting, look for someone who lets slip a strong, probably controversial opinion shortly after the conversation begins. It won't be delivered in a challenging way, just in a sort of offhand but very knowledgeable manner. If you want to disarm Aquarians, ask them to explain something to you and look interested while they go through all the endless details. If you want to annoy an Aquarian, ask how they feel. And if you want to know what all Aquarians have in common, the answer is nothing except a keen desire to be individuals, which is why many Aquarians dislike astrology. They hate being lumped together with other Aquarians!

PISCES
February 20 – March 20

Pisceans are the zodiac's magicians. They may not pull rabbits from hats, but they do perform acts of amazing transformation every day. The Piscean's greatest gift is the ability to turn despair into hope and fear into faith. Pisceans specialize in helping us to find the hidden wonder in that which we might be tempted to dismiss as ordinary.

PISCEANS don't miss much. They have a special inner radar which lets them tune into hidden messages, and somehow they always know what's really going on in people's hearts. You'll rarely find a Piscean abusing this gift, though, because Pisceans are as sensitive as they are sympathetic. It's just as well. If their ambitions were as ruthless as their instincts are sharp, there'd be no stopping a Piscean, ever.

Happily, nature has made most Pisceans content to value human warmth above material gain. There are, of course, exceptions to any rule, but even the occasional avaricious Piscean is prone to the same basic handicap as his or her less competitive cousin, an overactive imagination.

Pisceans are full of visionary enthusiasm. They daydream in Technicolor. Creativity comes as naturally to a Piscean as strength to an athlete. It's the sort of creativity which every poet, artist, musician, storyteller, or inventor needs. It's inspirational energy, but, while it's wonderful to have on tap, it's hard to control. Pisceans who don't have a creative job or hobby often find themselves overwhelmed by ideas which they can't put to use or emotions which they can't understand.

The best thing you can give your Piscean friends is an outlet for this imagination. Join them in their reveries, encourage their idealism, and, most important of all, help them see which of their fantasies should be followed and which should be ignored.

HOME

There's a chameleonlike quality to Pisceans. They usually manage to blend in with their surroundings no matter how much or how quickly these change.

Your Piscean home is, I'm sure, comfortable and cleverly furnished, but I'd like to bet it's also forever full of friends and neighbors in various states of severe distress. Who *are* these people who sit on your sofa, pouring their hearts out from morning till night, and then just pull out the cushions, turn it into a bed, snore loudly, and wake up to start sobbing on your shoulder all over again the next day? Where do they come from? And why do you encourage them? Their perpetual presence means your house is never quiet, dull, or empty, but it also means you never have time to live the domestic idyll you once intended.

You ideal house number is 1, to remind you of who you should be looking out for.

CLOTHES

Pisceans like to wear clothes which emphasize their romantic or idealistic aspirations. They can get away with very flamboyant, provocative outfits.

Pisces is a mysterious, exotic sign, so Pisceans ought to wear mysterious, exotic clothes. You were born to wander around in caftans and kimonos, saris and sarongs, pelerines and ponchos. Though you don't always wear such adventurous attire, you don't fool anyone when you dress more conventionally. Your faraway eyes still look as if they're longing to be set off by clothes from faraway places; so if you want to do yourself a real favor, let loose the poet in your soul. Find the courage to wear those long flowing robes and intricately patterned prints you're forever being tempted by.

CARS

For you, a car is a sort of elaborate mounting for your stereo speakers. You're so bothered about your sound system that, even when your car breaks down, you're more inclined to change the tape than the wheel. Other useful things in your car include a selection of mirrors in which to check your appearance. You suspect they have another purpose, but, offhand, you can't quite recall what it is. Such vagueness does, however, have its advantages. Salesmen give up when they ask what kind of vehicle you want, only to be told: "A nice blue one, please." Sadly, this makes you a liability on the road. You are, for example, supposed to use your turn signal to indicate that you are about to turn, not because you want to point out, to the motorist behind, a particularly pretty rose bush over there on the right!

FOOD

The ideal Piscean meal would probably take the form of a buffet table bulging with many colorful, exotic dishes on which to nibble slowly.

Pisceans are particularly fond of food that looks like it's going to taste of one thing but turns out to be entirely different. Rice that's been subtly flavored with coconut or lemon, white sauce that's been cleverly seasoned with cumin or coriander, cheese that has been matured with beer or onions would all be Piscean favorites. It's all related to being born under the influence of Neptune, the great celestial illusionist. You like your meals to be masterpieces and, to accompany them, you like wines full of character, wit, and subtlety. Your Piscean palate is tremendously sensitive, and you simply love having it stimulated.

MONEY

"The hardest thing in the world to understand is the income tax."

This quote comes from Albert Einstein, who was not just a genius but a Piscean genius. I have chosen it to begin your forecast partly because it's amusing to think of the person who gave the world $E = mc^2$ having trouble working out his tax return, and partly because I haven't been able to find an eminent Piscean economist to quote. I'm not too surprised, mind you. Yours is a creative sign. Creative people don't always do well in areas where people are expected to be dry, logical, and matter-of-fact. Einstein managed to get away with being a creative scientist, but even he couldn't bring himself to wrap his brilliant mind around such a dull matter as money. Creative people rarely can. When they do, it gets them into trouble. Creative economists are mistrusted, creative accountants frowned on, and creative financiers very often put into prison!

If you work in any of these fields, please don't take offense. I'm sure you're very good at following the rules all day, as long as you get to do something more inspiring by night. Even so, I maintain that if, as a Piscean, you really wish to *make* money, your best bet is to do something, well, creative! Long ago, you were very interested in a subject that circumstances eventually obliged you to move away from. Rediscover your old hobby, area of interest, or big idea. With a few modifications, it can become an important, profitable part of your future. You'll find yourself saying something like, "I never realized what a gold mine I was sitting on," or "Who would have thought that my interest in X would eventually lead to Y?" It should all result in a great deal of pleasure and satisfaction.

JUST THE JOB?

Anesthetist, artist, bartender, cartoonist, charity worker, chemist, clairvoyant, dancer, distiller, drug rehabilitation worker, escapologist, film director, fisherman, hydraulics engineer, impressionist, oceanographer, petroleum worker, photographer, plumber, poet, private eye, sailor, shoe repair person, spy.

Five ways to cash in
★ Write your life story (in the third person, with the names changed) as a best-selling romantic novel.
★ Cut back a little on that naughty and expensive habit.
★ Sell some of the shoes you no longer wear.
★ Pay as much attention to your banker as you normally do to your conscience.
★ Become a podiatrist or a reflexologist.

Five ways to branch out
★ Build your own multinational corporation from scratch.
★ Write beautiful, heartwarming poetry.
★ Breed exotic tropical fish in your own aquarium.
★ Take underwater photographs around gloriously exotic coral reefs.
★ Become a dream therapist.

LOVE

When a Piscean falls in love, the whole world turns rosy. Piscean fantasies can make a romantic novel look like a textbook on economics! In long-term relationships, boredom is rarely a problem for Pisceans. They can somehow make every day with their loved one seem new and exciting.

No Piscean is capable of giving his or her love exclusively and continuously to one person for an entire lifetime. This doesn't mean you cannot successfully maintain a joyous, monogamous relationship from now until the day you die or even (bearing in mind that you are a mystical Piscean) beyond. But it does mean that you have to recognize the limits of what any partnership can be expected to bring to you.

Because you're imaginative, idealistic and, to a degree at least, susceptible to the mythology with which we were all brought up, you cannot help but half-believe in the notion that two people can, if they try hard enough, become as one. It's a lovely idea, with a particular attraction to the poetic Piscean personality. But it's not necessarily quite so simple in reality.

Very often the most successful partnerships are those in which both participants have wide-ranging and very separate interests and commitments outside the relationship. To work successfully as a couple, they do not have to agree on every issue or area of interest. Indeed, they do not even have to tell each other every last detail of what they have been up to in their time apart. They do have to be honest, and they do have to have a bond of trust, but they also have to have enough commitment to and faith in one another not to feel obliged to weave a web of pretense. They do not have to (and should not try to) pretend to be fascinated in each others' hobbies or even jobs. Nor should they feel their relationship is only valid or worthwhile if they never argue, disagree, or differ.

Almost certainly you already know all this, in which case you are presumably well on the way to making your love last forever. But if it's lately begun to look as if this is not something that can or will ever happen, maybe it's time to look again at ways to separate, in your mind, the theoretical ideal from the pragmatic reality.

A SIDEWAYS LOOK AT YOUR SIGN

Pisceans are not just good fun to be with, it's never long before their amusing idiosyncrasies bubble to the surface. They're deeply sensitive and make loyal companions. Pisces is the twelfth sign of the zodiac, lying opposite Virgo in the celestial circle.

Pisces is a "water" sign, like Cancer and Scorpio. People born under the water signs tend to rely on their emotions rather than their intellects. They can be very brainy or academic, but deep down inside, they trust their feelings more than they trust their thoughts. Pisces is also a "mutable" sign, like Sagittarius, Gemini, and Virgo. People born under the water signs tend to be easygoing, flexible, and adaptable; they can also be lackadaisical or prone to changing horses in midstream. The "mutable water" sign Pisces produces people who are exceedingly sensitive and open to new ideas, and also people who could benefit from more discipline in their lives.

Pisces is symbolized by a pair of fish swimming away from each other. The idea is that one fish represents the world of material things and the other fish the world of the inner spirit. Pisceans supposedly don't belong to either world, but have one foot (or fish) in each camp. But there's something else in the symbol, water, which represents life itself. Pisceans are born not to struggle with themselves but to help others. Their message is that we must all learn to appreciate both worlds in order to be truly happy.

Pisceans don't just have strong instincts; they have accurate, long-range radar systems. Because they can rely on their sixth sense to guide them through life, they often act as if they don't know where they're going or what they're doing. Somehow, though, they always end up in the right place at just the right time. In fact, the endearing innocence which Pisceans project is a smoke screen, which is another reason why people born under this sign are so often successful. They disarm would-be adversaries by appearing to be lucky bumblers.

Because Pisceans are sensitive, sympathetic, and sweet-natured, they can sometimes be gullible. They are prone to pangs of guilt and are suckers for a sob story. A Piscean will always let you cry on his or her shoulder and will soak up your sorrow like a sponge. Then they'll walk around, carrying your burden and trying to solve your problems as well as their own. While this is a drawback to being a Piscean, it's also a part of a big advantage. The natural sixth sense protects them from harm, even when they make themselves dangerously responsible for the wrong people. It ensures that, even when they set out to help others, they end up coincidentally helping themselves.

Pisceans fear aggression, conflict, anger, confrontation, criticism, rejection, boredom, limitation, authority, competition, the commonplace, and being taken advantage of. They like to help other people, be thought of as wise, tell long stories, experiment with new ideas, wear fancy dress, be near the ocean, play at fortune-telling, be mysterious, and get carried away.

These are just some of the things which are traditionally ruled by Pisces: abstracts, alcohol, ambidexterity, anesthetics, aquariums, artists, bogs, boots, chaos, charity, cheats, chemistry, cisterns, clairvoyance, clouds, confinement, conspiracy, dance, disappointment, dissolution, escape, February, fog, gas, hermits, hospitals, institutions (of all kinds), intoxication, jellyfish, lilies (water), liquids, mediums, navies, nuns, oceans, opium, photography, podiatry, poetry, poison, retirement, sand, secrets, ships, sleep, suffering, time (power over), unconscious thought, wells, X-rays.

Chapter Two

THE MAGIC
OF YOUR
MOON SIGN

THE MAGIC OF YOUR MOON SIGN

Have you ever read about your zodiac sign but felt that, while you could identify with some of it, there wasn't enough to explain everything about you? Have you, perhaps, even felt a little insulted to hear an astrologer suggest that you share your personality with one-twelfth of the population? We're now going to look, not at what you have in common with those who share your sign, but at what makes you different.

THE REAL YOU

At the moment, all you really know about yourself in astrological terms is what Sun sign you were born under. Your Sun sign is the zodiac sign you turn to every day when you read your forecast in a daily column. It's the sign you share with everyone else who happens to have been born within the same thirty-day period of any year.

You can, if you like, consider your Sun sign to be the nationality under which you were born. Just as Americans tend to expect instant service while British people are more conditioned to expect a delay, so Aries and Virgo people tend, on the whole, to have contrasting ideas about what life ought to be offering them. You share, with everyone else born under your sign, certain influences which have shaped your outlook on life. They have given you an accent, an attitude, or a set of mannerisms. But you are more than your Sun sign, just as you are more than a product of your birthplace.

Between the sunny façade you put up for the benefit of others and the vulnerable, sincere individual you are in private, there's a gap as big as the difference between night and day. This is where your Moon sign comes in. If the Sun depicts the way you tend to be on the surface, the Moon describes what you are like deep down within. It tells you how you cope with problems, what you cling to for hope, plus when or why your moods are likely to alter. Your Moon sign, in other words, describes the kind of person you really are.

You may be wondering why nobody has ever told you about this before. To do the answer justice, I need to give you a brief history of popular astrology.

A HISTORY OF ASTROLOGY
IN TWO PAGES

Back in the distant past, if you'd asked an astrologer what sign you were, he or she would have told you your Moon sign, not your Sun sign. The Roman Emperor Augustus, for example, had the sign of Capricorn, the goat, embossed on the reverse of his coinage. But according to our modern way of looking at things, Augustus was actually a Libran born on 23 September 63 B.C. It just so happens, however, that on the day he was born, the Moon was in Capricorn. That was the part of his horoscope which he considered significant enough to show off.

Throughout the next two thousand years or so, nothing much changed. The great and the good all had an astrologer present at their birth. The rest of the population, meanwhile, were lucky if they even knew what year they were born in, let alone what month. When, or if, they consulted an astrologer, it would be to get a straight answer to a question such as "Who stole my sheep?" or "Will my son's ship return safely from foreign shores?" Astrologers would often answer these questions with surprising accuracy, but they would not consider the inquirer's date of birth. They simply got their answer from a chart of the sky as it stood at the precise moment of consultation.

This cosmic status quo prevailed throughout British astrology's long, proud history. From the Emperor Hadrian, who cast horoscopes between building walls, to King Henry VIII, who cast horoscopes between divorcing wives, to Queen Elizabeth I, who had horoscopes cast for her by the court "mathematician," the division remained simple. If you were "important," you got a full, personal "time of birth" horoscope. If you were not so well off, you got a form of cosmic "rune reading."

All this changed on July 1, 1837, with the Registration Act. All persons were obliged by law to have a record of their exact date of entry into the world. No longer were personal horoscopes exclusively reserved for the privileged few. The practice of astrology began to alter almost immediately, but still the Moon sign was seen as the most important factor within a chart.

That situation didn't change until 1930, when the *Sunday Express* began to print the first regular weekly column by a professional astrologer. R.H. Naylor's articles were rather dry to begin with, but he did once imply that the heavens were making air travel inauspicious. When the R101 airship crashed a few days later, Naylor's reputation was made. And history was made when

Naylor wrote a little piece called "What the Stars Foretell" for people born at various times of the year. This was an instant hit and had the public clamoring for more. So loudly did they clamor that the face of popular astrology was changed for good. I imagine the conversation between Naylor and Lord Beaverbrook, the proprietor of the *Express*, might have run something like this:

"Can you do more of this sort of thing, please?"

"Yes, indeed. We can work with people's Moon signs. You'll need to publish a few pages of tables so people can see what Moon sign they were born under. And then I can predict what sort of week they are going to have."

"I can't spare that sort of space. Do you think paper grows on trees? Can't we do anything that requires fewer tables and less space?"

"Er. . . [*reluctantly*] well, I suppose you could use Sun signs."

"Oh, yes? What are they?"

"Well, they're less specific indicators of personality and future, but they do have one distinct advantage. They're based on the movement of the Sun, which follows almost exactly the same pattern from year to year."

"So?"

"So instead of printing thousands of dates you only need to print twelve, thus saving loads of space."

"Splendid, old chap. Have a cigar!"

And so a star was born, or rather, twelve star signs were. Within weeks, American newspapers were on the bandwagon, and soon Sun sign columns were everywhere. The rest, as they say, is history. Except that it's not necessarily the sort of history about which all serious astrologers feel happy. "It's like," they say, "having a beautiful symphony you could play to people and then proceeding to hammer out a few passages with one hand on the piano." As an astrologer who once trained long and hard to learn the art of working with the full celestial orchestra, I have long wanted to be able to offer, if not the complete symphony, at least the left-hand piano part. And now, I can! All I need you to do, in order to make the magic happen, is to turn to page 256 and discover your Moon sign.

WHAT THE MOON REVEALS

There's just one more point I need to make. The Moon has a lot to do with the irrational, intuitive side of your nature. Unfortunately, just as society's statisticians and scientists feel it is their duty to provide a sensible explanation for everything, so most people have within their psyche a desire to refute the existence of the subconscious. It's the reason why we wake up after a vivid dream and try to shake it off, or why we all try so often to deny what we really feel. The Moon, being primarily an entity of the night, is all about dreams and feelings. To appreciate what I have to say about your Moon sign, you need to have a wish to explore your own dreams and feelings in more depth. You can gain a great deal more control over your destiny by understanding the urges that the Moon pulls like tides across your inner ocean. But first, you must be brave enough to look objectively and honestly at what these are.

A lot of people don't want to do this. They feel, perhaps, a little afraid that they may harbor a seething mass of emotional needs beneath the calm surface of their inner world. They even fear they may find, if they look, that they are a little crazy, or that others may think so.

I won't deny that there is a link between the Moon and craziness. The Latin word for Moon is *luna*, and it is from this that we get "lunacy." But actually, we don't get lunacy from looking at the Moon; we get it from denying its influence or trying to pretend that we are "normal." It's the constant stress of feeling socially obliged to repress a host of hidden feelings that causes most people to go over the edge. If we lived in a more honest, Moon-celebrating world, our asylums would probably mainly contain the people insensitive enough to imagine that they had no poetry in their soul. The way things stand in our Sun-centered, superficial society, it's often those with vision who cannot take the pace, while those without it set the pace!

"But what," you may say, "if I find, when I look at my Moon sign (or 'into my soul,' it amounts to the same thing) that I am not just mildly eccentric but dangerously deranged? Am I not in danger of opening up a Pandora's box?"

Maybe. But maybe you're potentially a lot more dangerous to yourself and others if you *don't* want to know what's within, and you just allow the steam of your inner pressure cooker to rise until it blows the lid! I promise not to take the top off of your Pandora's pressure cooker any further than you can immediately slam back down. But I do hope I'll show you something that helps you, even if at first you resent a little of what I have to say. If you *do* strongly object, it could be because the Moon itself is currently at the wrong phase in relation to your Moon sign, making you unreceptive to today's topic. Try rereading it in a few days' time.

YOUR MOON SIGN

Please remember the following information will make no sense unless you first turn to pages 253 and 256 and follow the simple instructions you will find there. N.B.: There is a one-in-twelve chance that when you turn to the tables on page 262 you will discover that your Moon sign is the same as your Sun sign. This simply means that you are, in some respects, extremely typical of your sign!

MOON IN ARIES

"Fools rush in where angels fear to tread." People with the Moon in Aries, however, cheerfully plunge into situations that even fools would think twice about! "Rash" is not the right word to describe the emotional side of your character. "Rash" implies someone who is sometimes just a little too hasty, reckless, and lacking in forethought. "Rash" also implies a problem that can be "cured" by removing certain irritants. You, however, are permanently, irrevocably, and quite unabashedly impulsive. Your notion of propriety is to keep a few clothes on while dancing drunkenly up to a policeman and inviting him to tango. Your idea of self-restraint means stopping short of actually sawing in half the broken meter that's preventing you from parking your car where you want to. And what's more, you're proud of all this!

If I were to make comments like these to anyone born under any other Moon sign, I'd cause them mortal offense. You, though, I suspect, are sitting there grinning, saying, "Go on, tell me more!" Well, OK then. You're crazy as a loon, mad as a hatter, and blind as a bat to anything you do not want to see. You are also, however, as sweet, as kind, and as forgiving a soul as the world has ever known. There's hardly an ounce of malice in your personality, and though you can be absolutely outrageous on the spur of the moment, you find it impossible to bear a grudge or keep up a feud for longer than half an hour.

Your greatest talent is the ability to think on your feet. You are spontaneous, witty, alert, and energetic, with a natural air of authority and purpose. Rarely does an opportunity pass you by unnoticed. Your eyes are constantly scanning the horizon for signs of imminent change which you might be able to turn to your advantage. If the horizon happens to be quiet, you simply go out and make what you need to happen, happen.

Your biggest fear is that one day the pace of life might slow down so much that you become obliged to think about where you're going and why. Were you ever to do this, you suspect you might realize that you have become like a driver so eager to pass the driver ahead of you that you have long since overshot your destination.

Arguably, your worst vice is laziness. Not the physical kind; nobody could accuse you of using energy sparingly. But you tend not to bother about the likely consequences of your actions. "Let's just give it a whirl and see what happens," you say to yourself as you hurl yourself into yet another half-baked scheme or ill-advised relationship. "Whoops!" is usually the comment that follows as you try to make light of the need to extricate yourself from the ensuing sticky situation.

"Whoops," however, is not the word your exasperated loved ones would necessarily apply. Their reactions to your escapades tend to be a little stronger, though they do need to be similarly brief. At the slightest suspicion that you are being given a lecture, you make your eyes look bright and attentive while you secretly close your ears to ensure that not a syllable enters your brain! Your favorite song is "Anything You Can Do, I Can Do Better." Fortunately, what you lack in self-restraint and diplomacy, you more than make up for in natural warmth. Friends, family members, and partners alike simply can't help admiring your audacity.

Somewhere deep within, you lust for power. You have it within you to be a ruthless conqueror, a shameless despot, a supreme ruler of not just your world but the whole world. When people cross you, your first impulse is usually to send your army to raze their city to the ground. Of course, it only lasts a few seconds before you control yourself, usually by remembering that you haven't got an army, they haven't got a city, and anyway it's probably all an extreme reaction. But it *is* a reaction that you often have. Your temper doesn't just flare, it erupts into a supernova.

Much the same can be said of your passion. When you really want something (or someone) you want it bad. It's why you're such a high achiever. And it's also why you're such a bad person to make an enemy of. You may not hold a grudge or even entertain a wild desire for long, but in the short time that it consumes you, you can cause plenty of damage!

The good news, however, is that you're better than you were. As a child you were absolutely impossible. Siblings and school friends probably need counseling to get over the profound impact that your fiery personality made on them as a child! And your teenage exploits are almost certainly not fit to repeat. The adults who were faced with the challenge of bringing you up deserve a medal. But then, so do you, for you have lived and coped with your own impetuous nature surprisingly well. You'll be glad to hear that the worst is over. People with the Moon in Aries always grow a little more mellow with each passing year.

MOON IN ARIES, *Sun in ...*

Aries You're the original human dynamo. Nothing stops you from getting what you want, apart, perhaps, from your occasional lack of foresight or self-restraint.

Taurus Underneath your cool, calm, collected exterior beats an impatient, irascible, but highly motivated and decisive heart.

Gemini Ideas come to your mind so fast that you can sometimes hardly even articulate them. You're bright, lively, witty, and endlessly energetic.

Cancer You're rarely relaxed about anything for long, but you're a very high achiever with great power and ability to do good in the world.

Leo You're warm and wise, charming and confident. But sometimes you can be just a little too sure of the wisdom of your own judgement.

Virgo Though you seem meek and mild-mannered enough on first impression, there's a raging tiger waiting to pounce on those who cross you.

Libra You're about as mellow and easygoing as a hippopotamus in heat! Once you have an idea in your head, you'll move mountains to see it through.

Scorpio You take your commitments exceedingly seriously. You passionately believe in fulfilling your promises, whatever it takes.

Sagittarius You're a barrel of laughs and a bundle of fun. Pragmatism? That's a long word for a short day. Why not fill it with adventure instead?

Capricorn You're very sure about where you want to live and who you want to live with. And you'll fight hard to protect the interests of your family.

Aquarius You may have a penchant for fast cars or yearn to learn speed reading. Something in you can never get from A to B quickly enough.

Pisces Because you're not afraid to put your money where your mouth is, others are often happy (and right) to put their money into your hands.

☀ MOON IN TAURUS ☀

YOU'LL probably want to cut out and keep this explanation of what it means to have the Moon in Taurus. But then, you tend to want to cut out and keep almost everything you see. You're an incorrigible collector. Where others are content to look at things and then let them go, you yearn to own them. Your home contains all the luxurious creature comforts that have ever been invented, plus spares in the closet "just in case." You're a hopeless hoarder and a salesperson's dream customer. Never mind what it costs, if it's fine, precious, special, and exquisite, you've got to have it. You're also breathtakingly stubborn. When you come under pressure to do something you don't feel inclined to do, you anchor yourself to the nearest immovable object and defy anyone to budge you.

But enough of your good points! What's wrong with you? Well, I have to point out that you're far too inventive a cook, too gifted a gardener, or too talented a creative artist for your own good. You're forever having to fend off requests for your time and energy from the many people who stand in awe of your skill. And though there are few to rival you as a *bon vivant*, there are occasions when your insatiable sensual appetite leads to trouble. You're such a connoisseur of the finest things in life that you cannot bear to have, or to give others, anything less than the best. And, of course, you're sensitive, cautious, and clever. Less blessed individuals are sometimes jealous of this.

The Moon in Taurus gives you an overwhelming need to be emotionally and financially secure. You'll put up with a lot of hassle, hardship, or aggravation before you feel inclined to rock the boat or to leave the devil you know for one you don't. This makes you exasperatingly set in your ways, but heart-warmingly loyal. A loved one has to be proven guilty of not one but a host of heinous crimes before you'll consider relinquishing the relationship. You hate to see any investment go to waste, so you'd rather not make one at all rather than make one you regret. As a result, you never give your love quickly or easily. Maybe it's the traditional Taurean association with horticulture that makes you so determined to give a person time to grow on you before you transplant them from the seedbed of fancy to the garden of your heart. Certainly you consider it important to nurture and nourish personal bonds before deciding to prize and protect them. You secretly worry about making the wrong choice or being sold a shallot instead of a daffodil bulb.

Though you actually have a great ability to spot the real gem within a mountain of fakes, you like to inspect the pile carefully. There's always the chance you'll find a rough diamond that you can gradually polish. This desire to get value for money from your every acquisition makes some people shy from you. They may be afraid that they can't afford to share your expensive tastes or that you want more from them than they can easily give. You are demanding; there's no doubt about it. But since all you ever demand from a person is that they do their very best (for themselves as much as for you), it's just as well if your attitude naturally deters impostors, ne'er-do-wells, and fly-by-nights. You need to save yourself for those with enough taste to appreciate yours, enough sincerity to match your own, and enough energy to fulfill your insatiable appetite for deep, warm, demonstrative communication.

You've been your own worst enemy on several occasions in the past and, though you've recently become more adept at controlling the tendency to want to cut off your nose to spite your face, it's still a fairly constant temptation. It all comes down to your reluctance to compromise. You feel that if you can't have exactly what you want, precisely when you want it, you'd rather not have anything at all. Time and again you've turned down openings that could have been turned into opportunities, simply because they weren't gift wrapped and clearly labeled as such.

You also suffer, aptly enough for someone whose Moon is linked to cattle, from "foot 'n' mouth" disease. Every so often you open your big mouth and put your foot in it! It's bullish instinct that causes you to do this, in much the same way as it inspires your four-legged namesake to charge relentlessly at strangers who stray into his territory. You sense a potential threat, no matter how small, and you don't wait to give it the benefit of the doubt. Down goes the head, up flare the nostrils, and out of your way (if he or she has any sense) runs the innocent holder of what you perceive to be a red flag.

This inclination to treat others as guilty until proven innocent has saved your hide once or twice before, but it's also been the reason why, to this day, there are people to whom you dare not speak because you once vented more rage than was reasonable on them. As a child, you were probably obedient. As an adolescent, you were probably sulky. As an adult, however, you grew those horns and discovered you could use them to great effect. Now, you need to learn to hold them high with pride instead of lowering them in anger so often.

MOON IN TAURUS, *Sun in ...*

Aries You're not as reckless or as hasty as you'd like others to think. You've got enough caution to counter your enthusiasm and to guarantee you success.

Taurus If you aren't a millionaire, you ought to be. You certainly know how to spend money, and you possess more than enough talent to make it.

Gemini You know how to make marvelous investments, not just of money, but of time and energy and in your choice of friends.

Cancer Some people call you overcautious, but you very rarely make mistakes. You can tell a person's or an object's true worth at a glance.

Leo It's useless trying to persuade you of anything once you've made up your mind. But since you're usually right, that's no problem.

Virgo It takes a lot to stir you into action, but when you've got a mission, there's no stopping you. And no criticizing you, either!

Libra You're so laid-back you're positively supine. You can take everything in your stride except, perhaps, too much pressure.

Scorpio You yearn for stability in your love life, to the point where you will often let your partner off a hook they ought to be hoisted by.

Sagittarius You're surprisingly serious for a Sagittarian. You take great care to do your duty diligently and to be a healing influence in this troubled world.

Capricorn You sometimes have a terrible weakness for pleasures of the flesh. It makes you great fun to know. You may be naughty, but you're very nice.

Aquarius It doesn't matter how chaotic the rest of your world is as long as your home is safe, secure, and full of people and objects you can relate to.

Pisces You know the value of a sound education. You may not care for academia, but you certainly love to acquire information.

MOON IN GEMINI

I DON'T hold out much hope that you'll agree with the following
description. People with the Moon in Gemini never agree with anything if they can help it. You court controversy and find heated debates
as comforting as most folk find heated towel bars. What do you mean, "Oh,
no I don't!" You see? You're quarreling now!

But let's not argue about this. After all, you never intend your outbursts
of devil's advocacy to be taken seriously, and you are often upset to find
they have thrown more sensitive souls off balance. You're always happy to
reach a compromise between two points of view or even to retract your
own entirely. It's the scent of an argument that excites you, never the taste
of victory.

Some people, noticing this, call you inconsistent. What can they mean?
Your habit of changing your mind more often than your socks is as reliable
as the rising of the Sun. Or, because we're considering lunar influences here,
perhaps we should say Moon. Only the Moon, of course, is not so constant.
It has its moods and phases. And so do you. One moment, you're as confident as a cuckoo; the next, as restless as a robin. Similarly, you can change
from being a mischievous magpie to a vulnerable partridge. I make these
ornithological references intentionally, for in many respects you are like a
bird. You were born to fly free from life's petty restrictions and to see the
world from a high perspective; and, more than anything else in life, you hate
to feel caged.

Having the Moon in Gemini makes you witty and bright, lively and good-
humored, but prone to occasional dark moods. These, oddly enough, are
usually triggered by trivia. Life's bigger challenges you can easily cope with,
but it's the silly little things that make you despair. By nature you're an
explorer, experimenter, and innovator, prepared to try almost anything

once. Your partner needs to be similarly open-minded if the relationship is to provide the challenge and constant stimulation you seem to require. Your family doesn't, however, have to try so hard to hold your interest. If there's no excitement or drama on the home front, you'll simply create it for everyone.

You love persuading people to do what you think is good for them, especially if you can do it subtly enough to make them think it was all their own idea. You've been known to lie awake at night thinking, "If I tell Fred this, point out such-and-such to Mabel, and leave Zelda's letter lying around where Cecil can see it, then Cecil will have to confront Mabel. This will force her to come clean with Fred, which will worry him enough to ask Zelda for the help he's afraid she'll refuse to give." Complicated? Not half as much as the actual workings of your inner mind. No wonder your emotional life is such a soap opera.

In fairness, your desire to control situations is not linked to a yearning to turn things to your own advantage. You just want to make sure that your loved ones' problems are solved as cleverly as possible. This is why you've always got so many questions to ask your nearest and dearest. If you don't know all the facts about everyone and everything, how can you possibly apply your brain to sorting things out for them?

Some astrologers might argue that, for greater happiness in love, you need to be less calculating and a little more relaxed. There is, however, another way to look at this: Maybe you ought to spend more time with people smart enough to appreciate how smart you are!

If you go around telling your friends that you have the Moon in the sign of the twins, they will no doubt nod wisely and say, "That explains a lot." Indeed it does. Solar Geminis are just a little prone to be different people on different days, but lunar Geminis are veritable Jekyll and Hydes. Well, almost. It's not from nice to nasty that you switch, but from tame to wild. Nor do you alter suddenly and dramatically. Nonetheless, if we rewind the video of your life, then run it fast forward on "Play," we can clearly see the trait. Your inner twins may take turns dominating on a weekly, monthly, or even yearly rotation, but it's hard to see how your history can be the handiwork of just one entity.

This in itself is not always a problem. The different aspects of your character are not so much at loggerheads as in cahoots, for they are, after all, twins, mutually supportive in their agreement to differ. But twins are famous for playing naughty tricks, like swapping places in class to see if the teacher notices. You have, you must confess, found yourself in many situations where you have felt very much like an impostor. And to a degree, you have been. It's no use asking the real you to please stand up. You *are* both the willful, wacky, and outrageous one *and* the goody two shoes. But you need to admit this rather than denying that your other half exists.

MOON IN GEMINI, *Sun in ...*

Aries You're a very bright spark, but you change your mind more often than your socks and fail to see why others can't keep up.

Taurus You've got good financial acumen and a way of appearing reasonable and fair, even when you're determinedly getting your own way!

Gemini You ought to work in the city. You're a great wheeler and dealer even if you do sometimes tie even yourself up in intellectual knots!

Cancer You're a much tougher cookie than you pretend to be, and you're exceedingly good at convincing friends and loved ones of your viewpoint.

Leo You've got a natural ability to see things from others' point of view as you gradually and cleverly talk them into your own.

Virgo Your trouble is that you think you've got all the answers. In fact, what you're really good at is making others ask all the questions!

Libra Your tendency to ask too many questions and never leave enough time for people to answer them is probably your only major fault.

Scorpio You're fascinated by social taboos. Things that polite people never discuss in public excite your desire to get at the truth.

Sagittarius You want a long and stable relationship, but you're not always sure with whom, so you're often tempted to find out by trial and error.

Capricorn You think hard about ways to help others help themselves. You're giving and considerate, if rather too clever for your own good at times.

Aquarius Life may not be one long round of joyous celebration, but it often seems this way when you're around to share a little sunshine.

Pisces Where you really feel at home and inspired is in a place full of bright, friendly people making interesting, intelligent conversation.

Moon in Cancer

To have the Moon in Cancer is to be as soft as a damp sponge and every bit as sentimental! It's to want, more than anything else in the world, to protect and care for the people, items, causes, and beliefs that mean the most to you. And it is also, oddly enough, to have a thick skin. The very fact that you recognize how vulnerable you are, deep inside, makes you determined not to be a sucker for every sob story. You pretend to be like the character in the Paul Simon song who says, "I am a rock.... I am an island." You often convince others and even yourself of this. But every so often that inner ocean of emotion sends a tidal wave crashing over a shore that's not so sure. Then your no-nonsense, "don't-mess-with-me" façade cracks to reveal a quivering bundle of concern. You'll do almost anything for anyone when you're in such a state, no matter how counterproductive.

A psychologist might say that all this has something to do with your mother. An astrologer would dispute whether the chicken came before the egg, but they both would agree that no male or female with the Moon in Cancer ever has an ambivalent relationship with the woman who gave birth to them. There may be extreme resentment or intense adoration, but there's certainly some tremendously powerful feeling. Which in turn, I suppose, is why you often find yourself needing to fight so hard against a sense of guilt, a constant need to earn approval, or an inappropriate desire to mother those around you.

Sensitivity is your middle name. Try though you may to shorten it to "sense" or to leave it off your signature completely, the tag comes back to haunt you. What other people feel about you counts for so much that you seem to spend the whole of your life erecting and maintaining complex self-defense mechanisms. Sometimes you try being bombastic. You figure if you're enough of an extrovert, nobody will be able to find the chink in your psychological armor. Sometimes, you go to the other extreme and withdraw completely, on the basis that if you don't ever have anything to do with anyone, you can't possibly cause offense. None of it works. Where some people have an insatiable appetite for sex, power, or money, the Moon in Cancer gives you an unquenchable thirst for reassurance. You even have to be reassured about the fact that it's all right to need reassurance! Unless your closest loved ones are all aspiring saints, they may occasionally tire of giving it to you.

None of this, I hasten to add, makes you a wimp. In a funny way, it might be better if it did. But, almost in spite yourself, you are forever making bold statements or embarking on adventurous escapades. This is because the Moon's influence comes and goes in phases. When you're on one of your "ups," there's no stopping you. You'll take on enemies twice your size and go to outrageous lengths to defend the rights of those you care for. But then you'll suddenly realize what you've done and stop yourself before you go too far (or before you've gone far enough, depending on how you look at it). Only when your protective instincts are awakened do you feel safe to open the emotional floodgates of your heart. Therefore, your partner needs to be weak enough to inspire you to do this, yet strong enough not to be a liability. And as for your family? They just need to be glad they've got such an endlessly giving person in their midst.

I'm sorry to have to ask you this, but, if we're going to make sense of your more unfathomable urges and impulses, I need to know how you really feel about your mother. Aha! I thought so. That deep intake of breath you just took was all the confirmation I required. You *have* got the Moon in Cancer. Your emotional outlook on life has been shaped, perhaps more than you care to admit, by the woman who brought you into the world. Maybe you feel devotion to her, and maybe you feel anger. I can only tell which by checking your lunar "aspects," and we are not going that far into astrology here. But you know that, whatever else it is, the relationship has always been intense. This is normal and natural. To a degree, it is so for all of us.

Freud, Jung, and the other great psychologists were mining a rich seam when they began to hypothesize that our behavior patterns can be traced back to very early childhood. But where most children go through a phase of being unable to separate their own identity from that of their primary parent, followed by a healthy stage of rejection before eventual reconciliation in adulthood, Lunar Cancerians take longer than most to arrive fully at this latter point. You may have traveled to the corners of the earth, or you may never have left home. Geography has nothing to do with this psychological tie, and there's nothing wrong with it unless it happens also to be the cause of a sense of guilt. Many positive celestial developments have already helped you move on in stages, and I predict you will eventually go through a series of experiences and inner-realization processes that will help you go a long way further towards letting yourself off the hook.

MOON IN CANCER, *Sun in ...*

Aries You are the original hard nut with a soft center. You are also a born leader, which is just as well, because you hate taking orders.

Taurus You care passionately and deeply about the people in your world. Your loyalty is unshakable, your generosity most impressive.

Gemini You like to pretend that your every decision is totally logical, but actually you're a tremendously intuitive and very successful operator.

Cancer You either wear your heart on your sleeve or never let anyone see it at all. You're very giving, but rarely agree to accept anything from anyone.

Leo Your Moon in the sign of the sensitive crab doesn't need a shell to retreat into. It just lets your tough Leo persona fend off all enemies.

Virgo You try hard not to let others realize you're so soft in case they take advantage of your good nature, but you usually fail to convince them.

Libra You go out of your way to protect those you love from things they don't need to know, such as how worried you often are.

Scorpio You love to learn as much as you can about what life is really all about. You're open-minded and at ease with yourself.

Sagittarius You're a deep philosopher, though you're also wise enough to recognize that none of us lives by theory alone. We have to trust what we feel.

Capricorn You're deeply loyal to those you love, and you're happy, if not actually to give a partner the upper hand, certainly to let him think he's got it!

Aquarius You worry a great deal about letting other people down. Consequently you're very dedicated and discriminating about what you promise.

Pisces You've got a sunny disposition and a desire to keep life light, happy, and simple. It's much appreciated by all around you.

MOON IN LEO

YOU don't need me to tell you what a wonderful person you are. If you've got the Moon in Leo, you already know it to be true beyond question. Nor is this the only thing about which you can feel certain. You know a great deal about a great many subjects, and your opinions are invariably right, or so, at least, you passionately believe. Actually, they usually are, but sometimes people resent this, partly because you tend to deliver your opinion in too knowing a tone of voice, and partly because they sense that, while you're very good at making suggestions, you're not so good at taking them. Nobody, but nobody, gets away with giving *you* advice. Nor do they give you orders!

Your biggest recurring fantasy involves the idea that one day you may get proof that your beloved parents are actually foster parents and you are actually Queen Elizabeth II's love child, secretly born two years before Prince Charles. One day the world will find out, and you will claim the throne! Or, at least, your attitude towards life suggests that you must think along such grandiose lines. Fortunately, despite your occasionally pompous posture, your smart aleck disposition, and your tendency to want to be the star of every show, you are also one of the kindest, warmest, most generous, and genuine individuals who have ever graced the face of this planet. And for this you can be forgiven a multitude of sins.

You can, I'm sure, heartily agree with Shakespeare's assertion that "all the world's a stage." You're very much a class act and a natural celebrity. You exude warmth, charisma, and confidence; it's no pretense. There's something about you that was born to shine.

Nonetheless, it's not quite the whole story. Like many of the greatest media personalities, you secretly suffer stage fright. No matter how many times you step in front of the spotlight to thunderous applause, it's always preceded by a period of nervous pacing around your dressing room. Those who live with and love you soon learn to make allowances for these sudden swings between anxiety and bravado. They have to be able to supply the necessary quota of postperformance "Darling, you were wonderful"'s, and they also need some theatrical blood of their own in order to costar with you in a succession of demanding roles.

Where some people's lives are soap operas and others just border on the farcical, the Moon in Leo is like a celestial agent who keeps booking you into good, old-fashioned melodramas. No problem is ever an ordinary problem; no emotional reaction is ever just a mild sensation. You either feel nothing, or you feel as if you are on fire. This is why you give yourself wholeheartedly to the projects you tackle and the people you care for. It is also, however, why you often go over the top, putting more into a situation or conversation than it actually warrants.

You're an incorrigible perfectionist, not because you have some perverse fascination with detail, but because you simply cannot bear the thought of being judged and found wanting. Yet you're always suspicious of being fobbed off with platitudinous praise. This, probably, is the greatest drawback or difficulty you have to overcome on the road to a happy love life. Like Groucho Marx, you can never feel quite comfortable about belonging to any club that would want to have you as a member!

As a child, you were probably precocious. As a teenager, you may well have been "old before your time," haughtily aloof from the trivial fascinations of your more immature peers, but also probably extroverted and confident. Who would have thought that, as an adult, you would entertain such intense self-doubts and insecurities about yourself? Probably only an astrologer familiar with the traits of a Lunar Leo.

Your Moon sign is a blessing in that it gives you a natural air of dignity and authority. It is, however, a curse insofar as it makes you desperately worried that you may one day lose the respect others have for you. Often, you will take refuge in righteousness or stick with tried and tested techniques rather than risk falling on your face as a result of exploring some unfamiliar maneuver. The result is that you become too easily set in your ways.

If all these ways were means to a worthwhile end, that would be no problem. But you have habits that could sorely do with being conquered and tendencies that really do you no favors. You're often so nervous about "getting it wrong" that you hold yourself back, even when you have a chance to "get it right." You're so hungry for approval that you'll court it in areas where, frankly, you'd be better off being condemned for not going. You're so fearful of criticism that you'll refuse to listen even to the most well-informed and sincerely meant advice, for fear you'd look silly taking it.

No, no. Of *course*, you're not like this all the time, just some of it, when the Moon happens to catch you in the wrong phase. But I draw it to your attention so mercilessly because you are able to do something very constructive about your worst emotional worries. Eventually, a career or creative project is going to take off like a rocket. When it does, give it all you've got, and you'll soon regain enough pride to allow yourself to be humble.

MOON IN LEO, *Sun in ...*

Aries You're calm and at ease with yourself and with most people, most of the time. You exude charm, confidence, and good humor.

Taurus You're proud of who you are and what you stand for. Others may see you as stubborn, but you simply cannot settle for less than the best.

Gemini You often say things for dramatic effect without thinking about their likely consequences. But you have a heart of pure gold.

Cancer You've got a winning way with people and money too. Somehow, you're never emotionally or financially insecure for very long.

Leo You're magnetically attractive and charismatic, though it has to be said that you fall for your own charms as much as everyone else!

Virgo Yet to be born is the person able to get the better of you in an argument or to talk you into anything you don't want to be talked into.

Libra Because you're so charming, few people realize how cleverly you have talked them into something. It's a good thing you have scruples.

Scorpio You're probably very ambitious to get to the top of the career ladder. Even if you're not, others want to put you there. And deservedly so.

Sagittarius You're not a graduate of the university of life; you're a perpetual student and proud of it. Every day's a glorious education.

Capricorn You're very conscious of your responsibility to others. You hate to see money go to waste. And you yearn to explore life's deeper mysteries.

Aquarius To take all you have to give, a partner must be very strong and special. But it's your very dear wish to find (or keep) such a person.

Pisces You take great pride in your work and even more in your ability to recognize what's wrong with someone and how to put it right.

☼ MOON IN VIRGO ☼

YOU may be a little nervous to read what it means to have the Moon in Virgo. You probably expect to have confirmed what you have long suspected: namely that you are a worthless individual, hopelessly lacking charm or originality. The only reason (you imagine) that you have been lucky enough to do at all well in life so far is because others have been either too blind or too kind to notice this.

I'm so glad you've finally identified your Moon sign, because it gives me the chance to say what you have long needed someone to walk up to you and shout in your ear. You are a marvelous, magnificent individual. The only thing "wrong" with you is that you have the Moon in Virgo. And this is not really "wrong." It's just that it often makes you doubt your skill, undervalue your contribution, and rip yourself to shreds with viciously sharp self-criticism.

Many people like the fact that you are so inclined. It allows them to exploit you, manipulate you, and hire your services for a fraction of their true value. It's only those who truly love you who are baffled and frustrated. Why are you so self-denigrating when it's clear to them that you are the most intelligent, sexy, sensitive, talented, and funny individual they have ever met? All you need do to reassure them (and yourself) is learn to laugh at your inherited astrological tendency to sell yourself short and become the wise, witty, and talented star you truly are.

Your Moon in Virgo makes you a very easy person to get along with. You are tolerant, considerate, and always willing to see the good in others. Most people, in turn, find you fair and thoughtful, wise and reasonable, bright and interesting. It's only fools you don't suffer gladly, and they, conveniently enough, tend to be similarly dismissive of you. A "fool," according to your definition at least, is someone who puts quantity before quality, style before substance, and money before happiness. As a highly principled person, you find such short-sighted, unprincipled behavior anathema. You consider it essential to keep away from such dangerously disruptive characters.

Unfortunately, in today's world, it is not always easy to do this. As a result, you frequently find yourself arguing with or being impeded by these noisy, presumptuous beings with their incessant stream of poor judgements. You grow tired of dealing with them, and your loved ones sometimes grow tired of dealing with the frustration you find so hard to hide. They often have to remind you not to let yourself be so bothered by what you consider to be waste or stupidity.

The Moon in Virgo makes you yearn to live in a world that makes sense, but the sad fact is that few things in life ever really do. An ability to appreciate the bizarre, funny, and ironic side of life is the psychological defense mechanism you need to put in place if you want to become more relaxed about your closest relationships. You probably also need to counter a tendency to undervalue what you have to offer others. You seem to swing between feeling that you're not good enough for anyone and (usually by way of overcompensating for this fear) that you're far too good for everyone. Concentrate on giving more and judging less, and you'll find all the emotional fulfillment you so richly deserve.

We've already discussed your tendency to be viciously self-critical and similarly critical about those you feel are wasting their potential in life. What we haven't discussed is the link between these traits.

Before we do, I must remind you of the many assets the Moon in Virgo bestows. Diligence, wisdom, and reliability are the most obvious. You have all three in abundance, plus the ability to be magnificently sensual, creative, and compassionate. What you lack is sufficient defiance, arrogance, and rebelliousness. More than all that, you find it almost impossible to voice the phrase "I couldn't care less." Sometimes, we all need to be able to say this. The trouble with you is that, no matter how trivial the scenario, you "couldn't care more." You may have a great sense of humor, but you only find some things funny. By and large, you take life and yourself too seriously. Your overwhelming sense of duty makes you yearn to do your best at every juncture. Because you have such impossibly high standards, you frequently fail to live up to them. Thus, you forever drive yourself harder and further forward. When you see others, who clearly need to do the same, resting on their laurels, it triggers resentment. You ask: "How come *they* can live with themselves when they have so far to go, while I don't seem able to?" But the solution is simple. You don't need therapy. You just need to relax, relax, and then relax some more!

MOON IN VIRGO, *Sun in ...*

Aries You're far from a typical Aries. You notice details and worry about problems *before* they arise. But you're very swift to adapt.

Taurus You're deeply sensual but determinedly pragmatic. Quality counts for everything, and details matter immensely to you.

Gemini You're very clever but can sometimes be too smart for your own good, talking yourself out of ideas that are actually worth pursuing.

Cancer You're careful, cautious, kind, and considerate. You're also extremely clever. Few ever manage to pull the wool over your eyes.

Leo You take pride in your ability to make the right decision. You worry more than you need to, for your instincts are rarely misleading.

Virgo You're so marvelously inscrutable that you won't even tell yourself what you really feel. Nonetheless, you're a very powerful person.

Libra You're witty, wise, and exceedingly good at understanding what really makes other people tick. Little escapes your notice.

Scorpio You have many friends who admire you for your great integrity, insight, and your ability to manifest both with even greater modesty.

Sagittarius You've got just enough seriousness to counterbalance your Sagittarian excessiveness without becoming too inflexible. You were born to succeed.

Capricorn You're rather fond of traveling. You like to go to new places and learn new ways of looking at life. And you have a deep, strong, natural faith.

Aquarius For a person with two key planets in supposedly "logical" signs, you're surprisingly compassionate, sensitive, and deeply intuitive.

Pisces You're an incorrigible romantic and not really a secret one, no matter how much you may claim to be logical in your choice of partner.

MOON IN LIBRA

ITH the Moon in Libra, you always know exactly how you feel. Unsure! No doubt you had to learn, long ago, how to live with constantly fluctuating emotions. The trick, in case you have yet to discover it, is to stop thinking about how you feel or at least to stop thinking you ought to feel the same way from day to day. Other than the fact that you're never quite clear whether you're worried or confident, happy or upset, energetic or apathetic, you're an absolutely A-1 human being.

This may sound contradictory, but then aren't *all* humans contradictory? Isn't the only real difference between you and everyone else the fact that you are happy to own up to your own contrariness, but most other people fight hard to hide theirs? And doesn't this make you more emotionally honest and, therefore, in an odd way, more straightforward?

Sorry to ask so many questions, but in doing so I'm only reflecting yet another classic Moon in Libra tendency. You delight in pondering the imponderable. Yet you get along in life pretty well despite it all. Why? Because having the Moon in Libra also makes you charming, affable, seductive, creative, fun to be with, and generally fascinating. And because you're so aware of your own faults, you're loath to condemn others for theirs. Which, naturally enough, makes you very popular.

Your biggest problem is that you're so easily able to make yourself absolutely irresistible to others. Not only have you got natural charisma, poise, and elegance, you've got something even more potentially devastating: adaptability. You can instinctively sense what a person wants you to be like and effortlessly alter your personality to supply it. Worse still, you actually want to do this. Little gives you greater pleasure than to provide what a loved one is looking for. Willingly and instantly, you will say what they want to hear you say, respond as they want you to respond, and, most appealingly of all, put the look into your eyes that they most want to see. How can anyone fail to fall hopelessly for someone who so accurately mirrors their own deepest and most secret desire?

It's all fine until they find out that in a different situation, with a different companion, you're a different person entirely! When they turn and ask if the "real you" will please stand up, you have to reply meekly, "Uh … which real me did you want me to show you?" Well, OK, maybe you're not quite *that* bad. But you do have a tendency to be an emotional chameleon, and it does have to be watched.

Members of your family sometimes grow fed up with your habit of weighing every pro and con so carefully that, by the time you've found a fair formula, the issue under discussion has become irrelevant. Friends are never quite sure where your loyalties lie. Romantic partners despair of ever getting a straight answer to anything. They'll all forgive you, because you're so good at turning on the charm that, even when you're letting someone down, you can make it seem as though you're offering them an opportunity. But if you want a happier love life, you have to become secure in yourself and not need to find your security by winning everyone's approval all the time.

You'll see that your Moon sign has been depicted as a precariously balanced tightrope walker. Meditate on it for a few minutes and you'll have the benefit of twice as much commentary as I'm giving to every other zodiac sign.

This should please you for, though your Moon may be in the sign of the balance, the desire to be fair to everyone all the time is not your primary concern. You're conscious of how nice it would be if you could, but you're more conscious of what you see as the less-than-ideal hand that fate has dealt you. A lot of your energy is spent attempting to redress this balance. You want what you haven't got but feel you ought to be entitled to. If there's a chance to get it, you'll go to almost any length. Tightrope? You'll walk along a piece of tightly stretched cotton if that's what's required.

One thing the Moon in Libra has surely provided you with is plenty of courage. If the odds of success are so slim as to deter most people, or the window of opportunity so small that only a contortionist could enter it, you consider yourself to be looking at a challenge that has your name stamped all over it! You have your Moon sign to thank for the occasions in your life when you have pulled off some magnificent coup. You also have it to blame for the rather greater number of times when you have failed in a big way. Much of your irrepressibility is, ironically, a reaction to the way you always felt you were being kept down as a child. If you want to learn how to make it work for, rather than against, you as an adult, you must come to terms with these memories. In the meantime, if you can't be good, at least be a little more careful.

MOON IN LIBRA, *Sun in ...*

Aries You have a very strong urge to constantly prove yourself though you aren't always sure how to go about doing so.

Taurus You've got a magnificent aesthetic eye. You appreciate colors, textures, and flavors, and you probably love to create them too.

Gemini You try so hard to rationalize and analyze everything in your world that your own spontaneous instincts often take you by surprise.

Cancer You go to great lengths to protect the people and principles you believe in. You are generous with both your time and your heart.

Leo Few can resist your silver tongue, your golden smile, and your eyes that usually twinkle like diamonds but can also give very cutting looks.

Virgo You sometimes feel sorry for those who try to pin you down because you know you can run rings round just about anyone.

Libra Rarely, if ever, do you give others reason to take offense, which really infuriates your more impassioned friends and loved ones.

Scorpio You're never quite sure whether you really feel what you feel or just think you feel it. But you're a person of great vision and strength.

Sagittarius Your social diary is never empty. You have more friends than you can keep track of, even though they can't quite keep track of you!

Capricorn You have a lot of charisma, which no doubt contributes to the fact that you so often seem to make such a success of all you do.

Aquarius If your mind were open any wider, jumbo jets could fly in formation through it. You believe anything is possible, and you may be right.

Pisces You have an endless hunger to discover the true meaning of life and are forever asking deep, searching, and highly valuable questions.

MOON IN SCORPIO

I HOPE, when you checked your date of birth in the Moon sign tables, that you didn't mark the page. You really don't want anyone else to know you've got the Moon in Scorpio. If there's someone looking over your shoulder now, quickly scan an adjacent definition and throw them off the scent. Come back and read the rest when you've made sure the door is locked, the curtains are drawn, and there are no hidden cameras.

Am I joking? Not especially. I'm simply trying to illustrate that the Moon in Scorpio makes people very sensitive about things they want nobody ever to find out about. They fear that they are unreasonably and exceptionally jealous, desirous, passionate, and competitive. So powerful, indeed, do they consider their inner emotions that they keep a very tight lid on them, often denying to others and even to themselves that they exist. These people pretend to be easygoing, light, and breezy, when all the time below the surface they are in a seething sea of angst, insecurity, and turmoil.

Recognize the syndrome? I thought you might. So let me tell you something else. You may be mean and moody, possessive and broody, incurably suspicious of other people's true motives, and insatiably hungry for emotionally intense encounters. But you're also deeply intuitive, magnificently creative, and awe-inspiringly, accurately sensitive to the things that other people think and feel. None of which is anything to be ashamed of.

You can tell whether people are worthy of respect from one look at their face or one word uttered on the telephone. Your instincts are never wrong, and, once a person has passed your instant but stringent "trust test," nobody, but nobody, is capable of giving them more support and care. Your compassion is deeper than a magician's pocket; your loyalty is stronger than a jeweler's safe. It's just a shame that your mind is sharper than a surgeon's knife.

As intense as the emotions you experience in your heart are the thoughts that pass through your head. Where other people have opinions, you have judgements. Where others have ideas, you have brainwaves. And where others have fears, you have nameless dread.

The first two differences are assets. Nobody would dispute this, not even those who sometimes find themselves being outdone by the superior might of your intellect. However, your capacity to conjure up so freely the angel of anxiety, the demon of doubt, and the specter of suspicion rather reduces your ability to let the good times roll.

Your loved ones are more than happy to make allowance for this. They have to be, for they are often more aware of your tendency to worry than you are yourself. This, of course, is because primarily you are worrying about them. Most of them appreciate being shown so much concern, but sometimes they wish you could take what you feel a little less seriously. Those who are wisest know that the best way to help you do this is to find you a good cause to fight for or a real threat to fend off. And an astrologer can always tell when a person with the Moon in Scorpio has got the right partner. An astrologer just looks for the one who is smiling because this person has managed to convert his or her lover's emotional energy into energy of an altogether more physical nature.

Before I tell you about the darker side of having the Moon in Scorpio, I need to level with you. I'm trained as an astrologer, not as a psychiatrist. The term I'm about to apply to you is one that I really have no right to bandy about, so you can reject it if you wish. If you choose to accept it, please do so only on the understanding that I'm not using it in a medical sense. It's only what it has come to mean in popular parlance that I wish to convey.

The word is "paranoid." Now before I qualify this, I want to level with you some more. I've got the Moon in Scorpio, too. So believe me, I'm not just saying this in order to get at you! You can see how nervously sensitive I am by the amount of stalling I've done before uttering that dreaded word. And you can also see how self-defeatingly honest the Moon in Scorpio makes me by the fact that I eventually went ahead and said it.

We Moon-in-Scorpios see far more than is good for us. We cannot deny what our instincts are telling us, no matter how much we would like to for the sake of a quiet life. We frequently find ourselves needing to say things that we know others don't want to hear. Not surprisingly, we live in fear of the reaction we're going to get. Often, when we confront others with the truths we have seen, they deny them. Some even actively try to discredit us in an attempt to defend the pretense they wish to keep up. So we close down, clam up, and either become recluses or find a more superficial aspect of our personality to hide behind. Are we really paranoid? No. But the defense mechanisms we are obliged to maintain for our own and others' good sometimes lead us to display all the classic symptoms.

Now, having confided all this, I have great news. Between now and the year 2008, Pluto, the ruler of our Moon sign, will be passing through Sagittarius, the most expansive and optimistic sign of the zodiac. With each passing year, we Lunar Scorpians find that we become less inclined to apologize for, or feel afraid of, our sensitivity and more easily able to apply our special brand of insight in a very powerful way.

MOON IN SCORPIO, *Sun in ...*

Aries Woe unto the person who ever crosses you. Both your Sun and Moon are ruled by Mars, planet of power, strength, and victory at all costs!

Taurus Though you are often a little emotionally restless and eager to assert your will, you are also extremely wise, sensitive, and intuitive.

Gemini Your breezy and bubbly Gemini "front" is a very convenient mask behind which to hide your deep insight and emotional sensitivity.

Cancer You're far too sensitive for your own good. You take too much to heart, but then you've got an awful lot of heart to take it all!

Leo There's an iron fist behind your velvet glove. It only comes out in self-defense, but those who underestimate you should take care.

Virgo If it were not for your devastating ability to be so self-critical, you'd probably rule the country, if not the world, by now.

Libra You're good at putting your tremendous insight to practical use. People usually find you wise, and money tends to find its way to you.

Scorpio Others can take you or leave you, for you are who you are, and there'll never be any changing you. Most, rightly, prefer to take you!

Sagittarius You're always surprised by how deep your emotions run: they sneak up on you sideways. But your intuition is almost invariably right.

Capricorn You are very selective about whom you will allow to be your friend, but those in your special circle are as close to you as your family.

Aquarius Your Scorpio Moon is very conscious of what others think, so it tones down your Aquarian excesses and causes many people to look up to you.

Pisces You don't really care where you're going as long as you're not forever staying in the same old place or frame of mind.

MOON IN SAGITTARIUS

THE astrological textbooks tell us that people with the Moon in Sagittarius are jolly and approachable, open-minded, adventurous, extravagant, and generous. In all this, they are right, but they are only telling half the story. While you may be the life and soul of every party, and you are the office or family clown or comedian, looking closer, we have to consider the words of that wise philosopher Smokey Robinson: "It's easy to trace ... the tracks of your tears." Your ebullience is an act; your magnanimity, a defense mechanism. You figure that, if you're always merry, nobody will realize how vulnerable you truly feel or how afraid you are of being rejected. Deep within, you're not so much a hotbed of emotion as a veritable inferno of unfulfilled (and arguably unfulfillable) passion.

Every so often, you find yourself unable to keep up the parade of quips a moment longer. The inner volcano simply has to erupt. It doesn't happen often but, when your heart wells up with longing, the "amplifying" influence of Sagittarius on your Moon causes you to go to extreme lengths to pursue what you yearn for. You take risks that nobody else would even dare to dream of. You make outrageous statements, you chase impossible rainbows, and you take it all exceedingly seriously. Luckily, it's never long before your sense of humor returns and your dangerous desires subside.

Sagittarius is an exuberant, energetic, humorous, and hearty sign. It is also a kind, compassionate one. The Moon, however, can sometimes feel a little "lost" here, in the same way that someone from a small village can feel lost in a big city. The Moon is a part of the personality that always wants to know where it stands. Sagittarius is a part of the zodiac that is perpetually changing. The ethos of the sign is "onwards and upwards," which doesn't always gel with the Moon's inclination to be steady and safe. The result is that a person with the Moon in Sagittarius can often feel restless and insecure, constantly on the lookout for something solid to cling to, yet never quite able to settle for what they've got.

Behind your buoyant, good-natured, confident persona, there's a competitive edge. Not only are you forever measuring yourself against others, you are frequently trying to improve on your own past record. You frequently pursue unrealistic goals or extravagant ideas which you pick to test your own nerve and courage.

Your loved ones can find it hard to live with such a driven individual. They might be able to understand it if your aim never wavered from one target, but your tendency to shift and change priorities confuses those in your family who are by nature more consistent. Your partner finds you fun to be with, but can't work out why one moment you're sweet, light, and bubbling with the desire to respond to the spur of the moment, yet the next moment you're sharp, serious, and flatly insistent on a particular point. Frankly, nor can you. It's the fact that you never really know what you want from your lover that makes it so hard for your lover to provide what you need. All of which is why you get along best with others when there's a challenge to rise to that's big enough to cause all concerned to forget about their feelings and work together to succeed against the odds.

You might find it hard to imagine how a sign as traditionally light, bright, joyous, and jolly as Sagittarius can possibly have a dark side. It's like contemplating curry-flavored corn flakes or a mugging on Sesame Street. There's definitely, however, a danger-loving streak in your Moon sign, albeit not an obvious one. It springs, ironically, from the very fact that you are so anxious to do what's right. Sometimes, you can become such a champion of justice as to turn into an angel of revenge. You can forgive almost anyone almost anything, and it takes a lot to turn your benevolence to malevolence. But if you really feel someone has done something beyond all excuse, you can be almost as inexcusable in the methods you employ to let them know how you feel.

I'm not talking about something that happens often, but it doesn't need to happen often in order to have a profound impact on your outlook. And while you rarely get such a large bee in your bonnet, you are forever getting a series of smaller bees in your cap. You frequently want to come to the rescue of those you feel are getting a raw deal. In the process, you bite off more than you can chew or, worse, find that the object of your act of heroism turns around and bites the hand that has come to feed it.

A lot of this stems from the desire to emulate a person who was a kind and supportive influence on you in early childhood. You may, however, do their memory more credit by learning to hold back your desire to see justice done and having more faith in the ability to let natural justice prevail. Focus on putting your inner world to rights before you set off with the intention of sorting out the wider one.

MOON IN SAGITTARIUS, *Sun in …*

Aries You're a reckless adventurer and a wild, free spirit. You do everything at the last minute, and you will do almost anything for a laugh.

Taurus Though you like to play it cool, deep down you are tremendously excitable, enthusiastic, and very often lucky.

Gemini Your trouble is that when you have an idea, no matter how far-fetched, you simply have to act on it. Happily, things usually work out well.

Cancer You'll willingly go out of your way to do someone a favor. You're adaptable, easygoing, and very warm-hearted.

Leo Others sometimes feel you lack common sense. But as you are usually so full of fun and appreciation for life, why should you care?

Virgo Little baffles or perplexes you for long. You've got an inquiring mind, an adaptable heart, and a healthy sense of the ridiculous.

Libra You're a bright and lively character full of great ideas, but you sometimes let the voice of enthusiasm drown out that of common sense.

Scorpio You've got a rather good relationship with money. You don't worry about it, and it runs after you to see why you're not bothered!

Sagittarius You're the original bouncing toy. No matter what knocks you over, you may wobble but you simply won't stay down!

Capricorn You like the idea of being part of a large, worthy organization or institution to which you can safely dedicate your heart.

Aquarius You're exceedingly affable and good-natured. Your Sun and Moon signs are so sociable, it's a wonder you ever get any work done.

Pisces Your exuberance and enthusiasm make you popular, but it's your ability to seize an opportunity that makes you so successful.

MOON IN CAPRICORN

MANY of history's greatest achievers have been born with the Moon in Capricorn. There's something about the influence of this sign that turns otherwise timid characters into despots, dictators, and tyrants. No doubt, you recognize that somewhere deep within, you, too, have a hunger for status, a desire to control, and a yearning to be treated with respect verging on awe. And you have probably allowed this to influence you in one of two ways. Either you have deliberately climbed to a position of great and unquestionable authority at work, within your social circle, or in your family; or you have spent most of your life repressing the urge so successfully as to become the ultimate underdog, allowing everyone to get the better of you rather than release your lust for supreme power.

Either way, you know that, when you really need to, you can manifest motivation that will brook no opposition or release rage that knows no bounds. Luckily, as treasurer of such a valuable inner resource, your personality is wise and responsible enough to expend it sparingly. Most of the time, you're the very model of calm, common sense, and restraint. Many people admire your levelheadedness and your ability to keep contentious issues in perspective. But when you've got a mission, a purpose, a justified battle to fight, or a mighty wrong to right, woe unto the person or organization that stands in your way!

Others see you as strong, self-assured, mature, responsible, and discriminating. What's most intriguing to an astrologer about the Moon in Capricorn is how it manages to make them think that, while simultaneously causing you to see yourself as weak, insecure, childish, careless, and thoughtless. Perhaps it's the very fact that you're so conscious of what you consider to be your many faults that you work so hard to compensate for them. Perhaps this is also why, occasionally, the tendency I have outlined above gets inverted. It's when you try too intently to manifest those positive traits that you end up drawing the negative ones to your loved ones' attention.

You have a strong need to control. Mainly you apply this to yourself, repressing powerful urges and restricting what you consider to be stray emotional weaknesses. At times, though, you become determined to act as a restraining influence in the lives of others, and you do so in what could only be called a very passionate fashion. Others are surprised to discover the extent of your feeling and the depth of your desire to do something about it, the more so because they are not used to the idea that anything ever bothers you. You're usually happy enough to let your partner take charge of day-to-day decisions, but only when (in your mind at least) your mate is playing the role of ship's captain to your admiral of the fleet.

You are very attracted to individuals who are powerful in their own right. As a "great commander," you want to be able to delegate with confidence. But tension can arise when a serious situation inspires you to leave your lofty office and take over the helm, obliging you to challenge your partner's notion about who is really in charge. The more confident you can become about how much power you really hold, the less you will ever need to prove the point, and the calmer your more tempestuous relationships will become.

It's surprising that you have an interest in astrology. One might have imagined that you were fed up with being told what you were destined to be. From an early age, you have been surrounded by people with clear ideas about your future. A certain authority figure, probably male, certainly determined, tried hard when you were but a small child to make an indelible impression on your memory. He or she left you in no doubt about what was expected of you, yet quite possibly in some considerable doubt about whether you might ever be able to live up to this person's ideal. If you got as much praise as blame or as much understanding as criticism, you were lucky.

Probably a softer person was also there to intervene on your behalf. But even if there were, you grew up torn between the desire to fulfill the ambition that the dominant character clearly had for you and the desire to rebel against it. A part of you wanted to prove something to this person; another part figured that, as you could probably never be good enough to please your hard taskmaster, you might as well give up. No matter how many years have passed since that day, you have still not fully managed to shake off that aspect of your upbringing. Perhaps you never will, and perhaps it doesn't matter.

What *does* matter, however, is that you understand the mark it has made on you. An aspect of your own psyche now plays that role of chastiser and disapprover. You keep yourself so firmly in line as to hold back a side of yourself that sorely needs to be let out. Of late, the desire to do this has been exceptionally strong. You've made magnificent headway in freeing yourself from redundant inhibitions; but you still have further to go, and far greater freedom than you have ever known before lies ahead for you.

MOON IN CAPRICORN, *Sun in ...*

Aries You want respect and work hard to reach a position of such power that people have to give it, no matter what they may think.

Taurus There's never any arguing with you. You find it easy to say "no," though you rarely wind up in situations where you need to!

Gemini You're very good at explaining things to people and persuading them to see your point of view, sometimes, indeed, a little *too* good at it.

Cancer You take your responsibilities exceedingly seriously, and you never quite feel satisfied until you know all your jobs are done.

Leo You can be very masterful when you want to be, and sometimes even when you don't. Many people are a bit in awe of you.

Virgo You doubt your own judgement more than you need to. It's just as well, or others would never stand a chance against your strong will.

Libra Home and family mean a great deal to you. Perhaps partly to compensate for a chaotic past, you're determined to ensure that all around you are safe.

Scorpio You've got a very strong intellect, capable of absorbing many complicated ideas. And you've got a very strong character to go with it.

Sagittarius You've got a magnificent ability to make farfetched ideas sound perfectly feasible and often to turn them into moneymakers, too.

Capricorn Your shell is as tough as titanium, but underneath it your heart is as soft as jelly. Your personality is even sweeter and more colorful.

Aquarius You tend not to remember the dreams you have when you're asleep, but you never stop working to fulfill your waking ones.

Pisces You take your friends and your friendships very seriously. And others know you're a rock to which they can always cling.

MOON IN AQUARIUS

Y OU may well be one of the most sensual, physically demonstrative, and intellectually astute people the world has ever known. But when it comes to emotions, you're as numb as a frozen finger. When you first began to notice that you were surrounded by people who could pour out the content of their hearts by turning on some inner tap, you began to fear you were less than a whole human being. "Let out your feelings," others would say. "How can I," you would reply, "when I don't know what they are?" And so despondent would your lack of sensitivity then make you feel that, privately, you would sob bitter tears of confusion into your pillow. Hmm ... what, pray tell, were those if not an expression of profound inner feeling?

I put it to you that you are not at all the robot you paint yourself to be. Far from being shallow, you are so full of sensitivity as to be mortally afraid of admitting the fact for fear of diving into a pool from which you might never emerge. Your Moon in Aquarius makes you not devoid of feeling but devoid (or almost devoid) of stupidity. You cannot help but question the logic of giving vent to passions that have not been fully thought through. But all emotions are, of course, ultimately irrational. So the fact that your feelings well up only intermittently, in response to some rather unlikely stimuli, makes you neither perverse nor cold. It simply makes you normal in the eyes of everyone except yourself.

What others love most about you is your eccentricity. They have no choice other than to adore or abhor it, for it is as integral a part of your personality as your nose is to your face. Those whose own emotional predilections naturally incline them towards a more conventional companion rarely get close enough to you to form a deep bond. After all, you hardly go to any great lengths to disguise your idiosyncrasy for the sake of making a good first impression. People have to take you as they find you, and, since they rarely find you the same from one day to the next, your world is full of folks who have vastly different ideas about what kind of a person you actually are.

This suits you fine, for variety is not just the spice in your recipe for a happy life, it's the meat. Having friends who not only don't know each other but who wouldn't, even if they happened to meet and talk about you, necessarily realize they were talking about the same person, amuses you greatly.

Fortunately, you don't need a partner who can adapt to all the facets of your wide-ranging personality. You're happy just to have someone who sits contentedly in the department marked "spouse," and who trusts you enough to know that you'll keep coming back once you've gone off and been who you are to everyone else. If you don't currently have such a companion, it shouldn't be hard to find one in time, for, while you may be unusual, you're also unusually vibrant, attractive, and fun to be with.

It's more with loved ones of a nonromantic nature, such as other members of your family, that personality clashes can arise. They don't have the freedom to choose when, how, or where they get involved with you, nor vice versa. Consequently, they can never be quite sure which of your personalities they are likely to encounter! Some acknowledgement of this on your part could improve these relationships a lot.

To have the Moon in Aquarius is to have two mutually incompatible aspirations battling for supremacy in your personality your whole life long. It's by no means a disadvantage: this kind of internal conflict often creates the material from which great characters are carved. However, to become the truly successful and contented person you would dearly love to be, you need to reconcile the difference in your own mind between that which makes you feel successful and that which makes you feel content. Success, to you, implies proving to yourself and the whole world that you are quite unlike any other being who ever walked the face of the earth. You don't care how many people have walked along a path like yours before and what tricks they employed to make it work. You're determined to be different, to do it your way, and to do it without compromising a single thing you stand for. You want others to look at you and say, "There goes one of a kind," and to say it with a note of awe and admiration in their voice.

All of which is fine except that you also yearn to be accepted, welcomed, loved, trusted, and introduced to a group of people to whom you feel you can fully belong! Nonconformists don't, by definition, find it easy to fit in, even with other avowed eccentrics. As a child, you were equally famous for your stubbornness and your exceptional gifts and talents. As a teenager, you went in search of love everlasting, and you still nurse the broken heart to which this quest led you. Now, as an adult, you have to accept yourself for who you are and be proud of it, rather than act out a series of roles designed to persuade others that they are safe to embrace you.

MOON IN AQUARIUS, *Sun in ...*

Aries You really couldn't care less what other people think of you, which is just as well, for most people don't know *what* to think of you!

Taurus Your home may be full of gadgets, or it may just be with relationships that the new, the daring, and the different excite you.

Gemini You like to consider yourself above the ordinary world and its silly problems. And in a funny sort of way, perhaps you are.

Cancer You never really know whether you are coming or going, and neither do your loved ones. But you're very perceptive about everyone else.

Leo Your somewhat imperious personality disguises (sometimes completely) the soft, warm heart that beats beneath.

Virgo You've got a unique way of looking at life and can always be relied on to come up with the one side of the story that nobody else has seen.

Libra You're an adventurer, an explorer, and a bit of a party animal, though you may enjoy debating the night away as much as dancing.

Scorpio You take pride in looking after the interests of loved ones carefully and cleverly. Only when you really feel at home do you let your feelings show.

Sagittarius You're certainly an original thinker. Few have a mind as brilliantly convoluted as yours, and even fewer can actually articulate such thoughts.

Capricorn You're a great innovator with a handy ability to anticipate future needs and to be ready for them. It all does your bank balance no harm.

Aquarius After they made you, they broke the mold, assuming there ever was one. You constantly amaze everyone, including yourself.

Pisces Your mind works in mysterious ways, mysterious, at least, to you. Others often seem to know what you feel more clearly than you do.

MOON IN PISCES

DO you yearn for a life on the ocean waves? If so, you are manifesting a typical tendency of people born under the Moon in
Pisces. So deep are your needs, so profound are your yearnings,
so passionate are your impulses that no relationship, no matter how intense
and committed, with any other human being will suffice to fulfill them. You
need a relationship with something vaster, more unfathomable, and more
mysterious—the sea, for example. Your heart constantly wants to sail, swim,
surf, and dive. If it can't feel safe or able to do that, it prefers to sit patiently doing nothing other than splash pathetically through some shallow pud-
dle.

This is why so many of your loved ones consider you an enigma. You often
reveal little or no trace of emotion, yet it is clear that you are far from being
heartless or insensitive. And no matter how successful you are at your job,
in your lifestyle, or in your family life, there's always something about you
that seems to be a "fish out of water." It may not be the actual ocean that
you require in order to find complete satisfaction. It could be a stimulating,
demanding role to play in some large organization or institution that fills the
gap you sense in your heart. But it's certainly true that Pisceans are not emotionally content unless they're in the process of trying to do the impossible
in an environment where anything can happen next, and probably will.

If you read the descriptions of some of the other Moon signs, you will see
that most follow a pattern. I begin by describing the assets of having the
Moon in a certain sign, go on to discuss the drawbacks, and end with an
appraisal of how these may cause problems in a person's love life. I cannot,
however, apply such a formula when writing about you.

There is, as far as I am aware, no romantic disadvantage to having been
born with the Moon in Pisces. Nor is there some particular attitude to life
that can make family relationships stressful. To have the Moon is Pisces is

to be everyone's friend, nobody's enemy, and some very lucky person's ideal partner.

Well, almost. I'm not trying to say you're perfect. But you're certainly harmless without being insipid, sympathetic without being sentimental, wise without being arrogant, and good-humored without being giddy. Your faults, if it's proper to call them such, are all connected with being "too good to be true." You can make even the most unself-critical companion feel unworthy of your love. You can be unreasonably reasonable, so fair that it's unfair, and so unresentfully self-sacrificing as to make others resent you!

Many people are simply not psychologically geared up to the challenge of coexisting with someone as nice as you are. When they try to probe you for weaknesses or to goad you into a heated emotional reaction, you don't even give them the satisfaction of feeling patronized by a refusal to respond. You bravely go through the motions of anger, jealousy, or angst in the sincere hope that this will help.

None of this is to say that you're devoid of emotion, far from it. You're tremendously deep and prone to profound inner feelings that sweep like tidal waves across your heart. It's just that, even when these feelings have more to do with despair than joy, you don't allow them to cause problems to others in your world. You're one of a very extraordinary Moon-in-Pisces kind.

Some people lust for power. Others crave money, love, or sensual fulfillment. You may not be entirely immune to such desires, but they hardly dominate your life. If they did, one way or another you'd have more of them, for you're not the kind of person to deny yourself anything you crave. What you crave, however, is something that the modern world seems to have in short supply: meaning. Your life must have a point and a purpose, though the conventional goals and aspirations that others strive for seem somehow petty to you. There has to be a sense of sublime transcendence before you're interested. Painting, poetry, music, or other creative activities fulfill this need in some Lunar Pisceans. Others find it through their devotion to a spiritual or charitable cause.

But if all this is beginning to sound like the light side of your Moon, hold on. There's a hunger in your soul for a strong, powerful experience. You simply cannot bear the commonplace, so you throw yourself into whatever you feel is most likely to provide you with an escape hatch from the ordinary world. You can all too easily become obsessive about your art, fanatical about your faith, or, worse still, convinced that even these are not sufficient to take you as far as you want to go. In the absence of a psychological anchor, you can become dangerously cavalier about your well-being, taking risks for the sheer thrill of seeing how close to the edge you can go. As a child you were inquisitive, as a teenager argumentative, and now, as an adult, you have to learn how to construct a lifestyle that satisfies rather than merely destroys the available options.

MOON IN PISCES, *Sun in ...*

Aries Others can't help but respect you for your wisdom and integrity, even if they find you a little too outspoken or pushy at times.

Taurus Though you try not to let the poetic side of your nature run away with you, you're more sentimental and more sensitive than you care to admit.

Gemini You're never one to let a prior engagement stand in the way of a good spur-of-the-moment idea. Hopefully, your friends are as flexible.

Cancer Most of the time you're at ease with yourself and with life in general. Somehow, your intuition always leads you to the right place.

Leo It's a good thing you can put up such a commanding front. If people knew how much fun you really were, they'd never take you seriously.

Virgo Tension in early childhood may have left you too ready to believe that dreams don't come true. Yet yours frequently do, despite this.

Libra You have a pronounced sense of duty. You work hard to keep your wilder impulses under control and at least give an impression of being sensible.

Scorpio You're a light and easygoing character most of the time. Your sense of humor is never far from the surface, no matter what's going on.

Sagittarius Though Sagittarians love to travel, something in you also loves to come home. Ideally, you'd have a home that was capable of travelling!

Capricorn You'd make a great teacher, largely because you're such an enthusiastic student of all that life has to offer. You have a permanent hunger for facts.

Aquarius The combination of a sensitive heart and a logical mind makes you an unbeatable force, as your bank manager will no doubt testify.

Pisces You're impossible! A law unto yourself, a living example of why there's an exception to every rule, and a very wonderful person.

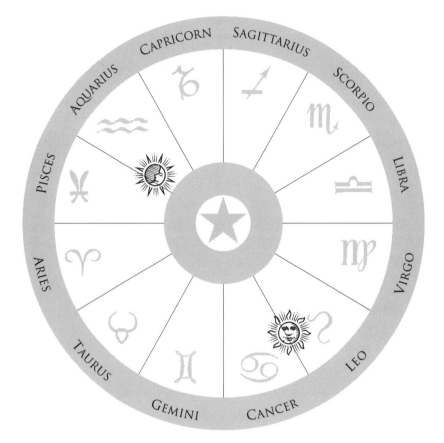

Chapter Three

YOUR UNIQUE
WHEEL OF
DESTINY

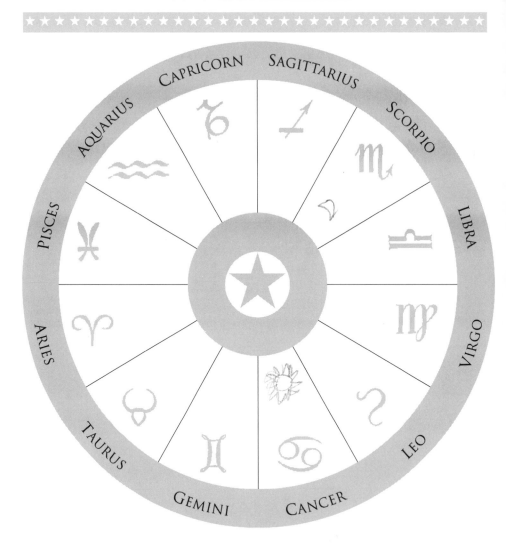

YOUR WHEEL OF DESTINY

Use this wheel to plot your own signs

YOUR WHEEL OF DESTINY

Now that you know your Moon sign as well as your Sun sign, I'm sure you're anxious to find out as much as possible about how the two factors work with one another. You may, indeed, be wondering why the previous chapter only contained a quick "one liner" about each Sun/Moon combination.

I could have said more. I could even, I suppose, have written 144 different chapters, one for each permutation. By keeping my comments brief, I'm really not trying to shortchange you. It's just that there's a better, more astrologically accurate way to look at this whole business.

Think for a moment about cans of paint in a range of colors. Why carry a full range of 144 different shades when you can mix to order any shade you want from a handful of "base" colors?

If you know the secret formula, you can pack an entire decorator's warehouse into a small suitcase. Likewise, if you know how astrology really works, you can dispense with a library full of reference books.

It's my aim in this chapter, and, indeed, throughout the remainder of this book, to teach you the ultimate trick of this trade. I want to free you from the need to keep looking things up in some astrological "book of rules" by explaining the simple principle on which the rule book itself has been based.

Welcome, then, to the wheel of destiny, a diagram of the sky which will reveal the secret of your personality and free your future potential. It's not difficult, nor is it time consuming, but it is very revealing because the principle I'm about to explain to you is, in essence, a simplified version of a full, traditional personal horoscope.

PLOTTING YOUR PLACE ON THE WHEEL

Step 1

This is easy, for it merely involves writing down a piece of information you already know. Turn to the blank chart wheel on page 132 and find the zodiac sign you always read when you look for your forecast. Then write "Sun" in the appropriate space, or, if you're feeling artistic and would like to do the job the same way we professional stargazers do it, draw a little Sun symbol. (You may want to copy a few extra wheels before you begin for future use.)

What you have just done

Congratulations! By entering on the wheel the approximate position of the Sun on the day you were born, you have taken your first step towards plotting a personal horoscope. Now you are ready for something a little more complicated.

Step 2

Turn once more to the wheel and this time look for the zodiac sign that corresponds to your Moon sign. Write the word "Moon" in the appropriate space or draw a little Lunar symbol. You may be among the one in twelve readers whose Sun and Moon are both in the same sign. In this case, you will have to squeeze them both into the same box.

What you have just done

You have now charted your second reference point on the wheel of destiny and are nearly ready to start putting it to work. You have also, by the way, followed in the footsteps of great scientific astrologers from Claudius Ptolemy through Galileo to Kepler, by plotting a diagrammatic map of the sky according to an ancient, mystical method. You now have only one more step to perform.

Step 3

Turn once more to your now not-so-blank chart wheel and count the number of spaces between your Sun and your Moon. Once you have done this, you are ready to find out what your wheel of destiny has to tell you.

By counting the spaces you will end up discovering that your Sun and Moon are one of the following:

★ In the same sign as one another
★ In the sign next door to one another
★ Two signs apart
★ Three signs apart
★ Four signs apart
★ Five signs apart
★ Six signs apart (i.e., opposite one another)
★ If they are more than six signs apart, please count around the wheel in the other direction!

WHAT IT ALL MEANS

 # SUN AND MOON IN THE SAME SIGN

Your childhood influences

Because you were born when both the Sun and the Moon were passing through the same sector of the sky, you tend to fluctuate between manifesting the very best and very worst traits of your sign. Being born under the new Moon makes you exceptional in a further way, for traditionally the maternity wards are much busier when the Moon is full. But though there may have been a shortage of light in the sky on the night preceding your birth, there has been no shortage of light in your life.

In many ways, you have led a charmed existence and have been helped to do so both by a succession of kind, supportive individuals and by the naturally even balance of your own temperament. None of this is to say that you are perfect (even though some people accuse you of seeing yourself as so), nor that your entire life has been a bed of roses (even though you have managed to come up smelling like them time after time). But on balance, you have somehow been "celestially protected" from many of the tough scenarios that your peers and contemporaries have to face.

You may or may not have been showered with parental affection, but you certainly spent most of your formative years free from too many challenges to your sense of security. Key factors remained stable, allowing you the luxury of being a child rather than feeling forced into premature maturity. Even when big events and changes did rock the boat of home and family life, you found a way to cope by turning your attention inwards and developing a sense of independence. You may have had an imaginary playmate who seemed very real, or you may have had a profound interest from an early age in some highly absorbing hobby.

You certainly developed some strong techniques to keep yourself at an emotional distance from the outside world, a way of protecting yourself from your own immense sensitivity. You feel a great deal more than you care to reveal, a fact which those you are close to know only too well, but which it suits you to keep hidden when you can.

One of your parents had a much stronger influence on you than the other, perhaps even to the point where you were left feeling estranged from the less dominant one. This, too, has had its part to play in creating the self-contained, quietly confident character which others tend to see you as today.

Your approach to relationships

When people want to criticize you, they usually begin by having a little dig at your tendency to be rather set in your ways. They accuse you of being too anxious to stick with tradition or too sure that your way is the right way. Up to a point, this may be a fair comment, but it doesn't mean you should feel obliged to adjust your personality drastically. Often our quirks and foibles are merely our special gifts and talents taken a step too far.

We can easily see the truth of this in your case. What is your resistance to change, other than a deep desire to be loyal and consistent? What is your occasional tendency to seem self-righteous, if not a natural sense of faith in what you feel and believe?

If you do need to alter some aspect of your character, it's almost certainly a need to change your tone of voice rather than redefine your actual message. Stressful developments in your key relationships usually come about when you fail to realize what an impact your words are having on others. Your humble requests sometimes end up sounding like demands. Your sincere attempts to offer advice can come across like lectures. Your wise preference for precedent can make you seem like a reactionary.

It's all a little ironic because, deep within, you're an exceedingly soft, small, approachable, even cuddly character. Harm a fly? Why, you'd even be tempted to put a wasp on probation. You're naturally inclined to see the best in everyone and will offer to forgive and forget with a frequency that your less tolerant friends find alarming.

It is, as a matter of fact, your very lack of guile that causes you to be so misunderstood. Because a hidden agenda is the very last thing you look for in others, it's the last thing you imagine others will be looking for when they encounter you. So you say what's on your mind without sufficient regard for what it's going to sound like when it reaches *their* mind. All you ever really want, from a lover, friend, or family member, is a little trust and cooperation. You're quite prepared to give as much back in return, so why should there be a problem in asking for it? The answer is, there shouldn't be. And there won't be, once you learn to think a little more carefully about how to ask for it.

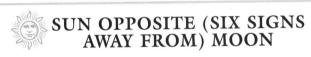

SUN OPPOSITE (SIX SIGNS AWAY FROM) MOON

Your childhood influences

Werewolves, witches, and vampires all traditionally come out when the Moon is full. Babies born under this astrological configuration don't, you'll be glad to hear, turn into any of the above, but they do have extremely strong, determined personalities and can certainly seem, to their long-suffering parents, like little devils! So the first thing we can conclude, from finding a full Moon in your wheel of destiny, is that you were no easy child to raise. You had a mind of your own from the moment you drew your first breath, and you have hardly stopped arguing from that day to this!

It's probably just as well that you were blessed with such a lively, inventive personality, because events in your early life created quite a powerful need for you to pit your wits against something and to prove to the world what you were capable of. You found yourself born into what could best be described as a somewhat unconventional family. Your parents lived in very different worlds, even if physically they remained under the same roof. They either agreed to differ (in which case you probably got off lightly), or they suffered from the straitlaced legacy of their generation and, while putting on a fine front in public, privately conducted a war of attrition. This was no doubt intended to go over your head, but in fact a lot of it went straight to your heart. It left you feeling unsure of how to please one without offending the other, or even feeling vaguely responsible for the rift between them.

Your uppity, idiosyncratic character was originally a sort of cosmic compensation for all this. It gave you the strength to blot out impressions that might have rendered you very weak had you been more sensitive by nature. It's served you well and helped you become the highly motivated, wise, and thoughtful bright spark that others tend to see you as today.

But deep within, you suffer from a couple of secret hang-ups. You're never quite sure whether you're coming or going; and, for all your outward air of confidence, you frequently suffer from agonizing bursts of profound self-doubt. And you yearn for the perfect partnership, yet try so hard to produce one that in the process you sometimes create unnecessary tension between yourself and your partner.

Your approach to relationships

You're a person of extremely strong opinions. Rarely, if ever, do you allow yourself to feel ambivalent about anything or anyone. This might be fine if you really knew why, but you sometimes develop unreasonable prejudices which you then see as perfectly justifiable likes and dislikes. We're all entitled to our preferences, and there's no law that these all must be thoroughly logical, but you're particularly "naughty." You tend, almost on principle, to develop ideas and beliefs that conflict with those held by your nearest and dearest. Mr. and Mrs. Jack Sprat may have made a good team with their differing tastes in meat, but your partner probably yearns to hear you say, "Actually, dear, I agree with you."

You say this a lot? Ah, but *do* you? Or do you just think it and then go on, in your next breath, to utter an argument? Could it be that you find it so easy to play devil's advocate that you step into the role without even noticing? Could it also be that loved ones have gotten so used to feeling challenged that, when they hear you beginning to think through both sides of an issue out loud, they automatically assume you are going to settle on a position contrary to their own?

Could all this be why your social, romantic, and family bonds are a tad too full of dynamic tension for comfort? A little variety adds spice to a relationship, but to make someone feel they are part of a perpetual tug of war is to tip a whole can of curry powder into the pot.

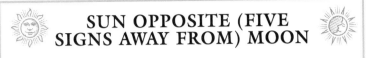

SUN OPPOSITE (FIVE SIGNS AWAY FROM) MOON

So should you learn how to compromise? No. You already know perfectly well how to do that (though you might benefit from learning how to do it without complaining quite so much). But really, it's not compromise you need more of in your life, it's confidence.

You're a thoroughly splendid, kind, incisive, and giving character who, deep down inside, rarely feels completely secure. To compensate, you posture and pretend when you really ought to confide and confess. Approach the other people in your world with a little less self-defensive certainty. You'll feel positively overwhelmed by the amount of affection, gratitude, and reciprocated honesty that begins to come your way.

Your childhood influences

On the day you were born, the Sun and Moon were five signs apart. The Moon, therefore, was almost but not quite full or just beginning to wane. If you want to know which, go back to the wheel and count again. Start with your Sun and work counterclockwise until you find your Moon. If, going this way around, it's five spaces away, you were born under a waxing Moon. If it's seven spaces away, your Moon was waning.

This factor doesn't make too much difference, except perhaps in one respect. If anything you read about yourself strikes you as especially true, yet at the same time significantly uncomfortable, you may want to make a conscious effort to alter certain habits. If you were born under a waxing Moon, the best way to do this is to reach a little further and try a little harder for what you feel tends to elude you. If, however, you were born under a waning Moon, your path to greater personal contentment probably has more to do with giving up a little and learning to relax.

And now let's return to what this particular five-sign-wide angle between the Sun and Moon in your wheel tells us about you. Chiefly, it says you're a born worrier; you find it impossible to rest on your laurels, or indeed on anything else! You can hardly ever sit still, leave things be, or believe that you are entitled to a life of comparative ease.

All this has something to do with a rather turbulent childhood. Your parents may have gotten along fine or lived in a state of mistrust, or perhaps their relationship swung between the two extremes. One thing's for sure, though: they had about as much in common as apples and cars. Thus, you grew up with two highly contrasting role models, and you never felt quite sure which you were more at home emulating. While this has made you exceedingly versatile as an adult, it has also left you with a slightly strange fascination. You constantly hunger to reconcile the irreconcilable, resolve the paradoxical, or explain the inexplicable. Up to a point, it's an exciting challenge. Sometimes, however, it's a very exhausting tendency.

Your approach to relationships

You're a thoroughly lovely person. About this much, at least, most of the world is in firm agreement. But as to quite why, or what it is that makes you so special, there are as many theories as you have friends.

You're a different person under different circumstances, not in any false way, but because you have such an impressive ability to adapt to what you can intuitively sense the person by your side requires. To some, you're a tower of strength and self-sufficiency; to others you're a soft, vulnerable soul. Between these two extremes are many more acquaintances who have each formed a different idea about what you have to offer and where they fit into your life.

Because you also take delight in spanning widely diverse social circles, it's feasible that if two of your closest companions were to meet on the street and discuss their mutual friend, neither would recognize you from the other's description. What makes this even more remarkable is that if you were then to stroll up and join in the conversation, neither you nor they would feel as though any great game were being given away.

You're not pretentious; you're genuinely versatile. Just occasionally, however, your ability to be casually chameleonlike can leave a loved one feeling flustered or threatened. Possessive characters secretly want to pin you down. When you honestly and innocently respond with, "Fine … pin this bit of me down if you like, but I'm afraid the other part of me has to go out now," they feel a little cheated.

If all of your relationships were with relaxed, easygoing characters, the ensuing tension would not arise. But something within you is drawn like a magnet to those with an intense disposition. You like a little fire and passion, and sometimes it seems easier to huddle around someone else's burning flame than to ignite one of your own. But if you ever feel a need to make some of your key relationships easier, you'll find the best way to take the heat off is to find some passion that's all your own and put it not into a person but into some great mission or vision. Let this be the primary source of warmth in your world, and then, as others come to gather around it, they will naturally offer to do things your way rather than expecting you to obey their rules.

SUN TRINE (FOUR SIGNS AWAY FROM) MOON

Your childhood influences

You were born under one of the most harmonious influences known to the world of astrology. Your Sun and Moon are 120 degrees (or one third of the wheel) apart and occupy mutually supportive signs of the same element. They're in a state of agreement with one another, and so you, by and large, are in a state of agreement with yourself. "Why?" you may ask. "What on earth else should I be?" and the answer to this is, "Nothing, but you're lucky, because a lot of people spend a great deal of time feeling anything but comfortable with who they are and what they have to offer."

You, however, have had the benefit of a relatively stable childhood during which, even if all was far from perfect in your environment, you never felt too far from one very special adult who treated you with constant love, kindness, and respect. Quite feasibly, there would have been more than one. Astrologers often find that people born under your particular cosmic alignment have been fortunate enough to enjoy what in modern times has become an increasingly rare phenomenon: a childhood home in which both parents lived in genuine harmony.

Even those who were brought up in less idyllic circumstances usually have genuinely happy memories of their youth. They recall at least some warm, wise, sympathetic adults who got along well with one another and with their children. They remember being given only gentle discipline and sweet encouragement, rather than being too harshly pushed and pulled. As a result, they now have less of an ax to grind in their day-to-day adult life. They naturally tend to look on the bright side and to trust that all in life will work out well in the end.

If you can identify with this, it may be why you are so popular, so easy to get along with, and so often entrusted with other people's secrets. It may also, however, be part of the reason why you don't always fight certain battles quite as determinedly as you could, or perhaps even as you should. Unless there are other extenuating factors in your personal chart, you probably feel more inclined to compromise than to court conflict. Just sometimes, however, you need a slightly harder, more ambitious edge in order to succeed in life. And so, just sometimes, you tend to feel your own easygoing nature is working against you.

Your approach to relationships

If a manufacturer of beauty products could capture the essence of what you've got, the company could bottle it and sell it for a fortune. To be born with your Sun and Moon positions so well balanced within the cosmic circle is to have oodles of what some call charisma and others, less delicately, refer to as sex appeal.

You weren't aware of possessing any such natural advantage? Come, come, surely you're being modest. You mean to say you've never noticed the impact you make on certain people from time to time? What did you think was causing all those wobbly knees and glazed eyes? Flu? Oh well, perhaps you did. Perhaps Mother Nature, in her endless struggle to strike an even balance, imbued you with drop-dead good looks with one hand while rendering you totally unconscious of their potential with the other. But if she did, she didn't manage to be fair to the rest of us, for this only gave you a meltingly innocent demeanor to go along with your air of subtly inviting promise.

It is even more annoying to those who would willingly give their eyeteeth for a small fraction of the magnetism you exude with every step, that you probably still aren't particularly interested in exploiting it, even now that you've had it pointed out to you. A part of you would far rather stay within the bosom of your family, tending to the needy or carrying out some other noble duty than be swept away by a tide of wild and exciting offers. Even if you do crave a life of adventure, you'd far rather have one that depended on something a little less nebulous than this "X factor."

Does all this ensure that in relationships, romantic and otherwise, your life will always be sweet and successful? Sadly not. Among members of your own sex, you have a tendency to evoke jealousy, no matter how hard you try to play down your assets. Among members of the opposite sex, there's always a slight doubt about whether you're being appreciated for your mind or your body. And can any spouse ever feel completely comfortable with a partner who turns more heads than an osteopath? Unless, of course, they were to be similarly celestially well-endowed? But then would you, with all your natural preference for a quiet life, really want to get involved with such potential trouble?

SUN SQUARE (THREE SIGNS AWAY FROM) MOON

Your childhood influences

On the day you were born, the Sun and Moon were forming a 90-degree angle to one another. Unfortunately, as far as astrologers are concerned, this is anything but a "right" angle. It's primarily an angle of tension, challenge, inner disquiet, and (often) external discord to boot. This is precisely why it's so often found in the horoscopes of the world's high achievers, from pop stars to politicians and from big business financiers to big-time celebrities.

If you think about it, it's obvious. To get ahead in life, you've got to have an "edge" to your personality. If you're naturally contented and relaxed, you're not going to have any motivation to prove yourself. You need a little psychological stimulus in your birth chart in order to become a major success. What's questionable, however, is whether you also need the constant disruption that tends to come with it.

You have never really known a quiet life. As a child, you were constantly pushing your luck and testing adults to see whether they meant the word "no." Not surprisingly, this led you into a strained relationship with at least one of your parents. You looked for examples of their hypocrisy with which to justify your defiance, and because, like all human beings, they were less than perfect, you found it. You also looked, indeed hunted like a hawk, for topics on which grownups disagreed. When they inevitably did, you slipped through as many of those disciplinary loopholes as you could.

Whether the authority figures in your formative years could have set a better example in the way they related to you (and to one another) is a moot point, but what's certainly clear is that you *felt* they could. All this left you with a healthy disrespect for petty rules but also, perhaps, an unhealthy tendency to challenge life's less trivial restrictions. So determined are you now not to take orders that you will sometimes balk against doing today what you decided to do yesterday. This doesn't make you the easiest person in the world to get along with, which is ironic, because deep down what you long for more than anything else is a life full of harmonious relationships.

Your approach to relationships

Most ancient mythologies saw the Moon as female and the Sun as male. Modern astrologers overwhelmingly agree with this view. You, however, may not be so willing to accept this notion, or indeed any other. Because you were born with the Sun and Moon approximately 90 degrees apart, you are not the kind of person to take anything at face value. You always want to know "Why?" You always want to know "What else?" And you often take special pleasure in supporting unconventional minority beliefs.

In deference to your desire to differ, I'll concede that certain historical civilizations perceived the Sun as a mother figure and the Moon as a patriarch. What's certain beyond question, though, is that no culture since the dawn of time has considered the Sun and Moon to be of the same sex. So any way you look at it, the key cosmic symbols of male and female energy are, in your wheel of fortune, aligned in mutually challenging positions.

This explains why you tend to be so restlessly argumentative, not just when dealing with others but when trying to make up your own mind. You're forever trying to reconcile distinctly incompatible inner yearnings: on the one hand, an urge to be sensible and assertive, on the other, a quest to be intuitive and adaptable.

The downside of all this, you already know. You're notorious among your friends, colleagues, and family for being an awkward so-and-so. They see you as erratic, unpredictable, and almost impossible to persuade. They may love and respect you, but they don't find you easy. Your key relationships are thus best described as "dynamic." They involve plenty of lively debate and tend to go through phases: periods of quiet, contented coexistence followed by conflict and upheaval.

The way to improve your relationships is, by happy coincidence, also the way to make your Sun/Moon configuration help you carve out a brighter career. It is to harness the immense creativity, inventive talent, and imagination that your wheel of destiny bestows. It is to learn to wrestle with concepts rather than people, to argue with artistic or scientific tradition rather than with routine. When you're busily asking pertinent, provocative questions on behalf of humanity as a whole, you're doing us all a favor and, in the bargain, using up excess emotional fighting energy that's far too potentially powerful to be squandered on some trivial personal battleground.

SUN SEXTILE (TWO SIGNS AWAY FROM) MOON

Your childhood influences

On the day you were born, the Sun and Moon were in zodiac signs approximately 60 degrees apart from one another. Astrologers call this particular angular relationship a sextile because it spans a sixth of the zodiac circle. It has long been regarded as a constructive influence. Indeed, the ancient astrologers used to believe that a person with such a link between their Sun and Moon was automatically destined for a life of good health and fortune.

Much though I hate to throw a monkey wrench in the works, I have to point out that this may not be quite so automatic in all cases today. We are working with slightly imprecise measurements, and, therefore, your sextile may be what we call a "weak aspect" (that is, one you have to reach for consciously rather than one that life has handed to you on some silver platter). But I can confirm that to have your Sun and Moon in the signs almost next door to each other is indeed to have a special celestial advantage operating in your life.

It suggests that you were probably blessed with a widely supportive family environment in your formative years, and, as a youngster, you were certainly much loved and protected by one very special parental figure. Even if not all in your childhood garden was rosy, someone went to great lengths to keep you safe from as much as they could. You will never forget the influence that this adult's sweet, generous nature had upon you. It's both the inspiration you draw on whenever you encounter conflict in your life today and the source of your motivation to help others, in your turn, wherever you can.

You're well-known and much admired for your even temper, sincerity, consistency, and creativity. You have a naturally philosophical way of coping with the slings and arrows of outrageous fate and of doing the best with what you've got without ever compromising your principles in the process. Even though you sometimes encounter misplaced jealousy from those who think you're a little too perfect to be true, you rarely rise to an emotionally baited hook. You prefer to find some way to understand what lies behind an individual's anger or bad behavior and, thus, to reach out to the better nature that you remain absolutely convinced can always be found in everyone, if only one looks hard enough for it.

Your approach to relationships

By and large you're an easygoing, affable character. You can snap and crackle rather fiercely sometimes, but it takes a lot to pop the bubble of goodwill that surrounds you. You're benign, trusting, sincere, and self-assured. You take pleasure in helping others and are even wise enough to recognize that this can't be done unless some effort is made to reach their level. So you work hard to be a good listener and a fair, open-minded friend. In theory all this ought to make you everyone's ideal choice for marriage, employment, or just social company. In practice? Well, it can, but there are drawbacks associated with your generous spirit. You have a tendency to mother or father people; you can rarely resist the urge to protect, nurture, guide, and console. It's a lovely trait, but it means that weak, unsettled characters are drawn towards you like moths to a flame. You've got one shoulder which is perpetually damp from the number of people who seem to think they have some right to cry on it, and another that constantly aches from the burdens it's ended up carrying.

All this you normally accept without complaint, though it's arguable whether sometimes you don't give certain people a little more support than they deserve, thus depriving them of a chance to learn their own lessons the hard way. But what really causes conflict in your world is another syndrome stemming from the same source.

Parental figures aren't always appreciated and honored: often they're resented and rebelled against. Some of the "lost souls" who seem to surround you take the unresolved issues that they have with their actual mothers or fathers and project these on to their relationship with you. They test your trust, tax your patience, or, worse, secretly complain about you to others. When you realize this is happening, you're left wondering what you've done wrong.

The answer is nothing, other perhaps than that you've cared a little more than you ought to have done. All you need, in order to develop a more settled, satisfactory personal life is to be a little more selective about whom you extend your protective wing to, and perhaps in the future to make a deliberate point of forging relationships on a distinctly adult-to-adult basis, where each person takes ultimate responsibility for his or her own problems.

SUN SEMI-SEXTILE (IN SIGN NEXT DOOR TO) MOON

Your childhood influences

You were born either just before or just after a new Moon. Before we go any further we ought to establish which, for it makes a slight difference to the rest of this reading. You can easily find this out by going back to your wheel of destiny for a moment and finding the segment containing your Sun. If your Moon is in the next sign reading clockwise, it had just begun to wax. If you have to look counterclockwise to find it, your Moon was still on the wane.

As a rule of thumb, people with waning Moons tend to hide the way in which they are being led through life by their emotions, feeling perhaps a little afraid of seeming silly. People with waxing Moons, on the other hand, are less inhibited about announcing that they are running on instinct. This is an important distinction to make in your case because, whether you were born while the Moon was waxing or waning, you were certainly born with a powerful sense of intuition. That's your blessing.

Your curse, if that's not too strong a word to use, is that the feelings which move you so strongly never seem to fit very logically into the lifestyle you lead on the outside. You either end up like the top accountant who secretly wants to be an artist (if your Moon is waning), or (if your Moon is waxing) like the great artist who proudly proclaims that a Bohemian lifestyle is a thing of the past and the avant-garde is to be found through double-entry bookkeeping. One way, you seem odd to yourself; the other, odd to others.

Either way, you're definitely an odd mixture, and, indeed, you've been so ever since you were born. Your parents were probably something of an odd couple, and your early lifestyle was probably an eccentric one. You've somehow been exposed to a series of logical non sequiturs all through life and have rather come to relish them. The way you lead your life may not make very much sense to you or anyone else, but it's fun and surprisingly successful, too. Furthermore, in your perpetual quest to find a compromise between wildly different impulses, you often manage to bring together the most unlikely ideas or people and make them work wonderfully well together.

Your approach to relationships

People can never be quite sure which side of your character they are going to see. Sometimes you can be tremendously down-to-earth, almost businesslike in your dealings with others. But every so often, you will reveal a very different, much deeper, and more emotionally vulnerable side of your character, even to those it might be considered inappropriate to show it to. Consequently, while you probably have some friends who feel safe in confiding great personal secrets to you because you in turn have been open with them, there are some members of your immediate family who feel unsure about approaching you on any topic more emotionally loaded than the color of their new sofa.

Even though you don't deliberately set out to make things go this way, a part of you may like the arrangement. For you're never quite sure how closely you want to get involved with anyone. Powerful inner feelings fascinate you in one way and worry you in another. You like life to be straightforward; complex emotions are usually anything but. Which is not to say that you deny their existence, either in yourself or in others, rather that you prefer to play a game of peek-a-boo with profound and intense matters, acknowledging their vast importance one moment but carrying on as if you have seen nothing to talk about the next.

It's all tied up with the way that your Sun and Moon, respectively representing the primary conscious and unconscious forces in your psyche, are aligned a little too closely for comfort. You find it hard to get a perspective on what's going on deep in your heart, for much the same reason that a driver who has passed another cannot always be sure when it's safe to return to the slower lane. Too much seems to take place in your psychological blind spot. This, in turn, is why you often find yourself surprised to hear that others have been upset by something you have said or done (or failed to say or do).

Your equivalent of an extra mirror needs to be a policy of asking your nearest and dearest to honk their horns when they feel you're in imminent danger of accidentally squeezing them off the road. And then they'll somehow be more able to accept and love your erratic behavior for what it actually is: the hallmark of a harmless, eccentric genius at work!

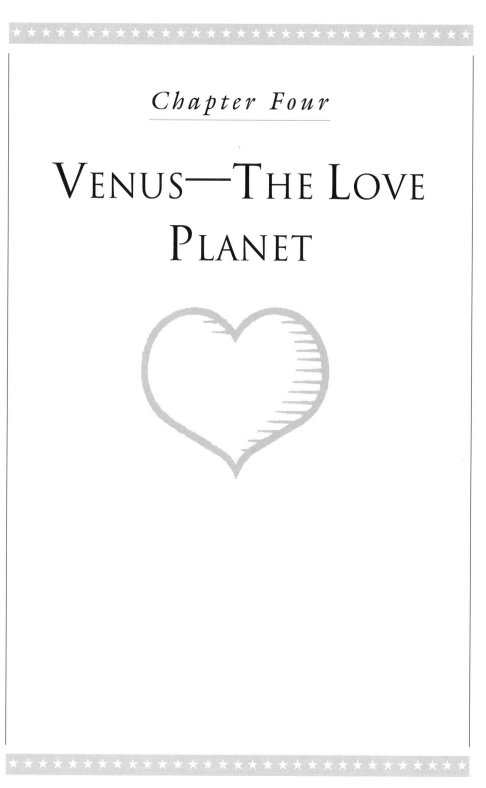

Chapter Four

VENUS—THE LOVE PLANET

VENUS—THE LOVE PLANET

For the purposes of this chapter, please forget all you know about the zodiac sign you normally consider you belong to. To discover what kind of lover you are, what kind of lover you really want, and what kind of love you may one day be able to enjoy in your life, I must ask you once more to look up your date of birth. This time do it in the Venus tables on page 313. These will tell you what sign Venus was in on the day you were born. It won't take you more than a moment to consult them, but the information they lead you to may change the way you see yourself forever!

The nature of Venus and the Venus sign

We're going to find out why some people cannot stand you, yet others feel so powerfully attracted to you that they simply cannot resist your charm. And, as Venus rules art and music as much as she rules romance, we're going to explore your instinctive aesthetic preferences. We're going to look at both the shapes and colors that strike your fancy, plus the figures and faces that fill your fantasies.

Venus is a planet for romantics. Her very name conjures up an image of mystery and sensuality, but she was a seductive symbol long before the Romans coined this name for her. The Babylonians called her Ishtar, Goddess of Fertility. The Sumerians knew her as Inanna, Queen of Thunder. To the Egyptians she was Isis, the Enchantress; and to the Greeks she was Aphrodite, ultimate icon of feminine charm and the mother of Cupid.

If you are a typical male, your Venus sign represents your ideal woman. Aphrodite wears many disguises. Today, you will see which she dons when she wants to capture your heart. If you are a woman, your Venus sign governs the kind of person you turn into when you exploit your feminine charm. I have to confess, though, that when reading romantic preference in a horoscope, all astrologers find female psychology more complicated.

Aphrodite was the ultimate free woman. She belonged to no man, yet she awakened a deep and profound spirit of desire in the heart of every man she encountered. She had passionate and fruitful romantic involvements with gods as diverse as the witty, intellectual Hermes; the silent, muscular Adonis; and the pompous, powerful Zeus. Throughout all this she also had a tolerant husband: aloof and irritable Hephaestus, the wounded craftsman. Forget for a moment any judgement you might feel inclined to make about her character. We are dealing here with a symbolic goddess, not a real human being, and we must view her in her proper context: as an icon of femininity. One day, I hope to write an entire book about her. For our purposes here, though, all we need to understand is that we are dealing with the image of a woman who is attractive to every type of man. A man's Venus sign tells us whether he is more likely to try and appeal to Aphrodite by acting like a Hermes, an Adonis, a Zeus, or a Hephaestus. A woman's Venus sign, however, does not tell us which of these four symbolic gods she is most likely to be drawn to. There is an image of an ideal man inside the mind of every woman, but to identify this using astrology, we have to look at a woman's Mars sign, not her Venus sign. That comes later in this book.

For now, while we're looking at the Venus sign, we simply need to remember that every woman has the spirit of Aphrodite somewhere within her and that her spirit is forever a free spirit. It reserves the right to pick and choose between all four types according to the mood of the moment.

In a man's horoscope, the Venus sign represents his ideal female fantasy figure: the guise in which he is most likely to perceive Aphrodite when he thinks of her and the way in which he would most like to relate to her. In a woman's horoscope, the Venus sign represents the way of being which is most likely to make her feel relaxed, at ease, sensual, confident, charming, and appealing. It tells us what kind of role in life is most likely to make her feel supremely free and feminine.

"Are two people with the same Venus sign compatible?" The short answer is, sometimes, yes, but please don't be misled, especially where you notice that the female description of a Venus sign appears to be a direct match for the male fantasy outlined below it. It's more a point in favor of the partnership's potential than a cast-iron guarantee.

Your Venus sign reveals a lot about your attitude to love, but it also speaks volumes about the way you relate to Mother Nature.

Mother Nature is a powerful entity. To some, she appears in an impersonal, scientific disguise. To others, she is very much a living individual with tastes and preferences, habits and hobbies. But to all, she is a source of inspiration and support. Without the environment that she so carefully creates, we would have no air to breathe, no water to drink, no sunshine to bathe in, and no world within which to pursue the love of one another.

We may not understand all that nature does, but we cannot help but appreciate how vast, powerful, and influential her activities are. Whether we take her for granted, live in awestruck appreciation of her strength, or actively seek a logical explanation of why she does what she does, we are bound to have a relationship with her. It is the particular quality of this constant relationship that your Venus sign describes.

Do you see yourself as needing to compensate for what nature has seemingly failed to endow you with? Or as overwhelmed by the generous gifts that she has bestowed? Do you see nature as an abundant force, constantly offering to supply whatever you need? Or as a weak, easily corrupted character, in need of sensitive protection? How you feel about the wider world you inhabit speaks volumes about your attitude toward other people. If you're naturally inclined to trust nature, you'll trust loved ones. If you're always suspicious that the elements are about to play some nasty trick, you'll be similarly guarded about giving too much to those close by. In these and a thousand other ways, the links between you and nature are as revealing as any session on a counselor's couch.

Venus is the second planet from the Sun and the nearest to our own. She is roughly the same size as Earth, but, as the planet is covered in clouds of sulfuric acid and has a surface temperature of 860°F (460°C), it is hardly the place you would want to go to for a holiday. Yet even astronomers have to concede that Venus has a bright, compelling beauty that makes you want to run to her. She may be a planet, but she twinkles like a star. She may have no gravitational effect on the human body, but she never fails to pull the heartstrings of any soul whose gaze wanders skyward. Venus's days may be four months long, but she is the ultimate symbol of nocturnal promise.

Those who are only prepared to see Venus as some distant ball of gas and rock can hardly be expected to recognize her power to influence events on Earth. There is, as yet, no satisfactory scientific explanation why Venus or any other planet should do this. But then, love itself is not a scientifically provable phenomenon. To experience it, you have to stop asking what it is and just give yourself over to something you feel to be true. If you're going to say that Venus is only a planet, you may as well say that a rainbow is nothing more than an intriguing phenomenon involving the refraction of light. Or that a kiss is only an expression of some primal urge to reproduce the species. Romance defies logical explanation, and so, to some degree, does astrology. But that doesn't make either of them any less real.

Now, if you have not already done so, please turn to the tables on page 313 and look up your Venus sign before you read on. Bear in mind that it is quite possible for your Venus sign to turn out to be the same as your Sun sign.

♡ VENUS IN ARIES ♡

YOU AND NATURE

T O have Venus in Aries is to have an admiration for earthquakes, an interest in infernos, a taste for tornadoes, and a respect for raging waters. You have no desire to live near nature at its most violent, but you can certainly empathize with the sheer energy it's capable of manifesting. You, too, yearn to move the immovable, inflame the impervious, whip up an enormous storm, or make waves that no one can resist.

To deny this is not just to suppress the fire in your soul but to risk unconsciously aligning yourself with others who will set the cat amongst pigeons you dare not disturb. If there's ever tension in your world, it's usually got a power struggle at its heart. You were born to lead rampaging armies, conduct exciting campaigns, fight furious battles, and awaken a sleepy world. You have to find some way, in this tame, restrained modern society, to pit your wits against the elements or put yourself at the head of some worthwhile, challenging enterprise.

If you can't or won't, you'll find your excess energy gets absorbed controlling the actions of some partner who both attracts you (by daring to do what you'd half like to) and horrifies you (by doing it clumsily or thoughtlessly). For as long as you feel you need to assert the kind of power over an individual that you ought more properly to be asserting over an environment, any companion will be in danger of becoming an adversary. But when you've got your work wisely cut out, you're too busy fulfilling a universal calling to contemplate personal conflict. As none can resist the magnetic appeal of a Venus-in-Aries person plowing ahead in a direction that truly makes sense, this is all you have to do if you want to surround yourself with love.

YOU AND YOUR CREATIVITY

Your greatest skills lie in starting things from scratch. Unlike some people, whose talents lie in refining or improving an existing idea, you're best at conjuring up the new from next to nothing. It's probably for this reason that you're drawn to primary colors, clearly defined textures, or strong, striking tastes. Life's more subtle nuances certainly don't escape you, but, as far as you're concerned, they're icing on the cake. First, the cake has to be baked. Others can have the joy of decorating it. They can even, if they wish, have the pleasure of beating the eggs. For you, the chief joy is in making a space in which magic can happen. It's in hunting down the ingredients, ordering up the materials, and then setting the creative process in motion. Just put you in charge of setting the ball rolling, and you'll rapidly sketch out brilliant blueprint after brilliant blueprint, which others can turn into reality at their leisure.

YOU AND ROMANCE

To have Venus in Aries is to be a powerhouse of passion. You've probably never spent a day wistfully yearning in your life. The only thing to do with a dream, as far as you're concerned, is to get out there in the world and do whatever it takes to make it a reality. If others think your plan is too risky, you merely try all the harder for the added joy of proving them wrong. You're competitive about all your conquests: romantic, creative, and financial. You need to perceive yourself as a winner (which is fine), but you're constantly comparing yourself to others and wondering why you haven't yet got what they've got (which is not quite so fine).

Your most attractive quality is your nerve. No matter how timid you may appear on the surface, you're rarely too shy to speak your mind or to make a bold proposition. You're spontaneous, strong, and charismatic, though rather too prone to do things in haste that you regret at leisure. Your eyes may sometimes flash with fire, but generally they sparkle with a kind of infectious enthusiasm that can melt the iciest heart. People tend to admire your confidence and resent your arrogance.

As you spend most of your life treading a thin line between the two, this makes for relationships that tend to be full of drama. You're one of those people who simply won't listen. Not only will you rush in where angels fear to tread, you'll rush right back in there again, even after someone has gone to a lot of trouble to get you out of trouble! As a lover you're adventurous, energetic, and deeply demonstrative, though your tendency to blow hot and cold can confuse those of a more stable disposition.

THE WAY YOU MANIFEST YOUR FEMININITY

Female

The day you flutter your eyelids helplessly and pretend that only a big strong man can help solve your problem is the day the coyote captures the road runner. You're not a weak Wendy, a lacy Tracy, or a flimsy Flora but a capable Caroline, a passionate Penelope, and an independent Eileen. You're strong, self-contained, and sensual, but you're a real woman and not one of those prepackaged, plastic Barbie dolls. Macho men don't impress you. You want someone who will treat you as an equal, respect your territory, and join you in a serious campaign to right the world's wrongs. If he's a little on the quiet side, that's fine as long as there's plenty of personality below the surface. The up-front performance, you can manage by yourself, if not all the better without some noisy, insensitive male constantly mishandling the conversational ball.

YOUR IDEAL WOMAN

Male

Your ideal woman has to be lively, powerful, and self-motivated. She must be quick on the uptake and quicker still on the trigger of the gun you envisage her holding at the end of her leather-clad arm: a sort of Annie Oakley with overtones of Mae West in her wit and refusal to let anyone get the better of her. You have a secret desire, if not to be dominated, certainly to be given a good run for your money. You don't want her to play hard to get, you want her to *be* hard to get. And ultimately, when you've run out of all possible ways to catch up with her, you want her to turn around and catch you! You're quite happy to play second fiddle to her first violin, but only if she's an absolute virtuoso. You'd rather be not quite secure with the wildest woman in the West than waited on hand and foot by some gorgeous geisha.

♡ VENUS IN TAURUS ♡

YOU AND NATURE

VENUS in Taurus means you ought to be a planter of acorns, a builder of windmills, a designer of reservoirs, or a mender of engines. You are in your element in any element, as long as you are patiently investing time, care, and skill in some enterprise to improve the quality of life. To seize efficiently the power of the earth (to grow trees), air (to harness power), rain (to irrigate), or fire (to propel) is to express perfectly the delicate, respectful relationship you have with nature: that of mutual servants, each providing what their partner most requires. A similarly purposeful balance is all you aspire to in love. The problem is, we live in a modern world. Unless you're lucky, you have little chance to interact with natural forces. You're more likely to be a consumer or end user than a person who can make what they need from start to finish. Even if you work with natural elements, you may feel more like a cog in the machine than someone with freedom to respond to the needs of your environment.

Domestically, too, similar artificial pressures may be creating tension and dissatisfaction. Neither you nor your partner may be free to live the lifestyles you might choose. It can all make you feel resentful, thus unwilling to let the love in your heart guide your life. The key to change lies in some means of self-expression (be it gardening, painting, sculpting, or basket weaving) that puts you in command of an entire natural process of transformation. By filling at least your leisure time with this activity, you can respond to the yearning of your Venus in Taurus for a joint creative venture with creation itself. If you can share the task with a soulmate, you really can lead a life abundant in joyous give and take.

YOU AND YOUR CREATIVITY

In this modern world of "make it fast, pile it high, sell it cheap," you're a genuine rarity: a person who believes in the old-fashioned ethos of care and craftsmanship. You'd far prefer to spend your life creating one outstanding novel, symphony, painting, sculpture, or garden than to churn out endless works of just-above-average quality. If you can't be sure you've got the time and resources to get something right, you'd rather not even try.

Subtle shades and textures make all the difference as far as you're concerned. No way can you stain pine dark and call it oak or pass off polyester for silk. Nor can you feel relaxed about entrusting responsibility to others. Unless you've got a promising apprentice you've personally trained, you'd far prefer to do your own dirty work and know you've done it to the highest standard. You're similarly discriminating when it comes to spending the money you've worked so hard to earn. One item of real quality is worth a house full of junk. But better still would be a collection of excellence. You're an exceedingly wise investor of time, skill, and money.

YOU AND ROMANCE

To have Venus in Taurus is to be almost breathtakingly responsive to physical stimuli. Where some people have photographic memories, you have full sensual recollection. You only have to touch, feel, taste, or hear something once to remember it forever. This is why the quality of your environment is so important to you. Just as an ecological campaigner hates the thought of some smokestack polluting the atmosphere, you cannot stand the idea of a substandard item or possession lowering the tone of your life. Everything has to be of the highest possible quality.

If you're selective about what you sit on, eat off of, sleep on, or listen to, you're even more choosy about the person you allow to awaken your deepest, most passionate urges. A lover who pays only lip service to your needs cannot be tolerated simply because they happen to be good company in other respects. When you give yourself to anything or anyone, you do so completely. Whether pursuing the enjoyment of art, music, literature, natural beauty, or romantic expression, you want to feel interest awaken slowly in the tips of your toes, rise gradually to the top of your head, and cause your whole body to writhe with endlessly powerful waves of involvement.

None of this is necessarily obvious to the casual observer. You rather like the idea of being a dark horse with a misleadingly bland persona. You're interested in what others do, not what they say, so you tend to appeal only to people who share an instinctive desire to put experience before philosophy. Those who cannot resist you recognize your capacity to meet them at a private and immensely deep level. Those who find your company difficult to deal with resent your refusal to act out false roles or put on social airs and graces.

THE WAY YOU MANIFEST
YOUR FEMININITY

Female

Some women go to great lengths to maximize their assets: for a date or special occasion they will dress up in an attempt to look appealing. But you find yourself needing to tone down your appearance in order not to radiate more sultry, sensual magic than already flows naturally out of your every pore. You're not so much glamorous (for that word implies a superficial glitz) as sumptuous, insofar as the ability to manifest deep feminine strength comes as a standard feature on your psychological operating system. You no more need a man to make you feel like a complete woman than a Rolls Royce needs a stripe to make it seem like a regular car. Consequently, you can pick and choose your partner from a wide range of willing applicants. The showoffs, the smart alecks, and the wise guys don't get past the first hurdle. You're only interested in someone deep, sensual, and sincere.

YOUR IDEAL WOMAN

Male

Your vision of loveliness wears a long gown with a wide hood. She's an angel of mercy, a figure of mystery, a radiant bestower of warmth and kindness. Quite how she's supposed to manage to juggle the nine kids that she's anxious to bear for you without a murmur of complaint while simultaneously tending to the needy and the sick who line up for her healing touch, plus (of course) fulfilling your every physical whim and fancy, is a puzzle, but somehow she'll do it all and more besides. She'll cook, clean, and make a comfortable home while selling the prize orchids she's grown on the back lawn for such high sums that you never need to work again. A difficult fantasy for any flesh-and-blood female to live up to? Indeed, but the one who comes (or appears to come) closest will always be the one who wins your heart.

♡ VENUS IN GEMINI ♡

YOU AND NATURE

To have Venus in Gemini is to be a connoisseur of variety and ingenuity. It is to appreciate, in people, plants, and animals alike, the subtle distinguishing features that make up the detail in life's rich tapestry. It is to want to communicate all you can see, to share your knowledge with others, and to absorb from them any additional information they may be able to supply. It is also, however, to risk becoming a critic rather than a commentator, a disenchanted pundit rather than an enthusiastic observer.

For when something captivates your heart, you want to know every little thing about it. So you tend to play about with it: to see how it responds under condition X or environment Y, or whether it will benefit from this change or that adjustment. Sometimes, you discover you can work minor miracles with your experiments, vastly improving the efficiency of a machine, the emotive impact of a piece of music, the taste of a recipe, or the sales potential of a product. And sometimes, like the child who dismembers an insect just to see what will happen, you tinker too much with your toy, disabling it beyond repair.

There is a very human (but nonetheless misplaced) tendency at such times to blame the failure on the fiddle rather than the fiddler. At which point, you become cynical: "Oh, I know all about such-and-such. It's useless." If this means you sometimes give up in an area of endeavor where you might have persevered to great success, that's a shame. If it's also the reason why you sometimes abandon faith in a relationship, it's a tragedy! To fill your life with loving acceptance, you simply have to overcome the tendency to fill your mind with negative dismissal. For while you have one, you simply have nowhere to put the other.

YOU AND YOUR CREATIVITY

You ought to consider becoming a writer, for you have a real way with words. You might also make a promising cartographer, for you can always find a clever way to get from A to B. Then again, a career in meteorology might suit you, for you're certainly fascinated by changing climates and conditions.

Yet for all your intelligence, wit, and fascination with detail, you're sometimes more inclined to help others display their genius than to use your own. You can find yourself interested in assisting absentminded professor types who have a lot to teach you and hopefully a lot to learn from your somewhat more substantial grasp of reality. Often, though, they end up talking you out of the common sense you're trying to talk them into. Venus in Gemini makes you willing to listen (which is good) but a little too easily persuaded (which is problematic).

For much the same reason, you have to take care in business matters. You have great ideas and a real talent for making ordinary things look special. But you're sometimes afraid to ask for what a thing is worth or a little too quick to agree to a deal that benefits the other participant more than it suits you.

YOU AND ROMANCE

Venus in Gemini makes you witty, perceptive, inventive, and vivacious. Given a straight, non-negotiable choice between a partner with devastating looks but a dull personality or one with, shall we say, an unusual appearance but a brilliant mind, you'd have no hesitation in opting for the intelligence. Ultimately, the quality of pillow talk matters far more to you than the quality of anything else that can happen in a bedroom.

This is not to say you're ambivalent about the physical side of romance nor that you've no appreciation of a fine face and figure. It's just that, to you, love is about good communication, or it's about nothing at all. In an ideal world, you'd have a lover with brains *and* beauty, or, dare I say it, you'd have one of each type. You can just about cope with the concept of monogamy, but only if the word never becomes confused with monotony, for you thrive on variety and change. Your partner, therefore, has to be lively and interesting enough to hold your interest and self-contained enough not to see your flirtatious personality as a threat.

It's the nature of Venus in Gemini never to be satisfied with anything, always to be looking out for something new, often to be questioning conventional ideas and expectations. People similarly stimulated by the desire to push back life's boundaries find you devastatingly attractive. You make them think, you make them fight, and, most of all, you make them laugh. People whose primary desire is to conform for the sake of a quiet life find you more likely to make them cry. Here you have to be careful, for, despite your general preference for thought over feeling, you are a soft and sensitive soul and a sucker for a sob story.

THE WAY YOU MANIFEST YOUR FEMININITY

Female

There may be a sexier woman on earth but you've yet to meet her. Once or twice you've come across someone superficially similar, but on closer inspection she's proved a little too dull, dreary, or desperate. It's a shame, really, because you could do with some competition, if only to enliven those tediously long days of fending off admirers. There's certainly not a man alive who can withstand your charm when you lay it on thick enough. With your sharp wit and infallible insight you can turn yourself, like a chameleon, into whomever you suspect your quarry happens to be dreaming of. But as you really want to be loved for who you are, your ideal man has to be smart enough to see through you without being quite smart enough to see past you. He also has to be good-looking (so others will envy you), but not so cute as to make you constantly nervous that he'll be stolen (not that he could be, of course, but it's just as well not to run the risk).

YOUR IDEAL WOMAN

Male

The siren of your secret dreams probably wears a mortarboard, a black academic gown, and precious little else. Before agreeing to respond to your amorous advances, she wants you to name the capital of Assyria, calculate π to ten decimal places, and list the Roman emperors in chronological order. Should you fail in any of these tasks, she will have to help you find some novel way to tease the answer into your memory.

It's debatable whether you really yearn for a seductress or an instructress, though, as the latter has overtones of punishment; we'd better add immediately that Venus in Gemini gives you no taste for stern discipline. The woman of your dreams needs to be lighthearted and good-humored about her role as educator and debater of topical issues. She simply has to be as bright as she is bubbly, as soft as she is sharp, and as attractively formed as she is impressively informed.

♡VENUS IN CANCER♡

YOU AND NATURE

To have Venus in Cancer is to be in love with the Moon. It is to be moved by its beauty, pulled by its gravity, and influenced by its phases. And it is to have an affinity with all in nature that is traditionally governed by this queen of the tides. In particular, it is to admire the oceans, lakes, and rivers, not just for their charm but for their historical claim to be the mother of all earthly life.

Our earliest ancestors were amphibians who gradually moved from the sea to the land. Some species (such as frogs, newts, and crabs, who symbolize your Venus sign) still need to keep in contact with their place of origin. Others pay only lip service to the relationship in the enjoyment of liquid refreshment or the occasional pleasure they take from a brief immersion. However, rather like the conscientious member of a large family who takes on the duty of calling to remind everyone that it's nearly Mom's birthday, people with Venus in Cancer are somehow cosmically required to remember, on behalf of the entire human race, what debt we owe to H_2O.

This is why, silly though it may sound, you need plenty of water in your world if you want plenty of love in your life. The more you float, bathe, swim, or sail, the more you will be in your element. And the more you share these activities with others, the more interpersonal tensions will somehow just be washed away.

YOU AND YOUR CREATIVITY

Venus (the artist) brings Cancer (the home lover) the ability to turn a humble abode into a glorious palace. But then Cancer (the unpretentious) brings to Venus (the great pretender) a determination to put comfort before style. So, while your chosen environment definitely conjures up a mood, it creates a real atmosphere, not an idealized, artificial but superficially impressive one.

Much the same balancing process takes place wherever you seek to express creative skills. You are a creature, first and foremost, of honesty, integrity, and intuition. You'd far rather take a chance on the truth than have a safe bet on a piece of deceit. So the cheap success that certain other people seem to get in life rarely comes your way. Your artistic, horticultural, healing, and people skills either get recognized for the valuable rarities they truly are, or they are taken for granted. Which it is matters little to you. Your interest is in doing what's right to the best of your ability and letting that satisfaction be its own reward.

It is only when pursuing success on behalf of others or in connection with some heartfelt cause that you feel inspired to be pushy. You cannot bear to stand by and watch others being ill-treated, so, when you see someone getting a raw deal, you seek ways to champion their cause, relieve their suffering, or rescue them from their predicament. In aid of some official charity or as part of some private campaign to help a friend, you will perform feats of creative genius that no amount of financial incentive alone could ever spur you on to do.

All of this is admirable and worthy, except that sometimes you will deny yourself an opportunity to which you are fully entitled simply because you don't feel that you should have it while others are suffering. Next time this syndrome crops up, think about how much more you might be able to do for others if you were in a position of greater power.

YOU AND ROMANCE

To have Venus in Cancer is to have an insatiable appetite for reassurance. You yearn to be loved, wanted, even needed. This may sound like a description of someone suffering from inner weakness, but it is actually the reason for your phenomenal strength. So anxious are you not to feel rejected that you think very carefully before ever putting your heart in a vulnerable position. Someone else with similar reservations might be destined to spend their life hiding behind a barrier of non-communication.

Venus in Cancer, however, compensates for its tendency to make you defensive by imbuing you with a vast capacity to give. Just as a wealthy person may donate $500 to charity without denting their bank balance while a poor one may only give $5 but will have to sacrifice to do so, you are rich in compassion and can afford to give generously. But poor people are always aware of their limits; rich ones can more easily assume they have endless reserves. If they make a mistake and draw too heavily on funds they cannot truly spare, they have much further to fall!

Your apparent emotional affluence coupled with your desire to be of real use to others naturally makes you a beacon in the night of this modern world. Fluttering around your attractive flame come all creatures seeking guidance or warmth. Moved by an equally strong urge to stay away, however, are not just those who prefer to be where it's cold and dark but sometimes those who want to create their own light rather than just take from yours. That's a shame, for it's among such people that you're most likely to find a lover worth letting past the psychological "No Entry" signs in the back room of your heart.

THE WAY YOU MANIFEST YOUR FEMININITY

Female

The idea of being a siren, seducer, vamp, or even a Venus appeals to you about as much as a vacation in a hospital. In fact, a charity ward seems like a better idea all around. There you could tend to the needy, protect the vulnerable, and fulfill the urge of your warm, caring heart to help others. While the idea of cynically exploiting your sexuality strikes you as ridiculous, the notion of clutching some poor soul to your bosom strikes straight to the core of your sincere psyche. This, of course, is precisely why certain people find you so desirable. Your honesty and integrity are as intoxicating to some men as fishnet stockings are to others. The only downside to this seemingly ideal arrangement is that, though the weak and weary beat a path to your door in droves, strong, self-sufficient types (who awaken less noble yearnings within you) tend to keep away lest they end up tied to your apron strings.

YOUR IDEAL WOMAN

Male

Venus in Cancer makes you deeply sensual and responsive to physical stimuli. But while most men dream of drowning in the mysterious haze of some exotically perfumed lover, you drool over the aroma of home-baked apple pie. The woman of your secret fantasy serves hot chocolate on cold nights before a roaring log fire. She takes a genuine interest in your work, sympathizes with your problems, and even acts fascinated when you talk about sports. Heaven is no higher or more distant than a giant train set in the basement, the tracks of which are being lovingly tended by your smiling soulmate, eagerly clutching a can of engine oil. For all you may make yourself out to be macho, you're a purring, domesticated pussycat. Only one thing turns you on more than the idea of a woman who's happy when you're happy, and that's a chance to prove that you understand the precise technique for making her very happy indeed!

♡ VENUS IN LEO ♡

YOU AND NATURE

NEXT time you get a chance to scan the cable or satellite channels, see if there's a station showing *Bewitched*. This sixties' TV series featured, as you may recall, a modern witch called Samantha. All she had to do was twitch her nose and whatever she wanted to happen, happened. Her husband, however, made her promise to accomplish everything by conventional means. So she struggled, as best she could, to do the hard way what she could do, if she chose, in an instant.

Does this description remind you of anyone? Males and females with Venus in Leo seem similarly bound by restrictions that they could easily defy if only they dared. How often have you found yourself tempted to take certain shortcuts, and how often have you denied yourself the opportunity, reflecting that it would be somehow wrong to use the power at your disposal?

You're laudably conscientious, but sometimes just a little too quick to see self-restraint as a virtue in its own right. There are occasions when you're fully entitled to go down the easy road. To refuse to contemplate those valid chances, just because you might then go on to take naughty ones, is as drastic as to ban toothpaste from your bathroom just in case the kids decide to eat it.

You may not have unearthly powers, but you certainly have impressive ones. There's very little on the material plane that you cannot achieve if you set your mind to it. There are very few people whose hearts will not succumb to your persuasive charm if you set out to melt them. In holding yourself back from what you could be capable of, you're also holding back some of the love that could be flooding into your world.

YOU AND YOUR CREATIVITY

The notion of a career in front of the cameras might (or might not) horrify you, but it would certainly suit you. You're terribly good at projecting a convincing, reassuring, capable, calm, and controlled image. If you could convince yourself that the viewers were not going to see the real you but only the act you were putting on, you'd take to the idea like a duck to water. This provision, however, is important, for you're afraid to make a fool of yourself in public.

This isn't to say that you can't or won't act the fool, but when you crack a joke, you aim it with all the precision of an expert archer at the funny bone of a carefully targeted audience. You're never afraid to take risks, but only if you're quite sure they're fully calculated. Whether dancing or designing, cooking or composing, innovating or restoring, your aim is to manifest grace and elegance, flair and finesse. Thus, you want to test the type of ground you're intending to tread on and ascertain how much weight it will bear before you go leaping on it with both feet.

You're determined to exercise a similar degree of precise control over every project you undertake. You don't just like to consider yourself an expert in your chosen field, you insist on making yourself one. You hold your every effort up to intense critical scrutiny, dismissing creations that others would consider minor masterpieces, and, when commissioned to do a job or perform a task, you take the clearest, straightest, most simply effective route to success. It very rarely fails, nor do you.

YOU AND ROMANCE

Venus in Leo makes you a popular person. People from all walks of life are drawn towards you by some inexplicable, magnetic impulse. Strangers feel inspired to tell you their life stories; friends feel safe to confide secrets they have been hiding even from themselves. It's almost as if your very presence has a hypnotic influence, yet this is not due to any conscious effort on your part. You often feel slightly estranged from society, happy enough to link up with friends if they want to make the effort, but equally at ease with your own company.

You come across as endearingly ambivalent, yet it's not true to say that you are without desires. The Lion in your birth chart is a lusty creature with a powerful urge to reign supreme in its chosen territory. Confident, however, of its own strength, it rarely needs to manifest aggression. Since none but a fool would risk challenging a Lion, you have little cause to feel the motivation of fear; nor do you always feel inclined to challenge yourself just for the sake of it. With Venus in Leo you can sometimes be a little too much like a furry, sleepy, sensual pussycat!

When it comes to choosing a partner, you have another potential celestial disadvantage to conquer. Lions easily draw admirers. Their equals, though, are usually clever enough to keep a distance. And what betters could they possibly have? So when it comes to romance, who is going to offer the Lion a worthwhile challenge? Again, none but a fool would risk it. So all hangs on you finding the right kind of fool. Does the right type really exist? Most definitely.

THE WAY YOU MANIFEST YOUR FEMININITY

Female

Men flutter round you like moths around a flame. If they get their wings burned, are you to blame? It depends on whether you're deliberately waving the lamp. Unlike some women who must spend hours in and out of the closet before they dare step out of the door, you can throw on any old rag and still attract admiring glances. It's something about the way you move. You carry yourself like a princess, even an empress. There's no deliberate effort. It just happens naturally, as does the inevitable reaction.

This is fine except that, if you're hot stuff when you're not even trying, you become an incendiary bomb when you do try! Every so often, you decide there's a man worth making an effort to attract. The lioness within you is a skilled huntress who rarely misses her quarry. But whether she still likes him once she's caught him is another matter. A greater part of you would rather be tamed than tempted.

YOUR IDEAL WOMAN

Male

You've got a bit of a thing about prima donnas. When a woman starts stamping her foot, laying down the law, and telling you what she will or won't put up with, you find it both amusing and exciting. It shows she has spirit, it makes her a challenge, and it obliges you either to comply with her wishes or to risk her wrath. Which you do depends on what else is in your horoscope. But the fact that such a fiery female fuels your fantasy is a point that no other cosmic condition can counteract. Your dream goddess is willful, powerful, charismatic, and aristocratic. She's also quarrelsome, sultry, and self-centered. But she's so hypnotically attractive that you can forgive or forget her faults and foibles. All you know is that, when she finally does get around to needing you, she envelops you in such a passionate embrace as to squeeze out every last drop of the love you have to express.

♡ VENUS IN VIRGO ♡

YOU AND NATURE

To have Venus in Virgo is to have not so much an empathy with nature as an encyclopedic understanding of it. It is to be able to see similarities between vastly different scenarios such as how a rising tide submerging an island mirrors a fire slowly suffusing a piece of coal. It is to be an observational scientist by disposition, if not by profession, a careful analyst of both nature and human nature.

Just as you watch creation with a sense of awe and wonder, rarely wanting to do anything more drastic than discuss your latest impressions, so you rarely seek to interfere in the activities of those you love. As long as they're doing fine, that's fine by you. Even when they seem to be making mistakes, you would rather wait until they ask for help than volunteer it prematurely. When pushed for your theory about what law a natural phenomenon is following, you'll give it, and research will usually prove you right. Likewise, when someone does want to know what they've been doing wrong, you'll tell them, gently and diplomatically but usually with uncanny accuracy.

Ironically, for all your natural wisdom you're afraid, afraid of speaking out of turn, afraid of rocking boats, afraid, perhaps, of being right but being resented for it. Yet you also fear being approached for an answer and failing to have one ready. So your life is often spent preparing for events that never happen and feeling resentful that though you took your violin to the party, nobody asked you to play. You deserve more, in career and love alike. If you want clients for your services and takers for the love, you have to give, to abandon your reservations or concerns about rejection, and to advertise.

YOU AND YOUR CREATIVITY

You have magnificent organizational skills, which is precisely why your world often seems a little chaotic. It's people with less than full confidence in their ability to cope who need to have everything marked up, written down, checked over, and filed away. You know what you've got and roughly where you've put it, so your time is better spent working on some new project than triple-checking the old one.

This explains why you're prolific as well as proficient. You design neither with a bullish broad brush nor with a nervously narrow nib, but with the happy medium of an implement which can, under the hand of a deft decorator, accomplish either stroke.

Having Venus in Virgo allows you to marry the charm of sensual Aphrodite with the wit and flexibility of businesslike Mercury. It also entitles you to claim the legacy of Chiron the cosmic Healer, hence your desire to be expedient and practical when expressing your creative urges. You see little point doing things the hard way just for the experience. If it's a tried and tested technique, why not use it? If it's not broken, why fix it? And if it's clearly popular with many people, why knock it? You'd prefer to praise what's good in someone else's work than rip what's bad to shreds. You're much more inclined to repair and renew than to knock something down and begin again from scratch.

A genuine willingness to adapt the way you impart your art without compromising its integrity is the reason you find your creative skills frequently complimented by everyone from the connoisseur to the inexperienced consumer. You are equally capable, potentially at least, of success in any field. Whether you paint, cook, garden, weave, knit, sing, dance, act, write, heal, mend, massage, measure, research, advise, or entertain, you do it with humble sincerity and dedication, and it does you proud.

YOU AND ROMANCE

To have Venus in Virgo is to possess not so much an eye for detail as an entire sensory system. It is the ability to hear the difference between a Bechstein and a Steinway, taste one between a King Edward and a Cara, feel one between silk and satin, even to smell the difference between a rat and a politician. To others, you can come across as a bit of a fusspot. Those who dislike you usually cite such a reason. Fortunately, these insensitive individuals are vastly outnumbered by the many who admire your discrimination, even if they don't share it.

While, however, your talent to apply subtle scrutiny stands you in excellent stead in the creative and aesthetic departments of life, it is not the primary reason for your popularity. Your fans and fanciers chiefly appreciate another talent that Venus in Virgo invariably bestows: the ability to defy the aging process. You may not be aware that anyone has ever given you the secret of eternal youth, but you undoubtedly know it instinctively. This is why you draw admiring glances from people half your age and presumably why you still insist on thinking, if not dressing, like a teenager. Your contemporaries get wrinkles, but you get laugh lines. Your peers get weighed down by worldly cares, but you get buoyed up by giddy ideas. You have no more intention of growing old gracefully than you have of being fobbed off with Coke when you specifically ordered Kahlua.

To be with you is to be with someone who is always fun, always fresh, and always full of enthusiasm for some new plan or project. It is also to be with someone who is deeply sensual, demonstrative, and emotionally attentive. The only thing it's not is dull!

THE WAY YOU MANIFEST YOUR FEMININITY

Female

Some women carry cosmetics in their handbags. You may have one or two beauty aids, but they're vastly outnumbered by other kinds of lotions and potions. A veritable dispensary of stomach settlers, headache dispellers, corn plasters, lip salves, antiseptics, and insect repellents cause you to rattle like an old car as you walk down the road. And that's nothing compared to the other useful items you constantly carry. It's not that you're neurotic: none of them are there for your personal use. It's in case you come across a hurt or sick body. You see yourself, not so much as a Florence Nightingale as a female Dr. Doolittle. You want to heal *all* creatures, great and small, because it's when you feel you're in a position to help someone that the waves of radiant womanhood emanate from you. Your ideal man is a patient physician's assistant. Yet all too often he just turns out to be another one of your physician's patients in need of assistance.

Your Ideal Woman

Male

The lady of your dreams has strict protocols to observe before she's prepared to embrace you. First, aphrodisiac candies must be washed down with honeyed mead. Then she must bathe in ox milk and anoint herself in flower essence while candles are lit to summon spirits of passion. Next, she must don robes and consult a crystal ball for proof of an auspicious moment. Only then can the magical mating ritual be properly performed. If, later, she climbs on a broomstick and flies to some hilltop meeting of her sisterhood, you're just happy to await the return of your mysterious medicine woman. Possibly, her love potions contain no more black magic than Cadbury's, and her mead is merely a martini. Perchance her ox milk is buttermilk, her flower essence Chanel, her light ceremony a deft flick of the dimmer switch. But even if her session with a crystal ball is only an indication that there's nothing good on TV, her broomstick only a hatchback, and her coven no more than a girl's night out, in essence it's the same. Your dream figure is a mistress of the environmental elements with an electric sense of timing.

VENUS IN LIBRA

YOU AND NATURE

THE question for you, with Venus in Libra, is not how to surround yourself with love but how to make more of the love that already constantly surrounds you. When you complain that you feel unwanted, rejected, or uncared for, it has much the same ring as an actress stepping back from the stage after her fourth standing ovation of the evening, in tears because one newspaper has savaged the show. But you can choose to hear genuine applause and ignore nitpicking criticism, partly by employing physical or psychological techniques and partly by simply allowing your ultimate asset, the will to survive, to guide you through life.

In nature, it's always persistence that most inspires you. When grass forces a crack in a concrete driveway, when fresh buds appear on the stump of a tired old oak, or when you sense the Sun waiting patiently for a chance to appear fleetingly through a gap in the clouds, your spirits rise. In love, in partnership, and in creativity, you simply have to apply the same refusal to be beaten. For almost invariably, what defeats you will not be some unconquerable problem but the fear of defeat itself. Conquer that, and the love that perpetually surrounds you will never take long to step forward and make its presence felt.

YOU AND YOUR CREATIVITY

You are good at everything you try your hand at, so you never know whether you ought to be doing this on the one hand or that on the other. Not only are you ambidextrous when it comes to creativity, you're double-jointed. Thus you are able to give yourself that most physically demanding of accolades, the pat on the back. Blessed as you also are with a fertile imagination, you can envisage, before you even lift a finger, the thumbs-up that your work is likely to get. So you finish before you start, deciding that, as you've already triumphed in your mind, you may as well try your hand at some other challenge.

If you were bereft of true talent, this capacity to be your own worst enemy might be your best friend. But as Venus in Libra is one of the most precious planetary gifts that a person can be handed, it's a shame. Others accomplish far more with less. Your talents could be winning you a big hand from an admiring audience, plus earning you cash in hand and allowing you to win the game of life hands down. But first, you have to put your hands up and admit that a bit more self-discipline would come in handy.

Probably the best way to achieve this is to form some kind of creative partnership. If you can work hand in glove with an expert at a skill complementary to your own, you will probably feel much more inspired to buckle down.

YOU AND ROMANCE

To have Venus in Libra is to be wickedly sensual and wildly indulgent at every opportunity. It goes without saying that you're hot stuff between the sheets. What's more remarkable is how you manage to fill the rest of the time obtaining paroxysms of pleasure from seemingly innocuous activity. Where some people might, for example, make themselves a quick sandwich when they feel hungry, you will disappear into the kitchen and come back with a gourmet creation. Where some might sink into a hot bath after a hard day, you will submerge yourself in an exotic cocktail of oils and essences. Where others will give their appearance a quick once-over in the mirror, you will preen yourself to perfection, departing the bathroom reluctantly with the sad thought that you won't see anyone quite so lovely until the next time you look in the glass!

You think a lot of yourself, and that's precisely why others think such a lot of you. You're a living refutation of the theory that self-praise is no recommendation. To the contrary, you believe there's no point keeping a sundial in the shade! You shamelessly flaunt your assets and rudely ignore your own bad points, and most people absolutely adore you for it. They like you even more because you are similarly uncritical about them in return, assuming (reasonably enough) that anyone who appreciates you must be worth liking in return! There are, of course, a few who remain singularly unimpressed by what they consider your lack of modesty, but, as these rather snooty characters tend to go out of their way to keep out of your way, you rarely have to be reminded of their existence. Nor need you be. With Venus in its home sign of Libra, it's a safe bet that you really are every bit as wonderful as you think you are.

THE WAY YOU MANIFEST YOUR FEMININITY

Female

You are a creator of illusions, a weaver of dreams, a tilter at windmills, and an architect of castles in the air. The rainbows you chase, however, you usually catch because your Venus position is a heavenly gift and not a cosmic curse. You can make ordinary things look incredibly special. You can turn mundane rooms into electric pleasure domes. And you can make yourself look like a million dollars, not necessarily by dressing cleverly but by summoning a certain sparkle to your eyes and subtly adjusting the way you walk or even talk. Men take one look at you and decide you're full of promise.

You may be, but whether that promise comes true depends on whether those men are buying into your image or tuning in to your true personality. Your dream is of a partner who is strong, true, and straightforward. Somehow, though, if you're not careful, you end up with complicated characters who mistake your ability to reflect their hopes for an ability to fulfill them.

YOUR IDEAL WOMAN

Male

They say it's a woman's prerogative to change her mind. You find that appealing, but you'd prefer to go one better and get one who frequently changes her entire personality. One moment you want her to be a free spirit, beckoning you towards the hayloft with a wild and seductive gaze of passion, but the next to be a studious companion, looking up knowingly from a textbook on law, engineering, or quantum mechanics. She needs to be as likely to cook your dinner, light your pipe, pour you a drink, and fetch your slippers one evening as she is to drag you next to a series of nightclubs where you'll dance nonstop until dawn. The only thing you expect her to be consistently is radiantly graceful. It's a tall order for any real-life partner to live up to.

But if you want anyone to come close, you could try looking at your own behavior and deciding to make it lighthearted and flexible enough to inspire an existing partner to be at her best.

♡ VENUS IN SCORPIO ♡

YOU AND NATURE

IMPRESSED though you may be by many aspects of nature, few sights inspire you more than the feat of wizardry displayed each time a caterpillar creates a cocoon from which to emerge as a butterfly, or the sight of some bare winter tree becoming a cascade of growth and life in the warmth of spring. Change excites and inspires you, especially when it's change that happens over time rather than distance. Those who adapt as they travel may be clever, but those who can stay in the same situation yet become something totally different are surely brilliant beyond praise.

Venus in Scorpio makes you something of an alchemist, bestowing the desire to find the psychological equivalent of the philosopher's stone. Gold from lead, you may not be able to produce, but this was only meant to be a metaphor. Transformation, you most certainly can achieve, and frequently do. You aspire to it in yourself, and you hope to find the tendency towards it in those you love. Hence the enthusiasm for sex exhibited by many people born with Venus in Scorpio. It transforms, although briefly, the body and mind.

To a degree, though, sex is a substitute for a far less base Venus-in-Scorpio aspiration: the desire to create a magical awakening of human potential. You merely want to bring forth what is most vibrant in everyone around you. Your efforts to do so, however, sometimes meet with objections. Some consider you too severe, demanding, or intense. To surround yourself with more love, you merely need to refine the technique of explaining to others why you really want them to go further, try harder, and reach deeper for life's truths. Perhaps, also, you need to be a little less unforgiving of what you sometimes feel to be failings within yourself.

YOU AND YOUR CREATIVITY

You really don't believe in wasting energy. If a job can be accomplished with the merest wave of a hand, why on earth get into a tizzy about it? Only if it cannot be done any way other than through sheer hard work, intense dedication, and near superhuman sacrifice will you muster all these qualities without a moment's reticence. It's because you know what incredible concentration you're capable of giving that you're extremely careful about what you agree to give yourself to. Once you allow a project, plan, or enterprise to matter, you surrender your life to it. You will leave absolutely no stone unturned, no angle uninvestigated, no obstacle in your path, or you'll collapse in the attempt.

People with Venus in Scorpio make especially good doctors, scientists, and company CEOs. But then they make equally good artists, writers, and musicians. For what they have is a burning desire, not to be the best but to *do* the best. Venus in Scorpio means you refuse to be fobbed off with phrases like "but it's not cost efficient" or "no one will ever notice if you cut a corner." You may find some clever way to reach a certain standard by subterfuge if there's no more direct alternative, but you certainly won't ever abandon your commitment to quality. You're a zealous perfectionist with a burning belief that, if something is worth doing at all, it's worth doing well. You may be enough of a realist to see the need for compromise, but you're not enough of a coward to see the need for giving up, ever!

YOU AND ROMANCE

You don't have to be a stargazer to know that Venus is a symbol of seduction. If you have even a passing familiarity with the zodiac, you will know what three-letter word the sign of Scorpio is synonymous with. So you don't have to be a genius to work out what the key fascination is likely to become when you mix these potent symbols. I shall leave you to digest this heavy hint while I tell you that, to an astrologer, Venus in Scorpio means much the same as a toddler in a candy shop, a rock star at a fan club concert, or a drinker in a distillery. Venus is *not* in its element in Scorpio. The toddler needs to be at nursery school, the rock star needs the challenge of a new audience, and the drinker needs to be where alcohol flows less freely. In all cases, there's a tempting opportunity for overindulgence combined with a possibility that things could go too far.

So do you have something to worry about? Probably not. By this point in your life, I'm sure you have learned either to restrain yourself or to live with the consequences of not doing so! But if you do feel the above strikes a painful chord, you might like to know that Venus is a symbol of creativity as well as procreativity, while Scorpio can govern a quest for spiritual, as well as physical, fulfillment. The way out of any predicament you ever get into is to channel excess energy into art, music, or poetry.

Whichever route you take to self-expression, however, you'll never be short of admirers. One thing that Venus in Scorpio inevitably imbues is the ability to render others awestruck by your power to trigger feelings within them that other signs cannot reach!

THE WAY YOU MANIFEST YOUR FEMININITY

Female

You are a very naughty girl. No matter how prim and proper you may choose to appear on the surface, there's mischief in your soul. You usually know what people are feeling, and you always know what men are thinking. You can manipulate this to your advantage so deftly as to make the other person totally unaware that they have been steered. It's true that you don't do this half as often as you could, but you still do it twice as often as you should.

You're potentially an extremely sexy person, but the sexiest part of your anatomy is your little finger. Around this, you effortlessly wrap the men in your life. Yet you yearn for a partner who won't fall for the trick. You want one who knows his own mind well enough to know yours, too. That's why you often fall for the rare character you cannot read like a book. Sometimes, though, you do so without checking whether this is because they are clever or just lacking real substance!

YOUR IDEAL WOMAN

Male

Some men dream of women who will dazzle their eyes with beauty, melt their hearts with compassionate understanding, or baffle their brains with sheer intelligence. Venus in Scorpio leads you to hope for one who will, not to put too fine a point on it, overwhelm you with an appetite for physical passion. You want her to have wicked ideas and make outrageous invitations on a daily (no, make that hourly) basis! Many adolescents entertain such vivid fantasies for a year or two at the height of their hormonal change. Venus in Scorpio seems to destine you to a lifetime of dreaming of very rude ladies.

Not true? Of course not. Sorry, silly me. I forgot. Venus in Scorpio also makes you extremely anxious to protect your privacy. The last thing you want is to see your X-rated imagination revealed in a national newspaper. So, um, it's all a joke, OK? Actually, you like women who are good at knitting.

♡ VENUS IN SAGITTARIUS ♡

YOU AND NATURE

TO have Venus in Sagittarius is to feel somewhat cheated by nature, for she has given you the spirit of a free, strong bird within a frail, earthbound body. You can compensate by traveling as far as possible and as much as possible and, unless extenuating circumstances forbid it, you probably do. But short of owning your own plane and having limitless funds to fly it, you're always going to have a sense of wanderlust. You can identify with migrating creatures from salmon to buffaloes or even with weather systems that have the flexibility to sweep across the globe in hours.

For you, love, like life, needs to be a journey. You need to feel that a partnership is going somewhere, leading to something, growing in some way; and you want to feel much the same way about all plans, activities, or involvements. What's the point in standing still, preserving the status quo, keeping to the same old paths, habits, and routines? None for you, perhaps. But if you want to surround yourself with love, you have to take into account the needs of some of your more pedestrian companions. You make certain people nervous. You represent a maverick force, a disruptive influence, a threat, even, to the stability and consistency they have worked so hard to achieve in their lives.

You cannot stop wanting to explore the new, the different, and the daring, but you can stop insisting that others are failing somehow if they don't follow you. Become more tolerant of what you consider to be your loved ones' great mistakes, and they in turn will become both less defensive and less inclined to point out yours. Anyway, how free can free spirits truly be if they won't grant themselves the freedom to stay in the same place for a while?

YOU AND YOUR CREATIVITY

Whatever you do, you do with gusto! Rather like Tigger in *Winnie the Pooh*, you're full of irrepressible enthusiasm and energy even if a little unsure of what it is you truly like best. Where Tigger tried Piglet's haycorns, Eeyore's thistles, and Pooh's honey before settling on the unlikely flavor of Roo's strengthening medicine, your tastes try the patience of those with less eclectic preferences. Today it's jazz-rap, tomorrow it's Bach. Today it's Gauguin, but yesterday it was Constable. Next week it may be hot baths, but this week you confidently prescribe cold showers to anyone with an ache or pain to cure. I exaggerate to make my point, but then again, sometimes so do you!

People with Venus in Sagittarius aren't exactly jacks of all trades, but they are certainly Renaissance men and women. Your Venus position makes you diligent and determined to reach high standards in every endeavor, but it sometimes makes it hard for you to know what you want your next endeavor to be. You never rest on your laurels or fall into a creative rut. Onwards and upwards is your motto. Often, it's also an apt description of your career path.

YOU AND ROMANCE

To have Venus in Sagittarius is to have an insatiable appetite for adventure—to live for the thrill of the different and daring, the bold and brave, the wild and free. Beyond all else, it's to be an absolute law unto yourself. You're a leader, not a follower; a prime subscriber to the motto, "Do as I say, not as I do." Others love you or hate you. You don't much care which, but you can't help but notice that both groups have something intriguing in common: a tendency to stand with their mouths agape as they watch you sail close to the wind time and time again, and seemingly get away with it! On the few occasions when you are defeated, it's usually in some spectacularly silly way. You'll perform a death-defying leap, emerge without a scratch, and then throw your back out bending down to pick up a flower thrown by some admirer in the crowd. Or you'll make a promise you can't possibly keep, backpedal in a rare moment of common sense, and discover that, had you persevered, you would have been the beneficiary of a lucky coincidence.

You may not be wealthy (though you could be if you really chose) but you've got a brilliant knack of turning up in the right place at the right time, time and time again. Lovers seeking a stable, predictable partner are better off plighting their troth to a tornado. Those who have enough sense of fun to appreciate a source of constant challenge and entertainment, however, will run for any chance to get near to you, even though they know they'll have to run even harder if they want to stay there.

THE WAY YOU MANIFEST
YOUR FEMININITY

Female

Braver, more adventurous women may exist, but where they're hiding, you'd love to know. You could do with a girlfriend who might egg you on rather than run nervously behind, alternately marveling at your courage and being terrified of it.

If your ability to be independent, fearless, and frank leaves most females flabbergasted, it has an even more devastating effect on men. In theory, you're the intelligent, fun-loving, uninhibited lass every red-blooded male dreams of. In practice? He can find your potential to be his equal intimidating. He may prefer to score cheap victories over wimpish women, seeing you only from the safety of a fantasy. If you're not careful, you'll wind up either with a devoted servant or an arrogant oaf who can't recognize your true worth. If you are careful, however, you can get the lover you need and deserve: a fellow traveler on the road that leads, via various dragons to be conquered and prisoners to be freed, to life's court of supreme justice.

YOUR IDEAL WOMAN

Male

Your dream woman has not a shred of uncertainty in her personality. What turns you on is a woman who knows what she wants, where she's going, and how she's going to get there. She has plenty of heart and soul, compassion and sensitivity, emotion and spirit, but she doesn't believe in wasting time feeling sorry for herself, crying over spilt milk, or worrying about things that might possibly go wrong one day. She tosses her head, summons a smile, and carries on bravely and determinedly with the difficult task she has set herself. Your role in her life is to be not just a supporter from the sidelines but an equal partner in the great adventure. You expect to argue with her occasionally, indeed you get something of a thrill out of hearing her make her case with conviction. And once in a blue moon or so, you hope to be able to draw her attention to some key point she's missed. But mainly you just like the idea of some wonder woman taking you by the hand and neither leading nor following, just sharing with you one great adventure after another.

♡ VENUS IN CAPRICORN ♡

YOU AND NATURE

VENUS in Capricorn gives you tremendous respect for nature, but it doesn't necessarily give you limitless faith in human nature. This is partly because you're very aware of some of creation's less savory facets: the law of the jungle, the bias towards survival of the fittest, the tendency for certain beings to devour their mates or to eat their young. You're not quite a cynic, but you're certainly a realist.

Not everything in the world's garden is rosy. Indeed, even the roses have sharp thorns. A cautious streak thus runs through your attitude to life and love. You don't feel able to trust that everything is always going to be all right. Experience has taught you that sometimes it just isn't. So contingency plans need to be prepared and undesirable developments guarded against. All of which is wise, as long as it's in perspective. But when you start looking at gorgeous rolling hills and wondering what they reveal about the tectonic fault line below or noticing some bright, beautiful star and wondering how long we have before our own sun goes into Supernova, it's time to control yourself. Similarly, when someone tells you they love you madly and forever, it's a bit much to envisage, in response, some day in the future when they'll be saying the same thing to someone else.

As all astrologers will testify, there's a phenomenon called self-fulfilling prophecy that has to be watched. Put simply: research has proved that people who expect good things to happen are more likely to find that they do, while those who are on the lookout for disaster normally find it. Venus in Capricorn makes you lovable, trustworthy, and worthwhile to be with. But until you start to believe this, how can you expect others to?

YOU AND YOUR CREATIVITY

Architectural and engineering skills are often found among people of both sexes with your Venus position. You tend to be fascinated by how things work and determined to construct durable items of practical use. This doesn't prevent you from being an impulsive artist or a free, creative spirit, but it certainly implies that, even if you are inclined this way, you won't allow your work to be bought cheap and sold at a high profit margin by some fancy agent. You have a good understanding of the value of money, based not on greed but on precisely the same natural desire you feel to understand the mechanics of any medium you ever happen to work with. If you paint, you like to know about the composition of the pigment. If you work in clay, you like to experiment with firing temperatures. If you play music, you like to know a little about sound waves. By the same token, you have an intelligent, inquiring, half-scientific/half-creative approach to many mundane occupations. The preparation of Sunday lunch becomes an exercise in attaining perfect roasting times. You can even turn doing the laundry into a fine art!

YOU AND ROMANCE

People with Venus in Capricorn are tremendously loyal. They'll quietly put up with dreadful conditions and terrible treatment as long as they feel they're fulfilling a worthwhile commitment. Their primary desire is to make themselves useful to others. Because they feel guilty about the idea of putting themselves first, they will often let people walk all over them before they finally declare that enough is enough.

Do you recognize a little something of yourself in the above? It is, I hope, only a little something, for there are bound to be other factors in your chart that prevent you from manifesting your full potential to become a martyr. Nonetheless, it's a tendency to watch, as is the tendency to draw towards you people with a need to dominate. It's not that you're weak, far from it. Your strength is enviable. But it's a carthorse's strength, not a bucking bronco's. All you ask is to be given a task you can perform with honor and integrity, yet we live in a world full of people seeking short-term solutions. Some of these take one look at you and see an eager willingness which they can turn to their advantage.

The great irony is that you could, if you chose, be a leader rather than a follower. You have all the right qualifications, except perhaps for a reticence to throw your weight about. At a creative level, Venus in Capricorn makes you a genuine craftsperson. You are as painstaking as you are perceptive, as discriminating as you are dedicated. But just as you often find that others profit from your work more than you do, you sometimes find yourself getting a raw deal in love, emotionally or physically. The worst (or best?) thing about you is that you're so big-hearted that you hardly mind.

THE WAY YOU MANIFEST YOUR FEMININITY

Female

Many women feel a great need to protect their dignity and composure. Because you have Venus in Capricorn, you can afford to play the "dizzy dame" and present yourself to the world as a wild, wacky, even slightly "dangerous" character. It's a bit of an act, but it's one you feel safe to play for much the same reason that a child feels safe sticking out his tongue at the school bully while holding his parent's hand. Knowing that, ultimately, you have vast reserves of common sense, you can push yourself to the limits of what's socially, morally, or emotionally acceptable. You know you'll never go over the brink!

Because you're in such rare control of yourself, you can afford the luxury of a partner whose grasp of reality is, shall we say, a little more tenuous. You may even deliberately overaccentuate your more bizarre qualities precisely to attract such a poet. And even if this means that you end up linked to a "head in the clouds" type, you're capable of turning him around and causing him to become a success in spite of himself. Indeed, you rather fancy the challenge.

YOUR IDEAL WOMAN

Male

Dithery, vacuous, silly-little-girl types hold no romantic fascination. Give you, if not a significantly older woman every time, at least a girl with a mature outlook and a no-nonsense look in her eyes. If she lays down certain rules and generally has a slightly stern demeanor, you're more likely to find this amusingly attractive than off-putting. Indeed, there are some males with Venus in Capricorn who find the idea of exceedingly strict women in positions of very direct control a definite turn-on. Quite how far down this road your fantasies take you depends on what else is in your horoscope. But even if you're not quite inclined to see Margaret Thatcher in much the same light as others see Claudia Schiffer, you're certainly far more inclined to prefer a woman who wears her common sense on the surface and hides her uncommon sensuality deep below. Strength and self-sufficiency appeal far more to you than any amount of hopeless, helpless femininity.

♡Venus in Aquarius♡

You and Nature

I N some households, the cats and dogs never fight. They eat from the same bowl and snuggle in the same basket. In some countries, there is hardly enough annual rainfall to fill a teacup, but by ingenious methods of irrigation or sea reclamation, life is supported. There are some birds that can't fly, yet some fish that can. And in some jungles, tiny carnivorous beasts live alongside enormous vegetarian elephants.

To you, with Venus in Aquarius, it's the anomalies, eccentricities, and downright oddities of nature which appeal most of all. When someone tells you a thing cannot be done, your question is, "Why not?" If the reply is, "There's no precedent," you'll find one or, better still, establish one. Little amuses you more than the chance to challenge convention, tradition, or even nature itself. And if you see the patterns within creation as frameworks to build on rather than boundaries never to cross, you see the structures within human relationships as starting points, not finishing ones.

This is fine so long as your loved ones are similarly attracted to the notion of pushing back frontiers. But when they want to remain within more familiar territory, you can feel a little trapped. And when they have the temerity to argue with your ideas and plans, you can become downright obstreperous. Your tendency to be assertively opinionated is one reason why your world is not as full of love as it might be. Your ability to clam up and refuse to hold a debate you're not sure you can win is another. Yet there are many people who admire you and would like to get close to you. To surround yourself with love, all you really need do is be more appreciative of the possible and less interested in always pursuing the impossible.

YOU AND YOUR CREATIVITY

You like to be at the cutting edge of fashion, thought, art, and/or technology. You want to feel you're doing today what the rest of the world will be doing in five years. Usually, five years later, once you've defended yourself against the doubters and experienced the stress of being a guinea pig, it turns out that this is precisely what you *were* doing. But by then you're busy being innovative in some other field.

Being innovative, mind you, doesn't always mean being futuristic. Your sensitive, creative antennae are often among the first to pick up the imminent revival of some old trend. It does mean, though, that if you're ever going to turn your best ideas into money, you're going to need the courage of your convictions and enough enthusiasm to convince others to take a risk. Those who don't understand you may question your need to lead such an eccentric lifestyle, to communicate with so many odd characters, or to spend your money on such unconventional items. But as Venus in Aquarius gives you an impressive ability to communicate cleverly when you want to, you can normally bring others around to accepting, if not quite believing, your unique point of view.

YOU AND ROMANCE

Venus in Aquarius makes you about as perverse a person as it is possible to be. Please don't misunderstand: I'm casting no aspersions here on your nocturnal preferences. It's quite possible (though not, I concede, usual) for people with your Venus sign to have perfectly unremarkable love lives. But regardless of what you may or may not be up to in areas beyond the scope of this family publication, you're certainly unconventional in your choice of friends and partners. You like to be surrounded by oddballs, eccentrics, innovators, and outcasts. It's almost as if you get a real sense of satisfaction when you hear a staid acquaintance saying, "Honestly. I really can't understand *what* you see in so-and-so." Then a part of you knows you've made the right choice, and you will do all you can to cement the relationship. "All that you can" often has to be quite a lot, for if there's one thing you like more than a peculiar person, it's an elusive or unattainable companion.

When it comes to love, it seems you'd far rather have half a dove, hovering precariously just above the bush, than any number of fine feathered friends in your hand. You have a similar attitude to creativity. You don't just feel you want to be good at what you do, you feel you want to be doing something that nobody else would ever dream of doing. One of your favorite tricks is to abandon a promising project just when it's starting to take off, because you'd like to take a stab at something that it's even harder to make a success of. Happily, you are talented and charming enough to do well in life and love, despite the tendency to be your own worst enemy.

THE WAY YOU MANIFEST YOUR FEMININITY

Female

You're a highly principled, confident character but also a little contrary. For example, while you are very sure of who you actually are, you get a kick out of pretending to be who you aren't. Venus in Aquarius gives you natural acting talent. You can, if it suits you, for example, manifest the kind of "come hither" look that would melt any red-blooded male, yet you can play the part of a sober, inscrutable businesswoman with equal conviction. Those who accuse you of blowing hot and cold tend to be types who like a lukewarm life. You simply have very specific tastes: in art, in music, in environment, and in men. You're either moved to the core or deeply ambivalent. Your eyes light up or glaze over accordingly unless (and this is what causes the confusion) you can see some fun to be had in feigning enthusiasm. The men who see you as deeply vibrant and sexy (and there are many of these) are not your ideal mates. It's the few who see beyond the façade and understand what you're really up to who fire your genuine passion.

YOUR IDEAL WOMAN

Male

It's not especially easy to define your ideal woman, for what you appreciate most in a female is her ability to surprise you. How can you ever be surprised if you know exactly what you're expecting? It's for this reason that you often find yourself drawn to rather crazy mixed-up types, or to women with something of a reputation for being difficult. You like the interesting challenge of a partner you can never be quite sure of. She needs to have either some very erratic, even inconsistent, behavior patterns or some deep mysterious secret in her past, or both. You think you want to understand her, and you certainly go to some impressive lengths to try, but ultimately you want to be hypnotized by her strong personality and even slightly in awe of it. Your relationships often appear to the outside observer a little volatile. It *looks* as if you're at loggerheads with your loved one, but in fact you thrive on a little creative tension and so, too, most definitely, does the siren of your secret dreams.

♡ VENUS IN PISCES ♡

YOU AND NATURE

FOR all our scientific knowledge and understanding, there are many things we understand no more nor less than our cave-dwelling ancestors. Quite why, for example, we need to spend a third of our lives asleep, oblivious and unconscious, is still not fully explained. Nor, for all our carefully charted territory, do we know very much about the vast majority of our planet which happens to lie under water. Venus in Pisces naturally draws you towards the aspects of nature which are shrouded in the most mystery. Why do some salmon swim so far upstream to spawn? Why do some creatures apparently choose to make their lives unduly difficult? And why, by contrast, do people seek their happiness in such shallow, unlikely places? How can humans expect to find true contentment in pursuits that cannot possibly ever bring more than momentary pleasure? How can they put their faith in such pretentious philosophies, empty dreams, artificial aspirations? How, for that matter, can they prefer plastic to wood, concrete to grass, fizzy cola to pure, clear water? Where in us humans, are the deep, instinctive, primeval urges? Where, in this oversanitized, civilized, officialized world of social taboos and market forces, are the opportunities to celebrate nature, express spontaneity, laugh from the tips of the toes, cry from the soul, and love from the heart?

If anyone knows, you do, or you intend to find out. To surround yourself with even more love than there surely already is in your world, all you have to do is discover the greatest secret of all. The fountain of youth, the reservoir of happiness, the ultimate source of all love and appreciation for life, lies not in some ideal policy, process, way of being, or relationship. It lies deep within you! Seek it, tap it, and let the good times roll.

YOU AND YOUR CREATIVITY

People with Venus in Pisces fall into two categories: those who are immensely musical and know it and those who are just as talented but don't. As members of the first group hardly need to be told about their skill, I will address the second here. Even in the unlikely event of your being stone deaf or even, for that matter, being totally deaf, there's still a vast amount of rhythm, harmony, and poetry in your soul. Deafness never stopped Beethoven. And as for being tone deaf, well, how many modern pop stars would you like me to cite?

Music is not just a matter of technical precision. Indeed, when that's all it involves, it becomes a branch of mathematics. Music is feeling, emotion, artistry, spontaneity, and the ability to create infectious, attractively subtle patterns in your environment. There's far more music in a finely tuned engine than in a poorly tuned guitar; more harmony in a well-chosen outfit than in any singer's ill-tailored arrangement; and more rhythm in a well-conducted car sale than in any badly conducted orchestra. You may never have touched a musical instrument in your life and may never feel the desire to do so, but in your ability to recognize life's most subtle sequences, turn random ideas into beautifully organized plans, and hear how a piece of material is crying out to be used, you are very much in touch with the unfolding, silent symphony of the universe. Respond to this call and you'll never be short of notes.

YOU AND ROMANCE

To have Venus in Pisces is to have the planet of romance in the sign of pure poetry. It's to be about as soft and sentimental as a person can possibly get, yet simultaneously to be perceptive, intuitive, and ingeniously creative. Only one thing in your life knows fewer bounds than your imagination, and that's your generosity. You'll bend over backwards to please others; and while that, plus your generally warm, physically demonstrative disposition may account for some of your popularity in the sphere of romance, it's nothing compared with how far you'll go to accommodate other people's creative, emotional, or spiritual needs. These, you rarely need to have pointed out to you. A sixth sense guides you, like an infallible inner radar system, straight to the heart of what another individual is thinking or feeling. A seventh sense then shows you, in a flash of inspiration, precisely what you can do to help their dearest dream come true.

You're not especially good at getting what you want for yourself in life, nor even at achieving consistently average success. But given someone else's trust in you and someone else's problem to solve, you turn instantly into a fairy godmother. (Male Pisceans, awkward about this image, can, if they prefer, see themselves as grinning leprechauns with three special wishes to grant.) Sometimes you do more for people than you ought to, and sometimes you do more for them than they need, depriving them of a chance to find out the hard way which of their own ideas are good and which are bad. But always your motives are sincere, your results are impressive, and your admirers many. The only people who don't like you very much are the grumps and pessimists who feel shamed and confronted by your open, friendly manner.

THE WAY YOU MANIFEST YOUR FEMININITY

Female

Years ago, the Zombies had a hit with "She's Not There." It was about an exceptionally elusive, ethereal woman. The singer could watch her in awe but never quite pin her down. Was she just a dream? Did she really exist? Or did she just have Venus in Pisces? You could be her or indeed, the mysterious, head-turning "Girl from Ipanema." It's got nothing to do with what you look like, what you wear, or any conscious effort you may make to be a certain way. It has to do with an unaffected but engaging air of mystery you cannot help but exude. You're Lennon's Lucy in the Sky, Dylan's Lady of the Lowlands, and Donovan's Jennifer Juniper all rolled into one. But while others may envy you the ability to inspire a thousand poets without even trying, a part of you wants to be treated like a real woman, not some goddess on a pedestal. Which perhaps explains why you sometimes go for the men who will do anything *but* worship you.

YOUR IDEAL WOMAN

Male

Your Venus comes rising out of watery Pisces like some mythical sea nymph. She's captivating and soft, yet dangerous and exciting in her role as emissary of some other world beyond comprehension. Abandon all to join her, and you may merge with some ocean of deep emotion from which you can never return. Ignore her, and you may spend your whole life yearning for another chance to glimpse her again. When you allow your fantasy to get as far as co-existence with this dream goddess, the communication is definitely "non-verbal" but still more psychic than physical. Intense telepathic waves of empathy bridge, at least temporarily, the gulf between your different worlds. Together you can act to rid the universe of its pain or to cleanse it of its selfishness. Does sex enter into this equation? Perhaps. But not sex as most people know it. The ecstasy of worldly transcendence is both the golden reward and enormous sacrifice that a man must make when he falls in love with a mermaid.

Chapter Five

ZODIAC ROMANCE AND ASTRO-COMPATIBILITY

ZODIAC ROMANCE
AND ASTRO-COMPATIBILITY

I S your most important relationship based mainly on physical attraction? Is it primarily platonic? Do you have a true bond of trust or a classic love-hate relationship? And what, if your partnership is less than ideal, can you do to improve it?

The fascinating answers to all these questions are revealed by your horoscope. To find them, however, we have to forget all about those twelve zodiac signs we have all come to know and love. We must explore, instead, the angular relationships between the planets in our own chart and the planets in our partner's chart. If this sounds complicated, don't worry. Angular relationships, otherwise known as "aspects," are precisely what we've been charting in our wheels of destiny so far. To proper astrologers, they're by far the most revealing factor in any birth chart. Having used them to reveal a little about your own personality, I now want to show you how to "marry" any two horoscopes, so that you can see precisely what kind of marriage the owners of those two horoscopes are likely to have!

To get right to the heart of what's in your heart, you'll need nothing more demanding than a pencil and a little patience. Just be aware that, though a personal chart wheel can be found on page 132, the techniques you are about to learn will place you in great demand. Many of your friends will want to know what the planets have to say about their relationships, so it may be wise to photocopy a few extra wheels before you fill anything in.

We are going to begin by looking at what the two of you have in common on, or just below the surface. By comparing your Sun and Moon positions, we shall see whether you are two of a kind or something of an odd couple. This will no doubt amuse you, but, as all who have ever delved into the realm of the heart know full well, it's no indication of your prospects for lasting harmony. Superficially perfect unions have been known to crumble just as often as strange combinations have withstood the test of time.

That's why we shall then go one step deeper and explore the creative connections plus the sensual preferences that are essential to a comfortable coexistence. Last, but by no means least, we'll assess the all-important animal magnetism between you and your loved one. Some of the tests we are about to perform involve Venus, some the Moon, and some the Sun. Take care not to plot the wrong planets on your wheel, or you'll get very misleading results!

ROMANTIC RAPPORT

Test 1:
TWO OF A KIND

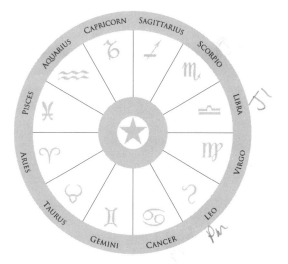

We shall begin our look at romantic rapport in the place where most other astrological features leave off, by comparing your Sun signs. Look at the wheel, find the empty space next to your zodiac sign, and write your initials in it. Next, look for the empty space next to your partner's sign and write his or her initials there. Now just count the number of spaces between your initials and your partner's and read the appropriate explanation below. If you are both born under the same sign, you must put both names in the same space. If you find more than five blank spaces between your name and your partner's, count around the wheel the other way.

IF YOU SHARE A SUN SIGN

Having a partner who shares your zodiac sign can be very much a mixed blessing. On the one hand, it gives you a lot in common; on the other, it tends to remove some of the mystery about how your loved one's mind works. You can end up so close that you feel like sister and brother, so mutually competitive that you fight like cats and dogs, or most interesting of all, you polarize, rather like twins tend to do. Little differences turn into big differences. One of you ends up manifesting all of your sign's best characteristics, while the other displays all the most excessive traits. On a scale of one to ten, sharing a Sun sign gives you a five.

 **IF YOUR SIGNS ARE NEXT
TO ONE ANOTHER**

Does the phrase "oil and water" mean anything to you? While it is quite possible that we shall uncover secret cosmic links between you and your partner which point to a magical, meaningful bond, on the basis of this factor alone you are about as likely to understand one another as a Swiss scientist and a South American samba dancer. Only if your minds are very open and your hearts are very mutually responsive do you stand a chance. Otherwise, on a scale of one to ten you get a cautious three.

**IF YOUR SIGNS ARE ONE
BLANK SPACE APART**

Most of the time, you enjoy a bright, lively rapport. As characters you complement one another, even if you do not always compliment each other. In a way, though, the fact that you do feel able gently to rib or criticize your companion is an indication of the ease and comfort of your rapport. You are like-minded enough to have plenty to say to one another, yet different enough not to end every conversation in a dull nod of agreement. If superficial compatibility were the only measure of success within a relationship, you would be a perfect pair. Whether you actually are, however, depends on how deep the other cosmic connections go. On a scale of one to ten, this aspect of your relationship warrants a hopeful seven.

IF YOUR SIGNS ARE TWO BLANK SPACES APART

Whether you are merely looking at this relationship as a possibility or striving to understand it because it is one to which you are committed, the very fact that you are entertaining a romantic interest in a person whose Sun sign forms a right angle to your own proves that you are a brave individual who thrives on challenge. People whose primary concern is a quiet life do not even contemplate relationships like this.

None of this is to be taken as an indication that the union does not or cannot work. It is potentially a healthy, dynamic sparring partnership that can bring out the very best in both parties. Rarely do you agree or even agree to differ, but if you both respect one another, you can have endless fun attempting to bring each other around to a very different point of view, as long as neither of you ever expects to win. On a scale of one to ten, this liaison deserves a suggestive six.

IF YOUR SIGNS ARE THREE BLANK SPACES APART

There's a delightful rapport between you and your loved one. You were born under signs of the same element, so you share a natural inclination to enjoy similar environments, experiences, and challenges. But this alone is no guarantee of a successful relationship. Indeed, it can be a problem insofar as it gives you a potentially false sense of security about one another. Your superficial similarities can disguise a host of deeper differences so well that it may be months or even years before either of you realizes how many cracks you have managed to paper over with a few glib exchanges. In conjunction with other, more important celestial links, however, to have your Sun signs in trine can be a tremendous asset. On a scale of one to ten, this partnership must be given the benefit of the doubt and awarded a generous nine.

IF YOUR SIGNS ARE FOUR BLANK SPACES APART

No matter how close you may be as lovers or partners, as friends you will always be less than fully in sympathy. You will never feel you really know or understand your other half, and may forever find yourself wishing that you could be at ease with them as naturally as you are with so many other companions.

This alone, however, is no reason to write the relationship off. If you are both well-adjusted individuals with reasonable expectations of what a relationship needs to be (that is, if you don't want to live permanently in one another's pocket), and if other links between your horoscopes offer the right potential for deeper communication, this superficial level of incompatibility can be a source of mutual amusement or a drawback easily overcome. On its own, however, it warrants on the scale of one to ten no higher than a two.

IF YOUR SIGNS ARE FIVE BLANK SPACES APART

You are born under opposite signs. Like magnets, you either attract each other so strongly as to make an astrologer's opinion irrelevant, or you repel each other with equal force. Unless, of course, you are like a pair of electromagnets between whom the current keeps alternating, so that one moment you are best buddies and the next mortal enemies! If so, you probably need a mutual common enemy to bind you together. Couples born under opposite signs often thrive together when times are tense and circumstances demanding, but grow apart when they have no special reason to join forces. To make this relationship work, it is essential for both parties to be characters who like to live life close to the edge. On a scale of one to ten, this cosmic link scores a debatable four.

Test 2:
WHAT DO YOU SECRETLY WANT?

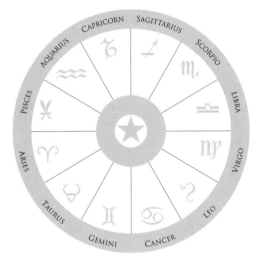

One good way to work out how well any two people are likely to get along is to consider them as individuals and decide what, deep down, they each expect a relationship to be like. This exercise is effectively a repetition of the trick we tried out back in Chapter 3. This time, though, we're going to compare your Sun and Moon with the specific purpose of clarifying your own definition of a "dream team." Then we're going to give it an interesting twist to see how closely your definition compares to that of your partner.

Place your Sun sign into the wheel above, just as you did in the previous exercise, only this time write the words, "My Sun." Now put your Moon sign into the appropriate space by writing the words, "My Moon." Then simply count the number of spaces between your Sun and Moon and read on.

If your Sun and Moon are in the same sign

Your idea of an ideal relationship is one in which the two partners are so close as to be almost joined at the hip! You want your partner to know you inside and out, and you want to feel equally sure that you know all there is to know about him or her. You feel it's important that you both agree about as much as possible and that you share as many experiences as you can. Some might consider this a recipe for boredom, but you don't worry about the risk of such a relationship growing stale. You believe that if your loved one is really the right person for you to be with, you'll always be able to stride through life together, side by side, in a state of constant close communication, enjoying each other's company every minute of every day.

If your Sun and Moon are in adjacent signs

It doesn't matter much to you if your loved one lives in a different world. In some ways, you far prefer this to the notion of having a partner who is forever in your pocket. You can easily identify with Kahlil Gibran's famous suggestion that a couple should: "Stand together yet not too near together: for the pillars of the temple stand apart and the Oak tree and the Cypress grow not in each other's shadow." For you, a degree of distance is healthy. You feel it's important to maintain a sense of being two distinctly separate people, each with a right to his or her own opinions and tastes. You have plenty of deep, sincere, consistent loving to give, but you don't feel that, to share it successfully, you or your partner has to keep proving the commitment to the other. Though you may have powerful passions, you feel trapped in any relationship that doesn't give you room to be yourself.

IF YOUR SUN AND MOON
ARE ONE BLANK SPACE APART

You are fundamentally an easygoing soul who finds it simple enough to get along with most people. This may be why you don't always notice immediately when a relationship is running into trouble; you somehow expect everything to be OK as long as it seems OK on the surface.

You can act as a stable foil to someone who thrives on tension or loves to argue, but you can also sometimes feel drained or unfairly picked on if you spend too much time in the company of such a soul. You certainly don't feel any need to be in a state of permanent semiwarfare in order to feel as though you have an exciting relationship. Often you find that you are the one who is doing all the compromising, the "propping up," or the smoothing over of rough edges.

IF YOUR SUN AND MOON
ARE TWO BLANK SPACES APART

You have a tendency to feel strongly attracted to people with whom you have little or nothing in common. If they happen to be erratic, changeable, and prone to unreasonable, bad-tempered outbursts, this only fascinates you more. It's almost as if you secretly feel that a relationship has to be painful to be real. As a result, you can, if you're not careful, either fall for very difficult characters or find yourself constantly goading a more mild-mannered partner into a display of obstreperousness! If you understand this inner predilection, you can work to get it under control, and thus improve your chances of finding harmony within your love life. It's worth the effort, for your heart is full of strong passion, and you have plenty that's special to share and give, if only you can overcome your mistrust of everything that seems safe.

IF YOUR SUN AND MOON ARE THREE BLANK SPACES APART

Although you are a very loving, giving, sweet, and stable soul, your relationships don't always contain quite as much fire as you might like them to have. Ironically, this is in part because you don't suffer so many pangs of desperate longing to be loved as most people do. By and large, you tend to be a contented, self-contained, and (some might even say) slightly self-satisfied character. You're not one to make a drama out of a crisis (which is good), but then there are times when an element of exaggeration can work wonders for a relationship that has become slightly too safe or set in its ways. If you were occasionally to allow yourself to worry or overreact more, you might avoid the tendency to make your partner wonder whether or not you truly need him or her!

IF YOUR SUN AND MOON ARE FOUR BLANK SPACES APART

You are either the most hopeless romantic ever to have walked on the face of the Earth, or the most incurable cynic. Either way, you have a tendency to spoil potentially great relationships either by being far too noncommittal or, worse, by swinging to the other extreme and being far too demanding.

This isn't much helped by your tendency to subscribe to the Groucho Marx philosophy of being deeply mistrustful of any society that would want to have you as a member. If someone likes you, you wonder what's wrong with him or her. It doesn't necessarily follow that you prefer to be treated like dirt, but your friends do often wonder why you take it upon yourself to pick partners with whom you can hardly expect life to be anything other than a constant struggle to find a single point in common.

IF YOUR SUN AND MOON ARE FIVE BLANK SPACES APART

Your craving for a soulmate is one of the strongest forces in your personality. It keeps you constantly looking for a better relationship than the one you currently have, or it makes you determined to stick with your existing partner no matter how stressful or awkward the partnership is becoming. For a partner to be ideal for you, he or she may need a hundred special qualifications, but the one thing needed most of all is an ability to be philosophical about your permanent sense of insecurity. When you're not worrying about being left, you're worrying about letting your loved one down. Ironically, the only thing likely to turn either of those remote possibilities into a reality is your tendency to worry so much about the idea that your partner needs to be a saint that you start behaving in ways likely to test a saint's patience!

Test 3:
WHAT DOES YOUR PARTNER
REALLY WANT?

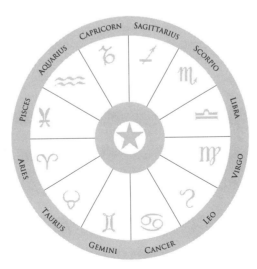

Now that you've read about the link between the Sun and Moon in your own horoscope, you need to see how it lines up in your partner's chart wheel. Do precisely what you did for your own date of birth, only this time put your partner's Sun sign into the appropriate space in the wheel by writing his or her name, followed by the word "Sun." Then place his or her Moon sign in the appropriate space. Count the spaces between the Sun and Moon, remembering that, if you find more than five blank spaces, you need to count again the other way around the wheel. Now go back and reread the relevant section in the previous set of interpretations.

There's a possibility that, even if your partner has a totally different Sun and Moon sign from your own, your mate may end up with the same reading that you did. If so, see this as an encouraging omen, but don't get carried away. It's not necessarily a promise that you were made for one another!

Test 4:
HOW DO YOU SEE EACH OTHER?
(PART 1)

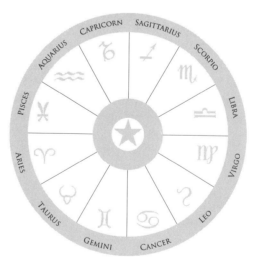

In the last test, we looked at how you and your partner each tend to treat relationships in general. It's now time to look at how you both respond to *this* relationship in particular. Because each of you is likely to see the relationship from a different perspective, we'll begin by looking at how you tend to think of your partner and then go on to see what your partner secretly tends to think about you.

Begin by putting your Moon sign into the appropriate empty space in the wheel by writing the words "My Moon." Then put your partner's Sun sign in the appropriate empty space by writing his or her name, followed by the word "Sun." Count the number of blank spaces between your Moon and your partner's Sun and read the relevant interpretation below. (Remember, if you find more than five blank spaces, you need to count around the wheel in the other direction!)

IF YOUR MOON IS
IN THE SAME SIGN AS YOUR
PARTNER'S SUN

You find it extremely easy to empathize with this person. Sometimes, indeed, you seem to know your partner almost a little too well. At times, you feel more like brother and sister than husband and wife. At times, too, you can't quite believe that your partner doesn't understand why he or she has said or done a certain thing, when to you it's all too obvious. Although you sometimes find the petty things your partner does more than a little annoying, by and large, you feel very proud of this person and extremely relaxed with him or her. There's an almost telepathic link between you. You can often instinctively tell how your partner is feeling, even when you're miles apart.

Together you can withstand a lot of worldly pressure; indeed, you feel very enthusiastic about the marvelous team you make when it's the two of you against the rest of the world. When it's the two of you against each other, however, you're not so comfortable. Thankfully, you rarely quarrel, for on the few occasions when you do, it seems you never quite understand why. All you know is that you don't just mildly disagree, you deeply (and occasionally bitterly) differ.

IF YOUR MOON IS ADJACENT TO YOUR PARTNER'S SUN

No matter how many years you spend in this person's company, there'll always be a sense of mystery insofar as there's something about your loved one that you simply cannot fathom.

You also suspect (unless there are other powerful links between your two horoscopes) that you, too, are often sorely misunderstood. Yet, though your partner doesn't always appreciate what makes you tick, he or she certainly knows how to wind you up!

The relationship is often what some astrologers call "challenging" and most other people call "exasperating." Nonetheless, it has its distinct advantages. You feel sure you're in no danger of ever settling into a dull, predictable routine, if only because you can never be quite sure what your partner is going to do or say next! What you can't cope with, your partner usually can, and vice versa!

IF YOUR MOON IS ONE BLANK SPACE FROM YOUR PARTNER'S SUN

No matter how well or badly you may get along at some levels, your relationship is greatly aided by the fact that you cannot help but see many qualities in your partner that you deeply admire. You feel a constant sense of warmth towards (and appreciation of) this person's general demeanor, which probably explains why you let him or her get away with so much more than you should. Your loved one has an instinctive way of putting you at your ease, defusing your anger, and encouraging you to see the funny side of whatever's worrying you.

Does this, then, make you a perfect pair? Not on its own. It depends on how well the celestial chemistry between you both is working elsewhere in the horoscope. Your tendency to want to forgive and tolerate this person can just as easily be the spoonful of sugar which makes an otherwise unpalatable dish seem as edible as the natural sweetness of a bond which is truly fruitful.

IF YOUR MOON IS TWO BLANK SPACES FROM YOUR PARTNER'S SUN

You more often see your loved one as an adversary than as an ally. For as long as you feel happy that you are both only play fighting, this can be a source of much amusement. The trouble comes when, instead of having a jovial joust with your spouse, you find yourself bitterly battling. After a while, your partner's tendency to disagree with you on principle, to engage in perpetual point-scoring or one-upmanship or to disapprove of so many of your friends, can become a little wearing. There's also a tendency for you both to lapse into role playing, with one of you acting the part of the stern parent to the other's naughty child.

That said, many people with this cosmic link find it an inconvenience that's well worth putting up with. As long as both sides make an effort to keep the relationship on an equal footing between two mature adults who can forgive each other for (and even laugh about) their respective differences, there's the potential for an almost never-ending source of mutual inspiration, motivation, and stimulation.

IF YOUR MOON IS THREE BLANK SPACES FROM YOUR PARTNER'S SUN

It's one thing to perceive your partner as bright, warm, and sunny, but quite another to imagine that the Sun actually shines out of any part of your spouse's anatomy. Watch out for your tendency to hang on to your loved one's every word or to follow this person trustingly wherever he or she leads, regardless of how debatable your partner's judgement. Though you may be steadfastly independent in all other circumstances, when the romantic mood sweeps over you, you can be putty in the hands of this particular person. You're not entirely blind to your partner's faults, but you're certainly in the habit of acknowledging them through the rosiest of tinted spectacles.

It's lovely that you have so much respect, affection, and pride in your beloved, and lovelier still if the beloved in question happens to deserve all this; but it's possibly wise to seek a second, more objective opinion if you want to be sure whether he or she does. Might you be projecting onto the screen of your partner's personality a magnificence that could be more aptly and properly recognized in yourself?

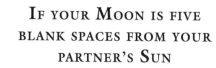

IF YOUR MOON IS FOUR BLANK SPACES FROM YOUR PARTNER'S SUN

Your loved one is an enigma, both fascinatingly mysterious and irritatingly difficult to understand. You cannot decide quite how you feel about this person, for you're never quite sure whether you know your partner well enough to be a fair judge of his or her character. This isn't likely to change, whether you're with this person for forty minutes or forty years. Nor, even if you've been with your spouse for forty years already, are you ever likely to feel sure whether you have forty more years or minutes left in the relationship; your partner doesn't exactly make you feel secure.

There may, though, be other reasons why you're happy to put up with (or even thrive on) this perpetual sense of uncertainty. In this particular person's company, you get constant excitement and interest: your partner helps you (or drives you) to do and feel things that you might otherwise never experience. A rare, precious, and highly constructive creative spark can be ignited by living your life with someone you can never quite bring yourself to believe you are actually living your life with!

IF YOUR MOON IS FIVE BLANK SPACES FROM YOUR PARTNER'S SUN

The success or failure of this relationship has a great deal to do with the success or failure of your relationship with your parents and of the nature of your partner's relationship with his or her own mother and father. There's a tendency for you both to play out the roles you saw enacted between the adults in your life when you were little, exacerbated by a tendency for you both to play out parent/child relationships in your partnership. You tend, no matter which sex you are, to mother your loved one by being overprotective or concerned for their well-being. Your partner, in turn, tends to father you by encouraging you to conquer challenges you might otherwise shy away from.

As long as this is just one facet of a multidimensional relationship, this can be magnificently healthy for you both. It's when it becomes the dominant, or even seemingly sole, behavior pattern that you can begin to yearn for someone with whom there's less friction. Two well-adjusted adults can enjoy a deeply fulfilling, mutually stimulating relationship with this Moon/Sun opposition between them. Two less well-adjusted adults will either find it difficult or will soon have to take steps to learn how to become more mature in their approach to one another.

Test 5:
HOW DO YOU SEE EACH OTHER?
(PART 2)

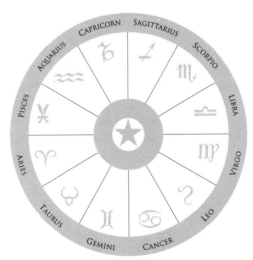

Having looked at how you see your partner, you now need to see how your partner sees you. On the wheel above, place your spouse's Moon in the appropriate space by writing his or her name followed by the word "Moon," and then write "my Sun" in the space next to your Sun sign. Count the spaces once more, remembering to go the other way around the wheel if you find more than five blank spaces.

Now go back and reread the relevant section in the previous set of interpretations. It's entirely possible (though somewhat unusual) for your partner's Moon to have the same angular relationship to your Sun as your Moon enjoys to his or her Sun. If you do find yourself led to the same interpretation that you've just read, see it as neither a good sign nor a bad sign, merely as a strong reinforcement of the trend described.

EMOTIONAL BALANCE

Test 6:
ARE YOU PROUD OF YOUR PARTNER?

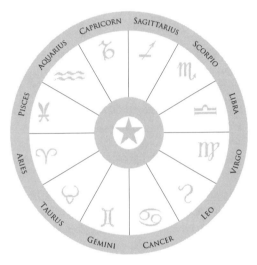

In the last test, we compared your Moon to your partner's Sun, after which we looked at the link between your partner's Moon and your Sun. The object was to gain an insight into how you secretly feel about one another by looking at your relationship from a Lunar point of view.

There is, however, another way to consider the way one person's Sun meshes with another person's Moon: this is to see it from what we astrologers grandly call a Solar perspective. Put simply, this means we ought to ask whether you fear that the private side of your relationship is a threat to your public image or whether you firmly believe that it's an enhancement of your personality. Put more simply still, we need to ask if you want to be like Tony and Charlene, a couple in which both partners enjoy equal lime-light, or are you more inclined to be a John and Norma, a couple in which one partner keeps a low profile while the other basks in all the glory?

To get a true answer, we have to ask each half of the couple separately. Maybe one of you is reluctantly hiding his or her light under a bushel. Or maybe that person feels pulled further into the spotlight than they want to be by the spouse's desire for both to be seen as a famous team.

If you're ready for what may (or may not) be a very revealing insight into the way you think your partner is best presented (or hidden) from the eyes of a watching world, here's what to do. Simply put your Sun into the wheel by writing the words "My Sun" into the empty space next to your zodiac sign, then put your partner's Moon into the wheel. Now count the number of empty spaces that separate your Sun from your partner's Moon. If you find more than five, go back around the wheel in the other direction.

IF YOUR SUN IS
IN THE SAME SIGN AS YOUR
PARTNER'S MOON

You tend to feel exceedingly proud of your partner, to the point where you can almost, if you're not careful, end up wanting to show off this person like a trophy, regardless of whether he or she relishes the attention. You certainly feel that if your spouse is good enough for you, he or she is good enough to present to anyone you meet, and woe unto anyone who dares to say different. You really like the idea of being spoken of in the same breath, and it is even possible, if you're honest, that one of the many reasons why you never want the relationship to end is that you aren't sure whether some people will still accept you without this wonderful asset on your arm.

IF YOUR SUN IS
IN THE ADJACENT SIGN TO
YOUR PARTNER'S MOON

No matter how much you may love or care for this person, you have no great desire to be introduced wherever you go as someone's "other half." Nor, perhaps more to the point, would you feel any great desire to have "his" and "hers" name tags on the windows of your car (even in the unlikely event that this was the height of fashion). You are neither ashamed of nor proud of your companion, merely conscious of the fact that you are two distinct individuals whose decision to share a private life puts neither of you under any obligation to share a public reputation. The fact that this is currently a very fashionable, even politically correct way to behave is purely coincidental. If, though, you're ever asked why you rarely introduce your loved one to anyone, you may be better off using this as your reason than just casually referring to him (or her).

IF YOUR SUN IS ONE
BLANK SPACE FROM YOUR
PARTNER'S MOON

Do you want your loved one to share so much of your life as to make it hard for even your closest friends to see you as separate entities? There's not much point in asking you. Your reply is probably, "I'm not sure. It depends what my partner wants." Something about this particular relationship tends to make you uncharacteristically amenable (or acquiescent, depending on how you look at it). Since most of the time the way you feel inclined to look at it, whatever it may happen to be, is from the same angle that your partner happens to be looking at it from, we'll make that "amenable" and hope your other half doesn't secretly yearn for someone who will argue more!

Conjecture and veiled criticism aside, your relationship is probably pretty healthy. You're proud of your partner for who he or she is, rather than for an ability to make you look good. You certainly don't worry that your partner may show you up in public.

IF YOUR SUN IS TWO
BLANK SPACES FROM YOUR
PARTNER'S MOON

You may well be proud of your partner, but you're certainly not anxious to be one of those couples who are never seen apart or described by others in such a way as to make your names run together as if they were one word. To say that you respect the right of your other half to a separate identity is putting it politely. It's probably more appropriate to say that you have no choice but to respect this, for you find it almost impossible to draw a discreet veil over your tendency to differ wildly in your beliefs, opinions, and preferences. Some of your friends do, it's true, tend to see you as a double act, but you rightly fear that they are more prone to perceive you as Punch and Judy rather than as Romeo and Juliet. Your private relationship may be wonderful, but your joint public reputation is sorely in need of a spin doctor.

IF YOUR SUN IS THREE BLANK SPACES FROM YOUR PARTNER'S MOON

The big question is not "Are you proud of your partner?" The answer to that, at least according to this crucial link between your horoscope and your mate's, is "Very." Even if you're not proud in the traditional sense, you're certainly happy to put up with, make endless excuses about, or blame others for this person's behavior. You usually feel so benignly disposed towards him or her as to be prone to see the most dreadful faults as glorious talents.

This, however, makes the following question crucial. "Is your partner so sweetly satisfied with you?" You had better not trust yourself to answer that. We've already established that, when it comes to this person in particular, you're capable of being very generous with the benefit of the doubt. Nor should you ask your friends. The spotlight of affection and tolerance that you shine on your partner is so bright as to blind all but the most cynical. You could try asking your other half, but as you'd be inclined to nod in agreement if this person told you the Moon was made of green cheese, your best bet is to ask your horoscope. Read the rest of this chapter carefully if you're brave enough to risk being disillusioned in your quest for reassurance.

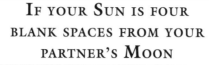

IF YOUR SUN IS FOUR BLANK SPACES FROM YOUR PARTNER'S MOON

How can you be proud of your partner when you're not particularly sure who your partner really is? Admittedly, you can hardly be ashamed, either, with so little information to go on. But the real wonder about your relationship is what on earth glues it together. It's certainly nothing superficial, which leads us to conclude that it must be something terribly deep, private, and intimate. Therefore, unless the two of you happen to be a pair of shameless exhibitionists, the issue of whether you have a partner who suits you in public or one that your friends can't stand the sight of makes not a bit of difference to you. Which is probably just as well.

IF YOUR SUN IS FIVE BLANK SPACES FROM YOUR PARTNER'S MOON

Your eyes probably lit up as soon as you read the title of this astrological exercise. The issue of whether or not you have a partner who makes you look good in public or one who makes you look a bit of a fool is a very hot potato indeed. Even if you're not normally the kind of person who gives a hoot about what other people think, there's something about the behavior of this particular partner that makes you slightly uneasy. You may love your spouse a lot, adore him or her even, but you're never quite sure that you bring out the best in this person, or vice versa.

You might ask yourself why this relationship makes you feel quite so determined to persuade your friends that you're part of a match made in heaven. Could it be because you secretly harbor doubts which might be assuaged if enough people were to tell you that they think your partner's wonderful? Your partner probably *is* wonderful. You most certainly *are* wonderful. The fundamental basis of the relationship may be wonderful too. On the basis of this astrological link alone, it's deeply unfair to make a judgement. But what we can safely conclude is that, when viewed as a couple by your friends and family, the most amazing thing about you both is the way you so often seem to drive one another bananas.

Test 7:
ARE YOU PROUD OF ONE
ANOTHER?

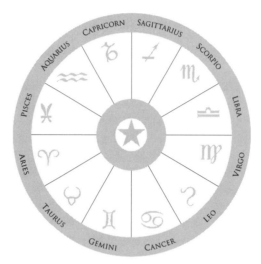

We now have half the story about your relationship's public image. If you feel bold enough to explore the other half, you need to take a look at your other half's horoscope. Simply put your partner's Sun into the wheel by writing his or her name, followed by the word "Sun," in the empty space next to this person's zodiac sign. Then put your own Moon into the wheel by writing "My Moon" in the appropriate space. Now count the number of empty spaces that separate your partner's Sun from your Moon. (If you find more than five, count around the wheel in the other direction.) Now go back and reread the relevant section in the previous set of interpretations.

Test 8:
ARE YOU IN COSMIC HARMONY?

Although you've now learned a lot about the way in which you and your partner get along, you're about to perform an exercise which counts for more than all the previous tests put together. The ultimate test of any couple's compatibility has to be a comparison between their Moon signs. Once we've performed this psychological health check, all that remains is to see how you match up at the more earthly, physical level. Animal magnetism without emotional empathy is, however, not much good for anything other than a very brief, shallow encounter. So draw a deep breath and be brave as we ask the sky for an honest answer to the question: "Are you in cosmic harmony?"

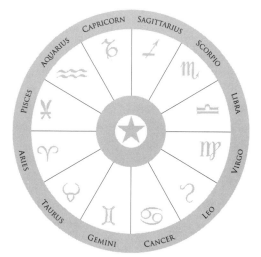

Plot your Moon sign in the appropriate space on the wheel in the usual way, then put your partner's Moon on the wheel. Now, as before, count the number of spaces between the two Moons, remembering, as always, that if you find more than five blank spaces, you need to count around the wheel in the opposite direction.

IF YOUR MOON IS IN THE SAME SIGN AS YOUR PARTNER'S MOON

You are in many ways magnificently compatible with this particular person. I don't use the word "soulmate" lightly, but this is an exceptional case. Even if every other astrological comparison between your two birth charts spells bad news, you have sufficient potential in this one positive link to overcome it if you feel so inclined. Almost certainly, you do feel so inclined. You can't help instinctively liking your partner, and he or she can't help thinking the world of you. Both of you, deep down, want the relationship to work so intently and sincerely as to turn a blind eye to a host of superficial incompatibilities.

The only serious downside to this combination is a tendency to be too close for comfort. When one of you is feeling low, the other is likely to be similarly despondent. You won't always enjoy quite the same ability to cheer one another up that some other couples have.

You may also have a problem if either of you, by nature, thrives on a degree of friction and tension. You may differ and disagree on the surface, but you should always be able to empathize deeply with your other half, and they with you. Soulmates, it must be remembered, sometimes make better friends than lovers.

IF YOUR MOON IS IN THE ADJACENT SIGN TO YOUR PARTNER'S MOON

You each have a dramatically different way of looking at life and of responding to emotional challenges. What one of you feels just fine about is often likely to be a source of great concern to the other. What one of you sees as an appropriate emotional response is likely to leave the other flabbergasted.

Your relationship may well have the potential to succeed, and to do so pretty happily too; but, if so, it must be because you both meet at some other level than the purely heartfelt. It could be an intellectual approach that you share, or a powerful physical attraction, or both. What it isn't going to provide naturally is a true sense of psychological belonging.

As such, the relationship may be vulnerable to the possibility of one or both partners eventually meeting someone with whom they click more instantly at an emotional level. This can be avoided or kept under control by a pact of honesty or a firm, frequently renewed promise of commitment. With determination on both sides, it can be made to work, but it's important to understand that this is a fire that needs to be constantly stoked with fresh fuel if it is not to burn out.

If your Moon is one blank space from your partner's Moon

You understand one another remarkably well. You may be far from a pair of bookends, but you certainly go together like a knife and fork or a table and chair! You naturally complement one another's personalities and are able, too, to prop each other up at times of stress or tension. There's not only an inspiring bond of empathy between you but a vibrant line of mutual attraction. You make each other feel at ease, most of the time at least, because neither of you feels much need to keep scoring points or establishing who's boss. Without trying too hard, you can share your deepest feelings and your most pressing responsibilities, too, trusting that each will respect and appreciate what the other considers truly important.

Does it all sound too good to be true? Perhaps it is. Perhaps other factors in the astrological relationship are not so helpful. It may be that you don't click mentally as well as you get along when all the words have run out. Or it may be that, overall, your partnership is more platonic than physical. Whatever the answer, you undoubtedly have the makings of a low-maintenance liaison with a high satisfaction quotient.

IF YOUR MOON IS TWO BLANK SPACES FROM YOUR PARTNER'S MOON

If yours is a marriage made in heaven, heaven must be a pretty competitive place! There's undoubtedly an exciting spark between you and your other half, but it's just as likely to ignite a flame of fury as to light a torch of undying affection. You empathize exceedingly well at some levels, but on the occasions when you disagree, you each fight hard to bring the other around to your own point of view. And neither of you takes easily to the notion of defeat. On the positive side, this ensures that the relationship is never dull. You won't become one of those couples who have so much in common that they run out of things to say to one another.

The other side of this coin, however, suggests that both of you have to keep your temper under control when you are together. If you're united in a common cause, or if you're both well-adjusted individuals who don't feel a perpetual need to score points off one another in anything other than the lightest, most good-humored way, this relationship can be a source of constant mutual stimulation and excitement. If, however, one or both of you are prone to feel a constant hunger for emotional reassurance, you will have to discover some way to learn to live with the fact that you may not always find it within this partnership.

IF YOUR MOON IS THREE BLANK SPACES FROM YOUR PARTNER'S MOON

No matter what you've read so far, you can rest assured that, in one key area of life at least, you and your partner are gloriously compatible. Your Moon signs are linked in such a way as to give you a deep and lasting empathy. For this reason you are cosmically suited, no matter how different your superficial personalities may be. You have a natural, easy rapport and an instinctive desire to treat one another with genuine respect.

If there *is* a potential problem with this planetary pairing, it lies in the possibility that your relationship can at times be a little too easy. You can both feel so safe together, or as if you have so little to prove, that there's a danger you may start taking each other for granted. You can also, if you're not careful, become a very insular couple. Because you gain so much contentment from being in one another's company, you may not always bother to keep up your outside interests and friendships. This can leave the relationship growing peacefully stale or cause you to seem like a rather uninteresting pair. It's a slight danger, but frankly not one worth worrying too much about.

Technically and officially, you need to check that other important connections between your two horoscopes are aligning as they should before you can be absolutely sure that you have done very well in choosing your other half. In fact, though, you knew before you even read this that you had something special going for you. And, indeed, you have.

If your Moon is four blank spaces from your partner's Moon

From an emotional point of view, you have about as much in common with one another as a fish and a bicycle. You are magnificently mismatched, and there's nothing much you can do about this other than to learn to see the funny side. Never, if you both try with all your might from now till the day that Oprah Winfrey takes a vow of silence, will either of you fully understand what makes the other tick! You will perpetually baffle, astound, and amaze your other half and, in turn, be flabbergasted, staggered, and surprised by him or her. Two peas in a pod does not describe the two of you, but then who seriously wants to live with a carbon copy?

Your relationship has plenty of potential for happiness, fulfillment, and success, provided both you and your loved one are prepared to celebrate all that's good within it while remaining philosophical about what it can never be. If you're both willing to find other, platonic friends with whom to share your deeper fears and feelings, you can fulfill the yearning for a confidant in another way, and you can decide to let your partner be the person with whom you perform an ever intriguing dance of disagreement. By constantly questioning your partner's attitude (as you are prone to do) and by accepting that your own deepest instincts will always be subject to healthy scrutiny in return (as they are undoubtedly bound to be) you can turn a possible problem into a unique advantage. What you have, if you can only see it from this angle, is a recipe for mutual growth within a partnership of two very different people who are nonetheless prepared to treat each other as equals.

IF YOUR MOON IS FIVE BLANK SPACES FROM YOUR PARTNER'S MOON

There's a very powerful emotional link between your horoscope and your partner's birth chart. This has the potential to make you an inseparable couple, each of whom constantly finishes one another's sentences, reads one another's minds, and feels very much like two halves of one whole. It also, however, has just as much potential to turn you into a pair who fight like cats and dogs.

It's the very fact that you *are* in some ways so similar that can make you both feel inclined on occasions to dwell on the little differences and turn them into big ones. But it's a way, if you can only see it as such, of protecting your own sense of identity. Twins do something similar when they decide, early in life, to separate into the dominant one and the passive one. By polarizing their personalities, they can each take the character traits they share to opposite extremes and turn two potentially similar lifestyles into dramatically different experiences.

The trouble is that you and your partner may never quite so easily agree about which one of you is going to lead and which one is going to be happy to follow. Your emotional make-up is so much the opposite of your partner's as to make the two of you feel like a mirror image of one another. When your partner is up, you're down. When your partner is all for it, you are totally against it.

You have, as I began by saying, a great deal in common. If you're both willing to accept this rather than fight against it, you can become delightfully close and remain so forever. But for as long as one of you insists on refusing to budge an inch, the other will feel inclined to be equally stubborn!

PHYSICAL ATTRACTION

Now we're going to take a look at the physical side of romance. I have left this until last in deference to the proprieties of courtship itself! While you don't have to be an astrologer to recognize that men and women often want very different things, this fact is certainly writ large in the laws of horoscope interpretation. Hence, our need now to consider the position of a new planet previously unmentioned in this book. We're going to look at Mars, the god of war and the ultimate symbol of male energy.

Mars in a woman's birth chart symbolizes something very different from Mars in the chart of a man. Similarly, as we discovered in Chapter 4, Venus has a double meaning. To understand what's going on in a relationship, it's essential to view each horoscope from both a male and female point of view. This, plus the fact that there are so many planetary factors to consider, makes the astrology of sex almost as complicated as the biology of it. This is reasonable enough, considering that what we're really trying to define is an elusive form of chemistry.

Test 9:
WHAT KIND OF LOVER DO YOU SEEK?

You now need to look up your Mars sign in the tables on page 317. If you're a woman, your Mars sign tells you what kind of a man you secretly want as a lover. If you're a man, your Mars sign describes the aspect of your personality that most women are likely to find most attractive.

MARS IN ARIES

Female The notion of a soft, sentimental "new age" man awakens little passion in you. You prefer to be swept off your feet by a tough, rugged, no-nonsense individual who isn't afraid of a fight or at least manifests an air of assertive authority when he needs to.

Male Women like your nerve, assurance, and ability to act on impulse.

Mars in Taurus

Female You fancy a man who is cool as a cucumber, solid as a rock, and strong as an ox. He must, of course, have a softer side, and preferably an artistic or musical streak, too. But he needs to be sure of himself if he is to be sure of you!

Male You score when you show your strength, especially when you also suggest that it stems from sensitivity rather than swagger.

Mars in Gemini

Female It's not what he looks like that you care about; it's how he talks and what he has to say. He needs to be witty, amusing, inventive, and knowledgeable. He also needs to be an adaptable, interesting character; you can't stand sticks-in-the-mud.

Male Women love your inquiring mind and your ability to address them as equals.

Mars in Cancer

Female For you, the notion of the "new age" holds a distinct appeal. You don't want him to be tied to the kitchen sink, but you do want compassion, tenderness, and sensitivity in a lover, far more than you want a hunk, a hulk, or a hard man.

Male It's your loyalty, integrity and obvious sincerity that women appreciate most of all.

Mars in Leo

Female You want a man who knows what he wants. You like the idea of a lover who sees himself as a king, partly because he will then treat you like a queen, but mainly because you find a great deal of satisfaction in being with someone who has supreme confidence.

Male You are sexiest when you simply relax and show others how charming you can be just by being yourself.

Mars in Virgo

Female Men who are all talk and no action do nothing for you. You like a man who can express himself physically, who can build machines or work with the earth, or show, even if he does do something more cerebral, that his hands are as sensitive as his heart!

Male Women like the way you can be so deep, patient, dependable, and diligent.

Mars in Libra

Female You generally go for the artistic type or for men who clearly appreciate the finer things in life. Your ideal man will take you into his confidence, involve you in his work, share with you his secrets, plus, most important of all, seek and take your advice.

Male Most women see your innate willingness to share as a sexier asset than all your other social skills.

Mars in Scorpio

Female You seek a go-getter, a hardworking man of substance who will brook no opposition when he believes he is right. When you see him dedicating himself to a subject with passion, you feel reassured that he will give himself to you with equal commitment.

Male It's your refusal to compromise that, oddly enough, makes most women want to compromise themselves for you!

Mars in Sagittarius

Female Your fantasy lover is a sort of Indiana Jones. He's probably a very physical, sporty type. He certainly doesn't shy away from a challenge. He's probably also very well traveled and experienced in the ways of the world. Your dream is to journey by his side.

Male Women are most drawn to your devil-may-care determination to explore all that life has to offer.

Mars in Capricorn

Female You like a man who is businesslike, masterful, and, not to put too fine a point on it, wealthy! This isn't because you want his money but because, if he's proved himself a success in the world, he'll have what it takes to conquer your reservations successfully.

Male You're most attractive to women when you show that you're not afraid to carry a heavy responsibility with dignity.

Mars in Aquarius

Female Your dream lover is someone who defies all attempts at categorization. You like idiosyncratic, even controversial types who can constantly surprise you and fulfill your desire to experience aspects of love and life that few but the boldest ever get to taste.

Male It's your ability to stand out from the crowd that most makes women want to give their hearts to you.

Mars in Pisces

Female If he's to stand a chance of winning your heart, he has to have the soul of a poet. You couldn't care less about his worldly achievements. You want someone who has a vivid imagination, a sensitive personality, and a deep, inspiring vision to share with you.

Male
It's your childlike enthusiasm for life and your deep faith in the dream of making the world more magical that women cannot resist.

Test 10:
WHAT KIND OF LOVER DOES YOUR PARTNER SEEK?

Now look up your partner's Mars sign and see what it says about that person. If it's the same as your own, or if it matches the description of your Venus sign as given in Chapter 4, this is probably a good omen. But we have more to explore before we can be sure.

Test 11:
DO YOU WANT DRAMA OR
DEVOTION?
(PART 1)

We must ask a crucial question before we directly compare the positions of your Venus and Mars to those of your partner. What kind of spark do you need to make a physical relationship come alive? Just as crucially, what kind of spark does your partner require? Two people are not necessarily well matched because their planets align harmoniously. If one or both of you secretly thrive on a sense of conflict, you may be more attracted to a lover whose planets inflame rather than soothe you!

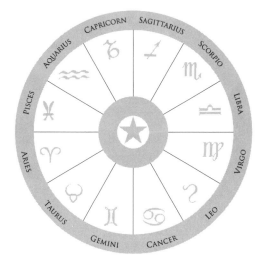

To find this out, we need to plot the relationship between your Mars and your Venus on the wheel. By now, you should have all the information you need from the tables. For wheel one, just write "Mars" in the space next to the appropriate sign and then do the same for your Venus. Now count the number of blank spaces between these two planets. (Remember, if you find more than five blank spaces, you need to count around the wheel in the opposite direction!)

IF YOUR VENUS AND MARS
ARE IN THE SAME SIGN

You're exceedingly selective about the kind of lover you want. Only a very particular type of person will do, and they'd better have plenty to give because shallow relationships have no appeal. You'll put up with a lot of tension but only because you're a stable character. You certainly don't need anger to spark your flame of passion. Trust is what you yearn for.

IF YOUR VENUS AND MARS
ARE IN ADJACENT SIGNS

You can adapt yourself well to most kinds of relationships. What you seek is neither a partner who will drive you into a frenzy nor one who'll provide endless support and succor, but simply a sensitive, adaptable soul who will understand that much of the time you're unsure about what you need and that this can change dramatically, depending on your mood and situation.

IF YOUR VENUS AND MARS
ARE ONE BLANK SPACE APART

Without a doubt, you prefer a cuddle to a battle. If your partner's Venus and/or Mars turns out to be forming antagonistic links to your own, you're far more likely to perceive this as a disadvantage to be overcome with good grace than as a stimulating aphrodisiac.

If your Venus and Mars are two blank spaces apart

You thrive on tension. If you can't successfully (and sometimes dramatically) argue with your partner, you feel you can't get quite as close to your partner as you would like. This doesn't necessarily destine you to a life of romantic conflict, but it does mean there has to be a healthy degree of combat or competition in your most important relationship.

If your Venus and Mars are three blank spaces apart

Though you probably prefer a partner who will whisper sweet nothings in your ear to one who will goad you with sharp comments, you can handle either in a pinch. Indeed, you can handle most things in life very well. You don't feel you need a partner to make you complete. This can make you easy to live with, and, on the other hand, it can make your loved one wonder why he or she bothers!

If your Venus and Mars are four blank spaces apart

Where most people want a lover to make them feel complete, you seem to want a lover in order to feel happily baffled. You don't much care for open conflict, yet you don't feel very comfortable about close harmony either. You like it when you're just not quite sure where you stand. You had better have a partner who similarly thrives on uncertainty and spontaneity.

IF YOUR VENUS AND MARS
ARE FIVE BLANK SPACES APART

You're emotionally well balanced, but more like a seesaw than a pair of scales. You feel uneasy when everything is still. You can accept a partner whose planets harmonize with your own, but you're probably better off with someone who appreciates the constant challenge in a game of love where the goalposts are always shifting within certain extreme parameters.

Test 12:
DO YOU WANT DRAMA OR
DEVOTION?
(PART 2)

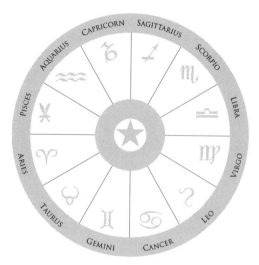

Now that you've read about yourself, plot your partner's Mars and Venus on the second wheel and count the spaces between them. Now go back to the preceding text to see, if you dare, what kind of dynamic your partner prefers!

Test 13:
SEXUAL COMPATIBILITY
(PART 1)

We've used our wheels to answer many interesting questions about the nature of your relationship. It's now time to ask the two most telling questions of all. How does your Mars line up with your partner's Venus? And how does your partner's Venus get along with your Mars?

From a woman's point of view, the first is by far the more important issue. From a man's standpoint, the second counts for much more. But because, of course, no relationship is ever going to work unless it works for both parties, we simply must have the answer to both questions.

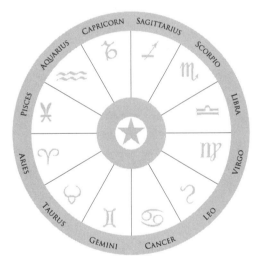

Use the wheel to plot your Venus and then your partner's Mars. Now count the number of blank spaces between these two planets. (Remember, if you find more than five blank spaces, you need to count around the wheel in the opposite direction.)

IF YOUR VENUS AND MARS ARE IN THE SAME SIGN

You undoubtedly have a strong rapport. Each of you can instinctively supply a great deal of what the other is looking for. The physical attraction between you is powerful and not especially likely to diminish over time, regardless of whether that time is spent together or apart. No matter what other differences may lie between you, it's relatively easy to be in one another's company, and, unless either of you has a deep psychological need to be partnered by someone more difficult or challenging, there's every reason to think that your love life together will be forever pleasing.

IF YOUR VENUS AND MARS ARE IN ADJACENT SIGNS

This particular celestial alignment isn't especially auspicious for a red-hot love life. That doesn't mean you can't enjoy one together, but it needs to come via some other cosmic link. Look to see if your partner's Venus is any better matched to your Mars. If it's not, don't despair. It could well be that your horoscopes are simply telling you that you don't have the kind of dangerous "fatal attraction" which can make a partnership sizzle by candlelight but fizzle out most depressingly when the light of reality finally dawns.

IF YOUR VENUS AND MARS ARE ONE BLANK SPACE APART

A most encouraging bond of empathy exists between you, which certainly makes you excellently matched for all creative undertakings. Whether it's similarly encouraging with regard to procreative activity depends on the answers you derived from Test 2. If this has told you that there's a hunger within either party for a more tense dynamic, you must hope that elsewhere in the relationship between your respective horoscopes there exists a nice, meaty bone of contention! Here, your problem (if you want to call it that) is simply that, when the two of you get close, everything is very sweet and tender. If sweetness and tenderness mean more to you than raw expressions of fierce passion, you don't have a problem at all!

IF YOUR VENUS AND MARS
ARE TWO BLANK SPACES APART

You and your partner have the ability to drive each other into a state of absolute frenzy. Those who like their personal love stories to reflect Danielle Steele more than Jackie Collins may find the heat, in this particular kitchen, a little too intense. It isn't, of course, the kitchen that we are interested in here so much as another room, usually found upstairs. Nonetheless, a point well worth remembering is that the force which creates such a steamy scenario in one area of life is highly likely to raise the temperature in other, not so enjoyable ways. The probable price you pay for having such an electric love life is a tendency for you both to short-circuit one another in areas of life where you might prefer to encounter less resistance.

IF YOUR VENUS AND MARS
ARE THREE BLANK SPACES APART

Your relationship is like a fireplace covered in crumpled up newspapers, above which a stack of kindling has been carefully built up. By the side of the fireplace, an endless supply of fuel has been placed. All that's missing is the vital spark to set it off. If this can be supplied by any other factor, no matter how otherwise insignificant in the various cosmic connections between your two horoscopes, you will have a roaring flame that never dies out. You are almost too well suited. You respect and admire each other almost too much. Even if you are a pair of folk who both like a quiet love life, you need just a little friction to set the necessary chemical reaction in motion. Find that, and you've found an ideal partner.

IF YOUR VENUS AND MARS
ARE FOUR BLANK SPACES APART

From a purely physical, totally animalistic point of view, you're not ideally suited. All this really means is that, where some people merely have to glance at one another in order to start a smoldering volcano erupting, you each have to work a little harder at learning how to supply what the other needs. Rather than feel disappointed by this less than glowing celestial report on your romantic potential, think about wine, or olives, or garlic. Acquired tastes are invariably more satisfying in the long run than those which come naturally to us, assuming, of course, that you're both willing to make enough effort to acquire a taste for another.

IF YOUR VENUS AND MARS
ARE FIVE BLANK SPACES APART

The electric currents that race between you and your partner carry an extremely high voltage. Assuming the connections are made correctly, you can transfer a great deal of energy and end up with a tremendously exciting, mutually fulfilling partnership that never loses its power to make you both light up. If, however, the links are loose, the wires are crossed, or the lines are subject to adverse environmental conditions, the relationship can become dangerously volatile. It's even possible that, if you and your partner enjoy life close to the edge, as you will both have to do if you are to make this work, innocent bystanders could end up getting an accidental shock if they unwittingly step into the middle of the highly charged field that the two of you create. All this needs to be monitored, and yet it may be that you're always so busy watching each other with awe, fascination, and hunger that you never feel inclined to worry about it.

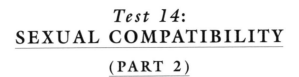

Test 14:
SEXUAL COMPATIBILITY
(PART 2)

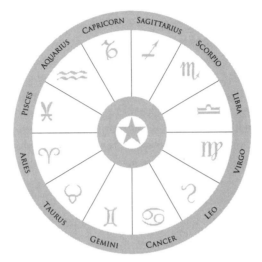

Here, on this wheel, we need to plot your Mars and your partner's Venus. Count around the wheel in the usual way, read the relevant explanation from earlier in the chapter, and then read the conclusion below.

CONCLUSION

You now know a great deal about the relationship between your horoscope and your partner's. If you feel reasonably content that you're astrologically compatible with your partner, read no further. If anything you've read so far has left you worried about your future with a certain person, I ought to stress that there's a great deal more to discover. For one thing, we are working with whole signs and not with degrees of signs, as a professional astrologer would do. For another, the planets Saturn, Jupiter, and Mercury can alter the picture tremendously and without printing tables for these, we can only guess. But if you *do* want to look more closely at your relationship, there's plenty more you can do with the information you've already been given. We haven't, for example, compared your Sun or Moon to your partner's Mars and Venus. Nor have we looked at the link between your Mars and your partner's Mars or Venus and your Venus. By using additional copies of the wheel, you can perform all these tests.

All you need to know is that, as a rule of thumb, it's an easy, encouraging link if the planets are in the same sign, one blank space apart, or three blank spaces apart. It's a challenging link if they are two or five blank spaces apart (but remember that some challenges can be healthy). And it's probably a bit of a nonstarter if the two planets turn out to be in adjacent signs or four blank spaces apart. Good luck!

Chapter Six

PREDICTING
THE
FUTURE

PREDICTING THE FUTURE

THEY say you should always save the best for last. Here, then, is the trick that I expect you've been waiting for me to show you since you first opened the book all that time ago. Thank you for your patience. And, if by chance, you haven't been patient at all and have had the effrontery to skip straight to this section, go away. Read the rest of the book in sequential order and don't you dare come back until you've performed every single exercise!

Honestly. Some people!

OK. Now that I'm hopefully addressing only the diligent reader, let's get down to the business of predicting the future.

You may think that all we've been doing so far is entering a couple of details onto a pretty little circle and counting the spaces between them. Actually, we've been plotting angular relationships between the positions occupied by key celestial bodies on the exact day of your birth. In other words, we've been following precisely the same principles employed by famous stargazers from the Emperor Hadrian to Nostradamus.

We are not going to use the Sun for our predictions, because that's what newspaper astrologers do all the time. There is no other option. When I'm writing in my newspaper column about what your future holds, I can only discuss the Sun; it's the only factor I know about you. But here, however, we now have the luxury of being able to compare the positions of some much more personal planets (such as the Moon and Venus) to the heavyweight outer planets that tend to have such a profound, long-term influence over so many people's lives.

In these forecasts, we're going to paint an outline picture of the challenges you're likely to face between April 2001 and the middle of the year 2003. If that seems like a long way into the future to be looking, don't worry, it will be here soon enough. But if that seems to you like a very reasonable period to be covering because it's the time you are currently living through, thank you. You've just proved my point about how fast the future becomes the present!

MOON AND SATURN

We're going to compare the position of the Moon on your day of birth (that is, your Moon sign) with the position that Saturn is due to occupy in the sky. Saturn entered the sign of Gemini in mid-August 2000. It slips back into Taurus for a few months at the end of 2000, returns to Gemini in April 2001, and then remains in Gemini until June 2003.

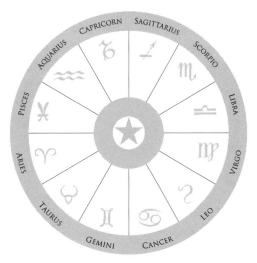

Find the segment labeled Gemini in the wheel. In it, write the word "Saturn" (or, if you want to be mystical, draw a Saturn symbol, which is a letter "h" with the top half of the vertical line crossed through). Now, simply write the word "Moon" or draw a little lunar symbol into the segment appropriate to your Moon sign. If your Moon sign is Gemini, squeeze your Moon into the same segment into which you've already placed Saturn and go on to read Saturn and Moon in the same sign below. Otherwise, find your Saturn and count, counterclockwise, the number of blank spaces between it and your Moon. If you find there are more than five spaces, go back to Saturn and count clockwise.

★ SATURN PASSING THROUGH YOUR MOON SIGN ★

Life for you at the moment is anything but frivolous. For some time, you've been going through what could most politely be called a challenging phase and might less deferentially be referred to as a seemingly endless series of frustrations. You've felt hurt, ignored, or even, at times, abandoned by certain people and organizations.

The cumulative effect has been to render you emotionally numb to the point where perhaps you now feel the world can go ahead and do its worst, for all you care, because you're already so far down you can't get much lower. You have my genuine sympathy, but you also have my genuine reassurance that things are not going to continue like this for very much longer. If they haven't already slowly started to take a turn for the better, they will within a few months.

Meanwhile, you will start to see what so far has often eluded you: the positive side of this debilitating era. You may be down, but you are not out, not by a long shot. And no matter how deprived or ripped off you feel, you really haven't been cheated. It's more that you've been given something whose true value you have yet to appreciate.

Hard though this may be to believe, there will come a day when you look back on all that's currently taking place and see it in a very different light. You'll realize that, though this was a time during which you had to face certain harsh realities and learn several difficult lessons, you also found a new and much more reliable source of inner strength. It was a time when you reached an emotional turning point and stopped looking to others for something that, all along, you knew you really ought to be supplying for yourself. And thus, it was a time in which you grew far more mature, made an essential series of long-overdue decisions, and resolved to set off on the next stage of your journey through life in a very different direction.

It may be a year or so before this perspective is granted, but, once it comes, I promise that you will feel glad of all you went through. For only one thing ever follows a period during which Saturn represses the energy of a person's Moon: a time during which hope is reborn, enthusiasm is regained, and the joy of success is rediscovered.

Saturn opposing
(five blank spaces from)
your Moon

A certain person currently seems to be doing everything within his or her power to make your life difficult. You can hardly believe you've allowed yourself to get so involved with someone so unyielding, unsympathetic, and dominating. Just possibly it's not an individual but an organization of some kind, yet the effect is much the same. You keep feeling crushed, squashed, and stifled, and it seems to be going on week after week.

What have you done to deserve this? What great error of judgement have you made? What possible way is there to alter the situation?

The answer to this last question depends on the answer you feel most inclined to give to the first two. For as long as you feel that somehow it's all your fault, you'll continue to lack the confidence you require to make things better. And in a funny sort of way, it's your sense of guilt, regret, or responsibility which is most directly contributing to this oppressive character's ability to hem you in.

Even if you're normally a person of great strength and independence, you've recently started to behave much more like the kid at school who always got picked on by the class bully. You've had such a draining sense of helplessness that you've virtually invited others to exert their will over your own. The more they've done so, the more the cycle has perpetuated itself. You've become more passive and accepting, while they've grown more outrageously assertive.

What's even more ironic, if you stop to think about it, is that this feeling of being small originally stemmed from your own, seemingly failed, attempt to be big. You sorely wanted to alter a certain person's plan or control a particular sequence of events. It didn't work out as you wished. Thus, the downward spiral began.

The good news is that unlike some celestial influences, which, like antibiotics, have to be allowed to work their natural course, Saturn/Moon oppositions can be conquered and the energy turned around. All you have to do is confront, not the person you feel so cheated by, as the part of yourself that won't take "Yes" for an answer. Force yourself to regain faith and confidence, little by little, day by day. Refuse to be daunted by the occasional setback. Just ensure that each step forward is as big as you dare make it. There will come a time, sooner than you think, when you are able to stand up tall and proud to anyone or anything. At that point, the constant sense of being hopelessly opposed will crumble quicker than a thug before a judge.

★ SATURN INCONJUNCT (FOUR BLANK SPACES FROM) YOUR MOON ★

Issues relating to health and well-being often crop up when Saturn is forming this kind of an alignment to a person's Moon. Note please, that I use the word issues, not problems. I know that you won't jump to the wrong conclusion, but there are some types of people who might. Astrologers soon learn by experience that even a casual mention of the word "health" can be sufficient to make a person's eyes widen with panic. "Why," they wonder, "is my cosmic advisor talking to me about the state of my body? Do the stars foretell some dreadful illness?" Paranoia, rather like flu, is easy to catch and hard to shake off. I therefore want to precede your prediction with a clear promise that there's no reason in the world why anything should go wrong with you, physically or mentally, in the period during which Saturn and the Moon are at this angle to one another. Is that understood? Completely? OK, then. Now I can explain. There's no reason to expect a problem, but there is a reason to expect increased sensitivity to the factors which might, one day, possibly cause a problem if they are not addressed. You may, for example, realize that you've got a habit which is doing you no favors. You may discover that certain foods don't agree with one part of your body, even though your tongue likes the taste. You could recognize the need to do more exercise, to get more sleep, or to supplement your diet with minerals or vitamins. It could also be that the development which brings you to this conclusion is a temporary state of malaise. This could manifest in more than one way, on more than one occasion. Hopefully though, now that you're on the lookout for it, you'll spot more quickly the message that your body has for you, and without becoming neurotic about it, you'll take sensible, reasonable steps to improve the level of care you take of yourself.

I must now address an alternative manifestation of the same astrological influence. Maybe you'll have no such warning symptoms, but the well-being of a loved one might give you cause for concern, and you'll want to "mother" this person and maybe the stress of feeling so responsible for him or her will sap a little of your own strength. I repeat my insistence that we're talking here about being alerted to something minor in plenty of time to take successful, positive action. I also remind you that if you are dealing with someone else's health, no matter how young or old they may be, you must not coddle them to the point that your own health begins to suffer. And now, after all that serious talk, here is something brighter to look forward to. You will discover during this phase that you grow stronger, more able to discipline yourself, more able to see what you truly need, and less inclined to worry unduly about irrelevant fears; all of which will work wonders for your confidence, your ability to succeed, your capacity to make wise choices, and your potential to enjoy life.

★ SATURN TRINE MOON ★
(THREE BLANK SPACES APART)

The current link between your ruler and Saturn is what we astrologers consider to be an especially harmonious one. In theory, you're going through a strengthening process, a period of consolidation, and a time of comparative emotional stability. In practice? Well, that's probably still a pretty fair overall assessment, even if it does rather glibly gloss over a lot of intense daily ups and downs that are also taking place. These, however, are ripples on the surface of a pond that, deep down below the surface, is surprisingly still. You know where you're going, you know why you're going there, and you rightly believe you have a good chance of making it all the way through to your destination. All you really need is consistency of approach, steady effort, and a refusal to be sidetracked by passing dramas. In this regard, you are definitely being helped by a constructive sky and, quite probably, by a constructive person, too.

You're lucky enough, at the moment, to have at least one person in your world who is solid as a rock and sensible, too. His or her advice and support are invaluable. You may feel a little concerned about how you'd manage if this person were suddenly withdrawn for any reason, but really you might as well worry about what you'd do if the Sun were to stop rising each morning. For as long as you really require assistance with your current, most worthwhile endeavors, you're going to find you get it, somehow, somewhere, from someone. And though you may have no need or reason to repay those who now seem to be giving you so much emotional backup, you're also at the moment in a nice position to pass the favor on to other, less centered or less confident characters who, in their turn, also require a bit of support.

You're currently being very kind to an unstable individual, and this sensitivity is much appreciated, even if the gratitude isn't always being very clearly demonstrated. As long as you continue to tread that delicate fine line between caring about and actually taking control of this person's problem, you will eventually have the satisfaction of seeing this person find his or her feet once more. It may sometimes be necessary to apply a little bit of "tough love" by refusing to wipe away every single tear or bail this person out every time he or she makes a mistake, but as long as you balance this with a lot of positive encouragement for your friend's better decisions, all will come out right in the end.

★ SATURN SQUARE MOON ★
(TWO BLANK SPACES APART)

Are you beginning to wonder if your guardian angel has taken an extended vacation and left you in the care of some bumbling apprentice? Do you seem to keep bumping into unforeseen obstacles and stumbling headlong into emotional quagmires, no matter how hard you try to walk carefully? Even if the situation has been going on for some time, it's not a permanent problem, nor have you been abandoned by any protective force. You're just caught in the cosmic crossfire between two celestial influences with different agendas.

The Moon in your personal chart represents your desire to sail sweetly through life on an ocean of emotion; it's the bit of you that wants to go wherever the warmest wind is blowing, following no other chart than your heart. But Saturn is a force that restricts without remorse, and it favors only those who are prepared to accept direction and discipline. Currently, it's forming a tense right angle to your Moon, creating the internal equivalent of storms to port and icebergs to starboard. Suddenly, there's a sense of danger and a growing need to check carefully your internal navigation equipment. The dynamic tension between these heavenly hotshots is making more waves than you can surf without getting seasick. Your luxury cruise on a gorgeous yacht is beginning to feel more like a rough ride on some dingy dinghy.

For now, you have little option other than to seek shelter. But this is not as easy as it sounds, for you are being pulled by a strong current that seems to be leading to anything but a safe harbor. You simply cannot, for the next few weeks, allow your intuition to be stronger than your intellect. If you are not to grow so tired of mounting a constant vigil that you end up being swept overboard by the conflict all around, you must sacrifice a little freedom for the sake of pragmatism.

If this involves swallowing sufficient pride to send out a mayday signal or even suffering the ignominy of being towed back to the nearest port, it's still wiser than trying to pretend you can go it alone. Especially since, once you do let go of whatever goal you feel so reluctant to relinquish, you'll discover that, far from having lost anything you need to keep, you have dropped only a burden you should never have been carrying in the first place. Once free from this misplaced sense of responsibility, you can set out on a new journey, this time with a far more pleasant course to follow and the help of a supportive crew.

★ ## Saturn sextile Moon
(ONE BLANK SPACE APART) ★

Many things in your world may be far from perfect, but at least you're not feeling desperately idealistic about your ideals. Instead of looking at life through rose-colored spectacles, you're wearing your commonsense glasses. You feel able to accept what you're sure you cannot alter, yet not so passive as to put up with what you know can be improved. Your current plan for progress involves a series of stepping stones. First you'll do this, then (opportunity allowing) you'll do that. All of which, in time, should lead to a chance to do something else. Unless, of course, when you reach the next decision point, you see other options. In which case, you will consider them on their merits, trusting that one will prove just right.

All this is why, though there may be big questions that you wouldn't mind having answered about your long-term future, you don't feel too concerned. Something within has already decided it's going to be pretty much OK. It's that, as much as anything else, which is going to be your guarantee that this prophecy comes true.

In light of this, I'd be reluctant to go into too much more detail, even if I had more to say. I wouldn't want to leave you with the impression that too much of what's to come is predestined at a time in your life when it's clear that the power to shape tomorrow rests very much in your own hands. So all I shall add is that you are due, soon, to see some encouraging developments on the domestic front. A key emotional relationship is going to deepen and strengthen. A sense of belonging is going to grow. A feeling that you are surrounded by stable, helpful, wise, and supportive characters is likely to increase significantly.

All this is going to help you find the courage to turn your relationship with a particularly oppressive, dominant force or figure into a more adult arrangement. Instead of feeling afraid to speak your mind, confront authority, or question an unfair code of practice, you're going to become something of a champion of the underdog. As you shake off your fear of being undermined or overlooked and discover what you want to stand up for and why in these next few months, you're going to turn into a quietly confident force to be reckoned with. As fast as you do, the petty fears and insecurities that now occasionally cut across your mood of calm like stray waves of radio interference spoiling a pleasant broadcast will die down to an unobtrusive minimum.

★ SATURN SEMI-SEXTILE MOON ★
(IN THE SIGN NEXT DOOR)

Do you really know the extent of your own strength? Are you fully aware of your greatest weakness? Don't be so sure. During the period in which Saturn forms a semi-sextile to your Moon, you may find that you have to seriously reappraise your own view of yourself. It would seem that you have been propping yourself up by indulging in a certain habit—or by fostering a particular attitude. This attitude or habit pattern is one that you are very fond of. It provides you with much psychological support and reassurance. It may not be at all unhealthy. It may even involve an adherence to high standards. Even so, there is something just a little awkward about the extent to which you use it as a crutch. It's like having a magic potion that you can take any time the world seems as if it were trying to threaten or destabilize you. One sip from the bottle and you are right as rain again. What's wrong with that? Nothing except that, if you want to be a free, fully grown, wise, conscious individual, you can't afford to rely too heavily on anything. Not even something "good." You have to be able to learn to live without it so that if it is ever taken away from you or if you ever find yourself in a situation where it is appropriate to act differently, you are capable of adapting. You don't like the sound of this, do you? You can't see why you *need* to give something up—especially not something that you are keen on and that doesn't really seem to be doing you any harm. That's understandable. But the cosmos has your best interests at heart. *It* wants you to be a free, fully grown, wise, conscious individual, even if *you* don't want to be!

The cosmos can't, of course, force you to become such a person. But it can at least put you in a situation where the opportunity exists. And that's what it is doing now. And it is what it will continue to do for most of the period during which Saturn is forming this 30-degree angle to your Moon. In the process, it will cause you to take a look at your biggest fear. What really winds you up? What is it that you cannot bear the thought of? What kind of event, scenario or situation do you tend to have an unreasonable, disproportionately bad reaction to? And *why?*

You are being asked, by the cosmos, to investigate this tendency within yourself. Because it is *this* tendency that you try to compensate for by leaning so heavily on your favorite, strength-giving attitude or behavior pattern. In order to free yourself from over-dependence on that "bottle of magic potion," you have to find out why you are so inclined to drink from it sometimes ... and *then* you can conquer the need.

Your life can continue much as normal, in most ways, if you want it to during this period. Or it can change dramatically. That's up to you—and how willing you are to learn something about yourself and about your relationship to the world at large. You are going to find yourself periodically encountering issues, situations and people that you don't much care for. You are going to want to alter your circumstances in order to escape this. Or you are going to want to draw even more deeply on that reassuring "psychological bottle." Do either of these things and you may end up feeling forced to instigate major change in your environment. But if, instead, you just decide to work out *what* it is you are so prone to be upset by and why—and if you then decide to develop a way of turning this into something that really doesn't phase or bother you anymore—you can take full advantage of this astrological aspect. You can use it in order to liberate an aspect of your personal potential that will help you achieve spectacular levels of spiritual and material progress in the future.

CONCLUSION

This is the end of the book. If you have arrived here at this page because you have now read everything else, congratulations and thank you. In a moment, I shall explain how to take your newfound expertise in astrology a stage further.

First, though, I must address a word to anyone who is reading this merely because they happen to be having an idle flip through the pages.

If you're standing in a bookshop wondering whether to buy this, stop dithering and get your credit card out. It's a purchase you won't regret.

If you're thumbing through someone else's copy, wondering whether or not you want to borrow this book, don't! You'll only want to keep it forever, and it's not worth spoiling a good friendship for. Buy your own copy instead!

OK. Now, as I'm sure you're aware, there's still an awful lot more to astrology than we've had a chance to cover in this book. You can dedicate a lifetime to studying the art and still only skim the surface. There are some good books by other authors that may well prove worth investing in, and you should also look out for a more advanced book by me called *How to Interpret a Horoscope*.

Make your way through the further reading list at your own pace and don't worry. I haven't recommended anything that isn't easy to read and learn from.

Oh, just one more thing. In the world of astrology there's absolutely no substitute for experience. If you really want to know what makes one horoscope different from another and to avoid the embarrassing mistake of looking at a chart and saying, "Aha!" only to realize, later, that you have gotten excited about some celestial alignment that almost everybody gets born with, you need to draw up and look at lots and lots of horoscopes. Work with your friends' dates of birth. Do your family. Look up famous people's birth details and cast horoscopes for them. Then do the people you loathe and detest; you may learn what it is they all really have in common!

And DO remember to have fun. That's what it's all about.

THE ZODIAC CHARTS

Use these charts to find your Sun sign, Moon sign, Venus sign, and Mars sign

THE ZODIAC CHARTS

The charts that follow may look terrifyingly complex, but they are simplicity itself to use.

1. Find your year of birth.

2. Now find the period that encompasses your date of birth. If you don't see your date of birth listed, go to the nearest date <u>before</u> the day when you were born. You've now found your Sun sign, Moon sign, Venus sign, or Mars sign, depending on which chart you are looking at.

3. Look to the right of that date and you will see the name of the sign of the zodiac. For example, if you were born on May 10, 1952, these tables show that the Sun was in Taurus from April 20 (at 03:37) until May 21 (at 03:04).

WHY HAVE THESE TABLES GOT TIMES OF DAY ON THEM?

You need only worry about the times given on these tables if your actual date of birth appears on the list. The dates and times given show the precise moment when the celestial body in question entered each zodiac sign. If you were born one minute earlier, the zodiac sign you need is the previous zodiac sign.

However, the times given are all GMT. In the United States and Canada you must add from three and a half to ten hours to your birth time to translate it to GMT. Thus if you were born in New York, which is EST, you would add five hours to your birth time before consulting the charts. In Newfoundland you would add three and a half, in Hawaii ten.

If you were born in summer during daylight savings time, when the clocks were one hour forward, then you would have to subtract one hour.

These charts go up to the year 2000. Please, though, think twice about calculating the horoscopes of children under 12. The interpretations in this book are intended only for adults. The art of reading a child's horoscope properly is subtly but crucially different. It deserves a book of its own and hopefully, one day, I will write one. Till then, if you must draw up a chart for a child, do it in a spirit of experimentation, not authority.

SUN CHARTS

1925
20 Jan	13.20	Aq
19 Feb	03.43	Pi
21 Mar	03.12	Ar
20 Apr	14.51	Ta
21 May	14.33	Ge
21 Jun	22.50	Ca
23 Jul	09.45	Le
23 Aug	16.33	Vi
23 Sep	13.44	Li
23 Oct	22.32	Sc
22 Nov	19.36	Sa
22 Dec	08.37	Cp

1926
20 Jan	19.13	Aq
19 Feb	09.35	Pi
21 Mar	09.01	Ar
20 Apr	20.36	Ta
21 May	20.15	Ge
22 Jun	04.30	Ca
23 Jul	15.25	Le
23 Aug	22.14	Vi
23 Sep	19.26	Li
24 Oct	04.18	Sc
23 Nov	01.28	Sa
22 Dec	14.33	Cp

1927
21 Jan	01.12	Aq
19 Feb	15.34	Pi
21 Mar	14.59	Ar
21 Apr	02.32	Ta
22 May	02.08	Ge
22 Jun	10.22	Ca
23 Jul	21.17	Le
24 Aug	04.06	Vi
24 Sep	01.17	Li
24 Oct	10.07	Sc
23 Nov	07.14	Sa
22 Dec	20.19	Cp

1928
21 Jan	06.57	Aq
19 Feb	21.19	Pi
20 Mar	20.44	Ar
20 Apr	08.17	Ta
21 May	07.52	Ge
21 Jun	16.06	Ca
23 Jul	03.02	Le
23 Aug	09.53	Vi
23 Sep	07.06	Li
23 Oct	15.55	Sc
22 Nov	13.01	Sa
22 Dec	02.04	Cp

1929
20 Jan	12.42	Aq
19 Feb	03.07	Pi
21 Mar	02.35	Ar
20 Apr	14.10	Ta
21 May	13.48	Ge
21 Jun	22.01	Ca
23 Jul	08.54	Le
23 Aug	15.41	Vi
23 Sep	12.52	Li
23 Oct	21.42	Sc
22 Nov	18.48	Sa
22 Dec	07.53	Cp

1930
20 Jan	18.33	Aq
19 Feb	08.59	Pi
21 Mar	08.29	Ar
20 Apr	20.06	Ta
21 May	19.42	Ge
22 Jun	03.53	Ca
23 Jul	14.42	Le
23 Aug	21.27	Vi
23 Sep	18.36	Li
24 Oct	03.26	Sc
23 Nov	00.35	Sa
22 Dec	13.40	Cp

1931
21 Jan	00.18	Aq
19 Feb	14.40	Pi
21 Mar	14.06	Ar
21 Apr	01.40	Ta
22 May	01.15	Ge
22 Jun	09.28	Ca
23 Jul	20.21	Le
24 Aug	03.10	Vi
24 Sep	00.24	Li
24 Oct	09.16	Sc
23 Nov	06.25	Sa
22 Dec	19.30	Cp

1932
21 Jan	06.07	Aq
19 Feb	20.29	Pi
20 Mar	19.54	Ar
20 Apr	07.28	Ta
21 May	07.06	Ge
21 Jun	15.22	Ca
23 Jul	02.18	Le
23 Aug	09.06	Vi
23 Sep	06.16	Li
23 Oct	15.04	Sc
22 Nov	12.10	Sa
22 Dec	01.14	Cp

1933
20 Jan	11.53	Aq
19 Feb	02.16	Pi
21 Mar	01.43	Ar
20 Apr	13.18	Ta
21 May	12.57	Ge
21 Jun	21.12	Ca
23 Jul	08.06	Le
23 Aug	14.52	Vi
23 Sep	12.01	Li
23 Oct	20.48	Sc
22 Nov	17.54	Sa
22 Dec	06.58	Cp

1934
20 Jan	17.37	Aq
19 Feb	08.02	Pi
21 Mar	07.28	Ar
20 Apr	19.00	Ta
21 May	18.35	Ge
22 Jun	02.48	Ca
23 Jul	13.42	Le
23 Aug	20.32	Vi
23 Sep	17.45	Li
24 Oct	02.36	Sc
22 Nov	23.44	Sa
22 Dec	12.50	Cp

1935
20 Jan	23.29	Aq
19 Feb	13.52	Pi
21 Mar	13.18	Ar
21 Apr	00.50	Ta
22 May	00.25	Ge
22 Jun	08.38	Ca
23 Jul	19.33	Le
24 Aug	02.24	Vi
23 Sep	23.38	Li
24 Oct	08.29	Sc
23 Nov	05.35	Sa
22 Dec	18.37	Cp

1936
21 Jan	05.12	Aq
19 Feb	19.33	Pi
20 Mar	18.58	Ar
20 Apr	06.31	Ta
21 May	06.07	Ge
21 Jun	14.22	Ca
23 Jul	01.18	Le
23 Aug	08.11	Vi
23 Sep	05.26	Li
23 Oct	14.18	Sc
22 Nov	11.26	Sa
22 Dec	00.27	Cp

1937
20 Jan	11.01	Aq
19 Feb	01.21	Pi
21 Mar	00.45	Ar
20 Apr	12.19	Ta
21 May	11.57	Ge
21 Jun	20.12	Ca
23 Jul	07.07	Le
23 Aug	13.58	Vi
23 Sep	11.13	Li
23 Oct	20.06	Sc
22 Nov	17.17	Sa
22 Dec	06.22	Cp

1938
20 Jan	16.59	Aq
19 Feb	07.20	Pi
21 Mar	06.43	Ar
20 Apr	18.15	Ta
21 May	17.50	Ge
22 Jun	02.03	Ca
23 Jul	12.57	Le
23 Aug	19.46	Vi
23 Sep	16.59	Li
24 Oct	01.54	Sc
22 Nov	23.03	Sa
22 Dec	12.14	Cp

1939
20 Jan	22.51	Aq
19 Feb	13.09	Pi
21 Mar	12.28	Ar
20 Apr	23.55	Ta
21 May	23.27	Ge
22 Jun	07.39	Ca
23 Jul	18.37	Le
24 Aug	01.31	Vi
23 Sep	22.50	Li
24 Oct	07.46	Sc
23 Nov	04.59	Sa
22 Dec	18.06	Cp

1940
21 Jan	04.44	Aq
19 Feb	19.04	Pi
20 Mar	18.24	Ar
20 Apr	05.51	Ta
21 May	05.29	Ge
21 Jun	13.36	Ca
23 Jul	00.34	Le
23 Aug	07.28	Vi
23 Sep	04.46	Li
23 Oct	13.39	Sc
22 Nov	10.49	Sa
21 Dec	23.55	Cp

1941
20 Jan	10.33	Aq
19 Feb	00.56	Pi
21 Mar	00.20	Ar
20 Apr	11.50	Ta
21 May	11.23	Ge
21 Jun	19.33	Ca
23 Jul	06.26	Le
23 Aug	13.17	Vi
23 Sep	10.33	Li
23 Oct	19.27	Sc
22 Nov	16.38	Sa
22 Dec	05.45	Cp

1942
20 Jan	16.24	Aq
19 Feb	06.47	Pi
21 Mar	06.11	Ar
20 Apr	17.39	Ta
21 May	17.09	Ge
22 Jun	01.16	Ca
23 Jul	12.07	Le
23 Aug	18.58	Vi
23 Sep	16.17	Li
24 Oct	01.15	Sc
22 Nov	22.30	Sa
22 Dec	11.40	Cp

1943
20 Jan	22.19	Aq
19 Feb	12.40	Pi
21 Mar	12.03	Ar
20 Apr	23.31	Ta
21 May	23.03	Ge
22 Jun	07.12	Ca
23 Jul	18.04	Le
24 Aug	00.55	Vi
24 Sep	22.12	Li
24 Oct	07.08	Sc
23 Nov	04.22	Sa
22 Dec	17.29	Cp

1944
21 Jan	04.07	Aq
19 Feb	18.27	Pi
20 Mar	17.48	Ar
20 Apr	05.18	Ta
21 May	04.51	Ge
21 Jun	13.02	Ca
22 Jul	23.56	Le
23 Aug	06.47	Vi
23 Sep	04.02	Li
23 Oct	12.56	Sc
22 Nov	10.08	Sa
22 Dec	23.15	Cp

1945
20 Jan	09.54	Aq
19 Feb	00.15	Pi
20 Mar	23.37	Ar
20 Apr	11.07	Ta
21 May	10.40	Ge
21 Jun	18.52	Ca
23 Jul	05.45	Le
23 Aug	12.35	Vi
23 Sep	09.50	Li
23 Oct	18.43	Sc
22 Nov	15.55	Sa
22 Dec	05.04	Cp

1946
20 Jan	15.45	Aq
19 Feb	06.08	Pi
21 Mar	05.33	Ar
20 Apr	17.02	Ta
21 May	16.34	Ge
22 Jun	00.44	Ca
23 Jul	11.37	Le
23 Aug	18.26	Vi
23 Sep	15.41	Li
24 Oct	00.35	Sc
22 Nov	21.47	Sa
22 Dec	10.53	Cp

1947
20 Jan	21.32	Aq
19 Feb	11.52	Pi
21 Mar	11.13	Ar
20 Apr	22.39	Ta
21 May	22.09	Ge
22 Jun	06.19	Ca
23 Jul	17.14	Le
24 Aug	00.09	Vi
23 Sep	21.29	Li
24 Oct	06.26	Sc
23 Nov	03.38	Sa
22 Dec	16.43	Cp

1948
21 Jan	03.19	Aq
19 Feb	17.37	Pi
20 Mar	16.57	Ar
20 Apr	04.25	Ta
21 May	03.57	Ge
21 Jun	12.11	Ca
22 Jul	23.08	Le
23 Aug	06.03	Vi
23 Sep	03.22	Li
23 Oct	12.18	Sc
22 Nov	09.29	Sa
21 Dec	22.34	Cp

1949
20 Jan	09.09	Aq
18 Feb	23.27	Pi
20 Mar	22.48	Ar
20 Apr	10.17	Ta
21 May	09.51	Ge
21 Jun	18.03	Ca
23 Jul	04.57	Le
23 Aug	11.48	Vi
23 Sep	09.06	Li
23 Oct	18.03	Sc
22 Nov	15.16	Sa
22 Dec	04.23	Cp

1950			1951			1952			1953			1954		
20 Jan	15.00	Aq	20 Jan	20.52	Aq	21 Jan	02.38	Aq	20 Jan	08.22	Aq	20 Jan	14.11	Aq
19 Feb	05.18	Pi	19 Feb	11.10	Pi	19 Feb	16.57	Pi	18 Feb	22.41	Pi	19 Feb	04.32	Pi
21 Mar	04.35	Ar	21 Mar	10.26	Ar	20 Mar	16.14	Ar	20 Mar	22.01	Ar	21 Mar	03.53	Ar
20 Apr	15.59	Ta	20 Apr	21.48	Ta	20 Apr	03.37	Ta	20 Apr	09.26	Ta	20 Apr	15.19	Ta
21 May	15.27	Ge	21 May	21.15	Ge	21 May	03.04	Ge	21 May	08.53	Ge	21 May	14.47	Ge
21 Jun	23.36	Ca	22 Jun	05.25	Ca	21 Jun	11.12	Ca	21 Jun	16.59	Ca	21 Jun	22.54	Ca
23 Jul	10.30	Le	23 Jul	16.21	Le	22 Jul	22.08	Le	23 Jul	03.52	Le	23 Jul	09.45	Le
23 Aug	17.23	Vi	23 Aug	23.16	Vi	23 Aug	05.03	Vi	23 Aug	10.45	Vi	23 Aug	16.36	Vi
23 Sep	14.44	Li	23 Sep	20.37	Li	23 Sep	02.24	Li	23 Sep	08.06	Li	23 Sep	13.55	Li
23 Oct	23.45	Sc	24 Oct	05.36	Sc	23 Oct	11.23	Sc	23 Oct	17.06	Sc	23 Oct	22.57	Sc
22 Nov	21.03	Sa	23 Nov	02.51	Sa	22 Nov	08.36	Sa	22 Nov	14.22	Sa	22 Nov	20.14	Sa
22 Dec	10.14	Cp	22 Dec	16.00	Cp	21 Dec	21.44	Cp	22 Dec	03.32	Cp	22 Dec	09.25	Cp

1955			1956			1957			1958			1959		
20 Jan	20.02	Aq	21 Jan	01.49	Aq	20 Jan	07.39	Aq	20 Jan	13.29	Aq	20 Jan	19.19	Aq
19 Feb	10.19	Pi	19 Feb	16.05	Pi	18 Feb	21.58	Pi	19 Feb	03.49	Pi	19 Feb	09.38	Pi
21 Mar	09.35	Ar	20 Mar	15.21	Ar	20 Mar	21.16	Ar	21 Mar	03.06	Ar	21 Mar	08.55	Ar
20 Apr	20.58	Ta	20 Apr	02.44	Ta	20 Apr	08.41	Ta	20 Apr	14.27	Ta	20 Apr	20.17	Ta
21 May	20.24	Ge	21 May	02.12	Ge	21 May	08.10	Ge	21 May	13.51	Ge	21 May	19.42	Ge
22 Jun	04.31	Ca	21 Jun	10.24	Ca	21 Jun	16.20	Ca	21 Jun	21.57	Ca	22 Jun	03.50	Ca
23 Jul	15.25	Le	22 Jul	21.20	Le	23 Jul	03.15	Le	23 Jul	08.51	Le	23 Jul	14.45	Le
23 Aug	22.19	Vi	23 Aug	04.15	Vi	23 Aug	10.08	Vi	23 Aug	15.46	Vi	23 Aug	21.44	Vi
23 Sep	19.41	Li	23 Sep	01.35	Li	23 Sep	07.26	Li	23 Sep	13.09	Li	23 Sep	19.09	Li
24 Oct	04.43	Sc	23 Oct	10.34	Sc	23 Oct	16.24	Sc	23 Oct	22.12	Sc	24 Oct	04.11	Sc
23 Nov	02.01	Sa	22 Nov	07.50	Sa	22 Nov	13.39	Sa	22 Nov	19.29	Sa	23 Nov	01.27	Sa
22 Dec	15.11	Cp	21 Dec	20.59	Cp	22 Dec	02.49	Cp	22 Dec	08.40	Cp	22 Dec	14.34	Cp

1960			1961			1962			1963			1964		
21 Jan	01.10	Aq	20 Jan	07.02	Aq	20 Jan	12.58	Aq	20 Jan	18.54	Aq	21 Jan	00.41	Aq
19 Feb	15.26	Pi	18 Feb	21.17	Pi	19 Feb	03.15	Pi	19 Feb	09.09	Pi	19 Feb	14.58	Pi
20 Mar	14.43	Ar	20 Mar	20.32	Ar	21 Mar	02.30	Ar	21 Mar	08.20	Ar	20 Mar	14.10	Ar
20 Apr	02.06	Ta	20 Apr	07.55	Ta	20 Apr	13.51	Ta	20 Apr	19.36	Ta	20 Apr	01.27	Ta
21 May	01.33	Ge	21 May	07.22	Ge	21 May	13.16	Ge	21 May	18.58	Ge	21 May	00.50	Ge
21 Jun	09.42	Ca	21 Jun	15.30	Ca	21 Jun	21.24	Ca	22 Jun	03.04	Ca	21 Jun	08.57	Ca
22 Jul	20.38	Le	23 Jul	02.24	Le	23 Jul	08.18	Le	23 Jul	13.59	Le	22 Jul	19.53	Le
23 Aug	03.35	Vi	23 Aug	09.19	Vi	23 Aug	15.13	Vi	23 Aug	20.58	Vi	23 Aug	02.51	Vi
23 Sep	00.59	Li	23 Sep	06.43	Li	23 Sep	12.35	Li	23 Sep	18.24	Li	23 Sep	00.17	Li
23 Oct	10.02	Sc	23 Oct	15.48	Sc	23 Oct	21.40	Sc	24 Oct	03.29	Sc	23 Oct	09.21	Sc
22 Nov	07.19	Sa	22 Nov	13.08	Sa	22 Nov	19.02	Sa	23 Nov	00.50	Sa	22 Nov	06.39	Sa
21 Dec	20.26	Cp	22 Dec	02.20	Cp	22 Dec	08.15	Cp	22 Dec	14.02	Cp	21 Dec	19.50	Cp

1965			1966			1967			1968			1969		
20 Jan	06.29	Aq	20 Jan	12.20	Aq	20 Jan	18.08	Aq	20 Jan	23.54	Aq	20 Jan	05.39	Aq
18 Feb	20.48	Pi	19 Feb	02.38	Pi	19 Feb	08.24	Pi	19 Feb	14.09	Pi	18 Feb	19.55	Pi
20 Mar	20.05	Ar	21 Mar	01.53	Ar	21 Mar	07.37	Ar	20 Mar	13.22	Ar	20 Mar	19.08	Ar
20 Apr	07.26	Ta	20 Apr	13.12	Ta	20 Apr	18.55	Ta	20 Apr	00.41	Ta	20 Apr	06.27	Ta
21 May	06.50	Ge	21 May	12.32	Ge	21 May	18.18	Ge	21 May	00.06	Ge	21 May	05.50	Ge
21 Jun	14.56	Ca	21 Jun	20.33	Ca	22 Jun	02.23	Ca	21 Jun	08.13	Ca	21 Jun	13.55	Ca
23 Jul	01.48	Le	23 Jul	07.24	Le	23 Jul	13.16	Le	22 Jul	19.08	Le	23 Jul	00.48	Le
23 Aug	08.43	Vi	23 Aug	14.18	Vi	23 Aug	20.12	Vi	23 Aug	02.03	Vi	23 Aug	07.44	Vi
23 Sep	06.06	Li	23 Sep	11.44	Li	23 Sep	17.38	Li	22 Sep	23.26	Li	23 Sep	05.07	Li
23 Oct	15.10	Sc	23 Oct	20.51	Sc	24 Oct	02.44	Sc	23 Oct	08.30	Sc	23 Oct	14.11	Sc
22 Nov	12.29	Sa	22 Nov	18.14	Sa	23 Nov	00.05	Sa	22 Nov	05.49	Sa	22 Nov	11.31	Sa
22 Dec	01.41	Cp	22 Dec	07.29	Cp	22 Dec	13.17	Cp	21 Dec	19.00	Cp	22 Dec	00.44	Cp

1970			1971			1972			1973			1974		
20 Jan	11.24	Aq	20 Jan	17.13	Aq	20 Jan	22.59	Aq	20 Jan	04.48	Aq	20 Jan	10.46	Aq
19 Feb	01.42	Pi	19 Feb	07.27	Pi	19 Feb	13.12	Pi	18 Feb	19.01	Pi	19 Feb	00.59	Pi
21 Mar	00.57	Ar	21 Mar	06.38	Ar	20 Mar	12.22	Ar	20 Mar	18.13	Ar	21 Mar	00.07	Ar
20 Apr	12.15	Ta	20 Apr	17.54	Ta	19 Apr	23.38	Ta	20 Apr	05.30	Ta	20 Apr	11.19	Ta
21 May	11.37	Ge	21 May	17.15	Ge	20 May	22.59	Ge	21 May	04.54	Ge	21 May	10.36	Ge
21 Jun	19.43	Ca	22 Jun	01.20	Ca	21 Jun	07.06	Ca	21 Jun	13.01	Ca	21 Jun	18.38	Ca
23 Jul	06.37	Le	23 Jul	12.15	Le	22 Jul	18.03	Le	22 Jul	23.55	Le	23 Jul	05.30	Le
23 Aug	13.34	Vi	23 Aug	19.15	Vi	23 Aug	01.03	Vi	23 Aug	06.54	Vi	23 Aug	12.29	Vi
23 Sep	10.59	Li	23 Sep	16.45	Li	22 Sep	22.33	Li	23 Sep	04.21	Li	23 Sep	09.59	Li
23 Oct	20.05	Sc	24 Oct	01.53	Sc	23 Oct	07.42	Sc	23 Oct	13.30	Sc	23 Oct	19.11	Sc
22 Nov	17.25	Sa	22 Nov	23.15	Sa	22 Nov	05.03	Sa	22 Nov	10.54	Sa	22 Nov	16.39	Sa
22 Dec	06.36	Cp	22 Dec	12.24	Cp	21 Dec	18.13	Cp	22 Dec	00.08	Cp	22 Dec	05.56	Cp

1975			1976			1977			1978			1979		
20 Jan	16.37	Aq	20 Jan	22.25	Aq	20 Jan	04.15	Aq	20 Jan	10.04	Aq	20 Jan	15.59	Aq
19 Feb	06.50	Pi	19 Feb	12.40	Pi	18 Feb	18.31	Pi	19 Feb	00.21	Pi	19 Feb	06.13	Pi
21 Mar	05.57	Ar	20 Mar	11.50	Ar	20 Mar	17.42	Ar	20 Mar	23.34	Ar	21 Mar	05.22	Ar
20 Apr	17.07	Ta	19 Apr	23.03	Ta	20 Apr	04.57	Ta	20 Apr	10.50	Ta	20 Apr	16.35	Ta
21 May	16.24	Ge	20 May	22.21	Ge	21 May	04.14	Ge	21 May	10.09	Ge	21 May	15.54	Ge
22 Jun	00.26	Ca	21 Jun	06.24	Ca	21 Jun	12.14	Ca	21 Jun	18.10	Ca	21 Jun	23.56	Ca
23 Jul	11.22	Le	22 Jul	17.18	Le	22 Jul	23.04	Le	23 Jul	05.00	Le	23 Jul	10.49	Le
23 Aug	18.24	Vi	23 Aug	00.18	Vi	23 Aug	06.00	Vi	23 Aug	11.57	Vi	23 Aug	17.47	Vi
23 Sep	15.55	Li	23 Sep	21.48	Li	23 Sep	03.30	Li	23 Sep	09.26	Li	23 Sep	15.17	Li
24 Oct	02.06	Sc	23 Oct	06.58	Sc	23 Oct	12.41	Sc	23 Oct	18.37	Sc	24 Oct	00.28	Sc
22 Nov	22.31	Sa	22 Nov	04.22	Sa	22 Nov	10.07	Sa	22 Nov	16.05	Sa	22 Nov	21.55	Sa
22 Dec	11.46	Cp	21 Dec	17.36	Cp	21 Dec	23.24	Cp	22 Dec	05.21	Cp	22 Dec	11.10	Cp

1980

20 Jan	21.49	Aq
19 Feb	12.02	Pi
20 Mar	11.10	Ar
19 Apr	22.23	Ta
20 May	21.42	Ge
21 Jun	05.47	Ca
22 Jul	16.42	Le
22 Aug	23.41	Vi
22 Sep	21.09	Li
23 Oct	06.18	Sc
22 Nov	03.42	Sa
21 Dec	16.56	Cp

1981

20 Jan	03.36	Aq
18 Feb	17.52	Pi
20 Mar	17.03	Ar
20 Apr	04.19	Ta
21 May	03.39	Ge
21 Jun	11.45	Ca
22 Jul	22.40	Le
23 Aug	05.38	Vi
23 Sep	03.05	Li
23 Oct	12.13	Sc
22 Nov	09.36	Sa
21 Dec	22.51	Cp

1982

20 Jan	09.31	Aq
18 Feb	23.47	Pi
20 Mar	22.56	Ar
20 Apr	10.07	Ta
21 May	09.23	Ge
21 Jun	17.23	Ca
23 Jul	04.16	Le
23 Aug	11.15	Vi
23 Sep	08.47	Li
23 Oct	17.58	Sc
22 Nov	15.24	Sa
22 Dec	04.39	Cp

1983

20 Jan	15.17	Aq
19 Feb	05.31	Pi
21 Mar	04.39	Ar
20 Apr	15.50	Ta
21 May	15.06	Ge
21 Jun	23.09	Ca
23 Jul	10.04	Le
23 Aug	17.08	Vi
23 Sep	14.42	Li
23 Oct	23.54	Sc
22 Nov	21.19	Sa
22 Dec	10.30	Cp

1984

20 Jan	21.05	Aq
19 Feb	11.16	Pi
20 Mar	10.24	Ar
19 Apr	21.38	Ta
20 May	20.58	Ge
21 Jun	05.02	Ca
22 Jul	15.58	Le
22 Aug	23.00	Vi
22 Sep	20.33	Li
23 Oct	05.46	Sc
22 Nov	03.11	Sa
21 Dec	16.23	Cp

1985

20 Jan	02.58	Aq
18 Feb	17.08	Pi
20 Mar	16.14	Ar
20 Apr	03.26	Ta
21 May	02.43	Ge
21 Jun	10.44	Ca
22 Jul	21.37	Le
23 Aug	04.36	Vi
23 Sep	02.08	Li
23 Oct	11.22	Sc
22 Nov	08.51	Sa
21 Dec	22.08	Cp

1986

20 Jan	08.47	Aq
18 Feb	22.58	Pi
20 Mar	22.03	Ar
20 Apr	09.12	Ta
21 May	08.28	Ge
21 Jun	16.30	Ca
23 Jul	03.25	Le
23 Aug	10.26	Vi
23 Sep	07.59	Li
23 Oct	17.14	Sc
22 Nov	14.45	Sa
22 Dec	04.03	Cp

1987

20 Jan	14.41	Aq
19 Feb	04.50	Pi
21 Mar	03.52	Ar
20 Apr	14.57	Ta
21 May	14.10	Ge
21 Jun	22.11	Ca
23 Jul	09.06	Le
23 Aug	16.10	Vi
23 Sep	13.45	Li
23 Oct	23.01	Sc
22 Nov	20.30	Sa
22 Dec	09.46	Cp

1988

20 Jan	20.25	Aq
19 Feb	10.35	Pi
20 Mar	09.39	Ar
19 Apr	20.45	Ta
20 May	19.57	Ge
21 Jun	01.49	Ca
22 Jul	14.51	Le
22 Aug	21.54	Vi
22 Sep	19.29	Li
23 Oct	04.45	Sc
22 Nov	02.12	Sa
21 Dec	15.28	Cp

1989

20 Jan	02.07	Aq
18 Feb	16.21	Pi
20 Mar	15.28	Ar
20 Apr	02.39	Ta
21 May	01.53	Ge
21 Jun	09.53	Ca
22 Jul	20.46	Le
23 Aug	03.46	Vi
23 Sep	01.20	Li
23 Oct	10.35	Sc
22 Nov	08.05	Sa
21 Dec	21.22	Cp

1990

20 Jan	08.02	Aq
18 Feb	22.14	Pi
20 Mar	21.19	Ar
20 Apr	08.26	Ta
21 May	07.37	Ge
21 Jun	15.33	Ca
23 Jul	02.22	Le
23 Aug	09.21	Vi
23 Sep	06.56	Li
23 Oct	16.14	Sc
22 Nov	13.47	Sa
22 Dec	03.07	Cp

1991

20 Jan	13.47	Aq
19 Feb	03.59	Pi
21 Mar	03.02	Ar
20 Apr	14.09	Ta
21 May	13.20	Ge
21 Jun	21.19	Ca
23 Jul	08.11	Le
23 Aug	15.13	Vi
23 Sep	12.48	Li
23 Oct	22.05	Sc
22 Nov	19.36	Sa
22 Dec	08.54	Cp

1992

20 Jan	19.33	Aq
19 Feb	09.44	Pi
20 Mar	08.48	Ar
19 Apr	19.57	Ta
20 May	19.12	Ge
21 Jun	03.14	Ca
22 Jul	14.09	Le
22 Aug	21.10	Vi
22 Sep	18.43	Li
23 Oct	03.57	Sc
22 Nov	01.26	Sa
21 Dec	14.43	Cp

1993

20 Jan	01.23	Aq
18 Feb	15.35	Pi
20 Mar	14.41	Ar
20 Apr	01.49	Ta
21 May	01.01	Ge
21 Jun	08.59	Ca
22 Jul	19.51	Le
23 Aug	02.51	Vi
23 Sep	00.23	Li
23 Oct	09.37	Sc
22 Nov	07.07	Sa
21 Dec	20.26	Cp

1994

20 Jan	07.08	Aq
18 Feb	21.22	Pi
20 Mar	20.28	Ar
20 Apr	07.36	Ta
21 May	06.48	Ge
21 Jun	14.48	Ca
23 Jul	01.41	Le
23 Aug	08.44	Vi
23 Sep	06.19	Li
23 Oct	15.36	Sc
22 Nov	13.06	Sa
22 Dec	02.23	Cp

1995

20 Jan	13.01	Aq
19 Feb	03.11	Pi
21 Mar	02.14	Ar
20 Apr	13.21	Ta
21 May	12.34	Ge
21 Jun	20.34	Ca
23 Jul	07.30	Le
23 Aug	14.35	Vi
23 Sep	12.13	Li
23 Oct	21.32	Sc
22 Nov	19.02	Sa
22 Dec	08.17	Cp

1996

20 Jan	18.53	Aq
19 Feb	09.01	Pi
20 Mar	08.03	Ar
19 Apr	19.10	Ta
20 May	18.23	Ge
21 Jun	02.24	Ca
22 Jul	13.19	Le
22 Aug	20.23	Vi
22 Sep	18.00	Li
23 Oct	03.19	Sc
22 Nov	00.50	Sa
21 Dec	14.06	Cp

1997

20 Jan	00.43	Aq
18 Feb	14.52	Pi
20 Mar	13.55	Ar
20 Apr	01.03	Ta
21 May	00.18	Ge
21 Jun	08.20	Ca
22 Jul	19.16	Le
23 Aug	02.19	Vi
22 Sep	23.56	Li
23 Oct	09.15	Sc
22 Nov	06.48	Sa
21 Dec	20.07	Cp

1998

20 Jan	06.46	Aq
18 Feb	20.55	Pi
20 Mar	19.55	Ar
20 Apr	06.57	Ta
21 May	06.05	Ge
21 Jun	14.02	Ca
23 Jul	00.56	Le
23 Aug	07.59	Vi
23 Sep	05.37	Li
23 Oct	14.59	Sc
22 Nov	12.35	Sa
22 Dec	01.57	Cp

1999

20 Jan	12.38	Aq
19 Feb	02.47	Pi
21 Mar	01.46	Ar
20 Apr	12.46	Ta
21 May	11.53	Ge
21 Jun	19.49	Ca
23 Jul	06.44	Le
23 Aug	13.51	Vi
23 Sep	11.32	Li
23 Oct	20.53	Sc
22 Nov	18.25	Sa
22 Dec	07.44	Cp

2000

20 Jan	18.24	Aq
19 Feb	08.34	Pi
20 Mar	07.36	Ar
19 Apr	18.40	Ta
20 May	17.50	Ge
21 Jun	01.48	Ca
22 Jul	12.43	Le
22 Aug	19.49	Vi
22 Sep	17.28	Li
23 Oct	02.48	Sc
22 Nov	00.20	Sa
21 Dec	13.38	Cp

MOON CHARTS

January 1925	
1st	3:01 am Aries
3rd	11:36 am Taurus
5th	10:54 pm Gemini
8th	11:34 am Cancer
11th	0:14 am Leo
13th	11:51 am Virgo
15th	9:31 pm Libra
18th	4:08 am Scorpio
20th	7:29 am Sagittarius
22nd	8:20 am Capricorn
24th	8:11 am Aquarius
26th	8:50 am Pisces
28th	12:05 pm Aries
30th	7:03 pm Taurus

February 1925	
2nd	5:35 am Gemini
4th	6:11 pm Cancer
7th	6:49 am Leo
9th	5:60 pm Virgo
12th	3:05 am Libra
14th	9:51 am Scorpio
16th	2:24 pm Sagittarius
18th	5:00 pm Capricorn
20th	6:21 pm Aquarius
22nd	7:37 pm Pisces
24th	10:22 pm Aries
27th	4:07 am Taurus

March 1925	
1st	1:29 pm Gemini
4th	1:37 am Cancer
6th	2:22 pm Leo
9th	1:24 am Virgo
11th	9:42 am Libra
13th	3:36 pm Scorpio
15th	7:51 pm Sagittarius
17th	11:07 pm Capricorn
20th	1:51 am Aquarius
22nd	4:34 am Pisces
24th	8:06 am Aries
26th	1:39 pm Taurus
28th	10:09 pm Gemini
31st	9:44 am Cancer

April 1925	
2nd	10:33 pm Leo
5th	9:52 am Virgo
7th	6:02 pm Libra
9th	11:04 pm Scorpio
12th	2:06 am Sagittarius
14th	4:33 am Capricorn
16th	7:25 am Aquarius
18th	11:04 am Pisces
20th	3:46 pm Aries
22nd	10:01 pm Taurus
25th	6:35 am Gemini
27th	5:47 pm Cancer
30th	6:35 am Leo

May 1925	
2nd	6:35 pm Virgo
5th	3:24 am Libra
7th	8:19 am Scorpio
9th	10:27 am Sagittarius
11th	11:32 am Capricorn
13th	1:11 pm Aquarius
15th	4:26 pm Pisces
17th	9:35 pm Aries
20th	4:42 am Taurus
22nd	1:53 pm Gemini
25th	1:07 am Cancer
27th	1:59 pm Leo
30th	2:34 am Virgo

June 1925	
1st	12:24 pm Libra
3rd	6:17 pm Scorpio
5th	8:31 pm Sagittarius
7th	8:45 pm Capricorn
9th	8:56 pm Aquarius
11th	10:41 pm Pisces
14th	3:06 am Aries
16th	10:19 am Taurus
18th	7:58 pm Gemini
21st	7:38 am Cancer
23rd	8:30 pm Leo
26th	9:19 am Virgo
28th	8:11 pm Libra

July 1925	
1st	3:29 am Scorpio
3rd	6:50 am Sagittarius
5th	7:22 am Capricorn
7th	6:51 am Aquarius
9th	7:10 am Pisces
11th	9:59 am Aries
13th	4:10 pm Taurus
16th	1:39 am Gemini
18th	1:35 pm Cancer
21st	2:33 am Leo
23rd	3:15 pm Virgo
26th	2:28 am Libra
28th	10:51 am Scorpio
30th	3:50 pm Sagittarius

August 1925	
1st	5:42 pm Capricorn
3rd	5:39 pm Aquarius
5th	5:24 pm Pisces
7th	6:50 pm Aries
9th	11:24 pm Taurus
12th	8:00 am Gemini
14th	7:40 pm Cancer
17th	8:41 am Leo
19th	9:12 pm Virgo
22nd	8:03 am Libra
24th	4:42 pm Scorpio
26th	10:49 pm Sagittarius
29th	2:17 am Capricorn
31st	3:40 am Aquarius

September 1925	
2nd	4:02 am Pisces
4th	5:03 am Aries
6th	8:31 am Taurus
8th	3:43 pm Gemini
11th	2:36 am Cancer
13th	3:29 pm Leo
16th	3:55 am Virgo
18th	2:14 pm Libra
20th	10:17 pm Scorpio
23rd	4:16 am Sagittarius
25th	8:34 am Capricorn
27th	11:27 am Aquarius
29th	1:19 pm Pisces

October 1925	
1st	3:06 pm Aries
3rd	6:21 pm Taurus
6th	0:34 am Gemini
8th	10:34 am Cancer
10th	11:09 pm Leo
13th	11:40 am Virgo
15th	9:56 pm Libra
18th	5:09 am Scorpio
20th	10:09 am Sagittarius
22nd	1:56 pm Capricorn
24th	5:11 pm Aquarius
26th	8:14 pm Pisces
28th	11:22 pm Aries
31st	3:30 am Taurus

November 1925	
2nd	9:47 am Gemini
4th	7:07 pm Cancer
7th	7:15 am Leo
9th	8:06 pm Virgo
12th	6:48 am Libra
14th	2:01 pm Scorpio
16th	6:10 pm Sagittarius
18th	8:38 pm Capricorn
20th	10:48 pm Aquarius
23rd	1:38 am Pisces
25th	5:32 am Aries
27th	10:48 am Taurus
29th	5:53 pm Gemini

December 1925	
2nd	3:19 am Cancer
4th	3:13 pm Leo
7th	4:12 am Virgo
9th	3:48 pm Libra
12th	0:04 am Scorpio
14th	4:20 am Sagittarius
16th	5:58 am Capricorn
18th	6:37 am Aquarius
20th	7:55 am Pisces
22nd	11:01 am Aries
24th	4:28 pm Taurus
27th	0:19 am Gemini
29th	10:29 am Cancer
31st	10:25 pm Leo

January 1926	
3rd	11:24 am Virgo
5th	11:42 pm Libra
8th	9:13 am Scorpio
10th	2:56 pm Sagittarius
12th	5:05 pm Capricorn
14th	5:06 pm Aquarius
16th	4:51 pm Pisces
18th	6:07 pm Aries
20th	10:17 pm Taurus
23rd	5:59 am Gemini
25th	4:33 pm Cancer
28th	4:52 am Leo
30th	5:48 pm Virgo

February 1926	
2nd	6:08 am Libra
4th	4:35 pm Scorpio
7th	0:02 am Sagittarius
9th	3:46 am Capricorn
11th	4:34 am Aquarius
13th	3:57 am Pisces
15th	3:50 am Aries
17th	6:14 am Taurus
19th	12:28 pm Gemini
21st	10:29 pm Cancer
24th	11:01 am Leo
26th	12:00 pm Virgo

March 1926	
1st	12:02 pm Libra
3rd	10:28 pm Scorpio
6th	6:37 am Sagittarius
8th	12:03 pm Capricorn
10th	2:37 pm Aquarius
12th	3:02 pm Pisces
14th	2:53 pm Aries
16th	4:11 pm Taurus
18th	8:44 pm Gemini
21st	5:33 am Cancer
23rd	5:37 pm Leo
26th	6:36 am Virgo
28th	6:25 pm Libra
31st	4:16 am Scorpio

April 1926	
2nd	12:06 pm Sagittarius
4th	6:00 pm Capricorn
6th	10:00 pm Aquarius
9th	0:03 am Pisces
11th	1:02 am Aries
13th	2:32 am Taurus
15th	6:25 am Gemini
17th	1:59 pm Cancer
20th	1:07 am Leo
22nd	1:58 pm Virgo
25th	1:53 am Libra
27th	11:17 am Scorpio
29th	6:19 pm Sagittarius

May 1926
1st 11:34 am Capricorn
4th 3:30 am Aquarius
6th 6:31 am Pisces
8th 8:55 am Aries
10th 11:36 am Taurus
12th 3:50 pm Gemini
14th 10:54 pm Cancer
17th 9:22 am Leo
19th 9:54 pm Virgo
22nd 10:01 am Libra
24th 7:40 pm Scorpio
27th 2:14 am Sagittarius
29th 6:23 am Capricorn
31st 9:19 am Aquarius

June 1926
2nd 11:54 am Pisces
4th 2:47 pm Aries
6th 6:30 pm Taurus
8th 11:44 pm Gemini
11th 7:18 am Cancer
13th 5:31 pm Leo
16th 5:49 am Virgo
18th 6:16 pm Libra
21st 4:38 am Scorpio
23rd 11:31 am Sagittariu
25th 3:15 pm Capricorr
27th 5:01 pm Aquarius
29th 6:15 pm Pisces

July 1926
1st 8:16 pm Aries
3rd 12:00 pm Taurus
6th 6:00 am Gemini
8th 2:21 pm Cancer
11th 0:50 am Leo
13th 1:08 pm Virgo
16th 1:52 am Libra
18th 1:02 pm Scorpio
20th 9:07 pm Sagittarius
23rd 1:27 am Capricorn
25th 2:47 am Aquarius
27th 2:47 am Pisces
29th 3:16 am Aries
31st 5:51 am Taurus

August 1926
2nd 11:30 am Gemini
4th 8:11 pm Cancer
7th 7:14 am Leo
9th 7:39 pm Virgo
12th 8:26 am Libra
14th 8:15 pm Scorpio
17th 5:35 am Sagittarius
19th 11:17 am Capricorn
21st 1:25 pm Aquarius
23rd 1:12 pm Pisces
25th 12:33 pm Aries
27th 1:30 pm Taurus
29th 5:43 pm Gemini

September 1926
1st 1:49 am Cancer
3rd 1:03 pm Leo
6th 1:41 am Virgo
8th 2:23 pm Libra
11th 2:15 am Scorpio
13th 12:17 pm Sagittarius
15th 7:33 pm Capricorn
17th 11:21 pm Aquarius
20th 0:05 am Pisces
21st 11:19 pm Aries
23rd 11:12 pm Taurus
26th 1:50 am Cancer
28th 8:38 am Cancer
30th 7:11 pm Leo

October 1926
3rd 7:47 am Virgo
5th 8:27 pm Libra
8th 7:57 am Scorpio
10th 5:52 pm Sagittarius
13th 1:46 am Capricorn
15th 6:58 am Aquarius
17th 9:25 am Pisces
19th 9:55 am Aries
21st 10:04 am Taurus
23rd 11:54 am Gemini
25th 5:11 pm Cancer
28th 2:31 am Leo
30th 2:43 pm Virgo

November 1926
2nd 3:20 am Libra
4th 2:34 pm Scorpio
6th 11:51 pm Sagittarius
9th 7:09 am Capricorn
11th 12:38 pm Aquarius
13th 4:20 pm Pisces
15th 6:26 pm Aries
17th 7:54 pm Taurus
19th 10:10 pm Gemini
22nd 2:56 am Cancer
24th 11:14 am Leo
26th 10:36 pm Virgo
29th 11:12 am Libra

December 1926
1st 10:38 pm Scorpio
4th 7:28 am Sagittariu
6th 1:48 pm Capricorn
8th 6:20 pm Aquarius
10th 9:44 pm Pisces
13th 0:32 am Aries
15th 3:23 am Taurus
17th 7:02 am Gemini
19th 12:23 pm Cancer
21st 8:18 pm Leo
24th 7:03 am Virgo
26th 7:29 pm Libra
29th 7:24 am Scorpio
31st 4:45 pm Sagittariu

January 1927
2nd 10:49 pm Capricorn
5th 2:09 am Aquarius
7th 4:06 am Pisces
9th 6:01 am Aries
11th 8:59 am Taurus
13th 1:33 pm Gemini
15th 8:01 pm Cancer
18th 4:32 am Leo
20th 3:10 pm Virgo
23rd 3:26 am Libra
25th 3:51 pm Scorpio
28th 2:18 am Sagittarius
30th 9:06 am Capricorn

February 1927
1st 12:17 pm Aquarius
3rd 1:05 pm Pisces
5th 1:22 pm Aries
7th 2:54 pm Taurus
9th 6:57 pm Gemini
12th 1:51 am Cancer
14th 11:14 am Leo
16th 10:17 pm Virgo
19th 10:31 am Libra
21st 11:08 pm Scorpio
24th 10:29 am Sagittarius
26th 6:51 pm Capricorn
28th 11:12 pm Aquarius

March 1927
3rd 0:05 am Pisces
4th 11:18 pm Aries
6th 11:07 pm Taurus
9th 1:30 am Gemini
11th 7:33 am Cancer
13th 4:55 pm Leo
16th 4:23 am Virgo
18th 4:50 pm Libra
21st 5:21 am Scorpio
23rd 5:04 pm Sagittari
26th 2:37 am Capricor
28th 8:34 am Aquariu
30th 10:48 am Pisces

April 1927
1st 10:28 am Aries
3rd 9:39 am Taurus
5th 10:31 am Gemini
7th 2:48 pm Cancer
9th 11:01 pm Leo
12th 10:11 am Virgo
14th 10:53 pm Libra
17th 11:19 am Scorpio
19th 10:09 pm Sagittarius
22nd 8:32 am Capricorn
24th 3:40 pm Aquarius
26th 7:34 pm Pisces
28th 8:42 pm Aries
30th 8:29 pm Taurus

May 1927
2nd 8:54 pm Gemini
4th 11:51 pm Cancer
7th 6:42 am Leo
9th 5:05 pm Virgo
12th 5:28 am Libra
14th 5:51 pm Scorpio
17th 4:56 am Sagittarius
19th 2:09 pm Capricorn
21st 9:15 pm Aquarius
24th 2:01 am Pisces
26th 4:36 am Aries
29th 5:51 am Taurus
30th 7:05 am Gemini

June 1927
1st 9:56 am Cancer
3rd 3:42 pm Leo
6th 0:55 am Virgo
8th 12:50 pm Libra
11th 1:16 am Scorpio
13th 12:14 pm Sagittarius
15th 8:50 pm Capricorn
18th 3:03 am Aquarius
20th 7:25 am Pisces
22nd 10:28 am Aries
24th 12:54 pm Taurus
26th 3:28 pm Gemini
28th 7:06 pm Cancer

July 1927
1st 0:50 am Leo
3rd 9:31 am Virgo
5th 8:48 pm Libra
8th 9:16 am Scorpio
10th 8:35 pm Sagittarius
13th 5:03 am Capricorn
15th 10:28 am Aquarius
17th 1:42 pm Pisces
19th 3:59 pm Aries
21st 6:25 pm Taurus
23rd 9:47 pm Gemini
26th 2:33 am Cancer
28th 9:04 am Leo
30th 5:45 pm Virgo

August 1927
2nd 4:45 am Libra
4th 5:16 pm Scorpio
7th 5:10 am Sagittarius
9th 2:18 pm Capricorn
11th 7:43 pm Aquarius
13th 10:04 pm Pisces
15th 10:58 pm Aries
18th 0:13 am Taurus
20th 3:10 am Gemini
22nd 8:23 am Cancer
24th 3:42 pm Leo
27th 0:57 am Virgo
29th 12:05 pm Libra

September 1927
1st 0:37 am Scorpio
3rd 1:08 pm Sagittarius
5th 11:28 pm Capricorn
8th 5:45 am Aquarius
10th 8:11 am Pisces
12th 8:17 am Aries
14th 8:06 am Taurus
16th 9:32 am Gemini
18th 1:53 pm Cancer
20th 9:15 pm Leo
23rd 7:04 am Virgo
25th 6:32 pm Libra
28th 7:07 am Scorpio
30th 7:54 pm Sagittarius

October 1927
3rd 7:10 am Capricorn
5th 3:01 pm Aquarius
7th 6:45 pm Pisces
9th 7:13 pm Aries
11th 6:18 pm Taurus
13th 6:15 pm Gemini
15th 8:52 pm Cancer
18th 3:09 am Leo
20th 12:45 pm Virgo
23rd 0:26 am Libra
25th 1:09 pm Scorpio
28th 1:48 am Sagittarius
30th 1:19 pm Capricorn

November 1927
1st 10:25 pm Aquarius
4th 3:51 am Pisces
6th 5:50 am Aries
8th 5:37 am Taurus
10th 5:06 am Gemini
12th 6:18 am Cancer
14th 10:54 am Leo
16th 7:15 pm Virgo
19th 6:41 am Libra
21st 7:26 pm Scorpio
24th 7:51 am Sagittarius
26th 6:58 pm Capricorn
29th 4:04 am Aquarius

December 1927
1st 10:33 am Pisces
3rd 2:16 pm Aries
5th 3:44 pm Taurus
7th 4:11 pm Gemini
9th 5:13 pm Cancer
11th 8:32 pm Leo
14th 3:27 am Virgo
16th 1:57 pm Libra
19th 2:30 am Scorpio
21st 2:56 pm Sagittarius
24th 1:35 am Capricorn
26th 9:51 am Aquarius
28th 3:57 pm Pisces
30th 8:17 pm Aries

January 1928
1st 11:14 pm Taurus
4th 1:20 am Gemini
6th 3:28 am Cancer
8th 6:55 am Leo
10th 12:57 pm Virgo
12th 10:17 pm Libra
15th 10:25 am Scorpio
17th 11:04 pm Sagittarius
20th 9:44 am Capricorn
22nd 5:23 pm Aquarius
24th 10:22 pm Pisces
27th 1:47 am Aries
29th 4:42 am Taurus
31st 7:49 am Gemini

February 1928
2nd 11:24 am Cancer
4th 3:55 pm Leo
6th 10:10 pm Virgo
9th 7:06 am Libra
11th 6:41 pm Scorpio
14th 7:29 am Sagittarius
16th 6:49 pm Capricorn
19th 2:44 am Aquarius .
21st 7:01 am Pisces
23rd 9:08 am Aries
25th 10:44 am Taurus
27th 1:10 pm Gemini
29th 5:07 pm Cancer

March 1928
2nd 10:39 pm Leo
5th 5:53 am Virgo
7th 3:08 pm Libra
10th 2:31 am Scorpio
12th 3:23 pm Sagittarius
15th 3:30 am Capricorn
17th 12:25 pm Aquarius
19th 5:15 pm Pisces
21st 6:51 pm Aries
23rd 7:06 pm Taurus
25th 7:55 pm Gemini
27th 10:43 pm Cancer
30th 4:06 am Leo

April 1928
1st 11:55 am Virgo
3rd 9:47 pm Libra
6th 9:29 am Scorpio
8th 10:20 pm Sagittarius
11th 10:53 am Capricorn
13th 9:05 pm Aquarius
16th 3:16 am Pisces
18th 5:37 am Aries
20th 5:35 am Taurus
22nd 5:11 am Gemini
24th 6:17 am Cancer
26th 10:16 am Leo
28th 5:30 pm Virgo

May 1928
1st 3:36 am Libra
3rd 3:39 pm Scorpio
6th 4:32 am Sagittarius
8th 5:07 pm Capricorn
11th 3:55 am Aquarius
13th 11:30 am Pisces
15th 3:25 pm Aries
17th 4:23 pm Taurus
19th 3:56 pm Gemini
21st 4:01 pm Cancer
23rd 6:20 pm Leo
26th 0:08 am Virgo
28th 9:39 am Libra
30th 9:41 pm Scorpio

June 1928
2nd 10:37 am Sagittarius
4th 11:00 pm Capricorn
7th 9:38 am Aquarius
9th 5:51 pm Pisces
11th 11:13 pm Aries
14th 1:45 am Taurus
16th 2:24 am Gemini
18th 2:36 am Cancer
20th 4:06 am Leo
22nd 8:33 am Virgo
24th 4:46 pm Libra
27th 4:18 am Scorpio
29th 5:14 pm Sagittarius

July 1928
2nd 5:23 am Capricorn
4th 3:30 pm Aquarius
6th 11:23 pm Pisces
9th 5:02 am Aries
11th 8:47 am Taurus
13th 10:50 am Gemini
15th 12:21 pm Cancer
17th 2:10 pm Leo
19th 5:56 pm Virgo
22nd 1:04 am Libra
24th 11:50 am Scorpio
27th 0:34 am Sagittarius
29th 12:43 pm Capricorn
31st 10:33 pm Aquarius

August 1928
3rd 5:33 am Pisces
5th 10:32 am Aries
7th 2:18 pm Taurus
9th 5:23 pm Gemini
11th 8:05 pm Cancer
13th 10:59 pm Leo
16th 3:10 am Virgo
18th 9:59 am Libra
20th 7:59 pm Scorpio
23rd 8:28 am Sagittarius
25th 8:58 pm Capricorn
28th 6:52 am Aquarius
30th 1:26 pm Pisces

September 1928
1st 5:25 pm Aries
3rd 8:08 pm Taurus
5th 10:44 pm Gemini
8th 1:54 am Cancer
10th 5:53 am Leo
12th 11:05 am Virgo
14th 6:16 pm Libra
17th 4:06 am Scorpio
19th 4:24 pm Sagittarius
22nd 5:14 am Capricorn
24th 3:57 pm Aquarius
26th 11:01 pm Pisces
29th 2:30 am Aries

October 1928
1st 3:59 am Taurus
3rd 5:10 am Gemini
5th 7:24 am Cancer
7th 11:21 am Leo
9th 5:17 pm Virgo
12th 1:15 am Libra
14th 11:32 am Scorpio
16th 11:46 pm Sagittarius
19th 12:50 pm Capricorn
22nd 0:34 am Aquarius
24th 8:45 am Pisces
26th 12:50 pm Aries
28th 2:14 pm Taurus
30th 2:13 pm Gemini

November 1928
1st 2:43 am Cancer
3rd 5:17 pm Leo
5th 10:42 pm Virgo
8th 7:07 am Libra
10th 5:55 pm Scorpio
13th 6:20 am Sagittarius
15th 7:25 pm Capricorn
18th 7:38 am Aquarius
20th 5:15 pm Pisces
22nd 11:14 pm Aries
25th 1:30 am Taurus
27th 1:23 am Gemini
29th 0:43 am Cancer

December 1928
1st 1:30 am Leo
3rd 5:20 am Virgo
5th 12:56 pm Libra
7th 11:46 pm Scorpio
10th 12:30 pm Sagittarius
13th 1:29 am Capricorn
15th 1:33 pm Aquarius
17th 11:48 pm Pisces
20th 7:10 am Aries
22nd 11:20 am Taurus
24th 12:37 pm Gemini
26th 12:17 pm Cancer
28th 12:10 pm Leo
30th 2:18 pm Virgo

January 1929
1st	8:11 pm	Libra
4th	6:11 am	Scorpio
6th	6:50 pm	Sagittarius
9th	7:49 am	Capricorn
11th	7:30 pm	Aquarius
14th	5:19 am	Pisces
16th	1:04 pm	Aries
18th	6:34 pm	Taurus
20th	9:42 pm	Gemini
22nd	10:52 pm	Cancer
24th	11:16 pm	Leo
27th	0:48 am	Virgo
29th	5:23 am	Libra
31st	1:50 pm	Scorpio

February 1929
3rd	1:58 am	Sagittarius
5th	2:58 pm	Capricorn
8th	2:32 am	Aquarius
10th	11:39 am	Pisces
12th	6:39 pm	Aries
15th	0:02 am	Taurus
17th	4:00 am	Gemini
19th	6:44 am	Cancer
21st	8:42 am	Leo
23rd	11:02 am	Virgo
25th	3:20 pm	Libra
27th	10:54 pm	Scorpio

March 1929
2nd	10:03 am	Sagittarius
4th	10:53 pm	Capricorn
7th	10:39 am	Aquarius
9th	7:40 pm	Pisces
12th	1:50 am	Aries
14th	6:03 am	Taurus
16th	9:22 am	Gemini
18th	12:24 pm	Cancer
20th	3:28 pm	Leo
22nd	7:05 pm	Virgo
25th	0:11 am	Libra
27th	7:52 am	Scorpio
29th	6:28 pm	Sagittarius

April 1929
1st	7:02 am	Capricorn
3rd	7:14 pm	Aquarius
6th	4:48 am	Pisces
8th	10:53 am	Aries
10th	2:13 pm	Taurus
12th	4:11 pm	Gemini
14th	6:04 pm	Cancer
16th	8:51 pm	Leo
19th	1:04 am	Virgo
21st	7:16 am	Libra
23rd	3:37 pm	Scorpio
26th	2:16 am	Sagittarius
28th	2:44 pm	Capricorn

May 1929
1st	3:18 am	Aquarius
3rd	1:46 pm	Pisces
5th	8:48 pm	Aries
8th	0:16 am	Taurus
10th	1:21 am	Gemini
12th	1:44 am	Cancer
14th	3:04 am	Leo
16th	6:35 am	Virgo
18th	12:56 pm	Libra
20th	9:55 pm	Scorpio
23rd	9:05 am	Sagittarius
25th	9:34 pm	Capricorn
28th	10:17 am	Aquarius
30th	9:36 pm	Pisces

June 1929
2nd	5:53 am	Aries
4th	10:29 am	Taurus
6th	11:54 am	Gemini
8th	11:35 am	Cancer
10th	11:28 am	Leo
12th	1:25 pm	Virgo
14th	6:42 pm	Libra
17th	3:34 am	Scorpio
19th	3:05 pm	Sagittarius
22nd	3:45 am	Capricorn
24th	4:23 pm	Aquarius
27th	3:57 am	Pisces
29th	1:16 pm	Aries

July 1929
1st	7:29 pm	Taurus
3rd	10:12 pm	Gemini
5th	10:20 pm	Cancer
7th	9:38 pm	Leo
9th	10:12 pm	Virgo
12th	1:55 am	Libra
14th	9:49 am	Scorpio
16th	9:02 pm	Sagittarius
19th	9:48 am	Capricorn
21st	10:20 pm	Aquarius
24th	9:37 am	Pisces
26th	7:12 pm	Aries
29th	2:24 am	Taurus
31st	6:40 am	Gemini

August 1929
2nd	8:13 am	Cancer
4th	8:12 am	Leo
6th	8:27 am	Virgo
8th	11:02 am	Libra
10th	5:27 pm	Scorpio
13th	3:45 am	Sagittarius
15th	4:20 pm	Capricorn
18th	4:48 am	Aquarius
20th	3:44 pm	Pisces
23rd	0:46 am	Aries
25th	7:53 am	Taurus
27th	12:50 pm	Gemini
29th	4:02 pm	Cancer
31st	5:27 pm	Leo

September 1929
2nd	6:29 pm	Virgo
4th	8:45 pm	Libra
7th	2:22 am	Scorpio
9th	11:42 am	Sagittarius
11th	11:44 pm	Capricorn
14th	12:14 pm	Aquarius
16th	11:06 pm	Pisces
19th	7:28 am	Aries
21st	1:43 pm	Taurus
23rd	6:24 pm	Gemini
25th	9:52 pm	Cancer
28th	0:29 am	Leo
30th	2:53 am	Virgo

October 1929
2nd	6:14 am	Libra
4th	11:45 am	Scorpio
6th	8:21 pm	Sagittarius
9th	7:52 am	Capricorn
11th	8:26 pm	Aquarius
14th	7:38 am	Pisces
16th	3:59 pm	Aries
18th	9:27 pm	Taurus
21st	0:54 am	Gemini
23rd	3:23 am	Cancer
25th	5:56 am	Leo
27th	9:11 am	Virgo
29th	1:42 pm	Libra
31st	8:05 pm	Scorpio

November 1929
3rd	4:50 am	Sagittarius
5th	4:00 pm	Capricorn
8th	4:34 am	Aquarius
10th	4:28 pm	Pisces
13th	1:42 am	Aries
15th	7:15 am	Taurus
17th	9:51 am	Gemini
19th	10:53 am	Cancer
21st	12:00 pm	Leo
23rd	2:35 pm	Virgo
25th	7:24 pm	Libra
28th	2:41 am	Scorpio
30th	12:11 pm	Sagittarius

December 1929
2nd	11:26 pm	Capricorn
5th	11:59 am	Aquarius
8th	0:28 am	Pisces
10th	10:53 am	Aries
12th	5:45 pm	Taurus
14th	8:47 pm	Gemini
16th	9:03 pm	Cancer
18th	8:35 pm	Leo
20th	9:23 pm	Virgo
23rd	1:03 am	Libra
25th	8:15 am	Scorpio
27th	6:13 pm	Sagittarius
30th	5:56 am	Capricorn

January 1930
1st	6:30 pm	Aquarius
4th	7:03 am	Pisces
6th	6:24 pm	Aries
9th	2:56 am	Taurus
11th	7:29 am	Gemini
13th	8:31 am	Cancer
15th	7:38 am	Leo
17th	7:01 am	Virgo
19th	8:51 am	Libra
21st	2:30 pm	Scorpio
23rd	11:56 pm	Sagittarius
26th	11:53 am	Capricorn
29th	0:34 am	Aquarius
31st	12:58 pm	Pisces

February 1930
3rd	0:23 am	Aries
5th	9:45 am	Taurus
7th	4:05 pm	Gemini
9th	6:52 pm	Cancer
11th	6:58 pm	Leo
13th	6:15 pm	Virgo
15th	6:54 pm	Libra
17th	10:46 pm	Scorpio
20th	6:52 am	Sagittarius
22nd	6:13 pm	Capricorn
25th	6:55 am	Aquarius
27th	7:11 pm	Pisces

March 1930
2nd	6:07 am	Aries
4th	3:16 pm	Taurus
6th	10:15 pm	Gemini
9th	2:33 am	Cancer
11th	4:25 am	Leo
13th	4:54 am	Virgo
15th	5:46 am	Libra
17th	8:51 am	Scorpio
19th	3:27 pm	Sagittarius
22nd	1:40 am	Capricorn
24th	2:03 pm	Aquarius
27th	2:22 am	Pisces
29th	12:56 pm	Aries
31st	9:22 pm	Taurus

April 1930
3rd	3:40 am	Gemini
5th	8:08 am	Cancer
7th	11:06 am	Leo
9th	1:10 pm	Virgo
11th	3:19 pm	Libra
13th	6:47 pm	Scorpio
16th	0:49 am	Sagittarius
18th	10:10 am	Capricorn
20th	9:57 pm	Aquarius
23rd	10:20 am	Pisces
25th	9:08 pm	Aries
28th	5:05 am	Taurus
30th	10:22 am	Gemini

★ ★

May 1930
2nd	1:51 pm	Cancer
4th	4:30 pm	Leo
6th	7:10 pm	Virgo
8th	10:29 pm	Libra
11th	3:07 am	Scorpio
13th	9:42 am	Sagittarius
15th	6:41 pm	Capricorn
18th	6:05 am	Aquarius
20th	6:34 pm	Pisces
23rd	5:52 am	Aries
25th	2:09 pm	Taurus
27th	7:03 pm	Gemini
29th	9:24 pm	Cancer
31st	10:44 pm	Leo

June 1930
3rd	0:36 am	Virgo
5th	4:04 am	Libra
7th	9:33 am	Scorpio
9th	4:58 pm	Sagittarius
12th	2:21 am	Capricorn
14th	1:41 pm	Aquarius
17th	2:11 am	Pisces
19th	2:11 pm	Aries
21st	11:36 pm	Taurus
24th	9:16 am	Gemini
26th	6:54 am	Cancer
28th	7:06 am	Leo
30th	7:30 am	Virgo

July 1930
2nd	9:51 am	Libra
4th	2:59 pm	Scorpio
6th	10:50 pm	Sagittarius
9th	8:50 am	Capricorn
11th	8:24 pm	Aquarius
14th	8:57 am	Pisces
16th	9:24 pm	Aries
19th	7:49 am	Taurus
21st	2:33 pm	Gemini
23rd	5:17 pm	Cancer
25th	5:17 pm	Leo
27th	4:36 pm	Virgo
29th	5:22 pm	Libra
31st	9:07 pm	Scorpio

August 1930
3rd	4:27 am	Sagittarius
5th	2:37 pm	Capricorn
8th	2:37 am	Aquarius
10th	3:02 pm	Pisces
13th	3:31 am	Aries
15th	2:34 pm	Taurus
17th	10:45 pm	Gemini
20th	2:59 am	Cancer
22nd	3:56 am	Leo
24th	3:15 am	Virgo
26th	3:00 am	Libra
28th	5:15 am	Scorpio
30th	11:09 am	Sagittarius

September 1930
1st	8:37 pm	Capricorn
4th	8:27 am	Aquarius
6th	9:06 pm	Pisces
9th	9:19 am	Aries
11th	8:17 pm	Taurus
14th	4:58 am	Gemini
16th	10:38 am	Cancer
18th	1:15 pm	Leo
20th	1:45 pm	Virgo
22nd	1:46 pm	Libra
24th	3:13 pm	Scorpio
26th	7:38 pm	Sagittarius
29th	3:52 am	Capricorn

October 1930
1st	3:10 pm	Aquarius
4th	3:48 am	Pisces
6th	3:51 pm	Aries
9th	2:13 am	Taurus
11th	10:26 am	Gemini
13th	4:27 pm	Cancer
15th	8:18 pm	Leo
17th	10:26 pm	Virgo
19th	11:44 pm	Libra
22nd	1:34 am	Scorpio
24th	5:28 am	Sagittarius
26th	12:33 pm	Capricorn
28th	10:55 pm	Aquarius
31st	11:24 am	Pisces

November 1930
2nd	11:34 pm	Aries
5th	9:34 am	Taurus
7th	4:55 pm	Gemini
9th	10:04 pm	Cancer
12th	1:44 am	Leo
14th	4:41 am	Virgo
16th	7:28 am	Libra
18th	10:39 am	Scorpio
20th	3:04 pm	Sagittarius
22nd	9:45 pm	Capricorn
25th	7:27 am	Aquarius
27th	7:35 pm	Pisces
30th	8:05 am	Aries

December 1930
2nd	6:30 pm	Taurus
5th	1:31 am	Gemini
7th	5:30 am	Cancer
9th	7:52 am	Leo
11th	10:05 am	Virgo
13th	1:07 pm	Libra
15th	5:21 pm	Scorpio
17th	10:55 pm	Sagittarius
20th	6:15 am	Capricorn
22nd	3:48 pm	Aquarius
25th	3:37 am	Pisces
27th	4:29 pm	Aries
30th	3:49 am	Taurus

January 1931
1st	11:30 am	Gemini
3rd	3:17 pm	Cancer
5th	4:31 pm	Leo
7th	5:08 pm	Virgo
9th	6:51 pm	Libra
11th	10:41 pm	Scorpio
14th	4:52 am	Sagittarius
16th	1:04 pm	Capricorn
18th	11:05 pm	Aquarius
21st	10:57 am	Pisces
23rd	11:56 pm	Aries
26th	12:06 pm	Taurus
28th	9:16 pm	Gemini
31st	2:09 am	Cancer

February 1931
2nd	3:24 am	Leo
4th	2:58 am	Virgo
6th	2:57 am	Libra
8th	5:07 am	Scorpio
10th	10:27 am	Sagittarius
12th	6:41 pm	Capricorn
15th	5:16 am	Aquarius
17th	5:24 pm	Pisces
20th	6:20 am	Aries
22nd	6:52 pm	Taurus
25th	5:10 am	Gemini
27th	11:42 am	Cancer

March 1931
1st	2:21 pm	Leo
3rd	2:20 pm	Virgo
5th	1:35 pm	Libra
7th	2:07 pm	Scorpio
9th	5:34 pm	Sagittarius
12th	0:38 am	Capricorn
14th	11:04 am	Aquarius
16th	11:26 pm	Pisces
19th	12:22 pm	Aries
22nd	0:44 am	Taurus
24th	11:16 am	Gemini
26th	7:02 pm	Cancer
28th	11:29 pm	Leo
31st	0:58 am	Virgo

April 1931
2nd	0:49 am	Libra
4th	0:51 am	Scorpio
6th	2:54 am	Sagittarius
8th	8:25 am	Capricorn
10th	5:42 pm	Aquarius
13th	5:48 am	Pisces
15th	6:46 pm	Aries
18th	6:47 am	Taurus
20th	4:53 pm	Gemini
23rd	0:41 am	Cancer
25th	6:00 am	Leo
27th	9:07 am	Virgo
29th	10:34 am	Libra

May 1931
1st	11:27 am	Scorpio
3rd	1:18 pm	Sagittarius
5th	5:40 pm	Capricorn
8th	1:38 am	Aquarius
10th	1:04 pm	Pisces
13th	1:57 am	Aries
15th	1:51 pm	Taurus
17th	11:24 pm	Gemini
20th	6:23 am	Cancer
22nd	11:24 am	Leo
24th	3:04 pm	Virgo
26th	5:49 pm	Libra
28th	8:07 pm	Scorpio
30th	10:47 pm	Sagittarius

June 1931
2nd	3:09 am	Capricorn
4th	10:28 am	Aquarius
6th	9:03 pm	Pisces
9th	9:44 am	Aries
11th	9:53 pm	Taurus
14th	7:17 am	Gemini
16th	1:33 pm	Cancer
18th	5:34 pm	Leo
20th	8:32 pm	Virgo
22nd	11:21 pm	Libra
25th	2:35 am	Scorpio
27th	6:27 am	Sagittarius
29th	11:38 am	Capricorn

July 1931
1st	6:59 pm	Aquarius
4th	5:11 am	Pisces
6th	5:40 pm	Aries
9th	6:12 am	Taurus
11th	4:09 pm	Gemini
13th	10:28 pm	Cancer
16th	1:40 am	Leo
18th	3:21 am	Virgo
20th	5:07 am	Libra
22nd	7:58 am	Scorpio
24th	12:20 pm	Sagittarius
26th	6:24 pm	Capricorn
29th	2:26 am	Aquarius
31st	12:48 pm	Pisces

August 1931
3rd	1:09 am	Aries
5th	2:02 pm	Taurus
8th	1:00 am	Gemini
10th	8:05 am	Cancer
12th	11:26 am	Leo
14th	12:24 pm	Virgo
16th	12:46 pm	Libra
18th	2:13 pm	Scorpio
20th	5:50 pm	Sagittarius
22nd	11:58 pm	Capricorn
25th	8:40 am	Aquarius
27th	7:28 pm	Pisces
30th	7:56 am	Aries

★ ★

September 1931
1st 8:57 pm Taurus
4th 8:39 am Gemini
6th 5:10 pm Cancer
8th 9:46 pm Leo
10th 11:03 pm Virgo
12th 10:44 pm Libra
14th 10:41 pm Scorpio
17th 0:40 am Sagittarius
19th 5:52 am Capricorn
21st 2:21 pm Aquarius
24th 1:28 am Pisces
26th 2:09 pm Aries
29th 3:06 am Taurus

October 1931
1st 3:00 pm Gemini
4th 0:37 am Cancer
6th 6:46 am Leo
8th 9:31 am Virgo
10th 9:49 am Libra
12th 9:20 am Scorpio
14th 9:57 am Sagittarius
16th 1:24 pm Capricorn
18th 8:42 pm Aquarius
21st 7:35 am Pisces
23rd 8:20 pm Aries
26th 9:10 am Taurus
28th 8:46 pm Gemini
31st 6:24 am Cancer

November 1931
2nd 1:35 pm Leo
4th 6:05 pm Virgo
6th 8:02 pm Libra
8th 8:22 pm Scorpio
10th 8:41 pm Sagittarius
12th 10:54 pm Capricorn
15th 4:44 am Aquarius
17th 2:37 pm Pisces
20th 3:09 am Aries
22nd 3:58 pm Taurus
25th 3:10 am Gemini
27th 12:07 pm Cancer
29th 7:03 pm Leo

December 1931
2nd 0:16 am Virgo
4th 3:43 am Libra
6th 5:43 am Scorpio
8th 7:07 am Sagittarius
10th 9:22 am Capricorn
12th 2:16 pm Aquarius
14th 10:52 pm Pisces
17th 10:52 am Aries
19th 11:46 pm Taurus
22nd 10:56 am Gemini
24th 7:20 pm Cancer
27th 1:16 am Leo
29th 5:39 am Virgo
31st 9:16 am Libra

January 1932
2nd 12:24 pm Scorpio
4th 3:17 pm Sagittarius
6th 6:39 pm Capricorn
8th 11:46 pm Aquarius
11th 7:54 am Pisces
13th 7:10 pm Aries
16th 8:02 am Taurus
18th 7:45 pm Gemini
21st 4:21 am Cancer
23rd 9:37 am Leo
25th 12:46 pm Virgo
27th 3:08 pm Libra
29th 5:45 pm Scorpio
31st 9:08 pm Sagittarius

February 1932
3rd 1:40 am Capricorn
5th 7:53 am Aquarius
7th 4:19 pm Pisces
10th 3:19 am Aries
12th 4:06 pm Taurus
15th 4:25 am Gemini
17th 1:58 pm Cancer
19th 7:47 pm Leo
21st 10:25 pm Virgo
23rd 11:23 pm Libra
26th 0:22 am Scorpio
28th 2:40 am Sagittarius

March 1932
1st 7:09 am Capricorn
3rd 2:03 pm Aquarius
5th 11:16 pm Pisces
8th 10:37 am Aries
10th 11:19 pm Taurus
13th 12:01 pm Gemini
15th 10:45 pm Cancer
18th 5:53 am Leo
20th 9:15 am Virgo
22nd 9:56 am Libra
24th 9:37 am Scorpio
26th 10:12 am Sagittarius
28th 1:14 pm Capricorn
30th 7:33 pm Aquarius

April 1932
2nd 5:06 am Pisces
4th 4:53 pm Aries
7th 5:43 am Taurus
9th 6:26 pm Gemini
12th 5:45 am Cancer
14th 2:17 pm Leo
16th 7:19 pm Virgo
18th 8:58 pm Libra
20th 8:34 pm Scorpio
22nd 7:50 pm Sagittarius
24th 9:18 pm Capricorn
27th 2:06 am Aquarius
29th 10:59 am Pisces

May 1932
1st 10:47 pm Aries
4th 11:45 am Taurus
7th 0:20 am Gemini
9th 11:32 am Cancer
11th 8:45 pm Leo
14th 3:10 am Virgo
16th 6:29 am Libra
18th 7:13 am Scorpio
20th 6:49 am Sagittarius
22nd 7:17 am Capricorn
24th 10:37 am Aquarius
26th 6:02 pm Pisces
29th 5:11 am Aries
31st 6:04 pm Taurus

June 1932
3rd 6:29 am Gemini
5th 5:18 pm Cancer
8th 2:13 am Leo
10th 9:02 am Virgo
12th 1:37 pm Libra
14th 3:57 pm Scorpio
16th 4:45 pm Sagittarius
18th 5:34 pm Capricorn
20th 8:16 pm Aquarius
23rd 2:28 am Pisces
25th 12:38 pm Aries
28th 1:09 am Taurus
30th 1:33 pm Gemini

July 1932
3rd 0:06 am Cancer
5th 8:15 am Leo
7th 2:30 pm Virgo
9th 7:10 pm Libra
11th 10:27 pm Scorpio
14th 0:37 am Sagittarius
16th 2:35 am Capricorn
18th 5:47 am Aquarius
20th 11:39 am Pisces
22nd 8:53 pm Aries
25th 8:55 am Taurus
27th 9:26 pm Gemini
30th 8:03 am Cancer

August 1932
1st 3:54 pm Leo
3rd 9:13 pm Virgo
6th 0:56 am Libra
8th 3:50 am Scorpio
10th 6:32 am Sagittarius
12th 9:40 am Capricorn
14th 1:57 pm Aquarius
16th 8:15 pm Pisces
19th 5:19 am Aries
21st 4:57 pm Taurus
24th 5:33 am Gemini
26th 4:47 pm Cancer
29th 1:03 am Leo
31st 5:55 am Virgo

September 1932
2nd 8:30 am Libra
4th 10:07 am Scorpio
6th 12:03 pm Sagittarius
8th 3:14 pm Capricorn
10th 8:18 pm Aquarius
13th 3:32 am Pisces
15th 1:02 pm Aries
18th 0:32 am Taurus
20th 1:13 pm Gemini
23rd 1:12 am Cancer
25th 10:28 am Leo
27th 4:03 pm Virgo
29th 6:20 pm Libra

October 1932
1st 6:44 pm Scorpio
3rd 7:05 pm Sagittarius
5th 9:02 pm Capricorn
8th 1:44 am Aquarius
10th 9:30 am Pisces
12th 7:37 pm Aries
15th 7:23 am Taurus
17th 8:03 pm Gemini
20th 8:24 am Cancer
22nd 6:54 pm Leo
25th 2:02 am Virgo
27th 5:13 am Libra
29th 5:29 am Scorpio
31st 4:42 am Sagittarius

November 1932
2nd 4:58 am Capricorn
4th 8:11 am Aquarius
6th 3:11 pm Pisces
9th 1:26 am Aries
11th 1:34 pm Taurus
14th 2:13 am Gemini
16th 2:31 pm Cancer
19th 1:34 am Leo
21st 10:02 am Virgo
23rd 3:02 pm Libra
25th 4:35 pm Scorpio
27th 3:59 pm Sagittarius
29th 3:21 pm Capricorn

December 1932
1st 4:53 pm Aquarius
3rd 10:10 pm Pisces
6th 7:39 am Aries
8th 7:43 pm Taurus
11th 8:26 am Gemini
13th 8:27 pm Cancer
16th 7:10 am Leo
18th 4:04 pm Virgo
20th 10:31 pm Libra
23rd 1:52 am Scorpio
25th 2:41 am Sagittarius
27th 2:33 am Capricorn
29th 3:26 am Aquarius
31st 7:23 am Pisces

January 1933			February 1933			March 1933			April 1933		
2nd	3:19 pm	Aries	1st	10:43 am	Taurus	3rd	7:18 am	Gemini	2nd	3:49 am	Cancer
5th	2:38 am	Taurus	3rd	11:05 pm	Gemini	5th	7:42 pm	Cancer	4th	3:13 pm	Leo
7th	3:20 pm	Gemini	6th	11:12 am	Cancer	8th	6:16 am	Leo	6th	11:34 pm	Virgo
10th	3:16 am	Cancer	8th	9:16 pm	Leo	10th	1:39 pm	Virgo	9th	3:50 am	Libra
12th	1:25 pm	Leo	11th	4:42 am	Virgo	12th	6:02 pm	Libra	11th	5:31 am	Scorpio
14th	9:41 pm	Virgo	13th	9:57 am	Libra	14th	8:28 pm	Scorpio	13th	5:54 am	Sagittarius
17th	4:01 am	Libra	15th	1:46 pm	Scorpio	16th	10:19 pm	Sagittarius	15th	6:58 am	Capricorn
19th	8:22 am	Scorpio	17th	4:42 pm	Sagittarius	19th	0:48 am	Capricorn	17th	10:07 am	Aquarius
21st	10:53 am	Sagittarius	19th	7:23 pm	Capricorn	21st	4:41 am	Aquarius	19th	3:58 pm	Pisces
23rd	12:19 pm	Capricorn	21st	10:29 pm	Aquarius	23rd	10:19 am	Pisces	22nd	0:13 am	Aries
25th	1:50 pm	Aquarius	24th	2:58 am	Pisces	25th	5:52 pm	Aries	24th	10:32 am	Taurus
27th	5:35 pm	Pisces	26th	9:47 am	Aries	28th	3:33 am	Taurus	26th	10:18 pm	Gemini
30th	0:21 am	Aries	28th	7:22 pm	Taurus	30th	3:15 pm	Gemini	29th	10:58 am	Cancer

May 1933			June 1933			July 1933			August 1933		
1st	11:06 pm	Leo	2nd	11:15 pm	Libra	2nd	10:50 am	Scorpio	2nd	9:40 pm	Capricorn
4th	8:36 am	Virgo	5th	2:23 am	Scorpio	4th	12:27 pm	Sagittarius	4th	10:22 pm	Aquarius
6th	2:12 pm	Libra	7th	2:32 am	Sagittarius	6th	12:16 pm	Capricorn	7th	0:10 am	Pisces
8th	4:04 pm	Scorpio	9th	1:35 am	Capricorn	8th	12:09 pm	Aquarius	9th	4:44 am	Aries
10th	3:44 pm	Sagittarius	11th	1:43 am	Aquarius	10th	2:08 pm	Pisces	11th	12:49 pm	Taurus
12th	3:20 pm	Capricorn	13th	4:55 am	Pisces	12th	7:35 pm	Aries	13th	11:58 pm	Gemini
14th	4:51 pm	Aquarius	15th	11:56 am	Aries	15th	4:52 am	Taurus	16th	12:32 pm	Cancer
16th	9:36 pm	Pisces	17th	10:13 pm	Taurus	17th	4:46 pm	Gemini	19th	0:23 am	Leo
19th	5:47 am	Aries	20th	10:27 am	Gemini	20th	5:24 am	Cancer	21st	10:04 am	Virgo
21st	4:28 pm	Taurus	22nd	11:07 pm	Cancer	22nd	5:17 pm	Leo	23rd	5:28 pm	Libra
24th	4:32 am	Gemini	25th	11:15 am	Leo	25th	3:34 am	Virgo	25th	10:44 pm	Scorpio
26th	5:11 pm	Cancer	27th	9:50 pm	Virgo	27th	11:41 am	Libra	28th	2:20 am	Sagittarius
29th	5:31 am	Leo	30th	6:06 am	Libra	29th	5:17 pm	Scorpio	30th	4:51 am	Capricorn
31st	4:03 pm	Virgo				31st	8:24 pm	Sagittarius			

September 1933			October 1933			November 1933			December 1933		
1st	7:01 am	Aquarius	2nd	10:50 pm	Aries	1st	1:54 pm	Taurus	1st	6:45 am	Gemini
3rd	9:46 am	Pisces	5th	6:19 am	Taurus	3rd	12:00 pm	Gemini	3rd	6:53 pm	Cancer
5th	2:19 pm	Aries	7th	4:19 pm	Gemini	6th	12:05 pm	Cancer	6th	7:56 am	Leo
7th	9:35 pm	Taurus	10th	4:29 am	Cancer	9th	0:56 am	Leo	8th	7:56 pm	Virgo
10th	8:03 am	Gemini	12th	5:00 pm	Leo	11th	12:19 pm	Virgo	11th	5:14 am	Libra
12th	8:26 pm	Cancer	15th	3:22 am	Virgo	13th	8:10 pm	Libra	13th	10:20 am	Scorpio
15th	8:28 am	Leo	17th	10:02 am	Libra	15th	11:52 pm	Scorpio	15th	11:45 am	Sagittarius
17th	6:10 pm	Virgo	19th	1:24 pm	Scorpio	18th	0:35 am	Sagittarius	17th	11:09 am	Capricorn
20th	0:51 am	Libra	21st	2:53 pm	Sagittarius	20th	0:24 am	Capricorn	19th	10:42 am	Aquarius
22nd	4:58 am	Scorpio	23rd	4:15 pm	Capricorn	22nd	1:21 am	Aquarius	21st	12:21 pm	Pisces
25th	7:48 am	Sagittarius	25th	6:51 pm	Aquarius	24th	4:53 am	Pisces	23rd	5:21 pm	Aries
26th	10:24 am	Capricorn	27th	11:18 pm	Pisces	26th	11:16 am	Aries	26th	1:45 am	Taurus
28th	1:27 pm	Aquarius	30th	5:42 am	Aries	28th	8:04 pm	Taurus	28th	12:46 pm	Gemini
30th	5:28 pm	Pisces							31st	1:07 am	Cancer

January 1934			February 1934			March 1934			April 1934		
2nd	1:55 pm	Leo	1st	7:59 am	Virgo	3rd	0:04 am	Libra	1st	1:34 pm	Scorpio
5th	2:08 am	Virgo	3rd	5:58 pm	Libra	5th	6:57 am	Scorpio	3rd	5:37 pm	Sagittarius
7th	12:15 pm	Libra	6th	1:31 am	Scorpio	7th	11:56 am	Sagittarius	5th	8:46 pm	Capricorn
9th	7:06 pm	Scorpio	8th	6:11 am	Sagittarius	9th	3:20 pm	Capricorn	7th	11:43 pm	Aquarius
11th	10:16 pm	Sagittarius	10th	8:22 am	Capricorn	11th	5:35 pm	Aquarius	10th	2:53 am	Pisces
13th	10:37 pm	Capricorn	12th	8:57 am	Aquarius	13th	7:27 pm	Pisces	12th	6:42 am	Aries
15th	9:57 pm	Aquarius	14th	9:30 am	Pisces	15th	10:01 pm	Aries	14th	11:59 am	Taurus
17th	10:19 pm	Pisces	16th	11:44 am	Aries	18th	2:48 am	Taurus	16th	7:44 pm	Gemini
20th	1:30 am	Aries	18th	5:08 pm	Taurus	20th	10:56 am	Gemini	19th	6:30 am	Cancer
22nd	8:32 am	Taurus	21st	2:18 am	Gemini	22nd	10:14 pm	Cancer	21st	7:11 pm	Leo
24th	6:57 pm	Gemini	23rd	2:24 pm	Cancer	25th	11:02 am	Leo	24th	7:18 am	Virgo
27th	7:25 am	Cancer	26th	3:15 am	Leo	27th	10:45 pm	Virgo	26th	4:29 pm	Libra
29th	8:12 pm	Leo	28th	2:45 pm	Virgo	30th	7:35 am	Libra	28th	10:08 pm	Scorpio

May 1934
1st	1:03 am	Sagittarius
3rd	2:55 am	Capricorn
5th	5:08 am	Aquarius
7th	8:29 am	Pisces
9th	1:10 pm	Aries
11th	7:26 pm	Taurus
14th	3:40 am	Gemini
16th	2:20 pm	Cancer
19th	2:55 am	Leo
21st	3:33 pm	Virgo
24th	1:42 am	Libra
26th	7:47 am	Scorpio
28th	10:26 am	Sagittarius
30th	11:13 am	Capricorn

June 1034
1st	11:59 am	Aquarius
3rd	2:11 pm	Pisces
5th	6:35 pm	Aries
8th	1:17 am	Taurus
10th	10:17 am	Gemini
12th	9:15 pm	Cancer
15th	9:53 am	Leo
17th	10:51 pm	Virgo
20th	9:54 am	Libra
22nd	5:20 pm	Scorpio
24th	8:47 pm	Sagittarius
26th	9:25 pm	Capricorn
28th	9:04 pm	Aquarius
30th	9:41 pm	Pisces

July 1934
3rd	0:41 am	Aries
5th	6:52 am	Taurus
7th	3:59 pm	Gemini
10th	3:22 am	Cancer
12th	4:07 pm	Leo
15th	5:06 am	Virgo
17th	4:44 pm	Libra
20th	1:28 am	Scorpio
22nd	6:22 am	Sagittarius
24th	8:01 am	Capricorn
26th	7:44 am	Aquarius
28th	7:24 am	Pisces
30th	8:51 am	Aries

August 1934
1st	1:32 pm	Taurus
3rd	9:51 pm	Gemini
6th	9:17 am	Cancer
8th	10:10 pm	Leo
11th	10:58 am	Virgo
13th	10:33 pm	Libra
16th	7:48 am	Scorpio
18th	2:06 pm	Sagittarius
20th	5:24 pm	Capricorn
22nd	6:16 pm	Aquarius
24th	6:08 pm	Pisces
26th	6:46 pm	Aries
28th	9:56 pm	Taurus
31st	4:59 am	Gemini

September 1934
2nd	3:43 pm	Cancer
5th	4:33 am	Leo
7th	5:15 pm	Virgo
10th	4:22 am	Libra
12th	1:17 pm	Scorpio
14th	8:03 pm	Sagittarius
17th	0:36 am	Capricorn
19th	3:05 am	Aquarius
21st	4:14 am	Pisces
23rd	5:15 am	Aries
25th	7:50 am	Taurus
27th	1:38 pm	Gemini
29th	11:15 pm	Cancer

October 1934
2nd	11:45 am	Leo
5th	0:30 am	Virgo
7th	11:17 am	Libra
9th	7:31 pm	Scorpio
12th	1:32 am	Sagittarius
14th	6:03 am	Capricorn
16th	9:31 am	Aquarius
18th	12:08 pm	Pisces
20th	2:29 pm	Aries
22nd	5:37 pm	Taurus
24th	10:58 pm	Gemini
27th	7:49 am	Cancer
29th	7:43 pm	Leo

November 1934
1st	8:34 am	Virgo
3rd	7:39 pm	Libra
6th	3:30 am	Scorpio
8th	8:31 am	Sagittarius
10th	11:56 am	Capricorn
12th	2:52 pm	Aquarius
14th	5:57 pm	Pisces
16th	9:27 pm	Aries
19th	1:47 am	Taurus
21st	7:51 am	Gemini
23rd	4:28 pm	Cancer
26th	3:55 am	Leo
28th	4:51 pm	Virgo

December 1934
1st	4:36 am	Libra
3rd	1:00 pm	Scorpio
5th	5:50 pm	Sagittarius
7th	8:08 pm	Capricorn
9th	9:34 pm	Aquarius
11th	11:32 pm	Pisces
14th	2:53 am	Aries
16th	8:00 am	Taurus
18th	3:01 pm	Gemini
21st	0:12 am	Cancer
23rd	11:39 am	Leo
26th	0:32 am	Virgo
28th	12:54 pm	Libra
30th	10:39 pm	Scorpio

January 1935
2nd	4:23 am	Sagittarius
4th	6:41 am	Capricorn
6th	7:04 am	Aquarius
8th	7:20 am	Pisces
10th	9:08 am	Aries
12th	1:31 pm	Taurus
14th	8:45 pm	Gemini
17th	6:40 am	Cancer
19th	6:28 pm	Leo
22nd	7:19 am	Virgo
24th	7:57 pm	Libra
27th	6:42 am	Scorpio
29th	2:04 pm	Sagittarius
31st	5:43 pm	Capricorn

February 1935
2nd	6:23 pm	Aquarius
4th	5:48 pm	Pisces
6th	5:53 pm	Aries
8th	8:26 pm	Taurus
11th	2:39 am	Gemini
13th	12:29 pm	Cancer
16th	0:37 am	Leo
18th	1:33 pm	Virgo
21st	2:03 am	Libra
23rd	1:01 pm	Scorpio
25th	9:39 pm	Sagittarius
28th	3:03 am	Capricorn

March 1935
2nd	5:14 am	Aquarius
4th	5:12 am	Pisces
6th	4:43 am	Aries
8th	5:48 am	Taurus
10th	10:18 am	Gemini
12th	6:55 pm	Cancer
15th	6:50 am	Leo
17th	7:52 pm	Virgo
20th	8:07 am	Libra
22nd	6:44 pm	Scorpio
25th	3:23 am	Sagittarius
27th	9:46 am	Capricorn
29th	1:39 pm	Aquarius
31st	3:13 pm	Pisces

April 1935
2nd	3:32 pm	Aries
4th	4:23 pm	Taurus
6th	7:39 pm	Gemini
9th	2:52 am	Cancer
11th	1:55 pm	Leo
14th	2:48 am	Virgo
16th	3:00 pm	Libra
19th	1:10 am	Scorpio
21st	9:05 am	Sagittarius
23rd	3:11 pm	Capricorn
25th	7:42 pm	Aquarius
27th	10:41 pm	Pisces
30th	0:26 am	Aries

May 1935
2nd	2:11 am	Taurus
4th	5:30 am	Gemini
6th	11:56 am	Cancer
8th	9:56 pm	Leo
11th	10:27 am	Virgo
13th	10:48 pm	Libra
16th	8:52 am	Scorpio
18th	4:11 pm	Sagittarius
20th	9:21 pm	Capricorn
23rd	1:10 am	Aquarius
25th	4:14 am	Pisces
27th	6:50 am	Aries
29th	10:01 am	Taurus
31st	2:15 pm	Gemini

June 1935
2nd	8:46 pm	Cancer
5th	6:22 am	Leo
7th	6:26 pm	Virgo
10th	6:58 am	Libra
12th	5:32 pm	Scorpio
15th	0:57 am	Sagittarius
17th	5:20 am	Capricorn
19th	7:56 am	Aquarius
21st	9:58 am	Pisces
23rd	12:25 pm	Aries
25th	3:57 pm	Taurus
27th	9:08 pm	Gemini
30th	4:29 am	Cancer

July 1935
2nd	2:15 pm	Leo
5th	2:10 am	Virgo
7th	2:51 pm	Libra
10th	2:14 am	Scorpio
12th	10:22 am	Sagittarius
14th	2:59 pm	Capricorn
16th	4:52 pm	Aquarius
18th	5:32 pm	Pisces
20th	6:36 pm	Aries
22nd	9:24 pm	Taurus
25th	2:46 am	Gemini
27th	10:47 am	Cancer
29th	9:07 pm	Leo

August 1935
1st	9:08 am	Virgo
3rd	9:54 pm	Libra
6th	9:53 am	Scorpio
8th	7:21 pm	Sagittarius
11th	1:08 am	Capricorn
13th	3:20 am	Aquarius
15th	3:19 am	Pisces
17th	2:58 am	Aries
19th	4:12 am	Taurus
21st	8:31 am	Gemini
23rd	4:22 pm	Cancer
26th	3:02 am	Leo
28th	3:22 pm	Virgo
31st	4:08 am	Libra

September 1935
2nd   4:21 pm Scorpio
5th   2:46 am Sagittarius
7th   10:03 am Capricorn
9th   1:39 pm Aquarius
11th   2:12 pm Pisces
13th   1:22 pm Aries
15th   1:15 pm Taurus
17th   3:52 pm Gemini
19th 10:29 pm Cancer
22nd   8:53 am Leo
24th   9:20 pm Virgo
27th 10:05 am Libra
29th 10:07 pm Scorpio

October 1935
2nd   8:39 am Sagittarius
4th   4:59 pm Capricorn
6th   10:19 pm Aquarius
9th   0:26 am Pisces
11th   0:19 am Aries
12th 11:54 pm Taurus
15th   1:18 am Gemini
17th   6:24 am Cancer
19th   3:38 pm Leo
22nd   2:45 am Virgo
24th   4:30 pm Libra
27th   4:14 am Scorpio
29th   2:16 pm Sagittarius
31st 10:31 pm Capricorn

November 1935
3rd   4:35 am Aquarius
5th   8:17 am Pisces
7th   9:52 am Aries
9th   10:30 am Taurus
11th 11:57 am Gemini
13th   4:01 pm Cancer
15th 11:50 pm Leo
18th 11:13 am Virgo
20th 11:52 pm Libra
23rd 11:33 am Scorpio
25th   9:08 pm Sagittarius
28th   4:27 am Capricorn
30th   9:57 am Aquarius

December 1935
2nd   2:01 pm Pisces
4th   4:52 pm Aries
6th   7:04 pm Taurus
8th   9:38 pm Gemini
11th   1:55 am Cancer
13th   9:10 am Leo
15th   7:34 pm Virgo
18th   7:57 am Libra
20th   8:00 pm Scorpio
23rd   5:41 am Sagittarius
25th 12:24 pm Capricorn
27th   4:44 pm Aquarius
29th   7:42 pm Pisces
31st 10:15 pm Aries

January 1936
3rd   1:12 am Taurus
5th   5:06 am Gemini
7th   10:32 am Cancer
9th   6:04 pm Leo
12th   4:06 am Virgo
14th   4:11 pm Libra
17th   4:36 am Scorpio
19th   3:06 pm Sagittarius
21st 10:17 pm Capricorn
24th   1:60 am Aquarius
26th   3:34 am Pisces
28th   4:37 am Aries
30th   6:40 am Taurus

February 1936
1st   10:43 am Gemini
3rd   5:02 pm Cancer
6th   1:27 am Leo
8th   11:51 am Virgo
10th 11:46 pm Libra
13th 12:23 pm Scorpio
15th 11:54 pm Sagittarius
18th   8:15 am Capricorn
20th 12:40 pm Aquarius
22nd   1:52 pm Pisces
24th   1:36 am Aries
26th   1:55 pm Taurus
28th   4:35 pm Gemini

March 1936
1st   10:27 am Cancer
4th   7:23 am Leo
6th   6:20 pm Virgo
9th   6:28 am Libra
11th   7:05 pm Scorpio
14th   7:03 am Sagittarius
16th   4:48 pm Capricorn
18th 10:51 pm Aquarius
21st   0:58 am Pisces
23rd   0:31 am Aries
24th 11:38 pm Taurus
27th   0:32 am Gemini
29th   4:56 am Cancer
31st   1:08 pm Leo

April 1936
3rd   0:08 am Virgo
5th   12:32 pm Libra
8th   1:06 am Scorpio
10th   1:01 pm Sagittarius
12th 11:24 pm Capricorn
15th   6:45 am Aquarius
17th 10:33 am Pisces
19th 11:18 am Aries
21st 10:39 am Taurus
23rd 10:43 am Gemini
25th   1:28 pm Cancer
27th   8:06 pm Leo
30th   6:25 am Virgo

May 1936
2nd   6:44 pm Libra
5th   7:17 am Scorpio
7th   6:55 pm Sagittarius
10th   4:55 am Capricorn
12th 12:44 pm Aquarius
14th   5:50 pm Pisces
16th   8:12 pm Aries
18th   8:49 pm Taurus
20th   9:14 pm Gemini
22nd 11:21 pm Cancer
25th   4:45 am Leo
27th   1:52 pm Virgo
30th   1:39 am Libra

June 1936
1st   2:12 pm Scorpio
4th   1:37 am Sagittarius
6th   11:01 am Capricorn
8th   6:15 pm Aquarius
10th 11:28 pm Pisces
13th   2:46 am Aries
15th   4:49 am Taurus
17th   6:32 am Gemini
19th   9:14 am Cancer
21st   2:19 pm Leo
23rd 10:17 pm Virgo
26th   9:26 am Libra
28th   9:53 pm Scorpio

July 1936
1st   9:24 am Sagittarius
3rd   6:32 pm Capricorn
6th   0:56 am Aquarius
8th   5:10 am Pisces
10th   8:11 am Aries
12th 10:48 am Taurus
14th   1:42 pm Gemini
16th   5:31 pm Cancer
18th 11:00 pm Leo
21st   6:58 am Virgo
23rd   5:33 pm Libra
26th   5:53 am Scorpio
28th   5:54 pm Sagittarius
31st   3:22 am Capricorn

August 1936
2nd   9:21 am Aquarius
4th   12:34 pm Pisces
6th   2:23 pm Aries
8th   4:15 pm Taurus
10th   7:15 pm Gemini
12th 11:53 pm Cancer
15th   6:24 am Leo
17th   2:49 pm Virgo
20th   1:18 am Libra
22nd   1:37 pm Scorpio
25th   2:09 am Sagittarius
27th 12:30 pm Capricorn
29th   7:08 pm Aquarius
31st 10:05 pm Pisces

September 1936
2nd   10:44 pm Aries
4th   11:05 pm Taurus
7th   0:55 am Gemini
9th   5:19 am Cancer
11th 12:17 pm Leo
13th   9:22 pm Virgo
16th   8:16 am Libra
18th   8:34 pm Scorpio
21st   9:24 am Sagittarius
23rd   8:51 pm Capricorn
26th   4:49 am Aquarius
28th   8:35 am Pisces
30th   9:08 am Aries

October 1936
2nd   8:28 am Taurus
4th   8:41 am Gemini
6th   11:34 am Cancer
8th   5:49 pm Leo
11th   3:02 am Virgo
13th   2:21 pm Libra
16th   2:48 am Scorpio
18th   3:38 pm Sagittarius
21st   3:37 am Capricorn
23rd 12:55 pm Aquarius
25th   6:24 pm Pisces
27th   8:06 pm Aries
29th   7:35 pm Taurus
31st   6:52 pm Gemini

November 1936
2nd   8:03 pm Cancer
5th   0:37 am Leo
7th   9:03 am Virgo
9th   8:16 pm Libra
12th   8:51 am Scorpio
14th   9:35 pm Sagittarius
17th   9:19 am Capricorn
19th   7:08 pm Aquarius
22nd   2:03 am Pisces
24th   5:33 am Aries
26th   6:28 am Taurus
28th   6:14 am Gemini
30th   6:44 am Cancer

December 1936
2nd   9:48 am Leo
4th   4:36 pm Virgo
7th   2:56 am Libra
9th   3:28 pm Scorpio
12th   4:06 am Sagittarius
14th   3:24 pm Capricorn
17th   0:43 am Aquarius
19th   7:42 am Pisces
21st 12:23 pm Aries
23rd   3:03 pm Taurus
25th   4:24 pm Gemini
27th   5:37 pm Cancer
29th   8:15 pm Leo

★ ★

January 1937
1st   1:46 am Virgo
3rd 10:58 am Libra
5th 10:57 pm Scorpio
8th 11:41 am Sagittarius
10th 10:52 pm Capricorn
13th 7:22 am Aquarius
15th 1:26 pm Pisces
17th 5:47 pm Aries
19th 9:06 pm Taurus
21st 11:55 pm Gemini
24th 2:40 am Cancer
26th 6:10 am Leo
28th 11:34 am Virgo
30th 7:51 pm Libra

February 1937
2nd 7:10 am Scorpio
4th 7:57 pm Sagittarius
7th 7:30 am Capricorn
9th 3:55 pm Aquarius
11th 9:08 pm Pisces
14th 0:12 am Aries
16th 2:35 am Taurus
18th 5:24 am Gemini
20th 9:07 am Cancer
22nd 1:54 pm Leo
24th 8:06 pm Virgo
27th 4:29 am Libra

March 1937
1st   3:26 pm Scorpio
4th 4:07 am Sagittarius
6th 4:19 pm Capricorn
9th 1:34 am Aquarius
11th 6:46 am Pisces
13th 8:57 am Aries
15th 9:55 am Taurus
17th 11:22 am Gemini
19th 2:29 pm Cancer
21st 7:38 pm Leo
24th 2:45 am Virgo
26th 11:50 am Libra
28th 10:52 pm Scorpio
31st 11:34 am Sagittarius

April 1937
3rd 0:16 am Capricorn
5th 10:34 am Aquarius
7th 4:54 pm Pisces
9th 7:25 pm Aries
11th 7:39 pm Taurus
13th 7:35 pm Gemini
15th 9:04 pm Cancer
18th 1:12 am Leo
20th 8:18 am Virgo
22nd 5:54 pm Libra
25th 5:22 am Scorpio
27th 6:06 pm Sagittarius
30th 6:56 am Capricorn

May 1937
2nd 6:06 pm Aquarius
5th 1:57 am Pisces
7th 5:44 am Aries
9th 6:31 am Taurus
11th 5:58 am Gemini
13th 6:03 am Cancer
15th 8:33 am Leo
17th 2:23 pm Virgo
19th 11:35 pm Libra
22nd 11:21 am Scorpio
25th 0:10 am Sagittarius
27th 12:51 pm Capricorn
30th 0:13 am Aquarius

June 1937
1st   8:54 am Pisces
3rd 2:17 pm Aries
5th 4:34 pm Taurus
7th 4:46 pm Gemini
9th 4:34 pm Cancer
11th 5:49 pm Leo
13th 10:04 pm Virgo
16th 6:11 am Libra
18th 5:34 pm Scorpio
21st 6:26 am Sagittarius
23rd 6:58 pm Capricorn
26th 5:52 am Aquarius
28th 2:35 pm Pisces
30th 8:50 pm Aries

July 1937
3rd 0:35 am Taurus
5th 2:17 am Gemini
7th 2:55 am Cancer
9th 4:03 am Leo
11th 7:22 am Virgo
13th 2:09 pm Libra
16th 0:36 am Scorpio
18th 1:21 pm Sagittarius
21st 1:51 am Capricorn
23rd 12:17 pm Aquarius
25th 8:21 pm Pisces
28th 2:15 am Aries
30th 6:31 am Taurus

August 1937
1st   9:30 am Gemini
3rd 11:35 am Cancer
5th 1:39 pm Leo
7th 4:59 pm Virgo
9th 10:59 pm Libra
12th 8:41 am Scorpio
14th 8:59 am Sagittarius
17th 9:36 am Capricorn
19th 8:03 pm Aquarius
22nd 3:27 am Pisces
24th 8:23 am Aries
26th 11:57 am Taurus
28th 3:03 pm Gemini
30th 6:06 pm Cancer

September 1937
1st   9:24 pm Leo
4th 1:36 am Virgo
6th 7:53 am Libra
8th 5:03 pm Scorpio
11th 5:01 am Sagittarius
13th 5:51 pm Capricorn
16th 4:48 am Aquarius
18th 12:14 pm Pisces
20th 4:28 pm Aries
22nd 6:49 pm Taurus
24th 8:46 pm Gemini
26th 11:26 pm Cancer
29th 3:17 am Leo

October 1937
1st   8:31 am Virgo
3rd 3:36 pm Libra
6th 0:57 am Scorpio
8th 12:47 pm Sagittarius
11th 1:47 am Capricorn
13th 1:35 pm Aquarius
15th 10:02 pm Pisces
18th 2:32 am Aries
20th 4:09 am Taurus
22nd 4:41 am Gemini
24th 5:49 am Cancer
26th 8:46 am Leo
28th 2:05 pm Virgo
30th 9:48 pm Libra

November 1937
2nd 7:51 am Scorpio
4th 7:48 pm Sagittarius
7th 8:51 am Capricorn
9th 9:18 pm Aquarius
12th 7:04 am Pisces
14th 12:55 pm Aries
16th 3:08 pm Taurus
18th 3:09 pm Gemini
20th 2:50 pm Cancer
22nd 4:00 pm Leo
24th 7:59 pm Virgo
27th 3:23 am Libra
29th 1:49 pm Scorpio

December 1937
2nd 2:06 am Sagittarius
4th 3:07 pm Capricorn
7th 3:40 am Aquarius
9th 2:18 pm Pisces
11th 9:53 pm Aries
14th 1:49 am Taurus
16th 2:42 am Gemini
18th 2:03 am Cancer
20th 1:50 am Leo
22nd 4:01 am Virgo
24th 9:58 am Libra
26th 7:46 pm Scorpio
29th 8:13 am Sagittarius
31st 9:17 pm Capricorn

January 1938
3rd 9:29 am Aquarius
5th 8:06 pm Pisces
8th 4:26 am Aries
10th 10:02 am Taurus
12th 12:47 pm Gemini
14th 1:20 pm Cancer
16th 1:11 pm Leo
18th 2:17 pm Virgo
20th 6:32 pm Libra
23rd 2:57 am Scorpio
25th 2:52 pm Sagittarius
28th 3:57 am Capricorn
30th 3:57 pm Aquarius

February 1938
2nd 1:57 am Pisces
4th 9:53 am Aries
6th 3:56 pm Taurus
8th 8:07 pm Gemini
10th 10:25 pm Cancer
12th 11:34 pm Leo
15th 0:57 am Virgo
17th 4:32 am Libra
19th 11:42 am Scorpio
21st 10:34 pm Sagittarius
24th 11:26 am Capricorn
26th 11:34 pm Aquarius

March 1938
1st   9:10 am Pisces
3rd 4:14 pm Aries
5th 9:29 pm Taurus
8th 1:33 am Gemini
10th 4:46 am Cancer
12th 7:24 am Leo
14th 10:07 am Virgo
16th 2:13 pm Libra
18th 8:56 pm Scorpio
21st 7:03 am Sagittarius
23rd 7:32 pm Capricorn
26th 7:52 am Aquarius
28th 5:48 pm Pisces
31st 0:33 am Aries

April 1938
2nd 4:41 am Taurus
4th 7:32 am Gemini
6th 10:08 am Cancer
8th 1:06 pm Leo
10th 4:52 pm Virgo
12th 10:03 pm Libra
15th 5:24 am Scorpio
17th 3:22 pm Sagittarius
20th 3:33 am Capricorn
22nd 4:09 pm Aquarius
25th 2:51 am Pisces
27th 10:03 am Aries
29th 1:57 pm Taurus

★ ★

May 1938
1st 3:43 pm Gemini
3rd 4:50 pm Cancer
5th 6:43 pm Leo
7th 10:17 pm Virgo
10th 4:07 am Libra
12th 12:19 pm Scorpio
14th 10:41 pm Sagittarius
17th 10:52 am Capricorn
19th 11:38 pm Aquarius
22nd 11:05 am Pisces
24th 7:32 pm Aries
27th 0:17 am Taurus
29th 1:51 am Gemini
31st 1:52 am Cancer

June 1938
2nd 2:10 am Leo
4th 4:24 am Virgo
6th 9:40 am Libra
8th 6:03 pm Scorpio
11th 4:58 am Sagittarius
13th 5:22 pm Capricorn
16th 6:07 am Aquarius
18th 6:01 pm Pisces
21st 3:38 am Aries
23rd 9:44 am Taurus
25th 12:21 pm Gemini
27th 12:26 pm Cancer
29th 11:48 am Leo

July 1938
1st 12:29 pm Virgo
3rd 4:14 pm Libra
5th 11:49 pm Scorpio
8th 10:49 am Sagittarius
10th 11:23 pm Capricorn
13th 12:05 pm Aquarius
15th 11:56 pm Pisces
18th 9:50 am Aries
20th 5:28 pm Taurus
22nd 9:42 pm Gemini
24th 10:55 pm Cancer
26th 10:27 pm Leo
28th 10:19 pm Virgo
31st 0:35 am Libra

August 1938
2nd 6:54 am Scorpio
4th 5:05 pm Sagittarius
7th 5:33 am Capricorn
9th 6:14 pm Aquarius
12th 5:43 am Pisces
14th 3:33 pm Aries
16th 11:27 pm Taurus
19th 4:50 am Gemini
21st 7:38 am Cancer
23rd 8:27 am Leo
25th 8:47 am Virgo
27th 10:33 am Libra
29th 3:33 pm Scorpio

September 1938
1st 0:28 am Sagittarius
3rd 12:31 pm Capricorn
6th 1:10 am Aquarius
8th 12:26 pm Pisces
10th 9:41 pm Aries
13th 4:54 am Taurus
15th 10:22 am Gemini
17th 2:08 pm Cancer
19th 4:27 pm Leo
21st 6:03 pm Virgo
23rd 8:23 pm Libra
26th 0:59 am Scorpio
28th 9:08 am Sagittarius
30th 8:23 pm Capricorn

October 1938
3rd 8:57 am Aquarius
5th 8:27 pm Pisces
8th 5:20 am Aries
10th 11:40 am Taurus
12th 4:09 pm Gemini
14th 7:31 pm Cancer
16th 10:20 pm Leo
19th 1:10 am Virgo
21st 4:46 am Libra
23rd 10:05 am Scorpio
25th 5:59 pm Sagittarius
28th 4:42 am Capricorn
30th 5:09 pm Aquarius

November 1938
2nd 5:09 am Pisces
4th 2:32 pm Aries
6th 8:40 pm Taurus
9th 0:03 am Gemini
11th 1:59 am Cancer
13th 3:52 am Leo
15th 6:40 am Virgo
17th 11:06 am Libra
19th 5:28 pm Scorpio
22nd 1:58 am Sagittarius
24th 12:42 pm Capricorn
27th 1:01 am Aquarius
29th 1:29 pm Pisces

December 1938
2nd 0:04 am Aries
4th 6:57 am Taurus
6th 10:15 am Gemini
8th 11:07 am Cancer
10th 11:20 am Leo
12th 12:42 pm Virgo
14th 4:31 pm Libra
16th 11:14 pm Scorpio
19th 8:34 am Sagittarius
21st 7:39 pm Capricorn
24th 7:50 am Aquarius
26th 8:42 pm Pisces
29th 8:10 am Aries
31st 4:44 pm Taurus

January 1939
2nd 9:18 pm Gemini
4th 10:19 pm Cancer
6th 9:33 pm Leo
8th 9:10 pm Virgo
10th 11:12 pm Libra
13th 4:57 am Scorpio
15th 2:13 pm Sagittarius
18th 1:45 am Capricorn
20th 2:16 pm Aquarius
23rd 2:51 am Pisces
25th 2:40 pm Aries
28th 0:30 am Taurus
30th 6:45 am Gemini

February 1939
1st 9:17 am Cancer
3rd 9:05 am Leo
5th 8:06 am Virgo
7th 8:35 am Libra
9th 12:28 pm Scorpio
11th 8:26 pm Sagittarius
14th 7:43 am Capricorn
16th 8:21 pm Aquarius
19th 8:51 am Pisces
21st 8:23 pm Aries
24th 6:17 am Taurus
26th 1:44 pm Gemini
28th 6:04 pm Cancer

March 1939
2nd 7:28 pm Leo
4th 7:17 pm Virgo
6th 7:29 pm Libra
8th 10:01 pm Scorpio
11th 4:26 am Sagittarius
13th 2:38 pm Capricorn
16th 3:00 am Aquarius
18th 3:29 pm Pisces
21st 2:38 am Aries
23rd 11:55 am Taurus
25th 7:13 pm Gemini
28th 0:19 am Cancer
30th 3:14 am Leo

April 1939
1st 4:39 am Virgo
3rd 5:50 am Libra
5th 8:26 am Scorpio
7th 1:52 pm Sagittarius
9th 10:46 pm Capricorn
12th 10:33 am Aquarius
14th 11:04 pm Pisces
17th 10:10 am Aries
19th 6:53 pm Taurus
22nd 1:14 am Gemini
24th 5:41 am Cancer
26th 8:52 am Leo
28th 11:26 am Virgo
30th 2:03 pm Libra

May 1939
2nd 5:39 pm Scorpio
4th 11:11 pm Sagittarius
7th 7:37 am Capricorn
9th 6:42 pm Aquarius
12th 7:08 am Pisces
14th 6:38 pm Aries
17th 3:26 am Taurus
19th 9:02 am Gemini
21st 12:19 pm Cancer
23rd 2:33 pm Leo
25th 4:51 pm Virgo
27th 8:06 pm Libra
30th 0:47 am Scorpio

June 1939
1st 7:18 am Sagittarius
3rd 3:52 pm Capricorn
6th 2:42 am Aquarius
8th 3:05 pm Pisces
11th 3:10 am Aries
13th 12:37 pm Taurus
15th 6:28 pm Gemini
17th 9:04 pm Cancer
19th 9:57 pm Leo
21st 10:56 pm Virgo
24th 1:30 am Libra
26th 6:28 am Scorpio
28th 1:41 pm Sagittarius
30th 10:54 pm Capricorn

July 1939
3rd 9:56 am Aquarius
5th 10:17 pm Pisces
8th 10:47 am Aries
10th 9:25 pm Taurus
13th 4:17 am Gemini
15th 7:12 am Cancer
17th 7:30 am Leo
19th 7:10 am Virgo
21st 8:14 am Libra
23rd 12:08 pm Scorpio
25th 7:12 pm Sagittarius
28th 4:52 am Capricorn
30th 4:16 pm Aquarius

August 1939
2nd 4:42 am Pisces
4th 5:21 pm Aries
7th 4:45 am Taurus
9th 1:01 pm Gemini
11th 5:17 pm Cancer
13th 6:07 pm Leo
15th 5:20 pm Virgo
17th 5:08 pm Libra
19th 7:24 pm Scorpio
22nd 1:15 am Sagittarius
24th 10:36 am Capricorn
26th 10:10 pm Aquarius
29th 10:43 am Pisces
31st 11:16 pm Aries

September 1939
3rd 10:45 am Taurus
5th 8:00 pm Gemini
8th 1:51 am Cancer
10th 4:11 am Leo
12th 4:09 am Virgo
14th 3:42 am Libra
16th 4:47 am Scorpio
18th 9:08 am Sagittarius
20th 5:15 pm Capricorn
23rd 4:24 am Aquarius
25th 4:59 pm Pisces
28th 5:21 am Aries
30th 4:27 am Taurus

October 1939
3rd 1:38 am Gemini
5th 8:14 am Cancer
7th 12:07 pm Leo
9th 1:44 pm Virgo
11th 2:18 pm Libra
13th 3:22 pm Scorpio
15th 6:40 pm Sagittarius
18th 1:24 am Capricorn
20th 11:44 am Aquarius
23rd 0:06 am Pisces
25th 12:27 pm Aries
27th 11:10 pm Taurus
30th 7:28 am Gemini

November 1939
1st 1:39 pm Cancer
3rd 5:50 pm Leo
5th 8:56 pm Virgo
7th 11:03 pm Libra
10th 1:15 am Scorpio
12th 4:46 am Sagittarius
14th 10:48 am Capricorn
16th 8:04 pm Aquarius
19th 8:02 am Pisces
21st 8:35 am Aries
24th 7:19 am Taurus
26th 3:05 pm Gemini
28th 8:10 pm Cancer
30th 11:34 pm Leo

December 1939
3rd 2:22 am Virgo
5th 5:23 am Libra
7th 8:60 am Scorpio
9th 1:35 pm Sagittarius
11th 7:54 pm Capricorn
14th 4:47 am Aquarius
16th 4:17 pm Pisces
19th 5:02 am Aries
21st 4:30 pm Taurus
24th 0:37 am Gemini
26th 5:02 am Cancer
28th 7:05 am Leo
30th 8:30 am Virgo

January 1940
1st 10:47 am Libra
3rd 2:40 pm Scorpio
5th 8:14 pm Sagittarius
8th 3:31 am Capricorn
10th 12:46 pm Aquarius
13th 0:04 am Pisces
15th 12:56 pm Aries
18th 1:16 am Taurus
20th 10:27 am Gemini
22nd 3:30 pm Cancer
24th 5:09 pm Leo
26th 5:14 pm Virgo
28th 5:46 pm Libra
30th 8:20 pm Scorpio

February 1940
2nd 1:37 am Sagittarius
4th 9:30 am Capricorn
6th 7:23 pm Aquarius
9th 7:01 am Pisces
11th 7:49 pm Aries
14th 8:33 am Taurus
16th 7:08 pm Gemini
19th 1:47 am Cancer
21st 4:17 am Leo
23rd 4:12 am Virgo
25th 3:31 am Libra
27th 4:17 am Scorpio
29th 7:59 am Sagittarius

March 1940
2nd 3:07 pm Capricorn
5th 1:07 am Aquarius
7th 1:08 pm Pisces
10th 1:60 am Aries
12th 2:44 pm Taurus
15th 1:53 am Gemini
17th 9:53 am Cancer
19th 2:11 pm Leo
21st 3:18 pm Virgo
23rd 2:49 pm Libra
25th 2:38 pm Scorpio
27th 4:36 pm Sagittarius
29th 10:02 pm Capricorn

April 1940
1st 7:15 am Aquarius
3rd 7:11 pm Pisces
6th 8:09 am Aries
8th 8:38 pm Taurus
11th 7:29 am Gemini
13th 4:01 pm Cancer
15th 9:43 pm Leo
18th 0:34 am Virgo
20th 1:23 am Libra
22nd 1:34 am Scorpio
24th 2:50 am Sagittarius
26th 6:54 am Capricorn
28th 2:44 pm Aquarius

May 1940
1st 1:55 am Pisces
3rd 2:51 pm Aries
6th 3:11 am Taurus
8th 1:29 pm Gemini
10th 9:31 pm Cancer
13th 3:20 am Leo
15th 7:15 am Virgo
17th 9:39 am Libra
19th 11:12 am Scorpio
21st 1:03 pm Sagittarius
23rd 4:39 pm Capricorn
25th 11:21 pm Aquarius
28th 9:42 am Pisces
30th 10:18 pm Aries

June 1940
2nd 10:41 am Taurus
4th 8:46 pm Gemini
7th 3:59 am Cancer
9th 8:58 am Leo
11th 12:38 pm Virgo
13th 3:41 pm Libra
15th 6:31 pm Scorpio
17th 9:33 pm Sagittarius
20th 1:45 am Capricorn
22nd 8:19 am Aquarius
24th 5:59 pm Pisces
27th 6:14 am Aries
29th 6:51 pm Taurus

July 1940
2nd 5:11 am Gemini
4th 12:05 pm Cancer
6th 4:09 pm Leo
8th 6:43 pm Virgo
10th 9:07 pm Libra
13th 0:07 am Scorpio
15th 4:06 am Sagittarius
17th 9:19 am Capricorn
19th 4:24 pm Aquarius
22nd 1:59 am Pisces
24th 2:02 pm Aries
27th 2:54 am Gemini
29th 1:59 pm Gemini
31st 9:30 pm Cancer

August 1940
3rd 1:20 am Leo
5th 2:50 am Virgo
7th 3:51 am Libra
9th 5:48 am Scorpio
11th 9:32 am Sagittarius
13th 3:17 pm Capricorn
15th 11:07 pm Aquarius
18th 9:12 am Pisces
20th 9:14 pm Aries
23rd 10:15 am Taurus
25th 10:12 pm Gemini
28th 6:49 am Cancer
30th 11:25 am Leo

September 1940
1st 12:54 pm Virgo
3rd 12:55 pm Libra
5th 1:20 pm Scorpio
7th 3:41 pm Sagittarius
9th 8:47 pm Capricorn
12th 4:53 am Aquarius
14th 3:27 pm Pisces
17th 3:43 am Aries
19th 4:45 pm Taurus
22nd 5:03 am Gemini
24th 2:54 pm Cancer
26th 9:07 pm Leo
28th 11:42 pm Virgo
30th 11:47 pm Libra

October 1940
2nd 11:12 pm Scorpio
4th 11:53 pm Sagittarius
7th 3:31 am Capricorn
9th 10:48 am Aquarius
11th 9:18 pm Pisces
14th 9:50 am Aries
16th 10:49 pm Taurus
19th 10:57 am Gemini
21st 9:17 pm Cancer
24th 4:47 am Leo
26th 9:06 am Virgo
28th 10:35 am Libra
30th 10:26 am Scorpio

November 1940
1st 10:26 am Sagittarius
3rd 12:29 pm Capricorn
5th 6:08 pm Aquarius
8th 3:49 am Pisces
10th 4:14 pm Aries
13th 5:12 am Taurus
15th 4:58 pm Gemini
18th 2:51 am Cancer
20th 10:35 am Leo
22nd 4:07 pm Virgo
24th 7:22 pm Libra
26th 8:45 pm Scorpio
28th 9:20 pm Sagittarius
30th 10:52 pm Capricorn

December 1940
3rd 3:16 am Aquarius
5th 11:41 am Pisces
7th 11:28 pm Aries
10th 12:26 pm Taurus
13th 0:08 am Gemini
15th 9:17 am Cancer
17th 4:14 pm Leo
19th 9:34 pm Virgo
22nd 1:36 am Libra
24th 4:30 am Scorpio
26th 6:37 am Sagittarius
28th 9:02 am Capricorn
30th 1:15 pm Aquarius

January 1941
1st   8:38 pm Pisces
4th   7:38 am Aries
6th   8:29 pm Taurus
9th   8:25 am Gemini
11th   5:31 pm Cancer
13th   11:40 am Leo
16th   3:46 am Virgo
18th   7:00 am Libra
20th   10:05 am Scorpio
22nd   1:18 am Sagittarius
24th   5:03 am Capricorn
26th   10:07 pm Aquarius
29th   5:38 am Pisces
31st   4:05 pm Aries

February 1941
3rd   4:41 am Taurus
5th   5:08 pm Gemini
8th   2:55 am Cancer
10th   9:05 am Leo
12th   12:20 pm Virgo
14th   2:08 pm Libra
16th   3:54 pm Scorpio
18th   6:39 pm Sagittarius
20th   10:55 pm Capricorn
23rd   5:03 am Aquarius
25th   1:21 pm Pisces
27th   11:54 pm Aries

March 1941
2nd   12:24 pm Taurus
5th   1:12 am Gemini
7th   11:59 am Cancer
9th   7:17 pm Leo
11th   10:52 pm Virgo
13th   11:52 pm Libra
16th   0:03 am Scorpio
18th   1:09 am Sagittarius
20th   4:27 am Capricorn
22nd   10:36 am Aquarius
24th   7:32 pm Pisces
27th   6:41 am Aries
29th   7:14 pm Taurus

April 1941
1st   8:05 am Gemini
3rd   7:42 pm Cancer
6th   4:23 am Leo
8th   9:17 am Virgo
10th   10:52 am Libra
12th   10:32 am Scorpio
14th   10:12 am Sagittarius
16th   11:45 am Capricorn
18th   4:36 pm Aquarius
21st   1:07 am Pisces
23rd   12:36 pm Aries
26th   1:21 am Taurus
28th   2:09 pm Gemini

May 1941
1st   1:55 am Cancer
3rd   11:29 am Leo
5th   6:02 pm Virgo
7th   9:10 pm Libra
9th   9:33 pm Scorpio
11th   8:51 pm Sagittarius
13th   9:07 pm Capricorn
16th   0:16 am Aquarius
18th   7:39 am Pisces
20th   6:36 pm Aries
23rd   7:25 am Taurus
25th   8:09 pm Gemini
28th   7:34 am Cancer
30th   5:13 pm Leo

June 1941
2nd   0:37 am Virgo
4th   5:14 am Libra
6th   7:10 am Scorpio
8th   7:23 am Sagittarius
10th   7:36 am Capricorn
12th   9:47 am Aquarius
14th   3:40 pm Pisces
17th   1:32 am Aries
19th   2:04 pm Taurus
22nd   2:43 am Gemini
24th   1:48 pm Cancer
26th   10:54 pm Leo
29th   6:00 am Virgo

July 1941
1st   11:13 am Libra
3rd   2:30 pm Scorpio
5th   4:11 pm Sagittarius
7th   5:22 pm Capricorn
9th   7:38 pm Aquarius
12th   0:43 am Pisces
14th   9:38 am Aries
16th   9:31 pm Taurus
19th   10:08 am Gemini
21st   9:13 pm Cancer
24th   5:45 am Leo
26th   12:00 pm Virgo
28th   4:39 pm Libra
30th   8:08 pm Scorpio

August 1941
1st   10:49 pm Sagittarius
4th   1:16 am Capricorn
6th   4:34 am Aquarius
8th   9:55 am Pisces
10th   6:14 pm Aries
13th   5:33 am Taurus
15th   6:09 pm Gemini
18th   5:34 am Cancer
20th   2:11 pm Leo
22nd   7:51 pm Virgo
24th   11:21 pm Libra
27th   1:49 am Scorpio
29th   4:14 am Sagittarius
31st   7:20 am Capricorn

September 1941
2nd   11:40 am Aquarius
4th   5:54 pm Pisces
7th   2:28 am Aries
9th   1:33 pm Taurus
12th   2:05 am Gemini
14th   2:06 pm Cancer
16th   11:36 pm Leo
19th   5:26 am Virgo
21st   8:14 am Libra
23rd   9:23 am Scorpio
25th   10:27 am Sagittarius
27th   12:48 pm Capricorn
29th   5:19 pm Aquarius

October 1941
2nd   0:17 am Pisces
4th   9:39 am Aries
6th   8:51 pm Taurus
9th   9:22 am Gemini
11th   9:52 pm Cancer
14th   8:25 am Leo
16th   3:31 pm Virgo
18th   6:51 pm Libra
20th   7:24 pm Scorpio
22nd   7:02 pm Sagittarius
24th   7:43 pm Capricorn
26th   11:02 pm Aquarius
29th   5:54 am Pisces
31st   3:40 pm Aries

November 1941
3rd   3:19 am Taurus
5th   3:52 pm Gemini
8th   4:24 am Cancer
10th   3:45 pm Leo
13th   0:29 am Virgo
15th   5:18 am Libra
17th   6:38 am Scorpio
19th   5:54 am Sagittarius
21st   5:15 am Capricorn
23rd   6:52 am Aquarius
25th   12:16 pm Pisces
27th   9:28 pm Aries
30th   9:19 am Taurus

December 1941
2nd   9:59 pm Gemini
5th   10:20 am Cancer
7th   9:41 pm Leo
10th   7:08 am Virgo
12th   1:41 pm Libra
14th   4:47 pm Scorpio
16th   5:08 pm Sagittarius
18th   4:30 pm Capricorn
20th   4:59 pm Aquarius
22nd   8:37 pm Pisces
25th   4:28 am Aries
27th   3:46 pm Taurus
30th   4:27 am Gemini

January 1942
1st   4:40 pm Cancer
4th   3:32 am Leo
6th   12:39 pm Virgo
8th   7:47 pm Libra
11th   0:24 am Scorpio
13th   2:30 am Sagittarius
15th   3:07 am Capricorn
17th   3:54 am Aquarius
19th   6:48 am Pisces
21st   1:14 pm Aries
23rd   11:21 pm Taurus
26th   11:45 am Gemini
29th   0:04 am Cancer
31st   10:35 am Leo

February 1942
2nd   6:56 pm Virgo
5th   1:18 am Libra
7th   5:55 am Scorpio
9th   9:06 am Sagittarius
11th   11:18 am Capricorn
13th   1:30 pm Aquarius
15th   4:55 pm Pisces
17th   10:47 pm Aries
20th   8:01 am Taurus
22nd   7:48 pm Gemini
25th   8:15 am Cancer
27th   7:05 pm Leo

March 1942
2nd   3:06 am Virgo
4th   8:21 am Libra
6th   11:49 am Scorpio
8th   2:29 pm Sagittarius
10th   5:10 pm Capricorn
12th   8:32 pm Aquarius
15th   1:10 am Pisces
17th   7:44 am Aries
19th   4:41 pm Taurus
22nd   4:02 am Gemini
24th   4:32 pm Cancer
27th   4:03 am Leo
29th   12:33 pm Virgo
31st   5:34 pm Libra

April 1942
2nd   7:55 pm Scorpio
4th   9:05 pm Sagittarius
6th   10:43 pm Capricorn
9th   1:58 am Aquarius
11th   7:21 am Pisces
13th   2:51 pm Aries
16th   0:18 am Taurus
18th   11:39 am Gemini
21st   0:10 am Cancer
23rd   12:19 pm Leo
25th   10:01 pm Virgo
28th   3:49 am Libra
30th   5:58 am Scorpio

★ ★

May 1942
2nd   6:04 am Sagittarius
4th   6:09 am Capricorn
6th   8:01 am Aquarius
8th 12:48 pm Pisces
10th   8:32 am Aries
13th   6:38 am Taurus
15th   6:16 pm Gemini
18th   6:49 am Cancer
20th   7:19 pm Leo
23rd   6:04 am Virgo
25th   1:15 pm Libra
27th   4:26 pm Scorpio
29th   4:38 pm Sagittarius
31st   3:47 pm Capricorn

June 1942
2nd   4:05 pm Aquarius
4th   7:18 pm Pisces
7th   2:14 am Aries
9th 12:18 pm Taurus
12th 12:12 am Gemini
14th 12:49 pm Cancer
17th   1:18 am Leo
19th 12:29 pm Virgo
21st   9:01 pm Libra
24th   1:49 am Scorpio
26th   3:06 am Sagittarius
28th   2:30 am Capricorn
30th   2:02 am Aquarius

July 1942
2nd   3:49 am Pisces
4th   9:16 am Aries
6th   6:25 pm Taurus
9th   6:12 am Gemini
11th   6:51 pm Cancer
14th   7:07 am Leo
16th   6:06 pm Virgo
19th   2:50 am Libra
21st   8:56 am Scorpio
23rd 11:53 am Sagittarius
25th 12:36 pm Capricorn
27th 12:39 pm Aquarius
29th   1:53 pm Pisces
31st   5:50 pm Aries

August 1942
3rd   1:49 am Taurus
5th 12:56 pm Gemini
8th   1:31 am Cancer
10th   1:37 pm Leo
13th   0:09 am Virgo
15th   8:29 am Libra
17th   2:35 pm Scorpio
19th   6:32 pm Sagittarius
21st   8:44 pm Capricorn
23rd 10:07 pm Aquarius
25th 11:55 pm Pisces
28th   3:40 am Aries
30th 10:33 am Taurus

September 1942
1st   8:41 pm Gemini
4th   9:00 am Cancer
6th   9:14 pm Leo
9th   7:28 am Virgo
11th   3:01 pm Libra
13th   8:18 pm Scorpio
15th 11:58 pm Sagittarius
18th   2:47 am Capricorn
20th   5:27 am Aquarius
22nd   8:35 am Pisces
24th 12:59 pm Aries
26th   7:35 pm Taurus
29th   5:06 am Gemini

October 1942
1st   5:04 pm Cancer
4th   5:33 am Leo
6th   4:10 pm Virgo
8th 11:33 pm Libra
11th   3:45 am Scorpio
13th   6:10 am Sagittarius
15th   8:13 am Capricorn
17th 11:03 am Aquarius
19th   3:06 pm Pisces
21st   8:36 pm Aries
24th   3:52 am Taurus
26th   1:20 pm Gemini
29th   0:59 am Cancer
31st   1:46 pm Leo

November 1942
3rd   1:18 am Virgo
5th   9:16 am Libra
7th   1:22 pm Scorpio
9th   2:45 pm Sagittarius
11th   3:19 pm Capricorn
13th   4:51 pm Aquarius
15th   8:30 pm Pisces
18th   2:32 am Aries
20th 10:39 am Taurus
22nd   8:35 pm Gemini
25th   8:17 am Cancer
27th   9:09 pm Leo
30th   9:25 am Virgo

December 1942
2nd   6:51 pm Libra
5th   0:07 am Scorpio
7th   1:32 am Sagittarius
9th   1:08 am Capricorn
11th   0:57 am Aquarius
13th   2:59 am Pisces
15th   8:09 am Aries
17th   4:20 pm Taurus
20th   2:47 am Gemini
22nd   2:57 pm Cancer
25th   3:35 am Leo
27th   4:07 pm Virgo
30th   2:41 am Libra

January 1943
1st   9:32 am Scorpio
3rd 12:28 pm Sagittarius
5th 12:33 pm Capricorn
7th 11:45 am Aquarius
9th 12:09 pm Pisces
11th   3:27 pm Aries
13th 10:24 pm Taurus
16th   8:42 am Gemini
18th   8:54 pm Cancer
21st   9:43 am Leo
23rd 10:02 pm Virgo
26th   8:44 am Libra
28th   4:46 pm Scorpio
30th   9:32 pm Sagittarius

February 1943
1st 11:14 pm Capricorn
3rd 11:11 pm Aquarius
5th 11:09 pm Pisces
8th   1:01 am Aries
10th   6:22 am Taurus
12th   3:29 pm Gemini
15th   3:25 am Cancer
17th   4:18 pm Leo
20th   4:19 am Virgo
22nd   2:28 pm Libra
24th 10:24 pm Scorpio
27th   3:58 am Sagittarius

March 1943
1st   7:17 am Capricorn
3rd   8:56 am Aquarius
5th   9:56 am Pisces
7th 11:46 am Aries
9th   3:34 pm Taurus
11th 11:39 pm Gemini
14th 10:53 am Cancer
16th 11:42 pm Leo
19th 11:41 am Virgo
21st   9:21 pm Libra
24th   4:23 am Scorpio
26th   9:22 am Sagittarius
28th   1:04 pm Capricorn
30th   3:57 pm Aquarius

April 1943
1st   6:28 pm Pisces
3rd   9:18 pm Aries
6th   1:39 am Taurus
8th   8:46 am Gemini
10th   7:04 pm Cancer
13th   7:39 am Leo
15th   7:59 pm Virgo
18th   5:39 am Libra
20th 12:01 pm Scorpio
22nd   3:55 pm Sagittarius
24th   6:40 pm Capricorn
26th   9:22 pm Aquarius
29th   0:36 am Pisces

May 1943
1st   4:40 am Aries
3rd   9:60 am Taurus
5th   5:18 pm Gemini
8th   3:19 am Cancer
10th   3:40 pm Leo
13th   4:20 am Virgo
15th   2:40 pm Libra
17th   9:18 pm Scorpio
20th   0:33 am Sagittarius
22nd   2:01 am Capricorn
24th   3:25 am Aquarius
26th   6:01 am Pisces
28th 10:20 am Aries
30th   4:26 pm Taurus

June 1943
2nd   0:31 am Gemini
4th 10:48 am Cancer
6th 11:03 pm Virgo
9th 12:01 pm Virgo
11th 11:21 pm Libra
14th   6:54 am Scorpio
16th 10:32 am Sagittarius
18th 11:29 am Capricorn
20th 11:36 am Aquarius
22nd 12:42 pm Pisces
24th   3:58 pm Aries
26th   9:54 pm Taurus
29th   6:30 am Gemini

July 1943
1st   5:15 pm Cancer
4th   5:40 am Leo
6th   6:43 pm Virgo
9th   6:41 am Libra
11th   3:34 pm Scorpio
13th   8:34 pm Sagittarius
15th 10:05 pm Capricorn
17th   9:46 pm Aquarius
19th   9:32 pm Pisces
21st 11:10 pm Aries
24th   3:56 am Taurus
26th 12:08 pm Gemini
28th 11:04 pm Cancer
31st 11:44 am Leo

August 1943
3rd   0:44 am Virgo
5th 12:48 pm Libra
7th 10:39 pm Scorpio
10th   5:04 am Sagittarius
12th   8:05 am Capricorn
14th   8:34 am Aquarius
16th   8:07 am Pisces
18th   8:36 am Aries
20th 11:46 am Taurus
22nd   6:38 pm Gemini
25th   5:09 am Cancer
27th   5:49 pm Leo
30th   6:47 am Virgo

★ ★

★★★

September 1943
1st   6:31 pm Libra
4th   4:19 pm Scorpio
6th   11:34 am Sagittarius
8th   4:09 pm Capricorn
10th 6:15 pm Aquarius
12th 6:45 pm Pisces
14th 7:09 pm Aries
16th 9:15 pm Taurus
19th 2:43 am Gemini
21st 12:13 pm Cancer
24th 0:33 am Leo
26th 1:29 pm Virgo
29th 0:56 am Libra

October 1943
1st   10:02 am Scorpio
3rd   5:01 pm Sagittarius
5th   10:10 pm Capricorn
8th   1:39 am Aquarius
10th 3:43 am Pisces
12th 5:12 am Aries
14th 7:27 am Taurus
16th 12:11 pm Gemini
18th 8:29 pm Cancer
21st 8:13 am Leo
23rd 9:08 pm Virgo
26th 8:33 am Libra
28th 5:11 pm Scorpio
30th 11:14 pm Sagittarius

November 1943
2nd   3:36 am Capricorn
4th   7:09 am Aquarius
6th   10:15 am Pisces
8th   1:11 pm Aries
10th 4:33 pm Taurus
12th 9:31 pm Gemini
15th 5:24 am Cancer
17th 4:28 pm Leo
20th 5:20 am Virgo
22nd 5:15 pm Libra
25th 2:07 am Scorpio
27th 7:31 am Sagittarius
29th 10:41 am Capricorn

December 1943
1st   1:01 pm Aquarius
3rd   3:36 pm Pisces
5th   7:01 pm Aries
7th   11:30 pm Taurus
10th 5:34 am Gemini
12th 1:49 pm Cancer
15th 0:36 am Leo
17th 1:20 pm Virgo
20th 1:54 am Libra
22nd 11:39 am Scorpio
24th 5:39 pm Sagittarius
26th 8:22 pm Capricorn
28th 9:21 pm Aquarius
30th 10:17 pm Pisces

January 1944
2nd   0:35 am Aries
4th   5:02 am Taurus
6th   11:48 am Gemini
8th   8:49 pm Cancer
11th 7:59 am Leo
13th 8:39 pm Virgo
16th 9:26 am Libra
18th 8:24 pm Scorpio
21st 3:49 am Sagittarius
23rd 7:22 am Capricorn
25th 8:07 am Aquarius
27th 7:49 am Pisces
29th 8:18 am Aries
31st 11:13 am Taurus

February 1944
2nd   5:22 am Gemini
5th   2:42 am Cancer
7th   2:22 pm Leo
10th 3:07 am Virgo
12th 3:53 pm Libra
15th 3:21 am Scorpio
17th 12:08 pm Sagittarius
19th 5:28 pm Capricorn
21st 7:23 pm Aquarius
23rd 7:07 pm Pisces
25th 6:33 pm Aries
27th 7:40 pm Taurus

March 1944
1st   0:06 am Gemini
3rd   8:42 am Cancer
5th   8:20 pm Leo
8th   9:19 am Virgo
10th 9:55 pm Libra
13th 9:10 am Scorpio
15th 6:29 pm Sagittarius
18th 1:12 am Capricorn
20th 4:53 am Aquarius
22nd 5:56 am Pisces
24th 5:42 am Aries
26th 6:04 am Taurus
28th 9:04 am Gemini
30th 4:04 pm Cancer

April 1944
2nd   2:56 am Leo
4th   3:49 pm Virgo
7th   4:22 am Libra
9th   3:10 pm Scorpio
12th 0:04 am Sagittarius
14th 6:54 am Capricorn
16th 11:44 am Aquarius
18th 2:26 pm Pisces
20th 3:35 pm Aries
22nd 4:31 pm Taurus
24th 7:03 pm Gemini
27th 0:49 am Cancer
29th 10:40 am Leo

May 1944
1st   11:05 pm Virgo
4th   11:38 am Libra
6th   10:18 pm Scorpio
9th   6:26 am Sagittarius
11th 12:32 pm Capricorn
13th 5:08 pm Aquarius
15th 8:34 pm Pisces
17th 11:03 pm Aries
20th 1:16 am Taurus
22nd 4:30 am Gemini
24th 10:09 am Cancer
26th 7:07 pm Leo
29th 6:59 am Virgo
31st 7:37 pm Libra

June 1944
3rd   6:29 am Scorpio
5th   2:25 pm Sagittarius
7th   7:41 pm Capricorn
9th   11:12 pm Aquarius
12th 1:50 am Pisces
14th 4:42 am Aries
16th 7:54 am Taurus
18th 12:14 pm Gemini
20th 6:32 pm Cancer
23rd 3:27 am Leo
25th 2:59 pm Virgo
28th 3:39 am Libra
30th 3:07 pm Scorpio

July 1944
2nd   11:38 pm Sagittarius
5th   4:40 am Capricorn
7th   7:13 am Aquarius
9th   8:40 am Pisces
11th 10:22 am Aries
13th 1:21 pm Taurus
15th 6:14 pm Gemini
18th 1:23 am Cancer
20th 10:55 am Leo
22nd 10:24 pm Virgo
25th 11:06 am Libra
27th 11:16 pm Scorpio
30th 8:44 am Sagittarius

August 1944
1st   2:37 pm Capricorn
3rd   5:07 pm Aquarius
5th   5:34 pm Pisces
7th   5:45 pm Aries
9th   7:23 pm Taurus
11th 11:39 pm Gemini
14th 7:07 am Cancer
16th 5:11 pm Leo
19th 5:03 am Virgo
21st 5:45 pm Libra
24th 6:11 am Scorpio
26th 4:47 pm Sagittarius
29th 0:12 am Capricorn
31st 3:42 am Aquarius

September 1944
2nd   4:13 am Pisces
4th   3:27 am Aries
6th   3:30 am Taurus
8th   6:18 am Gemini
10th 12:52 pm Cancer
12th 10:51 pm Leo
15th 11:01 am Virgo
17th 11:48 pm Libra
20th 12:11 pm Scorpio
22nd 11:17 pm Sagittarius
25th 7:51 am Capricorn
27th 1:04 pm Aquarius
29th 2:53 pm Pisces

October 1944
1st   2:28 pm Aries
3rd   1:49 pm Taurus
5th   3:05 pm Gemini
7th   7:58 pm Cancer
10th 5:04 am Leo
12th 5:05 pm Virgo
15th 5:53 am Libra
17th 6:02 pm Scorpio
20th 4:49 am Sagittarius
22nd 1:45 pm Capricorn
24th 8:17 pm Aquarius
26th 11:53 pm Pisces
29th 0:53 am Aries
31st 0:45 am Taurus

November 1944
2nd   1:29 am Gemini
4th   5:07 am Cancer
6th   12:48 pm Leo
8th   11:58 pm Virgo
11th 12:42 pm Libra
14th 0:47 am Scorpio
16th 10:50 am Sagittarius
18th 7:18 pm Capricorn
21st 1:46 am Aquarius
23rd 6:16 am Pisces
25th 8:54 am Aries
27th 10:22 am Taurus
29th 11:57 am Gemini

December 1944
1st   3:21 pm Cancer
3rd   9:53 pm Leo
6th   8:06 am Virgo
8th   8:28 pm Libra
11th 8:40 am Scorpio
13th 6:48 pm Sagittarius
16th 2:20 am Capricorn
18th 7:41 am Aquarius
20th 11:38 am Pisces
22nd 2:42 pm Aries
24th 5:25 pm Taurus
26th 8:26 pm Gemini
29th 0:43 am Cancer
31st 7:22 am Leo

★★★

January 1945
2nd 4:50 pm Virgo
5th 4:43 am Libra
7th 5:09 pm Scorpio
10th 3:51 am Sagittarius
12th 11:22 am Capricorn
14th 3:53 am Aquarius
16th 6:26 pm Pisces
18th 8:22 pm Aries
20th 10:49 pm Taurus
23rd 2:37 am Gemini
25th 8:08 am Cancer
27th 3:35 pm Leo
30th 1:09 am Virgo

February 1945
1st 12:46 pm Libra
4th 1:20 am Scorpio
6th 12:53 pm Sagittarius
8th 9:27 pm Capricorn
11th 2:09 am Aquarius
13th 3:51 am Pisces
15th 4:13 am Aries
17th 5:07 am Taurus
19th 8:05 am Gemini
21st 1:46 pm Cancer
23rd 10:00 pm Leo
26th 8:15 am Virgo
28th 7:57 pm Libra

March 1945
3rd 8:32 am Scorpio
5th 8:43 pm Sagittarius
8th 6:32 am Capricorn
10th 12:34 pm Aquarius
12th 2:44 pm Pisces
14th 2:30 am Aries
16th 1:57 pm Taurus
18th 3:09 pm Gemini
20th 7:35 pm Cancer
23rd 3:34 am Leo
25th 2:13 pm Virgo
28th 2:15 am Libra
30th 2:51 pm Scorpio

April 1945
2nd 3:07 am Sagittarius
4th 1:48 pm Capricorn
6th 9:28 pm Aquarius
9th 1:10 am Pisces
11th 1:37 am Aries
13th 0:39 am Taurus
15th 0:31 am Gemini
17th 3:16 am Cancer
19th 9:56 am Leo
21st 8:05 pm Virgo
24th 8:16 am Libra
26th 8:52 pm Scorpio
29th 8:55 am Sagittarius

May 1945
1st 7:39 pm Capricorn
4th 4:03 am Aquarius
6th 9:16 am Pisces
8th 11:21 am Aries
10th 11:24 am Taurus
12th 11:16 am Gemini
14th 12:57 pm Cancer
16th 6:01 pm Leo
19th 2:57 am Virgo
21st 2:43 pm Libra
24th 3:21 am Scorpio
26th 3:09 pm Sagittarius
29th 1:23 am Capricorn
31st 9:32 am

June 1945
2nd 3:22 pm Pisces
4th 6:48 pm Aries
6th 8:22 pm Taurus
8th 9:15 pm Gemini
10th 11:03 pm Cancer
13th 3:22 am Leo
15th 11:12 am Virgo
17th 10:06 pm Libra
20th 10:35 am Scorpio
22nd 10:27 pm Sagittarius
25th 8:13 am Capricorn
27th 3:34 pm Aquarius
29th 8:51 pm Pisces

July 1945
2nd 0:30 am Aries
4th 3:04 am Taurus
6th 5:21 am Gemini
8th 8:14 am Cancer
10th 12:48 pm Leo
12th 8:01 pm Virgo
15th 6:14 am Libra
17th 6:29 pm Scorpio
20th 6:33 am Sagittarius
22nd 4:25 pm Capricorn
24th 11:17 pm Aquarius
27th 3:26 am Pisces
29th 6:09 am Aries
31st 8:31 am Taurus

August 1945
2nd 11:27 am Gemini
4th 3:26 pm Cancer
6th 8:54 pm Leo
9th 4:26 am Virgo
11th 2:24 pm Libra
14th 2:24 am Scorpio
16th 2:54 pm Sagittarius
19th 1:30 am Capricorn
21st 8:26 am Aquarius
23rd 12:02 pm Pisces
25th 1:30 pm Aries
27th 2:36 pm Taurus
29th 4:50 pm Gemini
31st 9:02 pm Cancer

September 1945
3rd 3:22 am Leo
5th 11:40 am Virgo
7th 9:51 pm Libra
10th 9:49 am Scorpio
12th 10:37 pm Sagittarius
15th 10:07 am Capricorn
17th 6:15 pm Aquarius
19th 10:17 pm Pisces
21st 11:10 pm Aries
23rd 10:53 pm Taurus
25th 11:31 pm Gemini
28th 2:40 am Cancer
30th 8:50 am Leo

October 1945
2nd 5:35 pm Virgo
5th 4:19 am Libra
7th 4:26 pm Scorpio
10th 5:18 am Sagittarius
12th 5:31 pm Capricorn
15th 3:05 am Aquarius
17th 8:27 am Pisces
19th 10:05 am Aries
21st 9:30 am Taurus
23rd 8:53 am Gemini
25th 10:15 am Cancer
27th 2:60 pm Leo
29th 11:12 pm Virgo

November 1945
1st 10:08 am Libra
3rd 10:29 pm Scorpio
6th 11:18 am Sagittarius
8th 11:36 pm Capricorn
11th 9:55 am Aquarius
13th 5:01 pm Pisces
15th 8:21 pm Aries
17th 8:46 pm Taurus
19th 8:04 pm Gemini
21st 8:15 pm Cancer
23rd 11:11 pm Leo
26th 6:02 am Virgo
28th 4:20 pm Libra

December 1945
1st 4:42 am Scorpio
3rd 5:28 pm Sagittarius
6th 5:22 am Capricorn
8th 3:31 pm Aquarius
10th 11:20 pm Pisces
13th 4:12 am Aries
15th 6:27 am Taurus
17th 7:02 am Gemini
19th 7:30 am Cancer
21st 9:35 am Leo
23rd 2:49 pm Virgo
25th 11:45 pm Libra
28th 11:43 am Scorpio
31st 0:32 am Sagittarius

January 1946
2nd 12:07 pm Capricorn
4th 9:36 pm Aquarius
7th 4:45 am Pisces
9th 9:53 am Aries
11th 1:23 pm Taurus
13th 3:42 pm Gemini
15th 5:33 pm Cancer
17th 8:05 pm Leo
20th 0:40 am Virgo
22nd 8:35 am Libra
24th 7:40 pm Scorpio
27th 8:24 am Sagittarius
29th 8:15 pm Capricorn

February 1946
1st 5:20 am Aquarius
3rd 11:28 am Pisces
5th 3:37 pm Aries
7th 6:46 pm Taurus
9th 9:46 pm Gemini
12th 1:00 am Cancer
14th 4:51 am Leo
16th 10:06 am Virgo
18th 5:38 pm Libra
21st 4:04 am Scorpio
23rd 4:39 pm Sagittarius
26th 4:58 am Capricorn
28th 2:28 pm Aquarius

March 1946
2nd 8:22 pm Pisces
4th 11:23 pm Aries
7th 1:08 am Taurus
9th 3:13 am Gemini
11th 6:31 am Cancer
13th 11:16 am Leo
15th 5:33 pm Virgo
18th 1:42 am Libra
20th 12:07 pm Scorpio
23rd 0:31 am Sagittarius
25th 1:15 pm Capricorn
27th 11:50 pm Aquarius
30th 6:20 am Pisces

April 1946
1st 9:12 am Aries
3rd 9:55 am Taurus
5th 10:27 am Gemini
7th 12:25 pm Cancer
9th 4:40 pm Leo
11th 11:19 pm Virgo
14th 8:15 am Libra
16th 7:04 pm Scorpio
19th 7:32 am Sagittarius
21st 8:27 pm Capricorn
24th 7:53 am Aquarius
26th 3:49 pm Pisces
28th 7:42 pm Aries
30th 8:29 pm Taurus

May 1946
2nd 8:04 pm Gemini
4th 8:23 pm Cancer
6th 11:05 pm Leo
9th 4:60 am Virgo
11th 1:55 pm Libra
14th 1:08 am Scorpio
16th 1:47 pm Sagittarius
19th 2:41 am Capricorn
21st 2:29 pm Aquarius
23rd 11:39 pm Pisces
26th 5:01 am Aries
28th 7:01 am Taurus
30th 6:54 am Gemini

June 1946
1st 6:31 am Cancer
3rd 7:44 am Leo
5th 12:02 pm Virgo
7th 7:59 pm Libra
10th 7:06 am Scorpio
12th 7:52 pm Sagittarius
15th 8:38 am Capricorn
17th 8:14 pm Aquarius
20th 5:40 am Pisces
22nd 12:15 pm Aries
24th 3:52 pm Taurus
26th 5:06 pm Gemini
28th 5:12 pm Cancer
30th 5:51 pm Leo

July 1946
2nd 8:48 pm Virgo
5th 3:24 am Libra
7th 1:45 pm Scorpio
10th 2:20 am Sagittarius
12th 3:04 pm Capricorn
15th 2:17 am Aquarius
17th 11:13 am Pisces
19th 5:57 pm Aries
21st 10:15 pm Taurus
24th 1:19 am Gemini
26th 2:45 am Cancer
28th 3:59 am Leo
30th 6:37 am Virgo

August 1946
1st 12:11 pm Libra
3rd 9:24 pm Scorpio
6th 9:37 am Sagittarius
8th 10:23 pm Capricorn
11th 9:20 am Aquarius
13th 5:39 pm Pisces
15th 11:39 pm Aries
18th 3:59 am Taurus
20th 7:23 am Gemini
22nd 10:07 am Cancer
24th 12:41 pm Leo
26th 3:57 pm Virgo
28th 9:17 pm Libra
31st 5:52 am Scorpio

September 1946
2nd 5:32 pm Sagittarius
5th 6:22 am Capricorn
7th 5:38 pm Aquarius
10th 1:44 am Pisces
12th 6:47 am Aries
14th 10:03 am Taurus
16th 12:47 pm Gemini
18th 3:44 pm Cancer
20th 7:15 pm Leo
22nd 11:39 pm Virgo
25th 5:44 am Libra
27th 2:17 pm Scorpio
30th 1:33 am Sagittarius

October 1946
2nd 2:29 pm Capricorn
5th 2:27 am Aquarius
7th 11:03 am Pisces
9th 4:01 pm Aries
11th 6:19 pm Taurus
13th 7:37 pm Gemini
15th 9:23 pm Cancer
18th 0:35 am Leo
20th 5:38 am Virgo
22nd 12:36 pm Libra
24th 9:43 pm Scorpio
27th 9:06 am Sagittarius
29th 9:50 pm Capricorn

November 1946
1st 10:35 am Aquarius
3rd 8:31 pm Pisces
6th 2:27 am Aries
8th 4:48 am Taurus
10th 5:08 am Gemini
12th 5:18 am Cancer
14th 6:55 am Leo
16th 11:09 am Virgo
18th 6:15 pm Libra
21st 3:59 am Scorpio
23rd 3:46 pm Sagittarius
26th 4:39 am Capricorn
28th 5:29 pm Aquarius

December 1946
1st 4:28 am Pisces
3rd 11:59 am Aries
5th 3:44 pm Taurus
7th 4:27 pm Gemini
9th 3:51 pm Cancer
11th 3:50 pm Leo
13th 6:12 pm Virgo
16th 0:08 am Libra
18th 9:46 am Scorpio
20th 9:49 pm Sagittarius
23rd 10:49 am Capricorn
25th 11:30 am Aquarius
28th 10:41 am Pisces
30th 7:29 pm Aries

January 1947
2nd 1:05 am Taurus
4th 3:24 am Gemini
6th 3:27 am Cancer
8th 2:53 am Leo
10th 3:47 am Virgo
12th 7:59 am Libra
14th 4:19 pm Scorpio
17th 4:04 am Sagittarius
19th 5:09 pm Capricorn
22nd 5:35 am Aquarius
24th 4:21 pm Pisces
27th 1:10 am Aries
29th 7:42 am Taurus
31st 11:48 am Gemini

February 1947
2nd 1:36 pm Cancer
4th 2:01 pm Leo
6th 2:45 pm Virgo
8th 5:43 pm Libra
11th 0:27 am Scorpio
13th 11:17 am Sagittarius
16th 0:10 am Capricorn
18th 12:35 pm Aquarius
20th 10:57 pm Pisces
23rd 6:55 am Aries
25th 1:05 pm Taurus
27th 5:45 pm Gemini

March 1947
1st 8:59 pm Cancer
3rd 11:00 pm Leo
6th 0:47 am Virgo
8th 3:54 am Libra
10th 9:55 am Scorpio
12th 7:34 pm Sagittarius
15th 7:59 am Capricorn
17th 8:34 pm Aquarius
20th 6:53 am Pisces
22nd 2:18 pm Aries
24th 7:27 pm Taurus
26th 11:15 pm Gemini
29th 2:56 am Cancer
31st 5:23 am Leo

April 1947
2nd 8:32 am Virgo
4th 12:42 pm Libra
6th 6:59 pm Scorpio
9th 4:14 am Sagittarius
11th 4:09 pm Capricorn
14th 4:50 am Aquarius
16th 3:43 pm Pisces
18th 11:24 pm Aries
21st 3:53 am Taurus
23rd 6:26 am Gemini
25th 8:22 am Cancer
27th 10:45 am Leo
29th 2:17 pm Virgo

May 1947
1st 7:24 pm Libra
4th 2:37 am Scorpio
6th 12:12 pm Sagittarius
8th 11:54 pm Capricorn
11th 12:39 pm Aquarius
14th 0:19 am Pisces
16th 8:51 am Aries
18th 1:46 pm Taurus
20th 3:49 pm Gemini
22nd 4:26 pm Cancer
24th 5:10 pm Leo
26th 7:52 pm Virgo
29th 0:53 am Libra
31st 8:45 am Scorpio

June 1947
2nd 6:55 pm Sagittarius
5th 6:52 am Capricorn
7th 7:38 pm Aquarius
10th 7:44 am Pisces
12th 5:30 pm Aries
14th 11:46 pm Taurus
17th 2:20 am Gemini
19th 2:32 am Cancer
21st 2:07 am Leo
23rd 3:03 am Virgo
25th 6:55 am Libra
27th 2:21 pm Scorpio
30th 0:46 am Sagittarius

July 1947
2nd 1:03 pm Capricorn
5th 1:49 am Aquarius
7th 2:01 pm Pisces
10th 0:34 am Aries
12th 8:08 am Taurus
14th 12:12 pm Gemini
16th 1:12 pm Cancer
18th 12:35 pm Leo
20th 12:24 pm Virgo
22nd 2:39 pm Libra
24th 8:44 pm Scorpio
27th 6:42 am Sagittarius
29th 7:02 pm Capricorn

August 1947
1st 7:49 am Aquarius
3rd 7:48 pm Pisces
6th 6:18 am Aries
8th 2:40 pm Taurus
10th 8:16 pm Gemini
12th 10:49 pm Cancer
14th 11:06 pm Leo
16th 10:50 pm Virgo
19th 0:05 am Libra
21st 4:48 am Scorpio
23rd 1:39 pm Sagittarius
26th 1:31 am Capricorn
28th 2:16 pm Aquarius
31st 2:03 am Pisces

★ ★

September 1947
2nd 12:01 pm Aries
4th 8:09 pm Taurus
7th 2:19 am Gemini
9th 6:11 am Cancer
11th 8:02 am Leo
13th 8:53 am Virgo
15th 10:21 am Libra
17th 2:17 pm Scorpio
19th 9:51 pm Sagittarius
22nd 8:60 am Capricorn
24th 9:36 pm Aquarius
27th 9:22 am Pisces
29th 6:56 pm Aries

October 1947
2nd 2:15 am Taurus
4th 7:42 am Gemini
6th 11:46 am Cancer
8th 2:41 pm Leo
10th 4:58 pm Virgo
12th 7:33 pm Libra
14th 11:48 pm Scorpio
17th 6:57 am Sagittarius
19th 5:17 pm Capricorn
22nd 5:39 am Aquarius
24th 5:44 pm Pisces
27th 3:30 am Aries
29th 10:13 am Taurus
31st 2:34 pm Gemini

November 1947
2nd 5:32 pm Cancer
4th 8:04 pm Leo
6th 10:55 pm Virgo
9th 2:44 am Libra
11th 8:07 am Scorpio
13th 3:38 pm Sagittarius
16th 1:39 am Capricorn
18th 1:47 pm Aquarius
21st 2:17 am Pisces
23rd 12:50 pm Aries
25th 8:04 pm Taurus
27th 11:55 pm Gemini
30th 1:31 am Cancer

December 1947
2nd 2:32 am Leo
4th 4:26 am Virgo
6th 8:17 am Libra
8th 2:27 pm Scorpio
10th 10:50 pm Sagittarius
13th 9:17 am Capricorn
15th 9:17 pm Aquarius
18th 9:59 am Pisces
20th 9:35 pm Aries
23rd 6:07 am Taurus
25th 10:42 am Gemini
27th 12:00 pm Cancer
29th 11:43 am Leo
31st 11:52 am Virgo

January 1948
2nd 2:15 pm Libra
4th 7:53 pm Scorpio
7th 4:42 am Sagittarius
9th 3:43 pm Capricorn
12th 3:55 am Aquarius
14th 4:35 pm Pisces
17th 4:42 am Aries
19th 2:38 pm Taurus
21st 8:50 pm Gemini
23rd 11:22 pm Cancer
25th 10:59 pm Leo
27th 9:58 pm Virgo
29th 10:31 pm Libra

February 1948
1st 2:29 am Scorpio
3rd 10:30 am Sagittarius
5th 9:30 pm Capricorn
8th 9:59 am Aquarius
10th 10:37 pm Pisces
13th 10:36 am Aries
15th 9:07 pm Taurus
18th 4:53 am Gemini
20th 9:04 am Cancer
22nd 10:03 am Leo
24th 9:23 am Virgo
26th 9:10 am Libra
28th 11:30 am Scorpio

March 1948
1st 5:45 pm Sagittarius
4th 3:52 am Capricorn
6th 4:14 pm Aquarius
9th 4:51 am Pisces
11th 4:31 pm Aries
14th 2:39 am Taurus
16th 10:41 am Gemini
18th 4:11 pm Cancer
20th 6:56 pm Leo
22nd 7:42 pm Virgo
24th 8:02 pm Libra
26th 9:50 pm Scorpio
29th 2:48 am Sagittarius
31st 11:37 am Capricorn

April 1948
2nd 11:18 pm Aquarius
5th 11:54 am Pisces
7th 11:27 pm Aries
10th 8:55 am Taurus
12th 4:17 pm Gemini
14th 9:39 pm Cancer
17th 1:14 am Leo
19th 3:29 am Virgo
21st 5:17 am Libra
23rd 7:53 am Scorpio
25th 12:36 pm Sagittarius
27th 8:23 pm Capricorn
30th 7:17 am Aquarius

May 1948
2nd 7:44 pm Pisces
5th 7:25 am Aries
7th 4:44 pm Taurus
9th 11:19 pm Gemini
12th 3:35 am Cancer
14th 6:37 am Leo
16th 9:14 am Virgo
18th 12:08 pm Libra
20th 3:58 pm Scorpio
22nd 9:23 pm Sagittarius
25th 5:10 am Capricorn
27th 3:33 pm Aquarius
30th 3:46 am Pisces

June 1948
1st 3:53 pm Aries
4th 1:42 am Taurus
6th 8:01 am Gemini
8th 11:24 am Cancer
10th 1:11 pm Leo
12th 2:49 pm Virgo
14th 5:35 pm Libra
16th 10:03 pm Scorpio
19th 4:29 am Sagittarius
21st 12:53 pm Capricorn
23rd 11:15 pm Aquarius
26th 11:24 am Pisces
28th 11:56 pm Aries

July 1948
1st 10:35 am Taurus
3rd 5:43 pm Gemini
5th 9:04 pm Cancer
7th 9:51 pm Leo
9th 10:04 pm Virgo
11th 11:30 pm Libra
14th 3:30 am Scorpio
16th 10:14 am Sagittarius
18th 7:15 pm Capricorn
21st 6:04 am Aquarius
23rd 6:13 pm Pisces
26th 6:55 am Aries
28th 6:31 pm Taurus
31st 2:59 am Gemini

August 1948
2nd 7:15 am Cancer
4th 8:11 am Leo
6th 7:33 am Virgo
8th 7:33 am Libra
10th 10:01 am Scorpio
12th 3:53 pm Sagittarius
15th 0:51 am Capricorn
17th 12:03 pm Aquarius
20th 0:22 am Pisces
22nd 1:04 pm Aries
25th 1:03 am Taurus
27th 10:34 am Gemini
29th 4:29 pm Cancer
31st 6:38 pm Leo

September 1948
2nd 6:20 pm Virgo
4th 5:38 pm Libra
6th 6:38 pm Scorpio
8th 10:52 pm Sagittarius
11th 6:59 am Capricorn
13th 5:59 pm Aquarius
16th 6:26 am Pisces
18th 7:02 pm Aries
21st 6:44 am Taurus
23rd 4:38 pm Gemini
25th 11:47 pm Cancer
28th 3:33 am Leo
30th 4:40 am Virgo

October 1948
2nd 4:32 am Libra
4th 5:02 am Scorpio
6th 7:60 am Sagittarius
8th 2:37 pm Capricorn
11th 0:42 am Aquarius
13th 1:04 pm Pisces
16th 1:36 am Aries
18th 12:52 pm Taurus
20th 10:14 pm Gemini
23rd 5:18 am Cancer
25th 10:07 am Leo
27th 12:51 pm Virgo
29th 2:16 pm Libra
31st 3:34 pm Scorpio

November 1948
2nd 6:15 pm Sagittarius
4th 11:42 pm Capricorn
7th 8:46 am Aquarius
9th 8:34 pm Pisces
12th 9:12 am Aries
14th 8:22 pm Taurus
17th 4:59 am Gemini
19th 11:08 am Cancer
21st 3:31 pm Leo
23rd 6:47 pm Virgo
25th 9:33 pm Libra
28th 0:19 am Scorpio
30th 3:55 am Sagittarius

December 1948
2nd 9:22 am Capricorn
4th 5:37 pm Aquarius
7th 4:48 am Pisces
9th 5:30 pm Aries
12th 5:07 am Taurus
14th 1:40 pm Gemini
16th 6:59 pm Cancer
18th 10:02 pm Leo
21st 0:19 am Virgo
23rd 2:60 am Libra
25th 6:40 am Scorpio
27th 11:31 am Sagittarius
29th 5:49 pm Capricorn

★ ★

★ ★

January 1949
1st 2:10 am Aquarius
3rd 1:02 pm Pisces
6th 1:41 am Aries
8th 2:01 pm Taurus
10th 11:32 pm Gemini
13th 4:54 am Cancer
15th 7:07 am Leo
17th 7:54 am Virgo
19th 9:07 am Libra
21st 12:03 pm Scorpio
23rd 5:11 pm Sagittarius
26th 0:23 am Capricorn
28th 9:30 am Aquarius
30th 8:27 pm Pisces

February 1949
2nd 9:06 am Aries
4th 9:57 pm Taurus
7th 8:35 am Gemini
9th 3:17 pm Cancer
11th 5:58 pm Leo
13th 6:05 pm Virgo
15th 5:46 pm Libra
17th 6:57 pm Scorpio
19th 10:51 pm Sagittarius
22nd 5:53 am Capricorn
24th 3:27 pm Aquarius
27th 2:55 am Pisces

March 1949
1st 3:36 am Aries
4th 4:32 am Taurus
6th 4:01 pm Gemini
9th 0:21 am Cancer
11th 4:30 am Leo
13th 5:23 am Virgo
15th 4:41 am Libra
17th 4:28 am Scorpio
19th 6:36 am Sagittarius
21st 12:09 pm Capricorn
23rd 9:11 pm Aquarius
26th 8:50 am Pisces
28th 9:42 pm Aries
31st 10:27 am Taurus

April 1949
2nd 10:02 pm Gemini
5th 7:07 am Cancer
7th 12:55 pm Leo
9th 3:28 pm Virgo
11th 3:47 pm Libra
13th 3:29 pm Scorpio
15th 4:28 pm Sagittarius
17th 8:19 pm Capricorn
20th 4:02 am Aquarius
22nd 3:10 pm Pisces
25th 3:60 am Aries
27th 4:39 pm Taurus
30th 3:45 am Gemini

May 1949
2nd 12:40 pm Cancer
4th 7:07 pm Leo
6th 11:10 pm Virgo
9th 1:07 am Libra
11th 1:54 am Scorpio
13th 2:59 am Sagittarius
15th 6:02 am Capricorn
17th 12:24 pm Aquarius
19th 10:27 pm Pisces
22nd 11:02 am Aries
24th 11:42 pm Taurus
27th 10:22 am Gemini
29th 6:35 pm Cancer

June 1949
1st 0:35 am Leo
3rd 4:51 am Virgo
5th 7:55 am Libra
7th 10:12 am Scorpio
9th 12:25 pm Sagittarius
11th 3:43 pm Capricorn
13th 9:28 pm Aquarius
16th 6:42 am Pisces
18th 6:46 pm Aries
21st 7:28 am Taurus
23rd 6:16 pm Gemini
26th 1:60 am Cancer
28th 6:58 am Leo
30th 10:25 am Virgo

July 1949
2nd 1:21 pm Libra
4th 4:22 pm Scorpio
6th 7:45 pm Sagittarius
9th 0:02 am Capricorn
11th 6:12 am Aquarius
13th 3:04 pm Pisces
16th 2:42 am Aries
18th 3:34 pm Taurus
21st 2:55 am Gemini
23rd 10:46 am Cancer
25th 3:16 pm Leo
27th 5:35 pm Virgo
29th 7:19 pm Libra
31st 9:45 pm Scorpio

August 1949
3rd 1:26 am Sagittarius
5th 6:37 am Capricorn
7th 1:37 pm Aquarius
9th 10:47 pm Pisces
12th 10:20 am Aries
14th 11:17 pm Taurus
17th 11:19 am Gemini
19th 8:11 pm Cancer
22nd 1:07 am Leo
24th 2:55 am Virgo
26th 3:24 am Libra
28th 4:21 am Scorpio
30th 7:03 am Sagittarius

September 1949
1st 12:08 pm Capricorn
3rd 7:39 pm Aquarius
6th 5:27 am Pisces
8th 5:13 pm Aries
11th 6:11 am Taurus
13th 6:44 pm Gemini
16th 4:48 am Cancer
18th 10:59 am Leo
20th 1:30 pm Virgo
22nd 1:41 pm Libra
24th 1:23 pm Scorpio
26th 2:25 pm Sagittarius
28th 6:10 pm Capricorn

October 1949
1st 1:14 am Aquarius
3rd 11:21 am Pisces
5th 11:28 pm Aries
8th 12:25 pm Taurus
11th 1:02 am Gemini
13th 11:47 am Cancer
15th 7:32 pm Leo
17th 11:43 pm Virgo
20th 0:48 am Libra
22nd 0:19 am Scorpio
24th 0:08 am Sagittarius
26th 2:13 am Capricorn
28th 7:56 am Aquarius
30th 5:25 pm Pisces

November 1949
2nd 5:36 am Aries
4th 6:35 pm Taurus
7th 6:53 am Gemini
9th 5:33 pm Cancer
12th 1:58 am Leo
14th 7:38 am Virgo
16th 10:32 am Libra
18th 11:18 am Scorpio
20th 11:18 am Sagittarius
22nd 12:26 pm Capricorn
24th 4:30 pm Aquarius
27th 0:37 am Pisces
29th 12:21 pm Aries

December 1949
2nd 1:23 am Taurus
4th 1:27 pm Gemini
6th 11:31 pm Cancer
9th 7:25 am Leo
11th 1:27 pm Virgo
13th 5:42 pm Libra
15th 8:12 pm Scorpio
17th 9:33 pm Sagittarius
19th 11:02 pm Capricorn
22nd 2:28 am Aquarius
24th 9:26 am Pisces
26th 8:08 pm Aries
29th 8:58 am Taurus
31st 9:13 pm Gemini

January 1950
3rd 6:53 am Cancer
5th 1:55 pm Leo
7th 7:05 pm Virgo
9th 11:08 pm Libra
12th 2:28 am Scorpio
14th 5:17 am Sagittarius
16th 8:09 am Capricorn
18th 12:12 pm Aquarius
20th 6:46 pm Pisces
23rd 4:41 am Aries
25th 5:09 pm Taurus
28th 5:42 am Gemini
30th 3:47 pm Cancer

February 1950
1st 10:34 pm Leo
4th 2:36 am Virgo
6th 5:20 am Libra
8th 7:52 am Scorpio
10th 10:53 am Sagittarius
12th 2:47 pm Capricorn
14th 7:60 pm Aquarius
17th 3:14 am Pisces
19th 1:04 pm Aries
22nd 1:13 am Taurus
24th 2:02 pm Gemini
27th 1:02 am Cancer

March 1950
1st 8:27 am Leo
3rd 12:22 pm Virgo
5th 2:00 pm Libra
7th 2:57 pm Scorpio
9th 4:41 pm Sagittarius
11th 8:09 pm Capricorn
14th 1:53 am Aquarius
16th 10:02 am Pisces
18th 8:21 pm Aries
21st 8:33 am Taurus
23rd 9:28 pm Gemini
26th 9:13 am Cancer
28th 6:02 pm Leo
30th 11:01 pm Virgo

April 1950
2nd 0:42 am Libra
4th 0:37 am Scorpio
6th 0:38 am Sagittarius
8th 2:32 am Capricorn
10th 7:28 am Aquarius
12th 3:41 pm Pisces
15th 2:32 am Aries
17th 3:01 pm Taurus
20th 3:54 am Gemini
22nd 4:01 pm Cancer
25th 1:55 am Leo
27th 8:25 am Virgo
29th 11:21 am Libra

★ ★

MOON CHARTS

★ ★

May 1950
1st 11:36 am Scorpio
3rd 10:54 am Sagittarius
5th 11:14 am Capricorn
7th 2:28 pm Aquarius
9th 9:37 pm Pisces
12th 8:21 am Aries
14th 8:59 pm Taurus
17th 9:51 am Gemini
19th 9:49 pm Cancer
22nd 8:03 am Leo
24th 3:46 pm Virgo
26th 8:24 pm Libra
28th 9:60 pm Scorpio
30th 9:44 pm Sagittarius

June 1950
1st 9:29 pm Capricorn
3rd 11:19 pm Aquarius
6th 5:02 am Pisces
8th 2:48 pm Aries
11th 3:13 am Taurus
13th 4:04 pm Gemini
16th 3:42 am Cancer
18th 1:34 pm Leo
20th 9:29 pm Virgo
23rd 3:07 am Libra
25th 6:15 am Scorpio
27th 7:24 am Sagittarius
29th 7:50 am Capricorn

July 1950
1st 9:25 am Aquarius
3rd 1:58 pm Pisces
5th 10:26 pm Aries
8th 10:16 am Taurus
10th 11:01 pm Gemini
13th 10:30 am Cancer
15th 7:51 pm Leo
18th 3:04 am Virgo
20th 8:32 am Libra
22nd 12:24 pm Scorpio
24th 2:53 pm Sagittarius
26th 4:39 pm Capricorn
28th 6:57 pm Aquarius
30th 11:19 pm Pisces

August 1950
2nd 7:06 am Aries
4th 6:08 pm Taurus
7th 6:43 am Gemini
9th 6:25 pm Cancer
12th 3:34 am Leo
14th 10:00 am Virgo
16th 2:28 pm Libra
18th 5:49 pm Scorpio
20th 8:35 pm Sagittarius
22nd 11:23 pm Capricorn
25th 2:53 am Aquarius
27th 8:05 am Pisces
29th 3:48 pm Aries

September 1950
1st 2:18 am Taurus
3rd 2:45 pm Gemini
6th 2:52 am Cancer
8th 12:29 pm Leo
10th 6:52 pm Virgo
12th 10:27 pm Libra
15th 0:26 am Scorpio
17th 2:12 am Sagittarius
19th 4:50 am Capricorn
21st 9:02 am Aquarius
23rd 3:11 pm Pisces
25th 11:31 pm Aries
28th 10:09 am Taurus
30th 10:27 pm Gemini

October 1950
3rd 10:57 am Cancer
5th 9:39 pm Leo
8th 4:50 am Virgo
10th 8:25 am Libra
12th 9:30 am Scorpio
14th 9:47 am Sagittarius
16th 10:60 am Capricorn
18th 2:31 pm Aquarius
20th 8:55 pm Pisces
23rd 5:60 am Aries
25th 5:04 pm Taurus
28th 5:22 am Gemini
30th 6:03 pm Cancer

November 1950
2nd 5:35 am Leo
4th 2:16 pm Virgo
6th 7:07 pm Libra
8th 8:27 pm Scorpio
10th 7:52 pm Sagittarius
12th 7:29 pm Capricorn
14th 9:17 pm Aquarius
17th 2:40 am Pisces
19th 11:43 am Aries
21st 11:08 pm Taurus
24th 11:38 am Gemini
27th 0:12 am Cancer
29th 11:59 am Leo

December 1950
1st 9:51 pm Virgo
4th 4:26 am Libra
6th 7:15 am Scorpio
8th 7:19 am Sagittarius
10th 6:20 am Capricorn
12th 6:40 am Aquarius
14th 10:18 am Pisces
16th 6:04 pm Aries
19th 5:12 am Taurus
21st 5:49 pm Gemini
24th 6:17 am Cancer
26th 5:43 pm Leo
29th 3:39 am Virgo
31st 11:16 am Libra

January 1951
2nd 3:53 pm Scorpio
4th 5:35 pm Sagittarius
6th 5:32 pm Capricorn
8th 5:39 pm Aquarius
10th 7:60 pm Pisces
13th 2:09 am Aries
15th 12:15 pm Taurus
18th 0:36 am Gemini
20th 1:06 pm Cancer
23rd 0:13 am Leo
25th 9:24 am Virgo
27th 4:44 pm Libra
29th 10:02 pm Scorpio

February 1951
1st 1:17 am Sagittarius
3rd 2:53 am Aquarius
5th 4:06 am Aquarius
7th 6:33 am Pisces
9th 11:48 am Aries
11th 8:37 pm Taurus
14th 8:19 am Gemini
16th 8:51 pm Cancer
19th 7:60 am Leo
21st 4:41 pm Virgo
23rd 11:01 pm Libra
26th 3:32 am Scorpio
28th 6:50 am Sagittarius

March 1951
2nd 9:30 am Capricorn
4th 12:13 pm Aquarius
6th 3:49 pm Pisces
8th 9:19 pm Aries
11th 5:35 am Taurus
13th 4:38 pm Gemini
16th 5:06 am Cancer
18th 4:43 pm Leo
21st 1:40 am Virgo
23rd 7:19 am Libra
25th 10:35 am Scorpio
27th 12:42 pm Sagittarius
29th 2:53 pm Capricorn
31st 6:05 pm Aquarius

April 1951
2nd 10:46 pm Pisces
5th 5:18 am Aries
7th 1:55 pm Taurus
10th 0:42 am Gemini
12th 1:05 pm Cancer
15th 1:18 am Leo
17th 11:03 am Virgo
19th 5:10 pm Libra
21st 7:54 pm Scorpio
23rd 8:41 pm Sagittarius
25th 9:22 pm Capricorn
27th 11:33 pm Aquarius
30th 4:15 am Pisces

May 1951
2nd 11:29 am Aries
4th 8:47 pm Taurus
7th 7:51 am Gemini
9th 8:13 pm Cancer
12th 8:48 am Leo
14th 7:42 pm Virgo
17th 3:04 am Scorpio
19th 6:21 am Scorpio
21st 6:43 am Sagittarius
23rd 6:10 am Capricorn
25th 6:47 am Aquarius
27th 10:12 am Pisces
29th 4:57 pm Aries

June 1951
1st 2:35 am Taurus
3rd 2:04 pm Gemini
6th 2:32 am Cancer
8th 3:10 pm Leo
11th 2:44 am Virgo
13th 11:25 am Libra
15th 4:11 pm Scorpio
17th 5:23 pm Sagittarius
19th 4:39 pm Capricorn
21st 4:09 pm Aquarius
23rd 5:54 pm Pisces
25th 11:15 pm Aries
28th 8:21 am Taurus
30th 7:53 pm Gemini

July 1951
3rd 8:28 am Cancer
5th 8:59 pm Leo
8th 8:32 am Virgo
10th 6:01 pm Libra
13th 0:17 am Scorpio
15th 3:00 am Sagittarius
17th 3:13 am Capricorn
19th 2:44 am Aquarius
21st 3:31 am Pisces
23rd 7:28 am Aries
25th 3:12 pm Taurus
28th 2:09 am Gemini
30th 2:43 pm Cancer

August 1951
2nd 3:07 am Leo
4th 2:16 pm Virgo
6th 11:35 pm Libra
9th 6:21 am Scorpio
11th 10:26 am Sagittarius
13th 12:15 pm Capricorn
15th 12:53 pm Aquarius
17th 1:55 pm Pisces
19th 5:02 pm Aries
21st 11:27 pm Taurus
24th 9:30 am Gemini
26th 9:44 pm Cancer
29th 10:08 am Leo
31st 8:50 pm Virgo

★ ★

★ ★

September 1951			October 1951			November 1951			December 1951		
3rd	5:31 am	Libra	2nd	6:21 pm	Scorpio	1st	5:19 am	Sagittarius	2nd	3:48 pm	Aquarius
5th	11:47 am	Scorpio	4th	9:47 pm	Sagittarius	3rd	6:41 am	Capricorn	4th	6:12 pm	Pisces
7th	4:10 pm	Sagittarius	7th	0:30 am	Capricorn	5th	8:46 am	Aquarius	6th	11:19 pm	Aries
9th	7:05 pm	Capricorn	9th	3:20 am	Aquarius	7th	12:26 pm	Pisces	9th	7:07 am	Taurus
11th	9:12 pm	Aquarius	11th	6:48 am	Pisces	9th	5:54 pm	Aries	11th	4:56 pm	Gemini
13th	11:21 pm	Pisces	13th	11:21 am	Aries	12th	1:08 am	Taurus	14th	4:23 am	Cancer
16th	2:48 am	Aries	15th	5:39 pm	Taurus	14th	10:17 am	Gemini	16th	5:05 pm	Leo
18th	8:45 am	Taurus	18th	2:22 am	Gemini	16th	9:28 pm	Cancer	19th	5:50 am	Virgo
20th	5:49 pm	Gemini	20th	1:45 pm	Cancer	19th	10:11 am	Leo	21st	4:36 pm	Libra
23rd	5:35 am	Cancer	23rd	2:25 am	Leo	21st	10:34 pm	Virgo	23rd	11:39 pm	Scorpio
25th	6:07 pm	Leo	25th	1:58 pm	Virgo	24th	8:04 am	Libra	26th	2:26 am	Sagittarius
28th	5:03 am	Virgo	27th	10:24 pm	Libra	26th	1:27 pm	Scorpio	28th	2:24 am	Capricorn
30th	1:05 pm	Libra	30th	3:08 am	Scorpio	28th	3:17 pm	Sagittarius	30th	1:37 am	Aquarius
						30th	3:23 pm	Capricorn			

January 1952			February 1952			March 1952			April 1952		
1st	2:13 am	Pisces	1st	7:55 pm	Taurus	2nd	12:42 pm	Gemini	1st	7:42 am	Cancer
3rd	5:47 am	Aries	4th	4:59 am	Gemini	4th	11:40 pm	Cancer	3rd	8:10 pm	Leo
5th	12:49 pm	Taurus	6th	4:46 pm	Cancer	7th	12:31 pm	Leo	6th	8:40 am	Virgo
7th	10:44 pm	Gemini	9th	5:37 am	Leo	10th	0:53 am	Virgo	8th	6:55 pm	Libra
10th	10:36 am	Cancer	11th	6:02 pm	Virgo	12th	11:15 am	Libra	11th	2:14 am	Scorpio
12th	11:19 pm	Leo	14th	4:58 am	Libra	14th	7:20 pm	Scorpio	13th	7:07 am	Sagittarius
15th	11:59 am	Virgo	16th	1:42 pm	Scorpio	17th	1:15 am	Sagittarius	15th	10:42 am	Capricorn
17th	11:19 pm	Libra	18th	7:41 pm	Sagittarius	19th	5:18 am	Capricorn	17th	1:44 pm	Aquarius
20th	7:39 am	Scorpio	20th	10:49 pm	Capricorn	21st	7:54 am	Aquarius	19th	4:41 pm	Pisces
22nd	12:16 pm	Sagittarius	22nd	11:49 pm	Aquarius	23rd	9:40 am	Pisces	21st	7:58 pm	Aries
24th	1:36 pm	Capricorn	25th	0:02 am	Pisces	25th	11:37 am	Aries	24th	0:16 am	Taurus
26th	1:07 pm	Aquarius	27th	1:13 am	Aries	27th	3:10 pm	Taurus	26th	6:44 am	Gemini
28th	12:50 pm	Pisces	29th	5:05 am	Taurus	29th	9:37 pm	Gemini	28th	4:10 pm	Cancer
30th	2:39 pm	Aries									

May 1952			June 1952			July 1952			August 1952		
1st	4:14 am	Leo	2nd	12:21 pm	Libra	2nd	5:20 am	Scorpio	2nd	10:25 pm	Capricorn
3rd	4:56 pm	Virgo	4th	8:17 pm	Scorpio	4th	10:21 am	Sagittarius	4th	10:40 pm	Aquarius
6th	3:38 am	Libra	7th	0:22 am	Sagittarius	6th	12:00 pm	Capricorn	6th	10:06 pm	Pisces
8th	10:45 am	Scorpio	9th	1:47 am	Capricorn	8th	11:55 am	Aquarius	8th	10:35 pm	Aries
10th	2:49 pm	Sagittarius	11th	2:29 am	Aquarius	10th	12:04 pm	Pisces	11th	1:47 am	Taurus
12th	5:10 pm	Capricorn	13th	4:04 am	Pisces	12th	2:03 pm	Aries	13th	8:42 am	Gemini
14th	7:15 pm	Aquarius	15th	7:34 am	Aries	14th	6:50 pm	Taurus	15th	6:55 pm	Cancer
16th	10:07 pm	Pisces	17th	1:14 pm	Taurus	17th	2:40 am	Gemini	18th	7:21 am	Leo
19th	2:09 am	Aries	19th	9:05 pm	Gemini	19th	1:08 pm	Cancer	20th	8:23 pm	Virgo
21st	7:32 am	Taurus	22nd	7:07 am	Cancer	22nd	1:21 am	Leo	23rd	8:40 am	Libra
23rd	2:41 pm	Gemini	24th	7:03 pm	Leo	24th	2:24 pm	Virgo	25th	7:09 pm	Scorpio
26th	0:06 am	Cancer	27th	8:05 am	Virgo	27th	2:52 am	Libra	28th	2:51 am	Sagittarius
28th	12:01 pm	Leo	29th	8:16 pm	Libra	29th	12:58 pm	Scorpio	30th	7:19 am	Capricorn
31st	0:58 am	Virgo				31st	7:33 pm	Sagittarius			

September 1952			October 1952			November 1952			December 1952		
1st	8:60 am	Aquarius	2nd	7:34 am	Aries	1st	6:50 am	Taurus	3rd	3:10 am	Cancer
3rd	8:60 am	Pisces	4th	9:06 pm	Taurus	3rd	11:07 am	Gemini	5th	1:24 pm	Leo
5th	9:01 am	Aries	7th	1:15 am	Gemini	5th	6:15 pm	Cancer	8th	1:58 am	Virgo
7th	10:53 am	Taurus	9th	9:20 am	Cancer	8th	4:58 am	Leo	10th	2:32 pm	Libra
9th	4:10 pm	Gemini	11th	8:50 pm	Leo	10th	5:47 pm	Virgo	13th	0:39 am	Scorpio
12th	1:25 am	Cancer	14th	9:49 am	Virgo	13th	5:54 am	Libra	15th	6:55 am	Sagittarius
14th	1:40 pm	Leo	16th	9:44 pm	Libra	15th	3:15 pm	Scorpio	17th	10:15 am	Capricorn
17th	2:42 am	Virgo	19th	7:07 am	Scorpio	17th	9:32 pm	Sagittarius	19th	12:02 pm	Aquarius
19th	2:40 pm	Libra	21st	2:10 pm	Sagittarius	20th	1:39 am	Capricorn	21st	1:48 pm	Pisces
22nd	0:43 am	Scorpio	23rd	7:27 pm	Capricorn	22nd	4:51 am	Aquarius	23rd	4:33 pm	Aries
24th	8:31 am	Sagittarius	25th	11:27 pm	Aquarius	24th	7:55 am	Pisces	25th	8:48 pm	Taurus
26th	2:03 pm	Capricorn	28th	2:22 am	Pisces	26th	11:10 am	Aries	28th	2:50 am	Gemini
28th	5:21 pm	Aquarius	30th	4:34 am	Aries	28th	2:56 pm	Taurus	30th	10:57 am	Cancer
30th	6:51 pm	Pisces				30th	7:55 pm	Gemini			

★ ★

January 1953
1st 9:18 pm Leo
4th 9:42 am Virgo
6th 10:35 am Libra
9th 9:39 am Scorpio
11th 5:09 pm Sagittarius
13th 8:53 am Capricorn
15th 9:57 am Aquarius
17th 10:08 pm Pisces
19th 11:11 am Aries
22nd 2:23 am Taurus
24th 8:26 am Gemini
26th 5:10 pm Cancer
29th 4:08 am Leo
31st 4:36 pm Virgo

February 1953
3rd 5:31 am Libra
5th 5:18 pm Scorpio
8th 2:18 am Sagittarius
10th 7:27 am Capricorn
12th 9:12 am Aquarius
14th 8:58 am Pisces
16th 8:34 am Aries
18th 9:56 am Taurus
20th 2:33 pm Gemini
22nd 10:49 pm Cancer
25th 10:09 am Leo
27th 10:53 pm Virgo

March 1953
2nd 11:41 am Libra
4th 11:32 pm Scorpio
7th 9:16 am Sagittarius
9th 4:07 pm Capricorn
11th 7:35 pm Aquarius
13th 8:16 pm Pisces
15th 7:40 pm Aries
17th 7:48 pm Taurus
19th 10:37 pm Gemini
22nd 5:33 am Cancer
24th 4:18 pm Leo
27th 5:06 am Virgo
29th 5:51 pm Libra

April 1953
1st 5:19 am Scorpio
3rd 2:57 pm Sagittarius
5th 10:29 pm Capricorn
8th 3:26 am Aquarius
10th 5:48 am Pisces
12th 6:19 am Aries
14th 6:35 am Taurus
16th 8:33 am Gemini
18th 2:00 pm Cancer
20th 11:29 pm Leo
23rd 11:54 am Virgo
26th 0:42 am Libra
28th 11:50 am Scorpio
30th 8:52 pm Sagittarius

May 1953
3rd 3:55 am Capricorn
5th 9:11 am Aquarius
7th 12:45 pm Pisces
9th 2:48 pm Aries
11th 4:14 pm Taurus
13th 6:31 pm Gemini
15th 11:17 pm Cancer
18th 7:51 am Leo
20th 7:33 pm Virgo
23rd 8:16 am Libra
25th 7:31 pm Scorpio
28th 4:07 am Sagittarius
30th 10:16 am Capricorn

June 1953
1st 2:44 pm Aquarius
3rd 6:12 pm Pisces
5th 9:03 pm Aries
7th 11:41 pm Taurus
10th 3:05 am Gemini
12th 8:23 am Cancer
14th 4:31 pm Leo
17th 3:38 am Virgo
19th 4:17 pm Libra
22nd 3:56 am Scorpio
24th 12:44 pm Sagittarius
26th 6:27 pm Capricorn
28th 9:53 pm Aquarius

July 1953
1st 0:10 am Pisces
3rd 2:25 am Aries
5th 5:26 am Taurus
7th 9:46 am Gemini
9th 3:59 pm Cancer
12th 0:29 am Leo
14th 11:31 am Virgo
17th 0:04 am Libra
19th 12:14 pm Scorpio
21st 9:57 pm Sagittarius
24th 4:04 am Capricorn
26th 7:01 am Aquarius
28th 8:07 am Pisces
30th 8:59 am Aries

August 1953
1st 11:02 am Taurus
3rd 3:16 pm Gemini
5th 10:03 pm Cancer
8th 7:20 am Leo
10th 6:36 pm Virgo
13th 7:09 am Libra
15th 7:43 pm Scorpio
18th 6:27 am Sagittarius
20th 1:47 pm Capricorn
22nd 5:25 pm Aquarius
24th 6:10 pm Pisces
26th 5:47 pm Aries
28th 6:14 pm Taurus
30th 9:10 pm Gemini

September 1953
2nd 3:33 am Cancer
4th 1:09 pm Leo
7th 0:48 am Virgo
9th 1:28 pm Libra
12th 2:06 am Scorpio
14th 1:30 pm Sagittarius
16th 10:20 pm Capricorn
19th 3:28 am Aquarius
21st 5:04 am Pisces
23rd 4:31 am Aries
25th 3:47 am Taurus
27th 5:05 am Gemini
29th 10:01 am Cancer

October 1953
1st 6:57 pm Leo
4th 6:42 am Virgo
6th 7:28 pm Libra
9th 7:56 am Scorpio
11th 7:19 pm Sagittarius
14th 4:49 am Capricorn
16th 11:29 am Aquarius
18th 2:51 pm Pisces
20th 3:24 pm Aries
22nd 2:48 pm Gemini
24th 3:09 pm Gemini
26th 6:27 pm Cancer
29th 1:56 am Leo
31st 1:06 pm Virgo

November 1953
3rd 1:51 am Libra
5th 2:10 pm Scorpio
8th 1:07 am Sagittarius
10th 10:16 am Capricorn
12th 5:29 pm Aquarius
14th 10:16 pm Pisces
17th 0:34 am Aries
19th 1:14 am Taurus
21st 1:56 am Gemini
23rd 4:34 am Cancer
25th 10:45 am Leo
27th 8:43 pm Virgo
30th 9:06 am Libra

December 1953
2nd 9:30 pm Scorpio
5th 8:06 am Sagittarius
7th 4:30 pm Capricorn
9th 10:59 pm Aquarius
12th 3:44 am Pisces
14th 7:05 am Aries
16th 9:22 am Taurus
18th 11:30 am Gemini
20th 2:44 pm Cancer
22nd 8:25 pm Leo
25th 5:26 am Virgo
27th 5:11 pm Libra
30th 5:41 am Scorpio

January 1954
1st 4:37 pm Sagittarius
4th 0:45 am Capricorn
6th 6:07 am Aquarius
8th 9:42 am Pisces
10th 12:28 pm Aries
12th 3:12 pm Taurus
14th 6:31 pm Gemini
16th 11:02 pm Cancer
19th 5:27 am Leo
21st 2:16 pm Virgo
24th 1:31 am Libra
26th 2:01 pm Scorpio
29th 1:40 am Sagittarius
31st 10:21 am Capricorn

February 1954
2nd 3:34 am Aquarius
4th 6:02 pm Pisces
6th 7:15 pm Aries
8th 8:49 pm Taurus
10th 11:55 pm Gemini
13th 5:13 am Cancer
15th 12:39 pm Leo
17th 10:02 pm Virgo
20th 9:17 am Libra
22nd 9:44 pm Scorpio
25th 9:57 am Sagittarius
27th 7:54 pm Capricorn

March 1954
2nd 2:05 am Aquarius
4th 4:29 am Pisces
6th 4:40 am Aries
8th 4:35 am Taurus
10th 6:11 am Gemini
12th 10:42 am Cancer
14th 6:20 pm Leo
17th 4:22 am Virgo
19th 3:59 pm Libra
22nd 4:27 am Scorpio
24th 4:55 pm Sagittarius
27th 3:52 am Capricorn
29th 11:32 am Aquarius
31st 3:12 pm Pisces

April 1954
2nd 3:37 pm Aries
4th 2:44 pm Taurus
6th 2:45 pm Gemini
8th 5:33 pm Cancer
11th 0:06 am Leo
13th 10:06 am Virgo
15th 9:59 pm Libra
18th 10:34 am Scorpio
20th 10:56 pm Sagittarius
23rd 10:09 am Capricorn
25th 6:50 pm Aquarius
28th 0:22 am Pisces
30th 2:08 am Aries

May 1954
2nd 1:44 am Taurus
4th 1:08 am Gemini
6th 2:33 am Cancer
8th 7:34 am Leo
10th 4:27 pm Virgo
13th 4:04 am Libra
15th 4:43 pm Scorpio
18th 4:54 am Sagittarius
20th 3:48 pm Capricorn
23rd 0:48 am Aquarius
25th 7:06 am Pisces
27th 10:28 am Aries
29th 11:33 am Taurus
31st 11:44 am Gemini

June 1954
2nd 12:51 pm Cancer
4th 4:40 pm Leo
7th 0:08 am Virgo
9th 11:01 am Libra
11th 11:30 pm Scorpio
14th 11:37 am Sagittarius
16th 10:04 pm Capricorn
19th 6:25 am Aquarius
21st 12:35 pm Pisces
23rd 4:42 pm Aries
25th 7:09 pm Taurus
27th 8:44 pm Gemini
29th 10:38 pm Cancer

July 1954
2nd 2:19 am Leo
4th 9:01 am Virgo
6th 6:57 pm Libra
9th 7:04 am Scorpio
11th 7:19 pm Sagittarius
14th 5:38 am Capricorn
16th 1:16 pm Aquarius
18th 6:33 pm Pisces
20th 10:09 pm Aries
23rd 0:54 am Taurus
25th 3:32 am Gemini
27th 6:45 am Cancer
29th 11:15 am Leo
31st 5:54 pm Virgo

August 1954
3rd 3:17 am Libra
5th 3:04 pm Scorpio
8th 3:31 am Sagittarius
10th 2:16 pm Capricorn
12th 9:53 pm Aquarius
15th 2:17 am Pisces
17th 4:39 am Aries
19th 6:29 am Taurus
21st 8:50 am Gemini
23rd 12:54 pm Cancer
25th 6:26 pm Leo
28th 1:46 am Virgo
30th 11:16 am Libra

September 1954
1st 10:50 pm Scorpio
4th 11:32 am Sagittarius
6th 11:09 pm Capricorn
9th 7:26 am Aquarius
11th 11:51 am Pisces
13th 1:21 pm Aries
15th 1:47 pm Taurus
17th 2:59 pm Gemini
19th 6:17 pm Cancer
22nd 0:06 am Leo
24th 8:14 am Virgo
26th 6:14 pm Libra
29th 5:55 am Scorpio

October 1954
1st 6:43 pm Sagittarius
4th 7:02 am Capricorn
6th 4:41 pm Aquarius
8th 10:16 pm Pisces
10th 11:58 pm Aries
12th 11:33 pm Taurus
14th 11:10 pm Gemini
17th 0:50 am Cancer
19th 5:44 am Leo
21st 1:48 pm Virgo
24th 0:12 am Libra
26th 12:12 pm Scorpio
29th 1:01 am Sagittarius
31st 1:35 pm Capricorn

November 1954
3rd 0:23 am Aquarius
5th 7:30 am Pisces
7th 10:37 am Aries
9th 10:47 am Taurus
11th 9:53 am Gemini
13th 10:05 am Cancer
15th 1:09 pm Leo
17th 7:55 pm Virgo
20th 6:03 am Libra
22nd 6:14 pm Scorpio
25th 7:01 am Sagittarius
27th 7:24 pm Capricorn
30th 6:18 am Aquarius

December 1954
2nd 2:35 pm Pisces
4th 7:33 pm Aries
6th 9:22 pm Taurus
8th 9:16 pm Gemini
10th 9:08 pm Cancer
12th 10:49 pm Leo
15th 3:57 am Virgo
17th 12:56 pm Libra
20th 0:43 am Scorpio
22nd 1:34 pm Sagittarius
25th 1:40 am Capricorn
27th 11:58 am Aquarius
29th 8:08 pm Pisces

January 1955
1st 1:55 am Aries
3rd 5:23 am Taurus
5th 7:03 am Gemini
7th 8:02 am Cancer
9th 9:45 am Leo
11th 1:48 pm Virgo
13th 9:17 pm Libra
16th 8:15 am Scorpio
18th 9:01 pm Sagittarius
21st 9:06 am Capricorn
23rd 6:55 pm Aquarius
26th 2:11 am Pisces
28th 7:19 am Aries
30th 11:05 am Taurus

February 1955
1st 2:03 pm Gemini
3rd 4:37 pm Cancer
5th 7:30 pm Leo
7th 11:42 pm Virgo
10th 6:37 am Libra
12th 4:41 pm Scorpio
15th 5:06 am Sagittarius
17th 5:32 pm Capricorn
20th 3:30 am Aquarius
22nd 10:04 am Pisces
24th 2:04 pm Aries
26th 4:46 pm Taurus
28th 7:26 pm Gemini

March 1955
2nd 10:41 pm Cancer
5th 2:51 am Leo
7th 8:12 am Virgo
9th 3:24 pm Libra
12th 1:05 am Scorpio
14th 1:14 pm Sagittarius
17th 1:50 am Capricorn
19th 12:41 pm Aquarius
21st 7:41 pm Pisces
23rd 11:08 pm Aries
26th 0:31 am Taurus
28th 1:42 am Gemini
30th 4:07 am Cancer

April 1955
1st 8:23 am Leo
3rd 2:33 pm Virgo
5th 10:35 pm Libra
8th 8:41 am Scorpio
10th 8:44 pm Sagittarius
13th 9:40 am Capricorn
15th 9:20 pm Aquarius
18th 5:24 am Pisces
20th 9:25 am Aries
22nd 10:27 am Taurus
24th 10:25 am Gemini
26th 11:12 am Cancer
28th 2:12 pm Leo
30th 7:59 pm Virgo

May 1955
3rd 4:28 am Libra
5th 3:06 pm Scorpio
8th 3:19 am Sagittarius
10th 4:19 pm Capricorn
13th 4:28 am Aquarius
15th 1:48 pm Pisces
17th 7:18 pm Aries
19th 9:10 pm Taurus
21st 8:57 pm Gemini
23rd 8:34 pm Cancer
25th 9:55 pm Leo
28th 2:17 am Virgo
30th 10:12 am Libra

June 1955
1st 8:55 pm Scorpio
4th 9:25 am Sagittarius
6th 10:21 pm Capricorn
9th 10:28 am Aquarius
11th 8:31 pm Pisces
14th 3:21 am Aries
16th 6:47 am Taurus
18th 7:36 am Gemini
20th 7:18 am Cancer
22nd 7:41 am Leo
24th 10:32 am Virgo
26th 5:01 pm Libra
29th 3:06 am Scorpio

July 1955
1st 3:36 pm Sagittarius
4th 4:30 am Capricorn
6th 4:17 pm Aquarius
9th 2:09 am Pisces
11th 9:31 am Aries
13th 2:17 pm Taurus
15th 4:42 pm Gemini
17th 5:31 pm Cancer
19th 6:07 pm Leo
21st 8:09 pm Virgo
24th 1:18 am Libra
26th 10:23 am Scorpio
28th 10:25 pm Sagittarius
31st 11:18 am Capricorn

August 1955
2nd 10:51 pm Aquarius
5th 8:02 am Pisces
7th 2:59 pm Aries
9th 8:04 pm Taurus
11th 11:34 pm Gemini
14th 1:53 am Cancer
16th 3:36 am Leo
18th 6:02 am Virgo
20th 10:40 am Libra
22nd 6:42 pm Scorpio
25th 6:05 am Sagittarius
27th 6:56 pm Capricorn
30th 6:33 am Aquarius

MOON CHARTS

September 1955
1st 3:20 pm Pisces
3rd 9:24 pm Aries
6th 1:38 am Taurus
8th 4:50 am Gemini
10th 8:03 am Cancer
12th 11:05 am Leo
14th 2:37 pm Virgo
16th 7:40 pm Libra
19th 3:22 am Scorpio
21st 2:15 pm Sagittarius
24th 3:02 am Capricorn
26th 3:05 pm Aquarius
29th 0:13 am Pisces

October 1955
1st 5:45 am Aries
3rd 8:51 am Taurus
5th 10:50 am Gemini
7th 1:25 pm Cancer
9th 4:44 pm Leo
11th 9:13 pm Virgo
14th 3:16 am Libra
16th 11:29 am Scorpio
18th 10:09 pm Sagittarius
21st 10:54 am Capricorn
23rd 11:34 pm Aquarius
26th 9:33 am Pisces
28th 3:43 pm Aries
30th 6:28 pm Taurus

November 1955
1st 7:23 pm Gemini
3rd 8:13 pm Cancer
5th 10:20 pm Leo
8th 2:38 am Virgo
10th 9:19 am Libra
12th 6:15 pm Scorpio
15th 5:19 am Sagittarius
17th 6:02 pm Capricorn
20th 6:58 am Aquarius
22nd 6:08 pm Pisces
25th 1:47 am Aries
27th 5:24 am Taurus
29th 6:11 am Gemini

December 1955
1st 5:49 am Cancer
3rd 6:11 am Leo
5th 8:55 am Virgo
7th 2:53 pm Libra
9th 12:00 pm Scorpio
12th 11:36 am Sagittarius
15th 0:24 am Capricorn
17th 1:20 pm Aquarius
20th 1:02 am Pisces
22nd 10:01 am Aries
24th 3:28 pm Taurus
26th 5:31 pm Gemini
28th 5:17 pm Cancer
30th 4:39 pm Leo

January 1956
1st 5:35 pm Virgo
3rd 9:46 pm Libra
6th 6:03 am Scorpio
8th 5:35 pm Sagittarius
11th 6:33 am Capricorn
13th 7:18 pm Aquarius
16th 6:47 am Pisces
18th 4:15 pm Aries
20th 11:11 pm Taurus
23rd 3:05 am Gemini
25th 4:19 am Cancer
27th 4:07 am Leo
29th 4:21 am Virgo
31st 7:01 am Libra

February 1956
2nd 1:38 pm Scorpio
5th 0:12 am Sagittarius
7th 1:07 pm Capricorn
10th 1:51 am Aquarius
12th 12:49 pm Pisces
14th 9:49 pm Aries
17th 4:47 am Taurus
19th 9:48 am Gemini
21st 12:48 pm Cancer
23rd 2:10 pm Leo
25th 3:07 pm Virgo
27th 5:25 pm Libra
29th 10:45 pm Scorpio

March 1956
3rd 8:13 am Sagittarius
5th 8:33 pm Capricorn
8th 9:16 am Aquarius
10th 8:08 pm Pisces
13th 4:25 am Aries
15th 10:30 am Taurus
17th 3:10 pm Gemini
19th 6:47 pm Cancer
21st 9:32 pm Leo
23rd 11:53 pm Virgo
26th 3:02 am Libra
28th 8:23 am Scorpio
30th 4:50 pm Sagittarius

April 1956
2nd 4:38 am Capricorn
4th 5:23 pm Aquarius
7th 4:33 am Pisces
9th 12:42 pm Aries
11th 6:00 pm Taurus
13th 9:30 pm Gemini
16th 0:14 am Cancer
18th 3:00 am Leo
20th 6:18 am Virgo
22nd 10:39 am Libra
24th 4:48 pm Scorpio
27th 1:26 am Sagittarius
29th 12:46 pm Capricorn

May 1956
2nd 1:29 am Aquarius
4th 1:11 pm Pisces
6th 10:05 pm Aries
9th 3:22 am Taurus
11th 5:59 am Gemini
13th 7:20 am Cancer
15th 8:53 am Leo
17th 11:43 am Virgo
19th 4:27 pm Libra
21st 11:27 pm Scorpio
24th 8:49 am Sagittarius
26th 8:12 pm Capricorn
29th 8:53 am Aquarius
31st 9:09 pm Pisces

June 1956
3rd 7:01 am Aries
5th 1:16 pm Taurus
7th 4:06 pm Gemini
9th 4:41 pm Cancer
11th 4:47 pm Leo
13th 6:07 pm Virgo
15th 10:00 pm Libra
18th 5:05 am Scorpio
20th 2:59 pm Sagittarius
23rd 2:44 am Capricorn
25th 3:26 pm Aquarius
28th 3:54 am Pisces
30th 2:39 pm Aries

July 1956
2nd 10:25 pm Taurus
5th 2:24 am Gemini
7th 3:20 am Cancer
9th 2:43 am Leo
11th 2:36 am Virgo
13th 4:58 am Libra
15th 11:02 am Scorpio
17th 8:40 pm Sagittarius
20th 8:42 am Capricorn
22nd 9:28 pm Aquarius
25th 9:50 am Pisces
27th 8:53 pm Aries
30th 5:37 am Taurus

August 1956
1st 11:12 am Gemini
3rd 1:29 pm Cancer
5th 1:27 pm Leo
7th 12:53 pm Virgo
9th 1:57 pm Libra
11th 6:25 pm Scorpio
14th 3:01 am Sagittarius
16th 2:49 pm Capricorn
19th 3:38 am Aquarius
21st 3:45 pm Pisces
24th 2:30 am Aries
26th 11:21 am Taurus
28th 5:57 pm Gemini
30th 9:51 pm Cancer

September 1956
1st 11:14 pm Leo
3rd 11:22 pm Virgo
6th 0:05 am Libra
8th 3:30 am Scorpio
10th 10:51 am Sagittarius
12th 9:46 pm Capricorn
15th 10:27 am Aquarius
17th 10:33 pm Pisces
20th 8:46 am Aries
22nd 5:00 pm Taurus
24th 11:26 pm Gemini
27th 3:50 am Cancer
29th 6:48 am Leo

October 1956
1st 8:25 am Virgo
3rd 10:06 am Libra
5th 1:25 pm Scorpio
7th 7:51 pm Sagittarius
10th 5:51 am Capricorn
12th 6:10 pm Aquarius
15th 6:23 am Pisces
17th 4:33 pm Aries
20th 0:07 am Taurus
22nd 5:28 am Gemini
24th 9:22 am Cancer
26th 12:27 pm Leo
28th 3:11 pm Virgo
30th 6:12 pm Libra

November 1956
1st 10:27 pm Scorpio
4th 5:00 am Sagittarius
6th 2:30 pm Capricorn
9th 2:22 am Aquarius
11th 2:51 pm Pisces
14th 1:36 am Aries
16th 9:09 am Taurus
18th 1:43 pm Gemini
20th 4:16 pm Cancer
22nd 6:11 pm Leo
24th 8:34 pm Virgo
27th 0:11 am Libra
29th 5:37 am Scorpio

December 1956
1st 1:03 pm Sagittarius
3rd 10:38 pm Capricorn
6th 10:19 am Aquarius
8th 10:59 pm Pisces
11th 10:34 am Aries
13th 7:13 pm Taurus
16th 0:07 am Gemini
18th 1:52 am Cancer
20th 2:12 am Leo
22nd 2:58 am Virgo
24th 5:43 am Libra
26th 11:12 am Scorpio
28th 7:22 pm Sagittarius
31st 5:40 am Capricorn

★ ★

January 1957
2nd 5:26 pm Aquarius
5th 6:06 am Pisces
7th 6:21 pm Aries
10th 4:24 am Taurus
12th 10:39 am Gemini
14th 1:01 pm Cancer
16th 12:50 pm Leo
18th 12:08 pm Virgo
20th 1:02 pm Libra
22nd 5:07 pm Scorpio
25th 0:54 am Sagittarius
27th 11:34 am Capricorn
29th 11:42 pm Aquarius

February 1957
1st 12:21 pm Pisces
4th 0:44 am Aries
6th 11:34 am Taurus
8th 7:32 pm Gemini
10th 11:40 pm Cancer
13th 0:19 am Leo
14th 11:18 pm Virgo
16th 10:51 pm Libra
19th 1:07 am Scorpio
21st 7:28 am Sagittarius
23rd 5:29 pm Capricorn
26th 5:42 am Aquarius
28th 6:25 pm Pisces

March 1957
3rd 6:30 am Aries
5th 5:19 pm Taurus
8th 2:02 am Gemini
10th 7:42 am Cancer
12th 10:08 am Leo
14th 10:19 am Virgo
16th 10:03 am Libra
18th 11:20 am Scorpio
20th 3:59 pm Sagittarius
23rd 0:35 am Capricorn
25th 12:18 pm Aquarius
28th 0:58 am Pisces
30th 12:52 pm Aries

April 1957
1st 11:10 pm Taurus
4th 7:28 am Gemini
6th 1:35 pm Cancer
8th 5:21 pm Leo
10th 7:12 pm Virgo
12th 8:09 pm Libra
14th 9:46 pm Scorpio
17th 1:45 am Sagittarius
19th 9:13 am Capricorn
21st 7:55 pm Aquarius
24th 8:22 am Pisces
26th 8:20 pm Aries
29th 6:15 am Taurus

May 1957
1st 1:43 pm Gemini
3rd 7:06 pm Cancer
5th 10:53 pm Leo
8th 1:36 am Virgo
10th 3:57 am Libra
12th 6:50 am Scorpio
14th 11:17 am Sagittarius
16th 6:17 pm Capricorn
19th 4:14 am Aquarius
21st 4:22 pm Pisces
24th 4:32 am Aries
26th 2:39 pm Taurus
28th 9:45 pm Gemini
31st 2:04 am Cancer

June 1957
2nd 4:45 am Leo
4th 6:59 am Virgo
6th 9:47 am Libra
8th 1:43 pm Scorpio
10th 7:11 pm Sagittarius
13th 2:38 am Capricorn
15th 12:27 pm Aquarius
18th 0:16 am Pisces
20th 12:45 pm Aries
22nd 11:39 pm Taurus
25th 7:02 am Gemini
27th 10:56 am Cancer
29th 12:30 pm Leo

July 1957
1st 1:25 pm Virgo
3rd 3:18 pm Libra
5th 7:12 pm Scorpio
8th 1:22 am Sagittarius
10th 9:37 am Capricorn
12th 7:43 pm Aquarius
15th 7:34 am Pisces
17th 8:13 pm Aries
20th 7:54 am Taurus
22nd 4:29 pm Gemini
24th 9:02 pm Cancer
26th 10:15 pm Leo
28th 9:59 pm Virgo
30th 10:21 pm Libra

August 1957
2nd 1:02 am Scorpio
4th 6:51 am Sagittarius
6th 3:25 pm Capricorn
9th 2:01 am Aquarius
11th 2:03 pm Pisces
14th 2:46 am Aries
16th 2:59 pm Taurus
19th 0:51 am Gemini
21st 6:45 am Cancer
23rd 8:47 am Leo
25th 8:27 am Virgo
27th 7:46 am Libra
29th 8:51 am Scorpio
31st 1:12 pm Sagittarius

September 1957
2nd 9:07 pm Capricorn
5th 7:51 am Aquarius
7th 8:04 pm Pisces
10th 8:45 am Aries
12th 8:57 pm Taurus
15th 7:23 am Gemini
17th 2:45 pm Cancer
19th 6:28 pm Leo
21st 7:11 pm Virgo
23rd 6:35 pm Libra
25th 6:44 pm Scorpio
27th 9:30 pm Sagittarius
30th 4:03 am Capricorn

October 1957
2nd 2:07 pm Aquarius
5th 2:18 am Pisces
7th 2:56 pm Aries
10th 2:47 am Taurus
12th 12:58 pm Gemini
14th 8:53 pm Cancer
17th 1:59 am Leo
19th 4:23 am Virgo
21st 5:04 am Libra
23rd 5:35 am Scorpio
25th 7:38 am Sagittarius
27th 12:48 pm Capricorn
29th 9:35 pm Aquarius

November 1957
1st 9:20 am Pisces
3rd 10:01 am Aries
6th 9:36 am Taurus
8th 7:07 pm Gemini
11th 2:23 am Cancer
13th 7:34 am Leo
15th 11:05 am Virgo
17th 1:25 pm Libra
19th 3:20 pm Scorpio
21st 5:55 pm Sagittarius
23rd 10:33 pm Capricorn
26th 6:22 am Aquarius
28th 5:20 pm Pisces

December 1957
1st 5:57 am Aries
3rd 5:47 pm Taurus
6th 2:58 am Gemini
8th 9:13 am Cancer
10th 1:22 pm Leo
12th 4:28 pm Virgo
14th 7:23 pm Libra
16th 10:36 pm Scorpio
19th 2:33 am Sagittarius
21st 7:52 am Capricorn
23rd 3:23 pm Aquarius
26th 1:44 am Pisces
28th 2:14 pm Aries
31st 2:37 am Taurus

January 1958
2nd 12:18 pm Gemini
4th 6:19 pm Cancer
6th 9:21 pm Leo
8th 10:59 pm Virgo
11th 0:52 am Libra
13th 4:04 am Scorpio
15th 8:53 am Sagittarius
17th 3:16 pm Capricorn
19th 11:24 pm Aquarius
22nd 9:45 am Pisces
24th 10:04 pm Aries
27th 10:55 am Taurus
29th 9:47 pm Gemini

February 1958
1st 4:38 am Cancer
3rd 7:35 am Leo
5th 8:12 am Virgo
7th 8:28 am Libra
9th 10:08 am Scorpio
11th 2:16 pm Sagittarius
13th 8:57 pm Capricorn
16th 5:53 am Aquarius
18th 4:42 pm Pisces
21st 5:03 am Taurus
23rd 6:05 pm Taurus
26th 5:50 am Gemini
28th 2:12 pm Cancer

March 1958
2nd 6:24 pm Leo
4th 7:14 pm Virgo
6th 6:37 pm Libra
8th 6:38 pm Scorpio
10th 8:59 pm Sagittarius
13th 2:38 am Capricorn
15th 11:31 am Aquarius
17th 10:42 pm Pisces
20th 11:17 am Aries
23rd 0:16 am Taurus
25th 12:17 pm Gemini
27th 9:52 pm Cancer
30th 3:44 am Leo

April 1958
1st 5:59 am Virgo
3rd 5:54 am Libra
5th 5:19 am Scorpio
7th 6:11 am Sagittarius
9th 10:07 am Capricorn
11th 5:45 pm Aquarius
14th 4:40 am Pisces
16th 5:23 am Aries
19th 6:15 am Taurus
21st 6:01 pm Gemini
24th 3:44 am Cancer
26th 10:39 am Leo
28th 2:37 pm Virgo
30th 4:05 pm Libra

★ ★

★ ★

May 1958
2nd   4:14 pm Scorpio
4th   4:46 pm Sagittarius
6th   7:24 pm Capricorn
9th   1:31 am Aquarius
11th 11:30 am Pisces
13th 11:58 pm Aries
16th 12:48 pm Taurus
19th 0:13 am Gemini
21st 9:19 am Cancer
23rd 4:11 pm Leo
25th 8:58 pm Virgo
27th 11:55 pm Libra
30th 1:34 am Scorpio

June 1958
1st   2:55 am Sagittarius
3rd   5:26 am Capricorn
5th   10:40 am Aquarius
7th   7:27 pm Pisces
10th 7:22 am Aries
12th 8:12 pm Taurus
15th 7:28 am Gemini
17th 3:50 pm Cancer
19th 10:03 pm Leo
22nd 2:21 am Virgo
24th 5:41 am Libra
26th 8:30 am Scorpio
28th 11:12 am Sagittarius
30th 2:35 pm Capricorn

July 1958
2nd   7:47 pm Aquarius
5th   3:59 am Pisces
7th   3:20 pm Aries
10th 4:08 am Taurus
12th 3:43 pm Gemini
15th 0:14 am Cancer
17th 5:28 am Leo
19th 8:41 am Virgo
21st 11:12 am Libra
23rd 1:58 pm Scorpio
25th 5:26 pm Sagittarius
27th 9:53 pm Capricorn
30th 3:54 am Aqiarius

August 1958
1st   12:14 pm Pisces
3rd   11:14 pm Aries
6th   12:04 pm Taurus
9th   0:16 am Gemini
11th 9:19 am Cancer
13th 2:39 pm Leo
15th 5:05 pm Virgo
17th 6:16 pm Libra
19th 7:50 pm Scorpio
21st 10:48 pm Sagittarius
24th 3:40 am Capricorn
26th 10:30 am Aquarius
28th 7:27 pm Pisces
31st 6:36 am Aries

September 1958
2nd   7:23 pm Taurus
5th   8:04 am Gemini
7th   6:19 pm Cancer
10th 0:41 am Leo
12th 3:19 am Virgo
14th 3:45 am Libra
16th 3:51 am Scorpio
18th 5:19 am Sagittarius
20th 9:17 am Capricorn
22nd 4:06 pm Aquarius
25th 1:34 am Pisces
27th 1:08 pm Aries
30th 1:58 am Taurus

October 1958
2nd   2:48 pm Gemini
5th   1:50 am Cancer
7th   9:46 am Leo
9th   1:46 pm Virgo
11th 2:42 pm Libra
13th 2:13 pm Scorpio
15th 2:13 pm Sagittarius
17th 4:28 pm Capricorn
19th 10:07 pm Aquarius
22nd 7:22 am Pisces
24th 7:12 pm Aries
27th 8:07 am Taurus
29th 8:49 pm Gemini

November 1958
1st   8:06 am Cancer
3rd   4:59 pm Leo
5th   10:44 pm Virgo
8th   1:16 am Libra
10th 1:30 am Scorpio
12th 1:04 am Sagittarius
14th 1:57 am Capricorn
16th 5:59 am Aquarius
18th 2:02 pm Pisces
21st 1:29 am Aries
23rd 2:31 pm Taurus
26th 2:59 am Gemini
28th 1:48 pm Cancer
30th 10:39 pm Leo

December 1958
3rd   5:15 am Virgo
5th   9:27 am Libra
7th   11:26 am Scorpio
9th   12:02 pm Sagittarius
11th 12:51 pm Capricorn
13th 3:45 pm Aquarius
15th 10:16 pm Pisces
18th 8:50 am Aries
20th 9:39 pm Taurus
23rd 10:07 am Gemini
25th 8:31 pm Cancer
28th 4:32 am Leo
30th 10:38 am Virgo

January 1959
1st   3:19 pm Libra
3rd   6:41 pm Scorpio
5th   8:57 pm Sagittarius
7th   10:52 pm Capricorn
10th 1:54 am Aquarius
12th 7:46 am Pisces
14th 5:13 pm Aries
17th 5:34 am Taurus
19th 6:15 pm Gemini
22nd 4:45 am Cancer
24th 12:12 pm Leo
26th 5:12 pm Virgo
28th 8:55 pm Libra
31st 0:07 am Scorpio

February 1959
2nd   3:13 am Sagittarius
4th   6:31 am Capricorn
6th   10:44 am Aquarius
8th   4:55 pm Pisces
11th 1:56 am Aries
13th 1:48 pm Taurus
16th 2:40 am Gemini
18th 1:48 pm Cancer
20th 9:38 pm Leo
23rd 2:07 am Virgo
25th 4:29 am Libra
27th 6:16 am Scorpio

March 1959
1st   8:36 am Sagittarius
3rd   12:09 pm Capricorn
5th   5:19 pm Aquarius
8th   0:26 am Pisces
10th 9:57 am Aries
12th 9:37 pm Taurus
15th 10:31 am Gemini
17th 10:27 pm Cancer
20th 7:19 am Leo
22nd 12:25 pm Virgo
24th 2:25 pm Libra
26th 2:55 pm Scorpio
28th 3:35 pm Sagittarius
30th 5:53 pm Capricorn

April 1959
1st   10:43 pm Aquarius
4th   6:25 am Pisces
6th   4:35 pm Aries
9th   4:31 am Taurus
11th 5:25 pm Gemini
14th 5:46 am Cancer
16th 3:51 pm Leo
18th 10:27 pm Virgo
21st 1:20 am Libra
23rd 1:35 am Scorpio
25th 1:01 am Sagittarius
27th 1:36 am Capricorn
29th 5:01 am Aquarius

May 1959
1st   12:04 pm Pisces
3rd   10:19 pm Aries
6th   10:39 am Taurus
8th   11:34 pm Gemini
11th 11:55 am Cancer
13th 10:39 pm Leo
16th 6:34 am Virgo
18th 11:02 am Libra
20th 12:21 pm Scorpio
22nd 11:52 am Sagittarius
24th 11:29 am Capricorn
26th 1:17 pm Aquarius
28th 6:47 pm Pisces
31st 4:21 am Aries

June 1959
2nd   4:38 pm Taurus
5th   5:35 am Gemini
7th   5:43 pm Cancer
10th 4:16 am Leo
12th 12:45 pm Virgo
14th 6:38 pm Libra
16th 9:37 pm Scorpio
18th 10:14 pm Sagittarius
20th 10:02 pm Capricorn
22nd 11:02 pm Aquarius
25th 3:12 am Pisces
27th 11:34 am Aries
29th 11:12 pm Taurus

July 1959
2nd   12:04 pm Gemini
5th   0:04 am Cancer
7th   10:05 am Leo
9th   6:13 pm Virgo
12th 0:26 am Libra
14th 4:31 am Scorpio
16th 6:39 am Sagittarius
18th 7:42 am Capricorn
20th 9:09 am Aquarius
22nd 12:46 pm Pisces
24th 7:57 pm Aries
27th 6:44 am Taurus
29th 7:23 pm Gemini

August 1959
1st   7:21 am Cancer
3rd   5:06 pm Leo
6th   0:29 am Virgo
8th   5:55 am Libra
10th 9:58 am Scorpio
12th 12:57 pm Sagittarius
14th 3:19 pm Capricorn
16th 5:55 pm Aquarius
18th 10:00 pm Pisces
21st 4:54 am Aries
23rd 3:01 pm Taurus
26th 3:18 am Gemini
28th 3:30 pm Cancer
31st 1:33 am Leo

★ ★

September 1959
2nd 8:27 am Virgo
4th 12:54 pm Libra
6th 3:53 pm Scorpio
8th 6:20 pm Sagittarius
10th 9:05 pm Capricorn
13th 0:44 am Aquarius
15th 5:56 pm Pisces
17th 1:19 am Aries
19th 11:11 pm Taurus
22nd 11:16 am Gemini
24th 11:50 am Cancer
27th 10:32 am Leo
29th 6:01 pm Virgo

October 1959
1st 10:07 pm Libra
3rd 11:53 pm Scorpio
6th 0:54 am Sagittarius
8th 2:39 am Capricorn
10th 6:14 am Aquarius
12th 12:09 pm Pisces
14th 8:21 pm Aries
17th 6:40 am Taurus
19th 6:39 pm Gemini
22nd 7:21 am Cancer
24th 7:02 pm Leo
27th 3:46 am Virgo
29th 8:37 am Libra
31st 10:11 am Scorpio

November 1959
2nd 10:03 am Sagittarius
4th 10:10 am Capricorn
6th 12:19 pm Aquarius
8th 5:39 pm Pisces
11th 2:10 am Aries
13th 1:06 pm Taurus
16th 1:15 am Gemini
18th 1:55 pm Cancer
21st 2:02 am Leo
23rd 12:03 pm Virgo
25th 6:37 pm Libra
27th 9:20 pm Scorpio
29th 9:11 pm Sagittarius

December 1959
1st 8:14 pm Capricorn
3rd 8:38 pm Aquarius
6th 0:16 am Pisces
8th 8:04 am Aries
10th 6:57 pm Taurus
13th 7:25 am Gemini
15th 8:00 pm Cancer
18th 7:56 am Leo
20th 6:27 pm Virgo
23rd 2:27 am Libra
25th 6:57 am Scorpio
27th 8:13 am Sagittarius
29th 7:39 am Capricorn
31st 7:20 am Aquarius

January 1960
2nd 9:26 am Pisces
4th 3:28 pm Aries
7th 1:24 am Taurus
9th 1:46 pm Gemini
12th 2:24 am Cancer
14th 1:59 pm Leo
17th 0:04 am Virgo
19th 8:10 am Libra
21st 1:55 pm Scorpio
23rd 4:50 pm Sagittarius
25th 5:58 pm Capricorn
27th 6:21 pm Aquarius
29th 7:59 pm Pisces

February 1960
1st 0:41 am Aries
3rd 9:21 am Taurus
5th 9:01 pm Gemini
8th 9:36 am Cancer
10th 9:09 pm Leo
13th 6:33 am Virgo
15th 1:53 pm Libra
17th 7:23 pm Scorpio
19th 11:12 pm Sagittarius
22nd 1:40 am Capricorn
24th 3:34 am Aquarius
26th 6:06 am Pisces
28th 10:42 am Aries

March 1960
1st 6:22 pm Taurus
4th 5:09 am Gemini
6th 5:36 pm Cancer
9th 5:23 am Leo
11th 2:45 pm Virgo
13th 9:19 pm Libra
16th 1:37 am Scorpio
18th 4:39 am Sagittarius
20th 7:16 am Capricorn
22nd 10:12 am Aquarius
24th 2:05 pm Pisces
26th 7:31 pm Aries
29th 3:15 am Taurus
31st 1:34 pm Gemini

April 1960
3rd 1:47 am Cancer
5th 1:59 pm Leo
8th 0:04 am Virgo
10th 6:34 am Libra
12th 9:59 am Scorpio
14th 11:38 am Sagittarius
16th 1:04 pm Capricorn
18th 3:34 pm Aquarius
20th 7:57 pm Pisces
23rd 2:23 am Aries
25th 10:53 am Taurus
27th 9:16 pm Gemini
30th 9:24 am Cancer

May 1960
2nd 9:59 pm Leo
5th 8:55 am Virgo
7th 4:26 pm Libra
9th 8:05 pm Scorpio
11th 8:55 pm Sagittarius
13th 8:53 pm Capricorn
15th 9:54 pm Aquarius
18th 1:26 am Pisces
20th 7:59 am Aries
22nd 5:02 pm Taurus
25th 3:55 am Gemini
27th 4:07 pm Cancer
30th 4:50 am Leo

June 1960
1st 4:35 pm Virgo
4th 1:30 am Libra
6th 6:16 am Scorpio
8th 7:29 am Sagittarius
10th 6:50 am Capricorn
12th 6:28 am Aquarius
14th 8:24 am Pisces
16th 1:48 pm Aries
18th 10:35 pm Taurus
21st 9:48 am Gemini
23rd 10:11 pm Cancer
26th 10:50 am Leo
28th 10:52 pm Virgo

July 1960
1st 8:41 am Libra
3rd 3:02 pm Scorpio
5th 5:37 pm Sagittarius
7th 5:32 pm Capricorn
9th 4:45 pm Aquarius
11th 5:24 pm Pisces
13th 9:10 pm Aries
16th 4:51 am Taurus
18th 3:43 pm Gemini
21st 4:09 am Cancer
23rd 4:46 pm Leo
26th 4:30 am Virgo
28th 2:30 pm Libra
30th 9:53 pm Scorpio

August 1960
2nd 2:02 am Sagittarius
4th 3:24 am Capricorn
6th 3:21 am Aquarius
8th 3:43 am Pisces
10th 6:25 am Aries
12th 12:41 pm Taurus
14th 10:30 pm Gemini
17th 10:43 am Cancer
19th 11:18 pm Leo
22nd 10:39 am Virgo
24th 8:08 pm Libra
27th 3:22 am Scorpio
29th 8:16 am Sagittarius
31st 11:06 am Capricorn

September 1960
2nd 12:34 pm Aquarius
4th 1:53 pm Pisces
6th 4:29 pm Aries
8th 9:46 pm Taurus
11th 6:33 am Gemini
13th 6:12 pm Cancer
16th 6:45 am Leo
18th 6:05 pm Virgo
21st 2:57 am Libra
23rd 9:16 am Scorpio
25th 1:41 pm Sagittarius
27th 4:53 pm Capricorn
29th 7:32 pm Aquarius

October 1960
1st 10:13 pm Pisces
4th 1:47 am Aries
6th 7:11 am Taurus
8th 3:19 pm Gemini
11th 2:19 am Cancer
13th 2:54 pm Leo
16th 2:39 am Virgo
18th 11:27 am Libra
20th 5:03 pm Scorpio
22nd 8:15 pm Sagittarius
24th 10:28 pm Capricorn
27th 0:58 am Aquarius
29th 4:27 am Pisces
31st 9:13 am Aries

November 1960
2nd 3:28 pm Taurus
4th 11:43 pm Gemini
7th 10:27 am Cancer
9th 10:59 pm Leo
12th 11:20 am Virgo
14th 9:05 pm Libra
17th 2:51 am Scorpio
19th 5:15 am Sagittarius
21st 6:03 am Capricorn
23rd 7:07 am Aquarius
25th 9:53 am Pisces
27th 2:54 pm Aries
29th 10:01 pm Taurus

December 1960
2nd 7:02 am Gemini
4th 5:53 pm Cancer
7th 6:20 am Leo
9th 7:12 pm Virgo
12th 6:05 am Libra
14th 1:07 pm Scorpio
16th 4:02 pm Sagittarius
18th 4:15 pm Capricorn
20th 3:52 pm Aquarius
22nd 4:52 pm Pisces
24th 8:37 pm Aries
27th 3:34 am Taurus
29th 1:04 pm Gemini

January 1961
1st 0:22 am Cancer
3rd 12:55 pm Leo
6th 1:47 am Virgo
8th 1:26 pm Libra
10th 10:06 pm Scorpio
13th 2:38 am Sagittarius
15th 3:39 am Capricorn
17th 2:56 am Aquarius
19th 2:33 am Pisces
21st 4:31 am Aries
23rd 9:57 am Taurus
25th 6:54 pm Gemini
28th 6:25 am Cancer
30th 7:06 pm Leo

February 1961
2nd 7:48 am Virgo
4th 7:25 pm Libra
7th 4:48 am Scorpio
9th 10:56 am Sagittarius
11th 1:46 pm Capricorn
13th 2:13 pm Aquarius
15th 1:55 pm Pisces
17th 2:45 pm Aries
19th 6:26 pm Taurus
22nd 1:54 am Gemini
24th 12:52 pm Cancer
27th 1:35 am Leo

March 1961
1st 2:11 pm Virgo
4th 1:21 am Libra
6th 10:21 am Scorpio
8th 5:01 pm Sagittarius
10th 9:18 pm Capricorn
12th 11:30 pm Aquarius
15th 0:26 am Pisces
17th 1:34 am Aries
19th 4:28 am Taurus
21st 10:38 am Gemini
23rd 8:24 pm Cancer
26th 8:49 am Leo
28th 9:31 pm Virgo
31st 8:19 am Libra

April 1961
2nd 4:35 pm Scorpio
4th 10:35 pm Sagittarius
7th 2:52 am Capricorn
9th 6:02 am Aquarius
11th 8:32 am Pisces
13th 10:57 am Aries
15th 2:20 pm Taurus
17th 7:58 pm Gemini
20th 4:53 am Cancer
22nd 4:45 pm Leo
25th 5:30 am Virgo
27th 4:33 pm Libra
30th 0:29 am Scorpio

May 1961
2nd 5:24 am Sagittarius
4th 8:40 am Capricorn
6th 11:25 am Aquarius
8th 2:24 pm Pisces
10th 5:57 pm Aries
12th 10:25 pm Taurus
15th 4:36 am Gemini
17th 1:21 pm Cancer
20th 0:45 am Leo
22nd 1:38 pm Virgo
25th 1:17 am Libra
27th 9:30 am Scorpio
29th 2:08 pm Sagittarius
31st 4:20 pm Capricorn

June 1961
2nd 5:47 pm Aquarius
4th 7:52 pm Pisces
6th 11:25 pm Aries
9th 4:39 am Taurus
11th 11:44 am Gemini
13th 8:51 pm Cancer
16th 8:17 am Leo
18th 9:11 pm Virgo
21st 9:29 am Libra
23rd 6:47 pm Scorpio
26th 0:05 am Sagittarius
28th 1:50 am Capricorn
30th 2:18 am Aquarius

July 1961
2nd 2:55 am Pisces
4th 5:16 am Aries
6th 10:06 am Taurus
8th 5:31 pm Gemini
11th 3:15 am Cancer
13th 2:58 pm Leo
16th 3:54 am Virgo
18th 4:35 pm Libra
21st 3:01 am Scorpio
23rd 9:35 am Sagittarius
25th 12:24 pm Capricorn
27th 12:40 pm Aquarius
29th 12:15 pm Pisces
31st 1:01 pm Aries

August 1961
2nd 4:25 pm Taurus
4th 11:06 pm Gemini
7th 8:59 am Cancer
9th 9:01 pm Leo
12th 10:01 am Virgo
14th 10:43 pm Libra
17th 9:41 am Scorpio
19th 5:40 pm Sagittarius
21st 10:05 pm Capricorn
23rd 11:24 pm Aquarius
25th 11:02 pm Pisces
27th 10:49 pm Aries
30th 0:37 am Taurus

September 1961
1st 5:56 am Gemini
3rd 3:04 pm Cancer
6th 3:01 am Leo
8th 4:05 pm Virgo
11th 4:32 am Libra
13th 3:21 pm Scorpio
15th 11:54 pm Sagittarius
18th 5:38 am Capricorn
20th 8:40 am Aquarius
22nd 9:34 am Pisces
24th 9:41 am Aries
26th 10:46 am Taurus
28th 2:36 pm Gemini
30th 10:19 pm Cancer

October 1961
3rd 9:44 am Leo
5th 10:45 pm Virgo
8th 11:01 am Libra
10th 9:19 pm Scorpio
13th 5:19 am Sagittarius
15th 11:21 am Capricorn
17th 3:34 pm Aquarius
19th 6:08 pm Pisces
21st 7:34 pm Aries
23rd 9:07 pm Taurus
26th 0:23 am Gemini
28th 7:06 am Cancer
30th 5:32 pm Leo

November 1961
2nd 6:16 am Virgo
4th 6:40 pm Libra
7th 4:37 am Scorpio
9th 11:47 am Sagittarius
11th 4:58 pm Capricorn
13th 8:59 pm Aquarius
16th 0:19 am Pisces
18th 3:10 am Aries
20th 6:03 am Taurus
22nd 10:01 am Gemini
24th 4:24 pm Cancer
27th 2:01 am Leo
29th 2:24 pm Virgo

December 1961
2nd 3:06 am Libra
4th 1:24 pm Scorpio
6th 8:21 pm Sagittarius
9th 0:31 am Capricorn
11th 3:12 am Aquarius
13th 5:42 am Pisces
15th 8:45 am Aries
17th 12:40 pm Taurus
19th 5:49 pm Gemini
22nd 0:49 am Cancer
24th 10:28 am Leo
26th 10:29 pm Virgo
29th 11:24 am Libra
31st 10:40 pm Scorpio

January 1962
3rd 6:19 am Sagittarius
5th 10:19 am Capricorn
7th 11:58 am Aquarius
9th 12:55 pm Pisces
11th 2:37 pm Aries
13th 6:05 pm Taurus
15th 11:42 pm Gemini
18th 7:42 am Cancer
20th 5:52 pm Leo
23rd 5:54 am Virgo
25th 6:51 pm Libra
28th 6:50 am Scorpio
30th 3:54 pm Sagittarius

February 1962
1st 9:07 pm Capricorn
3rd 10:56 pm Aquarius
5th 10:52 pm Pisces
7th 10:51 pm Aries
10th 0:36 am Taurus
12th 5:22 am Gemini
14th 1:24 pm Cancer
17th 0:04 am Leo
19th 12:28 pm Virgo
22nd 1:21 am Libra
24th 1:34 pm Scorpio
26th 11:45 pm Sagittarius

March 1962
1st 6:33 am Capricorn
3rd 9:47 am Aquarius
5th 10:14 am Pisces
7th 9:34 am Aries
9th 9:45 am Taurus
11th 12:41 pm Gemini
13th 7:30 pm Cancer
16th 5:58 am Leo
18th 6:35 pm Virgo
21st 7:28 am Libra
23rd 7:28 pm Scorpio
26th 5:48 am Sagittarius
28th 1:41 pm Capricorn
30th 6:41 pm Aquarius

April 1962
1st 8:42 pm Pisces
3rd 8:40 pm Aries
5th 8:27 pm Taurus
7th 10:02 pm Gemini
10th 3:14 am Cancer
12th 12:39 pm Leo
15th 0:57 am Virgo
17th 1:54 pm Libra
20th 1:37 am Scorpio
22nd 11:26 am Sagittarius
24th 7:19 pm Capricorn
27th 1:08 am Aquarius
29th 4:39 am Pisces

May 1962
1st	6:12 am	Aries
3rd	6:50 am	Taurus
5th	8:21 am	Gemini
7th	12:34 pm	Cancer
9th	8:39 pm	Leo
12th	8:12 am	Virgo
14th	9:04 pm	Libra
17th	8:42 am	Scorpio
19th	6:01 pm	Sagittarius
22nd	1:08 am	Capricorn
24th	6:30 am	Aquarius
26th	10:28 am	Pisces
28th	1:15 pm	Aries
30th	3:17 pm	Taurus

June 1962
1st	5:43 pm	Gemini
3rd	9:50 pm	Cancer
6th	5:26 am	Leo
8th	4:14 pm	Virgo
11th	4:51 am	Libra
13th	4:43 pm	Scorpio
16th	2:03 am	Sagittarius
18th	8:28 am	Capricorn
20th	12:47 pm	Aquarius
22nd	3:59 pm	Pisces
24th	6:44 pm	Aries
26th	9:35 pm	Taurus
29th	1:10 am	Gemini

July 1962
1st	6:23 am	Cancer
3rd	2:00 pm	Leo
6th	0:22 am	Virgo
8th	12:48 pm	Libra
11th	1:05 am	Scorpio
13th	10:55 am	Sagittarius
15th	5:28 pm	Capricorn
17th	9:07 pm	Aquarius
19th	11:00 pm	Pisces
22nd	0:35 am	Aries
24th	2:50 am	Taurus
26th	7:00 am	Gemini
28th	1:05 pm	Cancer
30th	9:24 pm	Leo

August 1962
2nd	7:50 am	Virgo
4th	8:18 pm	Libra
7th	8:54 am	Scorpio
9th	7:46 pm	Sagittarius
12th	3:14 am	Capricorn
14th	7:03 am	Aquarius
16th	8:16 am	Pisces
18th	8:27 am	Aries
20th	9:24 am	Taurus
22nd	12:33 pm	Gemini
24th	6:38 pm	Cancer
27th	3:32 am	Leo
29th	2:38 pm	Virgo

September 1962
1st	3:02 am	Libra
3rd	3:46 pm	Scorpio
6th	3:25 am	Sagittarius
8th	12:15 pm	Capricorn
10th	5:21 pm	Aquarius
12th	6:59 pm	Pisces
14th	6:33 pm	Aries
16th	6:04 pm	Taurus
18th	7:32 pm	Gemini
21st	0:26 am	Cancer
23rd	9:11 am	Leo
25th	8:32 pm	Virgo
28th	9:09 am	Libra
30th	9:49 pm	Scorpio

October 1962
3rd	9:38 am	Sagittarius
5th	7:32 pm	Capricorn
8th	2:19 am	Aquarius
10th	5:25 am	Pisces
12th	5:38 am	Aries
14th	4:45 am	Taurus
16th	4:54 am	Gemini
18th	8:10 am	Cancer
20th	3:35 pm	Leo
23rd	2:31 am	Virgo
25th	3:13 pm	Libra
28th	3:48 am	Scorpio
30th	3:18 pm	Sagittarius

November 1962
2nd	1:17 am	Capricorn
4th	8:58 am	Aquarius
6th	1:47 pm	Pisces
8th	3:42 pm	Aries
10th	3:44 pm	Taurus
12th	3:47 pm	Gemini
14th	5:52 pm	Cancer
16th	11:40 pm	Leo
19th	9:36 am	Virgo
21st	9:58 pm	Libra
24th	10:30 am	Scorpio
26th	9:41 pm	Sagittarius
29th	6:58 am	Capricorn

December 1962
1st	2:23 pm	Aquarius
3rd	7:52 pm	Pisces
5th	11:16 pm	Aries
8th	0:59 am	Taurus
10th	2:07 am	Gemini
12th	4:24 am	Cancer
14th	9:24 am	Leo
16th	6:02 pm	Virgo
19th	5:41 am	Libra
21st	6:16 pm	Scorpio
24th	5:29 am	Sagittarius
26th	2:14 pm	Capricorn
28th	8:41 pm	Aquarius
31st	1:19 am	Pisces

January 1963
2nd	4:47 am	Aries
4th	7:34 am	Taurus
6th	10:16 am	Gemini
8th	1:44 pm	Cancer
10th	7:03 pm	Leo
13th	3:08 am	Virgo
15th	2:06 pm	Libra
18th	2:33 am	Scorpio
20th	2:16 pm	Sagittarius
22nd	11:23 pm	Capricorn
25th	5:11 am	Aquarius
27th	8:33 am	Pisces
29th	10:43 am	Aries
31st	12:56 pm	Taurus

February 1963
2nd	4:06 pm	Gemini
4th	8:42 pm	Cancer
7th	3:08 am	Leo
9th	11:39 am	Virgo
11th	10:19 pm	Libra
14th	10:37 am	Scorpio
16th	10:55 pm	Sagittarius
19th	8:54 am	Capricorn
21st	3:18 pm	Aquarius
23rd	6:13 pm	Pisces
25th	7:04 pm	Aries
27th	7:40 pm	Taurus

March 1963
1st	9:40 pm	Gemini
4th	2:09 am	Cancer
6th	9:18 am	Leo
8th	6:35 pm	Virgo
11th	5:36 am	Libra
13th	5:52 pm	Scorpio
16th	6:26 am	Sagittarius
18th	5:31 pm	Capricorn
21st	1:19 am	Aquarius
23rd	4:60 am	Pisces
25th	5:35 am	Aries
27th	4:58 am	Taurus
29th	5:16 am	Gemini
31st	8:18 am	Cancer

April 1963
2nd	2:49 pm	Leo
5th	0:22 am	Virgo
7th	11:51 am	Libra
10th	0:14 am	Scorpio
12th	12:48 pm	Sagittarius
15th	0:27 am	Capricorn
17th	9:30 am	Aquarius
19th	2:48 pm	Pisces
21st	4:25 pm	Aries
23rd	3:50 pm	Taurus
25th	3:09 pm	Gemini
27th	4:32 pm	Cancer
29th	9:26 pm	Leo

May 1963
2nd	6:16 am	Virgo
4th	5:43 pm	Libra
7th	6:16 am	Scorpio
9th	6:43 pm	Sagittarius
12th	6:13 am	Capricorn
14th	3:48 pm	Aquarius
16th	10:32 pm	Pisces
19th	1:46 am	Aries
21st	2:21 am	Taurus
23rd	1:55 am	Gemini
25th	2:31 am	Cancer
27th	6:03 am	Leo
29th	1:27 pm	Virgo

June 1963
1st	0:10 am	Libra
3rd	12:38 pm	Scorpio
6th	1:02 am	Sagittarius
8th	12:05 pm	Capricorn
10th	9:22 pm	Aquarius
13th	4:20 am	Pisces
15th	8:44 am	Aries
17th	10:53 am	Taurus
19th	11:45 am	Gemini
21st	12:51 pm	Cancer
23rd	3:50 pm	Leo
25th	9:58 pm	Virgo
28th	7:43 am	Libra
30th	7:48 pm	Scorpio

July 1963
3rd	8:10 am	Sagittarius
5th	7:02 pm	Capricorn
8th	3:35 am	Aquarius
10th	9:51 am	Pisces
12th	2:15 pm	Aries
14th	5:15 pm	Taurus
16th	7:28 pm	Gemini
18th	9:47 pm	Cancer
21st	1:16 am	Leo
23rd	7:11 am	Virgo
25th	4:06 pm	Libra
28th	3:38 am	Scorpio
30th	4:06 pm	Sagittarius

August 1963
2nd	3:11 am	Capricorn
4th	11:22 am	Aquarius
6th	4:44 pm	Pisces
8th	8:07 pm	Aries
10th	10:39 pm	Taurus
13th	1:17 am	Gemini
15th	4:41 am	Cancer
17th	9:20 am	Leo
19th	3:44 pm	Virgo
22nd	0:27 am	Libra
24th	11:41 am	Scorpio
27th	0:14 am	Sagittarius
29th	11:53 am	Capricorn
31st	8:35 pm	Aquarius

★ ★

September 1963	October 1963	November 1963	December 1963
3rd 1:37 am Pisces	2nd 1:44 pm Aries	1st 0:42 am Taurus	2nd 10:48 am Cancer
5th 3:52 am Aries	4th 1:50 pm Taurus	2nd 11:49 pm Gemini	4th 12:26 pm Leo
7th 5:04 am Taurus	6th 2:01 pm Gemini	5th 0:08 am Cancer	6th 5:30 pm Virgo
9th 6:49 am Gemini	8th 4:04 pm Cancer	7th 3:26 am Leo	9th 2:23 am Libra
11th 10:12 am Cancer	10th 8:55 pm Leo	9th 10:17 am Virgo	11th 2:05 pm Scorpio
13th 3:33 pm Leo	13th 4:36 am Virgo	11th 8:09 pm Libra	14th 2:52 am Sagittarius
15th 10:49 pm Virgo	15th 2:27 pm Libra	14th 7:57 am Scorpio	16th 3:20 pm Capricorn
18th 8:03 am Libra	18th 1:53 am Scorpio	16th 8:41 pm Sagittarius	19th 2:28 am Aquarius
20th 7:12 pm Scorpio	20th 2:33 pm Sagittarius	19th 9:22 am Capricorn	21st 11:25 am Pisces
23rd 7:51 am Sagittarius	23rd 3:20 am Capricorn	21st 8:50 pm Aquarius	23rd 5:37 pm Aries
25th 8:15 am Capricorn	25th 2:15 pm Aquarius	24th 5:28 am Pisces	25th 8:55 pm Taurus
28th 5:58 am Aquarius	27th 9:35 pm Pisces	26th 10:19 am Aries	27th 9:57 pm Gemini
30th 11:40 am Pisces	30th 9:39 am Aries	28th 11:46 am Taurus	29th 10:08 pm Cancer
		30th 11:15 am Gemini	31st 11:09 pm Leo

January 1964	February 1964	March 1964	April 1964
3rd 2:49 am Virgo	1st 7:28 pm Libra	2nd 1:57 pm Scorpio	1st 9:42 am Sagittarius
5th 10:14 am Libra	4th 5:14 am Scorpio	5th 1:46 am Sagittarius	3rd 10:37 pm Capricorn
7th 9:04 pm Scorpio	6th 5:34 pm Sagittarius	7th 2:32 pm Capricorn	6th 10:19 am Aquarius
10th 9:47 am Sagittarius	9th 6:07 am Capricorn	10th 1:33 am Aquarius	8th 6:42 pm Pisces
12th 10:12 pm Capricorn	11th 4:35 pm Aquarius	12th 9:00 am Pisces	10th 11:07 pm Aries
15th 8:44 am Aquarius	14th 0:07 am Pisces	14th 1:11 am Aries	13th 0:36 am Taurus
17th 5:01 pm Pisces	16th 5:08 am Aries	16th 3:30 pm Taurus	15th 1:05 am Gemini
19th 11:10 pm Aries	18th 8:44 am Taurus	18th 5:27 pm Gemini	17th 2:23 am Cancer
22nd 3:23 am Taurus	20th 11:48 am Gemini	20th 8:13 pm Cancer	19th 5:42 am Leo
24th 6:03 am Gemini	22nd 2:50 pm Cancer	23rd 0:16 am Leo	21st 11:20 am Virgo
26th 7:52 am Cancer	24th 6:12 pm Leo	25th 5:43 am Virgo	23rd 7:09 pm Libra
28th 9:47 am Leo	26th 10:30 pm Virgo	27th 12:50 pm Libra	26th 5:03 am Scorpio
30th 1:13 pm Virgo	29th 4:49 am Libra	29th 10:04 pm Scorpio	28th 4:47 pm Sagittarius

May 1964	June 1964	July 1964	August 1964
1st 5:42 am Capricorn	2nd 10:57 am Pisces	2nd 0:52 am Aries	2nd 3:27 pm Gemini
3rd 6:04 pm Aquarius	4th 5:50 pm Aries	4th 5:40 am Taurus	4th 5:13 pm Cancer
6th 3:40 am Pisces	6th 9:18 pm Taurus	6th 7:41 am Gemini	6th 6:12 pm Leo
8th 9:11 am Aries	8th 9:49 pm Gemini	8th 7:57 am Cancer	8th 7:52 pm Virgo
10th 11:05 am Taurus	10th 9:17 pm Cancer	10th 8:04 am Leo	10th 11:53 pm Libra
12th 11:01 am Gemini	12th 9:37 pm Leo	12th 9:49 am Virgo	13th 7:36 am Scorpio
14th 10:56 am Cancer	15th 0:27 am Virgo	14th 2:47 pm Libra	15th 6:45 pm Sagittarius
16th 12:36 pm Leo	17th 6:57 am Libra	16th 11:33 pm Scorpio	18th 7:38 am Capricorn
18th 5:06 pm Virgo	19th 4:52 pm Scorpio	19th 11:30 am Sagittarius	20th 7:37 pm Aquarius
21st 0:40 am Libra	22nd 5:05 am Sagittarius	22nd 0:28 am Capricorn	23rd 5:11 am Pisces
23rd 11:01 am Scorpio	24th 6:01 pm Capricorn	24th 12:28 pm Aquarius	25th 12:13 am Aries
25th 11:04 pm Sagittarius	27th 6:20 am Aquarius	26th 10:36 pm Pisces	27th 5:22 am Taurus
28th 12:00 pm Capricorn	29th 4:54 pm Pisces	29th 6:23 am Aries	29th 9:17 pm Gemini
31st 0:32 am Aquarius		31st 11:57 am Taurus	

September 1964	October 1964	November 1964	December 1964
1st 0:15 am Cancer	2nd 12:45 pm Virgo	1st 0:24 am Libra	3rd 1:24 am Sagittarius
3rd 2:38 am Leo	4th 5:47 pm Libra	3rd 8:28 am Scorpio	5th 1:55 pm Capricorn
5th 5:15 am Virgo	7th 0:59 am Scorpio	5th 6:46 pm Sagittarius	8th 2:58 am Aquarius
7th 9:24 am Libra	9th 11:06 am Sagittarius	8th 7:08 am Capricorn	10th 2:57 pm Pisces
9th 4:24 pm Scorpio	11th 11:34 pm Capricorn	10th 8:09 pm Aquarius	13th 0:13 am Aries
12th 2:49 am Sagittarius	14th 12:13 pm Aquarius	13th 7:26 am Pisces	15th 5:29 am Taurus
14th 3:29 pm Capricorn	16th 10:32 pm Pisces	15th 3:05 pm Aries	17th 7:18 am Gemini
17th 3:45 am Aquarius	19th 5:02 am Aries	17th 6:55 pm Taurus	19th 7:02 am Cancer
19th 1:18 pm Pisces	21st 8:22 am Taurus	19th 7:58 pm Gemini	21st 6:34 am Leo
21st 7:42 pm Aries	23rd 10:04 am Gemini	21st 8:04 pm Cancer	23rd 7:46 am Virgo
23rd 11:46 pm Taurus	25th 11:39 am Cancer	23rd 9:00 pm Leo	25th 12:10 pm Libra
26th 2:46 am Gemini	27th 2:17 pm Leo	26th 0:02 am Virgo	27th 8:12 pm Scorpio
28th 5:40 am Cancer	29th 6:27 pm Virgo	28th 5:57 am Libra	30th 7:22 am Sagittarius
30th 8:54 am Leo		30th 2:34 pm Scorpio	

★ ★

January 1965
- 1st 8:06 pm Capricorn
- 4th 9:03 am Aquarius
- 6th 9:05 pm Pisces
- 9th 7:05 am Aries
- 11th 2:05 pm Taurus
- 13th 5:44 pm Gemini
- 15th 6:32 pm Cancer
- 17th 5:58 pm Leo
- 19th 5:58 pm Virgo
- 21st 8:31 pm Libra
- 24th 3:03 am Scorpio
- 26th 1:34 pm Sagittarius
- 29th 2:21 am Capricorn
- 31st 3:16 pm Aquarius

February 1965
- 3rd 2:55 am Pisces
- 5th 12:41 pm Aries
- 7th 8:22 pm Taurus
- 10th 1:36 am Gemini
- 12th 4:12 am Cancer
- 14th 4:53 am Leo
- 16th 5:08 am Virgo
- 18th 6:50 am Libra
- 20th 11:51 am Scorpio
- 22nd 8:58 pm Sagittarius
- 25th 9:16 am Capricorn
- 27th 10:13 pm Aquarius

March 1965
- 2nd 9:34 am Pisces
- 4th 6:43 pm Aries
- 7th 1:50 am Taurus
- 9th 7:12 am Gemini
- 11th 11:01 am Cancer
- 13th 1:22 pm Leo
- 15th 2:57 pm Virgo
- 17th 5:07 pm Libra
- 19th 9:34 pm Scorpio
- 22nd 5:39 am Sagittarius
- 24th 5:09 pm Capricorn
- 27th 5:56 am Aquarius
- 29th 5:28 pm Pisces

April 1965
- 1st 2:17 am Aries
- 3rd 8:25 am Taurus
- 5th 12:53 pm Gemini
- 7th 4:22 pm Cancer
- 9th 7:24 pm Leo
- 11th 10:15 pm Virgo
- 14th 1:39 am Libra
- 16th 6:45 am Scorpio
- 18th 2:35 pm Sagittarius
- 21st 1:25 am Capricorn
- 23rd 2:03 pm Aquarius
- 26th 2:00 am Pisces
- 28th 11:06 am Aries
- 30th 4:59 pm Taurus

May 1965
- 2nd 8:25 pm Gemini
- 4th 10:38 pm Cancer
- 7th 0:49 am Leo
- 9th 3:48 am Virgo
- 11th 8:05 am Libra
- 13th 2:12 pm Scorpio
- 15th 10:32 pm Sagittarius
- 18th 9:21 am Capricorn
- 20th 9:50 am Aquarius
- 23rd 10:12 am Pisces
- 25th 8:16 am Aries
- 28th 2:47 am Taurus
- 30th 5:56 am Gemini

June 1965
- 1st 7:04 am Cancer
- 3rd 7:48 am Leo
- 5th 9:36 am Virgo
- 7th 1:33 pm Libra
- 9th 8:05 pm Scorpio
- 12th 5:12 am Sagittarius
- 14th 4:21 pm Capricorn
- 17th 4:52 am Aquarius
- 19th 5:28 pm Pisces
- 22nd 4:27 am Aries
- 24th 12:11 pm Taurus
- 26th 4:13 pm Gemini
- 28th 5:17 pm Cancer
- 30th 4:50 pm Leo

July 1965
- 2nd 5:14 pm Virgo
- 4th 7:45 pm Libra
- 7th 1:40 am Scorpio
- 9th 10:56 am Sagittarius
- 11th 10:30 pm Capricorn
- 14th 11:07 am Aquarius
- 16th 11:44 pm Pisces
- 19th 11:09 am Aries
- 21st 8:11 pm Taurus
- 24th 1:47 am Gemini
- 26th 3:52 am Cancer
- 28th 3:37 am Leo
- 30th 2:57 am Virgo

August 1965
- 1st 3:57 am Libra
- 3rd 8:26 am Scorpio
- 5th 4:53 pm Sagittarius
- 8th 4:23 am Capricorn
- 10th 5:08 pm Aquarius
- 13th 5:37 am Pisces
- 15th 4:55 pm Aries
- 18th 2:27 am Taurus
- 20th 9:17 am Gemini
- 22nd 1:00 pm Cancer
- 24th 1:59 pm Leo
- 26th 1:38 pm Virgo
- 28th 1:57 pm Libra
- 30th 4:50 pm Scorpio

September 1965
- 1st 11:60 pm Sagittarius
- 4th 10:54 am Capricorn
- 6th 11:34 pm Aquarius
- 9th 11:35 am Pisces
- 11th 10:50 pm Aries
- 14th 7:54 am Taurus
- 16th 3:03 pm Gemini
- 18th 8:00 pm Cancer
- 20th 10:35 pm Leo
- 22nd 11:31 pm Virgo
- 25th 0:17 am Libra
- 27th 2:50 am Scorpio
- 29th 8:47 am Sagittarius

October 1965
- 1st 6:31 pm Capricorn
- 4th 6:49 am Aquarius
- 6th 7:12 pm Pisces
- 9th 5:51 am Aries
- 11th 2:15 pm Taurus
- 13th 8:39 pm Gemini
- 16th 1:26 am Cancer
- 18th 4:50 am Leo
- 20th 7:14 am Virgo
- 22nd 9:24 am Libra
- 24th 12:37 pm Scorpio
- 26th 6:14 pm Sagittarius
- 29th 3:09 am Capricorn
- 31st 2:51 pm Aquarius

November 1965
- 3rd 3:23 am Pisces
- 5th 2:19 pm Aries
- 7th 10:30 pm Taurus
- 10th 3:52 am Gemini
- 12th 7:28 am Cancer
- 14th 10:14 am Leo
- 16th 12:55 pm Virgo
- 18th 4:11 pm Libra
- 20th 8:39 pm Scorpio
- 23rd 2:59 am Sagittarius
- 25th 11:49 am Capricorn
- 27th 11:06 pm Aquarius
- 30th 11:40 am Pisces

December 1965
- 2nd 11:23 pm Aries
- 5th 8:07 am Taurus
- 7th 1:24 pm Gemini
- 9th 3:55 pm Cancer
- 11th 5:08 pm Leo
- 13th 6:37 pm Virgo
- 15th 9:34 pm Libra
- 18th 2:42 am Scorpio
- 20th 10:04 am Sagittarius
- 22nd 7:29 pm Capricorn
- 25th 6:46 am Aquarius
- 27th 7:18 pm Pisces
- 30th 7:38 am Aries

January 1966
- 1st 5:42 pm Taurus
- 4th 0:07 am Gemini
- 6th 2:39 am Cancer
- 8th 2:50 am Leo
- 10th 2:37 am Virgo
- 12th 3:57 am Libra
- 14th 8:13 am Scorpio
- 16th 3:42 pm Sagittarius
- 19th 1:45 am Capricorn
- 21st 1:27 pm Aquarius
- 24th 1:59 am Pisces
- 26th 2:32 pm Aries
- 29th 1:41 am Taurus
- 31st 9:38 am Gemini

February 1966
- 2nd 1:35 pm Cancer
- 4th 2:11 pm Leo
- 6th 1:13 pm Virgo
- 8th 12:56 pm Libra
- 10th 3:20 pm Scorpio
- 12th 9:35 pm Sagittarius
- 15th 7:27 am Capricorn
- 17th 7:26 pm Aquarius
- 20th 8:05 am Pisces
- 22nd 8:29 pm Aries
- 25th 7:51 am Taurus
- 27th 4:59 pm Gemini

March 1966
- 1st 10:48 pm Cancer
- 4th 0:56 am Leo
- 6th 0:36 am Virgo
- 7th 11:49 pm Libra
- 10th 0:48 am Scorpio
- 12th 5:22 am Sagittarius
- 14th 1:50 pm Capricorn
- 17th 1:35 am Aquarius
- 19th 2:18 pm Pisces
- 22nd 2:33 am Aries
- 24th 1:29 pm Taurus
- 26th 10:41 pm Gemini
- 29th 5:21 am Cancer
- 31st 9:08 am Leo

April 1966
- 2nd 10:29 am Virgo
- 4th 10:41 am Libra
- 6th 11:35 am Scorpio
- 8th 2:59 pm Sagittarius
- 10th 10:03 pm Capricorn
- 13th 8:44 am Aquarius
- 15th 9:12 pm Pisces
- 18th 9:25 am Aries
- 20th 7:57 pm Taurus
- 23rd 4:24 am Gemini
- 25th 10:45 am Cancer
- 27th 3:06 pm Leo
- 29th 5:47 pm Virgo

May 1966
1st   7:31 pm Libra
3rd   9:24 pm Scorpio
6th   0:53 am Sagittarius
8th   7:17 am Capricorn
10th 4:54 am Aquarius
13th 4:55 am Pisces
15th 5:13 pm Aries
18th 3:45 am Taurus
20th 11:35 am Gemini
22nd 4:57 pm Cancer
24th 8:35 pm Leo
26th 11:21 pm Virgo
29th 1:59 am Libra
31st 5:12 am Scorpio

June 1966
2nd   9:41 am Sagittarius
4th   4:13 am Capricorn
7th   1:23 am Aquarius
9th 12:58 pm Pisces
12th 1:26 am Aries
14th 12:26 pm Taurus
16th 8:23 pm Gemini
19th 1:03 am Cancer
21st 3:27 am Leo
23rd 5:08 am Virgo
25th 7:24 am Libra
27th 11:06 am Scorpio
29th 4:33 pm Sagittarius

July 1966
1st 11:51 pm Capricorn
4th   9:16 am Aquarius
6th   8:40 pm Pisces
9th   9:15 am Aries
11th 9:01 pm Taurus
14th 5:46 am Gemini
16th 10:38 am Cancer
18th 12:24 pm Leo
20th 12:47 pm Virgo
22nd 1:41 pm Libra
24th 4:35 pm Scorpio
26th 10:06 pm Sagittarius
29th 6:06 am Capricorn
31st 4:03 pm Aquarius

August 1966
3rd   3:35 am Pisces
5th   4:14 pm Aries
8th   4:36 am Taurus
10th 2:33 pm Gemini
12th 8:38 pm Cancer
14th 10:49 pm Leo
16th 10:35 pm Virgo
18th 10:05 pm Libra
20th 11:23 pm Scorpio
23rd 3:53 am Sagittarius
25th 11:40 am Capricorn
27th 9:56 pm Aquarius
30th 9:48 am Pisces

September 1966
1st 10:27 pm Aries
4th 10:57 am Taurus
6th   9:50 pm Gemini
9th   5:23 am Cancer
11th 8:57 am Leo
13th 9:24 am Virgo
15th 8:36 am Libra
17th 8:38 am Scorpio
19th 11:27 am Sagittarius
21st 5:56 pm Capricorn
24th 3:48 am Aquarius
26th 3:48 pm Pisces
29th 4:29 am Aries

October 1966
1st   4:45 pm Taurus
4th   3:42 am Gemini
6th 12:08 pm Cancer
8th   5:21 pm Leo
10th 7:25 pm Virgo
12th 7:30 pm Libra
14th 7:24 pm Scorpio
16th 9:01 pm Sagittarius
19th 1:58 am Capricorn
21st 10:46 am Aquarius
23rd 10:21 pm Pisces
26th 11:02 am Aries
28th 11:04 pm Taurus
31st 9:25 am Gemini

November 1966
2nd   5:40 pm Cancer
4th 11:35 pm Leo
7th   3:08 am Virgo
9th   4:54 am Libra
11th 5:56 am Scorpio
13th 7:41 am Sagittarius
15th 11:43 am Capricorn
17th 7:08 pm Aquarius
20th 5:55 am Pisces
22nd 6:32 pm Aries
25th 6:35 am Taurus
27th 4:28 pm Gemini
29th 11:49 pm Cancer

December 1966
2nd   4:59 am Leo
4th   8:46 am Virgo
6th 11:42 am Libra
8th   2:18 pm Scorpio
10th 5:15 pm Sagittarius
12th 9:34 pm Capricorn
15th 4:23 am Aquarius
17th 2:22 pm Pisces
20th 2:40 am Aries
22nd 3:06 pm Taurus
25th 1:14 am Gemini
27th 7:55 am Cancer
29th 11:55 am Leo
31st 2:33 pm Virgo

January 1967
2nd   5:04 pm Libra
4th   8:17 pm Scorpio
7th   0:28 am Sagittarius
9th   5:55 am Capricorn
11th 1:10 pm Aquarius
13th 10:46 pm Pisces
16th 10:49 am Aries
18th 11:40 pm Taurus
21st 10:34 am Gemini
23rd 5:48 pm Cancer
25th 9:20 pm Leo
27th 10:37 pm Virgo
29th 11:34 pm Libra

February 1967
1st   1:45 am Scorpio
3rd   5:58 am Sagittarius
5th 12:14 pm Capricorn
7th   8:19 pm Aquarius
10th 6:21 am Pisces
12th 6:19 pm Aries
15th 7:18 am Taurus
17th 7:13 pm Gemini
20th 3:46 am Cancer
22nd 8:01 am Leo
24th 9:03 am Virgo
26th 8:47 am Libra
28th 9:14 am Scorpio

March 1967
2nd 11:58 am Sagittarius
4th   5:38 pm Capricorn
7th   2:04 am Aquarius
9th 12:44 pm Pisces
12th 0:53 am Aries
14th 1:54 pm Taurus
17th 2:18 am Gemini
19th 12:06 pm Cancer
21st 6:01 pm Leo
23rd 8:06 pm Virgo
25th 7:49 pm Libra
27th 7:13 pm Scorpio
29th 8:11 pm Sagittarius

April 1967
1st   0:11 am Capricorn
3rd   7:52 am Aquarius
5th   6:30 pm Pisces
8th   6:56 am Aries
10th 7:54 pm Taurus
13th 8:12 am Gemini
15th 6:33 pm Cancer
18th 1:53 am Leo
20th 5:39 am Virgo
22nd 6:39 am Libra
24th 6:20 am Scorpio
26th 6:31 am Sagittarius
28th 8:59 am Capricorn
30th 3:02 pm Aquarius

May 1967
3rd   0:48 am Pisces
5th   1:10 pm Aries
8th   2:09 am Taurus
10th 2:03 pm Gemini
13th 0:09 am Cancer
15th 7:46 am Leo
17th 12:48 pm Virgo
19th 3:27 pm Libra
21st 4:29 pm Scorpio
23rd 5:08 pm Sagittarius
25th 7:01 pm Capricorn
27th 11:46 pm Aquarius
30th 8:22 am Pisces

June 1967
1st   8:08 pm Aries
4th   9:03 am Taurus
6th   8:49 pm Gemini
9th   6:14 am Cancer
11th 1:16 pm Leo
13th 6:21 pm Virgo
15th 9:57 pm Libra
18th 0:25 am Scorpio
20th 2:20 am Sagittarius
22nd 4:48 am Capricorn
24th 9:15 am Aquarius
26th 4:53 pm Pisces
29th 3:54 am Aries

July 1967
1st   4:42 pm Taurus
4th   4:36 am Gemini
6th   1:42 pm Cancer
8th   7:56 pm Leo
11th 0:07 am Virgo
13th 3:19 am Libra
15th 6:17 am Scorpio
17th 9:23 am Sagittarius
19th 12:50 pm Capricorn
21st 6:01 pm Aquarius
24th 1:28 am Pisces
26th 12:02 pm Aries
29th 0:41 am Taurus
31st 12:56 pm Gemini

August 1967
2nd 10:30 pm Cancer
5th   4:23 am Leo
7th   7:34 am Virgo
9th   9:34 am Libra
11th 11:45 am Scorpio
13th 2:54 pm Sagittarius
15th 7:19 pm Capricorn
18th 1:17 am Aquarius
20th 9:20 am Pisces
22nd 7:48 pm Aries
25th 8:21 am Taurus
27th 9:07 pm Gemini
30th 7:30 am Cancer

September 1967
1st	2:02 pm	Leo
3rd	5:04 pm	Virgo
5th	6:02 pm	Libra
7th	6:45 pm	Scorpio
9th	8:41 pm	Sagittarius
12th	0:43 am	Capricorn
14th	7:10 am	Aquarius
16th	3:55 pm	Pisces
19th	2:46 am	Aries
21st	3:19 pm	Taurus
24th	4:19 am	Gemini
26th	3:42 pm	Cancer
28th	11:42 pm	Leo

October 1967
1st	3:37 am	Virgo
3rd	4:34 am	Libra
5th	4:15 am	Scorpio
7th	4:34 am	Sagittarius
9th	7:08 am	Capricorn
11th	12:49 pm	Aquarius
13th	9:39 pm	Pisces
16th	8:58 am	Aries
18th	9:40 pm	Taurus
21st	10:36 am	Gemini
23rd	10:27 pm	Cancer
26th	7:36 am	Leo
28th	1:14 pm	Virgo
30th	3:27 pm	Libra

November 1967
1st	3:26 pm	Scorpio
3rd	2:54 pm	Sagittarius
5th	3:50 pm	Capricorn
7th	7:49 pm	Aquarius
10th	3:45 am	Pisces
12th	3:01 pm	Aries
15th	3:52 am	Taurus
17th	4:39 pm	Gemini
20th	4:11 am	Cancer
22nd	1:43 pm	Leo
24th	8:44 pm	Virgo
27th	0:48 am	Libra
29th	2:13 am	Scorpio

December 1967
1st	2:11 am	Sagittarius
3rd	2:27 am	Capricorn
5th	5:03 am	Aquarius
7th	11:26 am	Pisces
9th	9:45 pm	Aries
12th	10:32 am	Taurus
14th	11:18 pm	Gemini
17th	10:20 am	Cancer
19th	7:19 pm	Leo
22nd	2:20 am	Virgo
24th	7:24 am	Libra
26th	10:34 am	Scorpio
28th	12:08 pm	Sagittarius
30th	1:14 pm	Capricorn

January 1968
1st	3:29 pm	Aquarius
3rd	8:40 pm	Pisces
6th	5:50 am	Aries
8th	6:05 pm	Taurus
11th	6:54 am	Gemini
13th	5:51 pm	Cancer
16th	2:09 am	Leo
18th	8:10 am	Virgo
20th	12:46 pm	Libra
22nd	4:27 pm	Scorpio
24th	7:25 pm	Sagittarius
26th	9:57 pm	Capricorn
29th	1:08 am	Aquarius
31st	6:21 am	Pisces

February 1968
2nd	2:44 pm	Aries
5th	2:16 am	Taurus
7th	3:08 pm	Gemini
10th	2:33 am	Cancer
12th	10:47 am	Leo
14th	4:01 pm	Virgo
16th	7:22 pm	Libra
18th	10:00 pm	Scorpio
21st	0:49 am	Sagittarius
23rd	4:13 am	Capricorn
25th	8:40 am	Aquarius
27th	2:46 pm	Pisces
29th	11:16 pm	Aries

March 1968
3rd	10:29 am	Taurus
5th	11:17 pm	Gemini
8th	11:18 am	Cancer
10th	8:26 pm	Leo
13th	1:51 am	Virgo
15th	4:23 am	Libra
17th	5:34 am	Scorpio
19th	6:57 am	Sagittarius
21st	9:39 am	Capricorn
23rd	2:20 pm	Aquarius
25th	9:16 pm	Pisces
28th	6:34 am	Aries
30th	5:55 pm	Taurus

April 1968
2nd	6:41 am	Gemini
4th	7:12 pm	Cancer
7th	5:25 am	Leo
9th	12:00 pm	Virgo
11th	2:58 pm	Libra
13th	3:32 pm	Scorpio
15th	3:26 pm	Sagittarius
17th	4:28 pm	Capricorn
19th	7:50 pm	Aquarius
22nd	2:47 am	Pisces
24th	12:34 pm	Aries
27th	0:22 am	Taurus
29th	1:10 pm	Gemini

May 1968
2nd	1:50 am	Cancer
4th	12:50 pm	Leo
6th	8:57 pm	Virgo
9th	1:20 am	Libra
11th	2:29 am	Scorpio
13th	1:54 am	Sagittarius
15th	1:33 am	Capricorn
17th	3:27 am	Aquarius
19th	8:59 am	Pisces
21st	6:18 pm	Aries
24th	6:17 am	Taurus
26th	7:12 pm	Gemini
29th	7:41 am	Cancer
31st	6:52 pm	Leo

June 1968
3rd	3:50 am	Virgo
5th	9:44 am	Libra
7th	12:25 pm	Scorpio
9th	12:40 pm	Sagittarius
11th	12:09 pm	Capricorn
13th	12:53 pm	Aquarius
15th	4:49 pm	Pisces
18th	0:51 am	Aries
20th	12:27 pm	Taurus
23rd	1:23 am	Gemini
25th	1:41 pm	Cancer
28th	0:31 am	Leo
30th	9:22 am	Virgo

July 1968
2nd	4:06 pm	Libra
4th	8:18 pm	Scorpio
6th	10:04 pm	Sagittarius
8th	10:24 pm	Capricorn
10th	11:04 pm	Aquarius
13th	2:05 am	Pisces
15th	8:57 am	Aries
17th	7:33 pm	Taurus
20th	8:13 am	Gemini
22nd	8:31 pm	Cancer
25th	6:53 am	Leo
27th	3:07 pm	Virgo
29th	9:31 pm	Libra

August 1968
1st	2:10 am	Scorpio
3rd	5:09 am	Sagittarius
5th	6:57 am	Capricorn
7th	8:39 am	Aquarius
9th	11:50 am	Pisces
11th	5:57 pm	Aries
14th	3:37 am	Taurus
16th	3:52 pm	Gemini
19th	4:13 am	Cancer
21st	2:36 pm	Leo
23rd	10:19 pm	Virgo
26th	3:43 am	Libra
28th	7:37 am	Scorpio
30th	10:40 am	Sagittarius

September 1968
1st	1:22 pm	Capricorn
3rd	4:30 pm	Aquarius
5th	8:29 pm	Pisces
8th	2:51 am	Aries
10th	12:08 pm	Taurus
12th	11:54 pm	Gemini
15th	12:27 pm	Cancer
17th	11:25 pm	Leo
20th	7:11 am	Virgo
22nd	11:57 am	Libra
24th	2:37 pm	Scorpio
26th	4:31 pm	Sagittarius
28th	6:46 pm	Capricorn
30th	10:11 pm	Aquarius

October 1968
3rd	3:22 am	Pisces
5th	10:37 am	Aries
7th	8:07 pm	Taurus
10th	7:44 am	Gemini
12th	8:24 pm	Cancer
15th	8:05 am	Leo
17th	4:54 pm	Virgo
19th	10:04 pm	Libra
22nd	0:06 am	Scorpio
24th	0:32 am	Sagittarius
26th	1:15 am	Capricorn
28th	3:45 am	Aquarius
30th	8:58 am	Pisces

November 1968
1st	4:53 pm	Aries
4th	3:02 am	Taurus
6th	2:48 pm	Gemini
9th	3:26 am	Cancer
11th	3:43 pm	Leo
14th	1:53 am	Virgo
16th	8:21 am	Libra
18th	11:01 am	Scorpio
20th	11:03 am	Sagittarius
22nd	10:24 am	Capricorn
24th	11:08 am	Aquarius
26th	2:58 pm	Pisces
28th	10:27 pm	Aries

December 1968
1st	9:00 am	Taurus
3rd	9:05 pm	Gemini
6th	2:48 pm	Cancer
8th	10:02 pm	Leo
11th	8:54 am	Virgo
13th	5:04 pm	Libra
15th	9:30 pm	Scorpio
17th	10:27 pm	Sagittarius
19th	9:33 pm	Capricorn
21st	9:03 pm	Aquarius
23rd	11:02 pm	Pisces
26th	5:08 am	Aries
28th	3:01 pm	Taurus
31st	3:12 am	Gemini

January 1969
2nd   3:52 pm Cancer
5th   3:53 am Leo
7th   2:39 pm Virgo
9th 11:32 pm Libra
12th   5:29 am Scorpio
14th   8:15 am Sagittarius
16th   8:38 am Capricorn
18th   8:20 am Aquarius
20th   9:27 am Pisces
22nd   1:50 pm Aries
24th 10:16 pm Taurus
27th   9:56 am Gemini
29th 10:37 pm Cancer

February 1969
1st 10:28 am Leo
3rd   8:41 pm Virgo
6th   4:59 am Libra
8th 11:16 am Scorpio
10th   3:20 pm Sagittarius
12th   5:27 pm Capricorn
14th   6:32 pm Aquarius
16th   8:05 pm Pisces
18th 11:49 pm Aries
21st   7:06 am Taurus
23rd   5:44 pm Gemini
26th   6:12 am Cancer
28th   6:12 am Leo

March 1969
3rd   4:06 am Virgo
5th 11:32 am Libra
7th   4:55 pm Scorpio
9th   8:48 pm Sagittarius
11th 11:41 pm Capricorn
14th   2:10 am Aquarius
16th   5:07 am Pisces
18th   9:32 am Aries
20th   4:24 am Taurus
23rd   2:13 am Gemini
25th   2:18 am Cancer
28th   2:36 am Leo
30th 12:51 pm Virgo

April 1969
1st   8:02 pm Libra
4th   0:24 am Scorpio
6th   2:59 am Sagittarius
8th   5:05 am Capricorn
10th   7:49 am Aquarius
12th 11:44 am Pisces
14th   5:15 pm Aries
17th   0:44 am Taurus
19th 10:31 am Gemini
21st 10:17 pm Cancer
24th 10:50 am Leo
26th   9:56 pm Virgo
29th   5:42 am Libra

May 1969
1st   9:46 am Scorpio
3rd 11:18 am Sagittarius
5th 11:60 am Capricorn
7th   1:32 pm Aquarius
9th   5:08 pm Pisces
11th 11:09 pm Aries
14th   7:30 am Taurus
16th   5:43 pm Gemini
19th   5:31 am Cancer
21st   6:12 pm Leo
24th   6:04 am Virgo
26th   3:02 pin Libra
28th   8:03 pm Scorpio
30th   9:29 pm Sagittarius

June 1969
1st   9:08 pm Capricorn
3rd   9:07 pm Aquarius
5th 11:16 pm Pisces
8th   4:41 am Aries
10th   1:10 pm Taurus
12th 11:48 pm Gemini
15th 11:54 am Cancer
18th   0:34 am Leo
20th 12:51 pm Virgo
22nd 11:03 pm Libra
25th   5:27 am Scorpio
27th   7:55 am Sagittarius
29th   7:44 am Capricorn

July 1969
1st   6:53 am Aquarius
3rd   7:33 am Pisces
5th 11:23 am Aries
7th   6:58 pm Taurus
10th   5:33 am Gemini
12th   5:48 pm Cancer
15th   6:29 am Leo
17th   6:41 pm Virgo
20th   5:16 am Libra
22nd 12:58 pm Scorpio
24th   5:05 pm Sagittarius
26th   6:06 pm Capricorn
28th   5:35 pm Aquarius
30th   5:34 pm Pisces

August 1969
1st   7:58 pm Aries
4th   2:05 am Taurus
6th 11:53 am Gemini
8th 11:58 pm Cancer
11th 12:38 pm Leo
14th   0:33 am Virgo
16th 10:48 am Libra
18th   6:52 pm Scorpio
21st   0:12 am Sagittarius
23rd   2:47 am Capricorn
25th   3:36 am Aquarius
27th   4:04 am Pisces
29th   6:01 am Aries
31st 10:55 am Taurus

September 1969
2nd   7:26 pm Gemini
5th   6:57 am Cancer
7th   7:35 pm Leo
10th   7:18 am Virgo
12th   4:50 pm Libra
15th   0:25 am Scorpio
17th   5:40 am Sagittarius
19th   9:12 am Capricorn
21st 11:30 am Aquarius
23rd   1:23 pm Pisces
25th   3:57 pm Aries
27th   8:30 pm Taurus
30th   4:08 am Gemini

October 1969
2nd   2:55 pm Cancer
5th   3:24 am Leo
7th   3:19 pm Virgo
10th   0:48 am Libra
12th   7:16 am Scorpio
14th 11:32 am Sagittarius
16th   2:35 pm Capricorn
18th   5:22 pm Aquarius
20th   8:26 pm Pisces
23rd   0:18 am Aries
25th   5:34 am Taurus
27th   1:03 pm Gemini
29th 11:13 pm Cancer

November 1969
1st 11:35 am Leo
3rd 12:00 pm Virgo
6th   9:54 am Libra
8th   4:13 pm Scorpio
10th   7:28 pm Sagittarius
12th   9:09 pm Capricorn
14th 10:53 pm Aquarius
17th   1:53 am Pisces
19th   6:34 am Aries
21st 12:54 pm Taurus
23rd   9:00 pm Gemini
26th   7:12 am Cancer
28th   7:23 pm Leo

December 1969
1st   8:11 am Virgo
3rd   7:13 pm Libra
6th   2:28 am Scorpio
8th   5:40 am Sagittarius
10th   6:21 am Capricorn
12th   6:30 am Aquarius
14th   8:00 am Pisces
16th 12:01 pm Aries
18th   6:38 pm Taurus
21st   3:29 am Gemini
23rd   2:11 pm Cancer
26th   2:22 am Leo
28th   3:19 pm Virgo
31st   3:16 am Libra

January 1970
2nd 11:56 am Scorpio
4th   4:28 pm Sagittarius
6th   5:27 pm Capricorn
8th   4:49 pm Aquarius
10th   4:42 pm Pisces
12th   6:52 pm Aries
15th   0:22 am Taurus
17th   9:11 am Gemini
19th   8:15 pm Cancer
22nd   8:41 am Leo
24th   9:32 pm Virgo
27th   9:40 am Libra
29th   7:32 pm Scorpio

February 1970
1st   1:48 am Sagittarius
3rd   4:19 am Capricorn
5th   4:18 am Aquarius
7th   3:39 am Pisces
9th   4:21 am Aries
11th   8:05 am Taurus
13th   3:34 pm Gemini
16th   2:19 am Cancer
18th   2:56 pm Leo
21st   3:43 am Virgo
23rd   3:28 pm Libra
26th   1:22 am Scorpio
28th   8:35 am Sagittarius

March 1970
2nd 12:50 pm Capricorn
4th   2:32 pm Aquarius
6th   2:49 pm Pisces
8th   3:20 pm Aries
10th   5:48 pm Taurus
12th 11:38 pm Gemini
15th   9:23 am Cancer
17th   9:40 pm Leo
20th 10:29 am Virgo
22nd   9:57 pm Libra
25th   7:08 am Scorpio
27th   2:05 pm Sagittarius
29th   6:59 pm Capricorn
31st 10:08 pm Aquarius

April 1970
3rd   0:02 am Pisces
5th   1:33 am Aries
7th   4:04 am Taurus
9th   9:07 am Gemini
11th   5:37 pm Cancer
14th   5:16 am Leo
16th   6:08 pm Virgo
19th   5:33 am Libra
21st   2:13 pm Scorpio
23rd   8:15 pm Sagittarius
26th   0:27 am Capricorn
28th   3:43 am Aquarius
30th   6:38 am Pisces

★★

May 1970
2nd   9:34 am Aries
4th   1:08 pm Taurus
6th   6:21 pm Gemini
9th   2:20 am Cancer
11th   1:25 pm Leo
14th   2:11 am Virgo
16th   2:00 pm Libra
18th 10:49 pm Scorpio
21st   4:10 am Sagittarius
23rd   7:13 am Capricorn
25th   9:28 am Aquarius
27th 12:02 pm Pisces
29th   3:29 pm Aries
31st   8:05 pm Taurus

June 1970
3rd   2:11 am Gemini
5th 10:30 am Cancer
7th   9:19 pm Leo
10th 10:02 am Virgo
12th 10:28 pm Libra
15th   7:58 am Scorpio
17th   1:35 pm Sagittarius
19th   4:03 pm Capricorn
21st   5:02 pm Aquarius
23rd   6:14 pm Pisces
25th   8:55 pm Aries
28th   1:37 am Taurus
30th   8:28 am Gemini

July 1970
2nd   5:25 pm Cancer
5th   4:27 am Leo
7th   5:11 pm Virgo
10th   6:01 am Libra
12th   4:36 pm Scorpio
14th 11:24 pm Sagittarius
17th   2:19 am Capricorn
19th   2:45 am Aquarius
21st   2:39 am Pisces
23rd   3:46 am Aries
25th   7:24 am Taurus
27th   1:58 pm Gemini
29th 11:15 pm Cancer

August 1970
1st 10:48 am Leo
3rd 11:36 pm Virgo
6th 12:30 pm Libra
8th 11:56 pm Scorpio
11th   8:02 am Sagittarius
13th 12:19 pm Capricorn
15th   1:28 pm Aquarius
17th   1:02 pm Pisces
19th 12:54 pm Aries
21st   2:51 pm Taurus
23rd   8:07 pm Gemini
26th   5:00 am Cancer
28th   4:40 pm Leo
31st   5:38 am Virgo

September 1970
2nd   6:25 pm Libra
5th   5:53 am Scorpio
7th   2:54 pm Sagittarius
9th   8:48 pm Capricorn
11th 11:33 pm Aquarius
13th 11:57 pm Pisces
15th 11:35 pm Aries
18th   0:20 am Taurus
20th   4:06 am Gemini
22nd 11:46 am Cancer
24th 10:54 pm Leo
27th 11:54 am Virgo
30th   0:34 am Libra

October 1970
2nd 11:34 am Scorpio
4th   8:31 pm Sagittarius
7th   3:09 am Capricorn
9th   7:23 am Aquarius
11th   9:28 am Pisces
13th 10:12 am Aries
15th 11:02 am Taurus
17th   1:48 pm Gemini
19th   8:02 pm Cancer
22nd   6:15 am Leo
24th   6:57 pm Virgo
27th   7:35 am Libra
29th   6:12 pm Scorpio

November 1970
1st   2:24 am Sagittarius
3rd   8:31 am Capricorn
5th   1:08 pm Aquarius
7th   4:31 pm Pisces
9th   6:51 pm Aries
11th   8:50 pm Taurus
13th 11:48 pm Gemini
16th   5:26 am Cancer
18th   2:39 pm Leo
21st   2:51 am Virgo
23rd   3:38 pm Libra
26th   2:23 am Scorpio
28th   9:58 am Sagittarius
30th   3:04 pm Capricorn

December 1970
2nd   6:43 pm Aquarius
4th   9:56 pm Pisces
7th   1:03 am Aries
9th   4:26 am Taurus
11th   8:36 am Gemini
13th   2:36 pm Cancer
15th 11:21 pm Leo
18th 11:06 am Virgo
21st   0:02 am Libra
23rd 11:22 am Scorpio
25th   7:23 pm Sagittarius
28th   0:02 am Capricorn
30th   2:24 am Aquarius

January 1971
1st   4:08 am Pisces
3rd   6:29 am Aries
5th 10:04 am Taurus
7th   3:11 pm Gemini
9th 10:11 pm Cancer
12th   7:27 am Leo
14th   6:58 pm Virgo
17th   7:51 am Libra
19th   8:01 pm Scorpio
22nd   5:10 am Sagittarius
24th 10:27 am Capricorn
26th 12:33 pm Aquarius
28th   1:02 pm Pisces
30th   1:39 pm Aries

February 1971
1st   3:54 pm Taurus
3rd   8:38 pm Gemini
6th   4:10 am Cancer
8th   2:10 pm Leo
11th   1:59 am Virgo
13th   2:51 pm Libra
16th   3:20 am Scorpio
18th   1:40 pm Sagittarius
20th   8:33 pm Capricorn
22nd 11:43 pm Aquarius
25th   0:05 am Pisces
26th 11:30 pm Aries
28th 11:55 pm Taurus

March 1971
3rd   3:05 am Gemini
5th   9:52 am Cancer
7th   7:48 pm Leo
10th   8:13 am Virgo
12th   9:07 pm Libra
15th   9:30 am Scorpio
17th   8:23 pm Sagittarius
20th   4:34 am Capricorn
22nd   9:24 am Aquarius
24th 11:04 am Pisces
26th 10:45 am Aries
28th 10:19 am Taurus
30th 11:50 am Gemini

April 1971
1st   4:56 pm Cancer
4th   2:07 am Leo
6th   2:19 pm Virgo
9th   3:18 am Libra
11th   3:28 pm Scorpio
14th   2:04 am Sagittarius
16th 10:35 am Capricorn
18th   4:44 pm Aquarius
20th   8:06 pm Pisces
22nd   9:09 pm Aries
24th   9:07 pm Taurus
26th 10:01 pm Gemini
29th   1:45 am Cancer

May 1971
1st   9:40 am Leo
3rd   9:05 pm Virgo
6th   9:59 am Libra
8th 10:05 pm Scorpio
11th   8:07 am Sagittarius
13th   4:09 pm Capricorn
15th 10:20 pm Aquarius
18th   2:40 am Pisces
20th   5:11 am Aries
22nd   6:32 am Taurus
24th   8:05 am Gemini
26th 11:33 am Cancer
28th   6:20 pm Leo
31st   4:51 am Virgo

June 1971
2nd   5:27 pm Libra
5th   5:35 am Scorpio
7th   3:26 pm Sagittarius
9th 10:45 pm Capricorn
12th   4:03 am Aquarius
14th   8:02 am Pisces
16th 11:06 am Aries
18th   1:40 pm Taurus
20th   4:27 am Gemini
22nd   8:34 pm Cancer
25th   3:15 am Leo
27th   1:10 pm Virgo
30th   1:23 am Libra

July 1971
2nd   1:43 pm Scorpio
4th 11:60 pm Sagittarius
7th   7:01 am Capricorn
9th 11:25 am Aquarius
11th   2:15 pm Pisces
13th   4:35 pm Aries
15th   7:13 pm Taurus
17th 10:49 pm Gemini
20th   3:50 am Cancer
22nd 11:21 am Leo
24th   9:12 pm Virgo
27th   9:13 am Libra
29th   9:49 pm Scorpio

August 1971
1st   8:45 am Sagittarius
3rd   4:28 pm Capricorn
5th   8:45 pm Aquarius
7th 10:35 pm Pisces
9th 11:27 pm Aries
12th   0:57 am Taurus
14th   4:15 am Gemini
16th   9:54 am Cancer
18th   6:02 pm Leo
21st   4:22 am Virgo
23rd   4:24 pm Libra
26th   5:09 am Scorpio
28th   4:54 pm Sagittarius
31st   1:52 am Capricorn

★★

MOON CHARTS

***

September 1971
2nd   6:59 am Aquarius
4th   8:48 am Pisces
6th   8:44 am Aries
8th   8:41 am Taurus
10th 10:31 am Gemini
12th 3:26 pm Cancer
14th 11:39 pm Leo
17th 10:32 am Virgo
19th 10:49 pm Libra
22nd 11:34 am Scorpio
24th 11:44 pm Sagittarius
27th 9:49 am Capricorn
29th 4:34 pm Aquarius

October 1971
1st   7:33 pm Pisces
3rd   7:39 pm Aries
5th   6:44 pm Taurus
7th   6:56 pm Gemini
9th 10:12 pm Cancer
12th 5:34 am Leo
14th 4:18 pm Virgo
17th 4:48 am Libra
19th 5:31 pm Scorpio
22nd 5:32 am Sagittarius
24th 4:03 pm Capricorn
27th 0:11 am Aquarius
29th 4:53 am Pisces
31st 6:24 am Aries

November 1971
2nd   5:56 am Taurus
4th   5:31 am Gemini
6th   7:20 am Cancer
8th   1:02 pm Leo
10th 10:45 pm Virgo
13th 11:05 am Libra
15th 11:50 pm Scorpio
18th 11:28 am Sagittarius
20th 9:36 pm Capricorn
23rd 5:50 am Aquarius
25th 11:44 am Pisces
27th 2:50 pm Aries
29th 4:06 pm Taurus

December 1971
1st   4:26 pm Gemini
3rd   5:55 pm Cancer
5th 10:18 pm Leo
8th   6:44 am Virgo
10th 6:21 pm Libra
13th 7:00 am Scorpio
15th 6:35 pm Sagittarius
18th 4:05 am Capricorn
20th 11:30 am Aquarius
22nd 5:09 pm Pisces
24th 9:08 pm Aries
26th 11:45 pm Taurus
29th 1:38 am Gemini
31st 4:03 am Cancer

January 1972
2nd   8:26 am Leo
4th   3:54 pm Virgo
7th   2:34 am Libra
9th   3:03 pm Scorpio
12th 2:55 am Sagittarius
14th 12:51 pm Capricorn
16th 7:01 pm Aquarius
18th 11:27 pm Pisces
21st 2:36 am Aries
23rd 5:18 am Taurus
25th 8:16 am Gemini
27th 12:05 pm Cancer
29th 5:25 pm Leo

February 1972
1st   0:56 am Virgo
3rd 11:09 am Libra
5th 11:18 pm Scorpio
8th 11:33 am Sagittarius
10th 9:48 pm Capricorn
13th 4:33 am Aquarius
15th 8:07 am Pisces
17th 9:51 am Aries
19th 11:14 am Taurus
21st 1:39 pm Gemini
23rd 5:56 pm Cancer
26th 0:17 am Leo
28th 8:43 am Virgo

March 1972
1st   7:03 pm Libra
4th   7:02 am Scorpio
6th   7:36 pm Sagittarius
9th   6:46 am Capricorn
11th 2:37 pm Aquarius
13th 6:36 pm Pisces
15th 7:35 pm Aries
17th 7:29 pm Taurus
19th 8:15 pm Gemini
21st 11:27 pm Cancer
24th 5:50 am Leo
26th 2:51 pm Virgo
29th 1:44 am Libra
31st 1:51 pm Scorpio

April 1972
3rd   2:29 am Sagittarius
5th   2:18 pm Capricorn
7th 11:37 pm Aquarius
10th 4:54 am Pisces
12th 6:30 am Aries
14th 5:55 am Taurus
16th 5:20 am Gemini
18th 6:50 am Cancer
20th 11:53 am Leo
22nd 8:26 pm Virgo
25th 7:36 am Libra
27th 7:58 pm Scorpio
30th 8:32 am Sagittarius

May 1972
2nd   8:29 pm Capricorn
5th   6:32 am Virgo
7th   1:23 pm Pisces
9th   4:31 pm Aries
11th 4:46 pm Taurus
13th 3:59 pm Gemini
15th 4:21 pm Cancer
17th 7:42 pm Leo
20th 2:59 am Virgo
22nd 1:40 pm Libra
25th 2:01 am Scorpio
27th 2:34 pm Sagittarius
30th 2:13 am Capricorn

June 1972
1st 12:13 pm Aquarius
3rd   7:51 pm Pisces
6th   0:29 am Aries
8th   2:14 am Taurus
10th 2:26 am Gemini
12th 2:48 am Cancer
14th 5:15 am Leo
16th .11:09 am Virgo
18th 8:40 pm Libra
21st 8:44 am Scorpio
23rd 9:15 pm Sagittarius
26th 8:35 am Capricorn
28th 6:01 pm Aquarius

July 1972
1st   1:19 am Pisces
3rd   6:21 am Aries
5th   9:24 am Taurus
7th 11:06 am Gemini
9th 12:33 pm Cancer
11th 3:11 pm Leo
13th 8:19 pm Virgo
16th 4:53 am Libra
18th 4:16 pm Scorpio
21st 4:46 am Sagittarius
23rd 4:08 pm Capricorn
26th 1:08 am Aquarius
28th 7:28 am Pisces
30th 11:51 am Aries

August 1972
1st   2:59 pm Taurus
3rd   5:36 pm Gemini
5th   8:21 pm Cancer
7th 11:58 pm Leo
10th 5:27 am Virgo
12th 1:32 pm Libra
15th 0:20 am Scorpio
17th 12:48 pm Sagittarius
20th 0:39 am Capricorn
22nd 9:38 am Aquarius
24th 3:26 pm Pisces
26th 6:40 pm Aries
28th 8:45 pm Taurus
30th 10:58 pm Gemini

September 1972
2nd   2:14 am Cancer
4th   6:57 am Leo
6th   1:19 pm Virgo
8th   9:39 pm Libra
11th 8:19 am Scorpio
13th 8:44 pm Sagittarius
16th 9:05 am Capricorn
18th 7:02 pm Aquarius
21st 1:09 am Pisces
23rd 3:44 am Aries
25th 4:28 am Taurus
27th 5:17 am Gemini
29th 7:42 am Cancer

October 1972
1st 12:30 pm Leo
3rd   7:34 pm Virgo
6th   4:38 am Libra
8th   3:31 pm Scorpio
11th 3:54 am Sagittarius
13th 4:44 pm Capricorn
16th 3:49 am Aquarius
18th 11:07 am Pisces
20th 2:18 pm Aries
22nd 2:36 pm Taurus
24th 2:06 pm Gemini
26th 2:49 pm Cancer
28th 6:17 pm Leo
31st 1:01 am Virgo

November 1972
2nd 10:29 am Libra
4th   9:48 pm Scorpio
7th 10:19 am Sagittarius
9th 11:11 pm Capricorn
12th 11:00 am Aquarius
14th 7:54 pm Pisces
17th 0:43 am Aries
19th 1:52 am Taurus
21st 1:06 am Gemini
23rd 0:33 am Cancer
25th 2:14 am Leo
27th 7:29 am Virgo
29th 4:19 pm Libra

December 1972
2nd   3:44 am Scorpio
4th   4:24 pm Sagittarius
7th   5:06 am Capricorn
9th   4:53 pm Aquarius
12th 2:32 am Pisces
14th 8:55 am Aries
16th 11:54 am Taurus
18th 12:65 pm Gemini
20th 11:59 am Cancer
22nd 12:40 pm Leo
24th 4:08 pm Virgo
26th 11:22 pm Libra
29th 10:13 am Scorpio
31st 10:51 pm Sagittarius

***

January 1973
3rd 11:29 am Capricorn
5th 10:48 pm Aquarius
8th 8:01 am Pisces
10th 2:55 pm Aries
12th 7:23 pm Taurus
14th 9:41 pm Gemini
16th 10:39 pm Cancer
18th 11:40 pm Leo
21st 2:26 am Virgo
23rd 8:21 am Libra
25th 5:55 pm Scorpio
28th 6:10 am Sagittarius
30th 6:52 pm Capricorn

February 1973
2nd 5:52 am Aquarius
4th 2:19 pm Pisces
6th 8:28 pm Aries
9th 0:53 am Taurus
11th 4:10 am Gemini
13th 6:45 am Cancer
15th 9:14 am Leo
17th 12:35 pm Virgo
19th 6:02 pm Libra
22nd 2:37 am Scorpio
24th 2:14 pm Sagittarius
27th 3:03 am Capricorn

March 1973
1st 2:18 pm Aquarius
3rd 10:30 pm Pisces
6th 3:35 am Aries
8th 6:51 am Taurus
10th 9:32 am Gemini
12th 12:31 pm Cancer
14th 4:09 pm Leo
16th 8:44 pm Virgo
19th 2:50 am Libra
21st 11:19 am Scorpio
23rd 10:26 pm Sagittarius
26th 11:15 am Capricorn
28th 11:13 pm Aquarius
31st 7:50 am Pisces

April 1973
2nd 12:43 pm Aries
4th 2:56 pm Taurus
6th 4:12 pm Gemini
8th 6:06 pm Cancer
10th 9:33 pm Leo
13th 2:47 am Virgo
15th 9:53 am Libra
17th 6:53 pm Scorpio
20th 6:04 am Sagittarius
22nd 6:50 pm Capricorn
25th 7:19 am Aquarius
27th 5:06 pm Pisces
29th 10:52 pm Aries

May 1973
2nd 1:01 am Taurus
4th 1:15 am Gemini
6th 1:35 am Cancer
8th 3:39 am Leo
10th 8:16 am Virgo
12th 3:34 pm Libra
15th 1:11 am Scorpio
17th 12:44 pm Sagittarius
20th 1:30 am Capricorn
22nd 2:16 pm Aquarius
25th 1:06 am Pisces
27th 8:09 am Aries
29th 11:24 am Taurus
31st 11:51 am Gemini

June 1973
2nd 11:23 am Cancer
4th 11:53 am Leo
6th 2:57 pm Virgo
8th 9:19 pm Libra
11th 6:54 am Scorpio
13th 6:45 pm Sagittarius
16th 7:37 am Capricorn
18th 8:19 pm Aquarius
21st 7:26 am Pisces
23rd 3:45 pm Aries
25th 8:35 pm Taurus
27th 10:17 pm Gemini
29th 10:09 pm Cancer

July 1973
1st 9:57 pm Leo
3rd 11:32 pm Virgo
6th 4:27 am Libra
8th 1:10 pm Scorpio
11th 0:49 am Sagittarius
13th 1:47 pm Capricorn
16th 2:15 am Aquarius
18th 1:06 pm Pisces
20th 9:44 pm Aries
23rd 3:39 am Taurus
25th 6:57 am Gemini
27th 8:11 am Cancer
29th 8:32 am Leo
31st 9:40 am Virgo

August 1973
2nd 1:19 pm Libra
4th 8:39 pm Scorpio
7th 7:39 am Sagittarius
9th 8:31 pm Capricorn
12th 8:51 am Aquarius
14th 7:13 pm Pisces
17th 3:17 am Aries
19th 9:13 am Taurus
21st 1:26 pm Gemini
23rd 4:08 pm Cancer
25th 5:51 pm Leo
27th 7:36 pm Virgo
29th 10:54 pm Libra

September 1973
1st 5:22 am Scorpio
3rd 3:28 pm Sagittarius
6th 4:02 am Capricorn
8th 4:28 pm Aquarius
11th 2:39 am Pisces
13th 9:53 am Aries
15th 2:59 pm Taurus
17th 6:49 pm Gemini
19th 10:02 pm Cancer
22nd 0:58 am Leo
24th 4:01 am Virgo
26th 8:05 am Libra
28th 2:25 pm Scorpio
30th 11:48 pm Sagittarius

October 1973
3rd 12:04 pm Capricorn
6th 0:50 am Aquarius
8th 11:19 am Pisces
10th 6:26 pm Aries
12th 10:36 pm Taurus
15th 1:09 am Gemini
17th 3:29 am Cancer
19th 6:26 am Leo
21st 10:21 am Virgo
23rd 3:32 pm Libra
25th 10:31 pm Scorpio
28th 8:02 am Sagittarius
30th 7:50 pm Capricorn

November 1973
2nd 8:59 am Aquarius
4th 8:26 pm Pisces
7th 4:18 am Aries
9th 8:22 am Taurus
11th 9:59 am Gemini
13th 10:48 am Cancer
15th 12:23 pm Leo
17th 3:45 pm Virgo
19th 9:17 pm Libra
22nd 5:09 am Scorpio
24th 3:15 pm Sagittarius
27th 3:15 am Capricorn
29th 4:18 pm Aquarius

December 1973
2nd 4:32 am Pisces
4th 1:46 pm Aries
6th 7:06 pm Taurus
8th 8:57 pm Gemini
10th 8:53 pm Cancer
12th 8:47 pm Leo
14th 10:23 pm Virgo
17th 2:55 am Libra
19th 10:48 am Scorpio
21st 9:22 pm Sagittarius
24th 9:43 am Capricorn
26th 10:45 pm Aquarius
29th 11:08 am Pisces
31st 9:33 am Aries

January 1974
3rd 4:35 am Taurus
5th 7:57 am Gemini
7th 8:26 am Cancer
9th 7:44 am Leo
11th 7:47 am Virgo
13th 10:28 am Libra
15th 4:59 pm Scorpio
18th 3:14 am Sagittarius
20th 3:48 pm Capricorn
23rd 4:49 am Aquarius
25th 4:59 pm Pisces
28th 3:31 am Aries
30th 11:37 am Taurus

February 1974
1st 4:51 pm Gemini
3rd 7:04 pm Cancer
5th 7:11 pm Leo
7th 6:53 pm Virgo
9th 8:14 pm Libra
12th 0:59 am Scorpio
14th 10:05 am Sagittarius
16th 10:16 pm Capricorn
19th 11:20 am Aquarius
21st 11:15 pm Pisces
24th 9:11 am Aries
26th 5:10 pm Taurus
28th 11:10 pm Gemini

March 1974
3rd 2:50 am Cancer
5th 4:49 am Leo
7th 5:35 am Virgo
9th 6:56 am Libra
11th 10:46 am Scorpio
13th 6:24 pm Sagittarius
16th 5:42 am Capricorn
18th 6:37 pm Aquarius
21st 6:30 am Pisces
23rd 3:59 pm Aries
25th 11:09 pm Taurus
28th 4:32 am Gemini
30th 8:38 am Cancer

April 1974
1st 11:40 am Leo
3rd 1:57 pm Virgo
5th 4:25 pm Libra
7th 8:28 pm Scorpio
10th 3:30 am Sagittarius
12th 1:60 pm Capricorn
15th 2:34 am Aquarius
17th 2:41 pm Pisces
20th 0:20 am Aries
22nd 6:50 am Taurus
24th 11:08 am Gemini
26th 2:17 pm Cancer
28th 5:04 pm Leo
30th 7:50 pm Virgo

May 1974
2nd 11:39 pm Libra
5th 4:45 am Scorpio
7th 12:09 pm Sagittarius
9th 10:16 pm Capricorn
12th 10:36 am Aquarius
14th 11:04 pm Pisces
17th 9:15 am Aries
19th 4:07 pm Taurus
21st 7:52 pm Gemini
23rd 9:45 pm Cancer
25th 11:12 pm Leo
28th 1:26 am Virgo
30th 5:17 am Libra

June 1974
1st 11:13 am Scorpio
3rd 7:24 pm Sagittarius
6th 5:50 am Capricorn
8th 6:04 pm Aquarius
11th 6:43 am Pisces
13th 5:50 pm Aries
16th 1:45 am Taurus
18th 5:55 am Gemini
20th 7:19 am Cancer
22nd 7:30 am Leo
24th 8:15 am Virgo
26th 11:02 am Libra
28th 4:43 pm Scorpio

July 1974
1st 1:22 am Sagittarius
3rd 12:22 pm Capricorn
6th 0:41 am Aquarius
8th 1:25 pm Pisces
11th 1:10 am Aries
13th 10:17 am Taurus
15th 3:50 pm Gemini
17th 5:53 pm Cancer
19th 5:43 pm Leo
21st 5:12 pm Virgo
23rd 6:23 pm Libra
25th 10:47 pm Scorpio
28th 7:03 am Sagittarius
30th 6:12 pm Capricorn

August 1974
2nd 6:47 am Aquarius
4th 7:26 pm Pisces
7th 7:14 am Aries
9th 5:10 pm Taurus
12th 0:16 am Gemini
14th 3:47 am Cancer
16th 4:26 am Leo
18th 3:45 am Virgo
20th 3:48 am Libra
22nd 6:43 am Scorpio
24th 1:40 pm Sagittarius
27th 0:16 am Capricorn
29th 12:53 pm Aquarius

September 1974
1st 1:30 am Pisces
3rd 12:56 pm Aries
5th 10:51 pm Taurus
8th 6:34 am Gemini
10th 11:37 am Cancer
12th 1:52 pm Leo
14th 2:13 pm Virgo
16th 2:22 pm Libra
18th 4:20 pm Scorpio
20th 9:48 pm Sagittarius
23rd 7:26 am Capricorn
25th 7:39 pm Aquarius
28th 8:13 am Pisces
30th 7:25 pm Aries

October 1974
3rd 4:38 am Taurus
5th 11:59 am Gemini
7th 5:28 pm Cancer
9th 9:02 pm Leo
11th 10:57 pm Virgo
14th 0:12 am Libra
16th 2:27 am Scorpio
18th 7:21 am Sagittarius
20th 3:50 pm Capricorn
23rd 3:22 am Aquarius
25th 3:57 pm Pisces
28th 3:12 am Aries
30th 11:57 am Taurus

November 1974
1st 6:22 pm Gemini
3rd 11:01 pm Cancer
6th 2:30 am Leo
8th 5:19 am Virgo
10th 8:01 am Libra
12th 11:28 am Scorpio
14th 4:44 pm Sagittarius
17th 0:45 am Capricorn
19th 11:43 am Aquarius
22nd 0:14 am Pisces
24th 11:57 am Aries
26th 9:04 pm Taurus
29th 2:57 am Gemini

December 1974
1st 6:21 am Cancer
3rd 8:32 am Leo
5th 10:42 am Virgo
7th 1:45 pm Libra
9th 6:16 pm Scorpio
12th 0:35 am Sagittarius
14th 9:09 am Capricorn
16th 7:52 pm Aquarius
19th 8:14 am Pisces
21st 8:36 pm Aries
24th 6:42 am Taurus
26th 1:12 pm Gemini
28th 4:13 pm Cancer
30th 5:05 pm Leo

January 1975
1st 5:35 pm Virgo
3rd 7:25 pm Libra
5th 11:39 pm Scorpio
8th 6:43 am Sagittarius
10th 4:01 pm Capricorn
13th 3:04 am Aquarius
15th 3:26 pm Pisces
18th 4:04 am Aries
20th 3:17 pm Taurus
22nd 11:23 pm Gemini
25th 3:20 am Cancer
27th 3:50 am Leo
29th 3:16 am Virgo
31st 3:17 am Libra

February 1975
2nd 5:58 am Scorpio
4th 12:16 pm Sagittarius
6th 9:44 pm Capricorn
9th 9:18 am Aquarius
11th 9:47 pm Pisces
14th 10:22 am Aries
16th 10:09 pm Taurus
19th 7:31 am Gemini
21st 1:14 pm Cancer
23rd 3:09 pm Leo
25th 2:36 pm Virgo
27th 1:43 pm Libra

March 1975
1st 2:40 pm Scorpio
3rd 7:10 pm Sagittarius
6th 3:41 am Capricorn
8th 3:11 pm Aquarius
11th 3:49 am Pisces
13th 4:18 pm Aries
16th 3:53 am Taurus
18th 1:40 pm Gemini
20th 8:47 pm Cancer
23rd 0:31 am Leo
25th 1:21 am Virgo
27th 0:53 am Libra
29th 1:10 am Scorpio
31st 4:13 am Sagittarius

April 1975
2nd 11:13 am Capricorn
4th 9:45 pm Aquarius
7th 10:16 am Pisces
9th 10:44 pm Aries
12th 9:51 am Taurus
14th 7:13 pm Gemini
17th 2:27 am Cancer
19th 7:11 am Leo
21st 9:40 am Virgo
23rd 10:41 am Libra
25th 11:43 am Scorpio
27th 2:25 pm Sagittarius
29th 8:12 pm Capricorn

May 1975
2nd 5:36 am Aquarius
4th 5:35 pm Pisces
7th 6:01 am Aries
9th 5:00 pm Taurus
12th 1:43 am Gemini
14th 8:05 am Cancer
16th 12:35 pm Leo
18th 3:44 pm Virgo
20th 6:04 pm Libra
22nd 8:26 pm Scorpio
24th 11:51 pm Sagittarius
27th 5:35 am Capricorn
29th 2:14 pm Aquarius

June 1975
1st 1:33 am Pisces
3rd 2:01 pm Aries
6th 1:19 am Taurus
8th 3:17 am Gemini
10th 6:43 pm Cancer
12th 9:10 pm Leo
14th 11:40 pm Virgo
16th 2:59 am Libra
19th 7:37 am Scorpio
21st 1:59 am Sagittarius
23rd 10:34 pm Capricorn
25th 9:35 pm Aquarius
28th 10:03 am Pisces
30th pm Aries

July 1975
3rd 9:51 am Taurus
5th 6:55 pm Gemini
8th 0:22 am Cancer
10th 2:49 am Leo
12th 3:56 am Virgo
14th 5:24 am Libra
16th 8:26 am Scorpio
18th 1:35 pm Sagittarius
20th 8:46 pm Capricorn
23rd 5:58 am Aquarius
25th 4:50 pm Pisces
28th 5:27 am Aries
30th 5:53 pm Taurus

August 1975
2nd 3:50 am Gemini
4th 10:11 am Cancer
6th 12:40 pm Leo
8th 12:53 pm Virgo
10th 12:54 pm Libra
12th 2:34 pm Scorpio
14th 7:02 pm Sagittarius
17th 2:26 am Capricorn
19th 12:11 pm Aquarius
21st 11:32 pm Pisces
24th 12:02 pm Aries
27th 0:44 am Taurus
29th 11:49 am Gemini
31st 7:33 pm Cancer

September 1975
2nd 11:08 pm Leo
4th 11:30 pm Virgo
6th 10:38 pm Libra
8th 10:47 pm Scorpio
11th 1:41 am Sagittarius
13th 8:15 am Capricorn
15th 5:53 pm Aquarius
18th 5:32 am Pisces
20th 6:08 pm Aries
23rd 6:43 am Taurus
25th 6:12 pm Gemini
28th 3:05 am Cancer
30th 8:16 am Leo

October 1975
2nd 10:00 am Virgo
4th 9:41 am Libra
6th 9:13 am Scorpio
8th 10:42 am Sagittarius
10th 3:35 pm Capricorn
13th 0:10 am Aquarius
15th 11:42 am Pisces
18th 0:20 am Aries
20th 12:42 pm Taurus
22nd 11:52 pm Gemini
25th 8:54 am Cancer
27th 3:16 pm Leo
29th 6:44 pm Virgo
31st 7:55 pm Libra

November 1975
2nd 8:10 pm Scorpio
4th 9:13 pm Sagittarius
7th 0:47 am Capricorn
9th 8:06 am Aquarius
11th 6:45 pm Pisces
14th 7:17 am Aries
16th 7:37 pm Taurus
19th 6:12 am Gemini
21st 2:33 pm Cancer
23rd 8:47 pm Leo
26th 1:05 am Virgo
28th 3:47 am Libra
30th 5:38 am Scorpio

December 1975
2nd 7:37 am Sagittarius
4th 11:04 am Capricorn
6th 5:18 pm Aquarius
9th 2:55 am Pisces
11th 3:09 pm Aries
14th 3:40 am Taurus
16th 2:10 pm Gemini
18th 9:49 pm Cancer
21st 2:53 am Leo
23rd 6:27 am Virgo
25th 9:27 am Libra
27th 12:29 pm Scorpio
29th 3:55 pm Sagittarius
31st 8:19 pm Capricorn

January 1976
3rd 2:35 am Aquarius
5th 11:40 am Pisces
7th 11:22 pm Aries
10th 12:09 pm Taurus
12th 11:21 pm Gemini
15th 6:57 am Cancer
17th 11:13 am Leo
19th 1:25 pm Virgo
21st 3:12 pm Libra
23rd 5:50 pm Scorpio
25th 9:52 pm Sagittarius
28th 3:25 am Capricorn
30th 10:38 am Aquarius

February 1976
1st 7:50 pm Pisces
4th 7:20 am Aries
6th 8:14 pm Taurus
9th 8:13 am Gemini
11th 4:55 pm Cancer
13th 9:31 pm Leo
15th 10:50 pm Virgo
17th 11:15 pm Libra
20th 0:15 am Scorpio
22nd 3:20 am Sagittarius
24th 8:58 am Capricorn
26th 4:50 pm Aquarius
29th 2:44 am Pisces

March 1976
2nd 2:24 pm Aries
5th 3:19 am Taurus
7th 3:55 pm Gemini
10th 1:58 am Cancer
12th 7:52 am Leo
14th 9:56 am Virgo
16th 9:45 am Libra
18th 9:22 am Scorpio
20th 10:39 am Sagittarius
22nd 2:54 pm Capricorn
24th 10:20 pm Aquarius
27th 8:35 am Pisces
29th 8:35 am Aries

April 1976
1st 9:34 am Taurus
3rd 10:15 pm Gemini
6th 9:04 am Cancer
8th 4:33 pm Leo
10th 8:15 pm Virgo
12th 8:54 pm Libra
14th 8:16 pm Scorpio
16th 8:18 pm Sagittarius
18th 10:45 pm Capricorn
21st 4:51 am Aquarius
23rd 2:31 pm Pisces
26th 2:36 am Aries
28th 3:36 pm Taurus

May 1976
1st 4:02 am Gemini
3rd 2:51 pm Cancer
5th 11:08 pm Leo
8th 4:18 am Virgo
10th 6:37 am Libra
12th 7:03 am Scorpio
14th 7:06 am Sagittarius
16th 8:37 am Capricorn
18th 1:10 pm Aquarius
20th 9:30 pm Pisces
23rd 9:09 am Aries
25th 10:08 pm Taurus
28th 10:19 am Gemini
30th 8:37 pm Cancer

June 1976
2nd 4:35 am Leo
4th 10:17 am Virgo
6th 1:56 pm Libra
8th 3:57 pm Scorpio
10th 5:07 pm Sagittarius
12th 6:47 pm Capricorn
14th 10:32 pm Aquarius
17th 5:49 am Pisces
19th 4:35 pm Aries
22nd 5:22 am Taurus
24th 5:35 pm Gemini
27th 3:27 am Cancer
29th 10:36 am Leo

July 1976
1st 3:44 pm Virgo
3rd 7:33 pm Libra
5th 10:32 pm Scorpio
8th 1:06 am Sagittarius
10th 3:50 am Capricorn
12th 7:57 am Aquarius
14th 2:41 pm Pisces
17th 0:40 am Aries
19th 1:11 pm Taurus
22nd 1:40 am Gemini
24th 11:35 am Cancer
26th 6:16 pm Leo
28th 10:22 pm Virgo
31st 1:13 am Libra

August 1976
2nd 3:56 am Scorpio
4th 7:04 am Sagittarius
6th 10:56 am Capricorn
8th 3:59 pm Aquarius
10th 11:00 pm Pisces
13th 8:52 am Aries
15th 9:06 pm Taurus
18th 9:52 am Gemini
20th 8:31 pm Cancer
23rd 3:28 am Leo
25th 7:01 am Virgo
27th 8:42 am Libra
29th 10:06 am Scorpio
31st 12:32 pm Sagittarius

September 1976
2nd 4:32 pm Capricorn
4th 10:20 pm Aquarius
7th 6:14 am Pisces
9th 4:20 pm Aries
12th 4:31 am Taurus
14th 5:31 pm Gemini
17th 5:03 am Cancer
19th 1:06 pm Leo
21st 5:13 pm Virgo
23rd 6:27 pm Libra
25th 6:34 pm Scorpio
27th 7:24 pm Sagittarius
29th 10:15 pm Capricorn

October 1976
2nd 3:51 am Aquarius
4th 12:51 pm Pisces
6th 10:51 pm Aries
9th 11:12 am Taurus
12th 0:14 am Gemini
14th 12:21 pm Cancer
16th 9:49 pm Leo
19th 3:23 am Virgo
21st 5:24 am Libra
23rd 5:17 am Scorpio
25th 4:52 am Sagittarius
27th 5:50 am Capricorn
29th 10:11 am Aquarius
31st 5:56 pm Pisces

November 1976
3rd 4:47 am Aries
5th 5:23 pm Taurus
8th 6:20 am Gemini
10th 6:27 pm Cancer
13th 4:34 am Leo
15th 11:40 am Virgo
17th 3:30 pm Libra
19th 4:29 pm Scorpio
21st 4:06 pm Sagittarius
23rd 4:09 pm Capricorn
25th 6:36 pm Aquarius
28th 0:50 am Pisces
30th 11:06 am Aries

December 1976
2nd 11:42 pm Taurus
5th 12:36 pm Gemini
8th 0:21 am Cancer
10th 10:09 am Leo
12th 5:53 pm Virgo
14th 11:13 pm Libra
17th 2:02 am Scorpio
19th 2:54 am Sagittarius
21st 3:14 am Capricorn
23rd 4:53 am Aquarius
25th 9:43 am Pisces
27th 6:37 pm Aries
30th 6:45 am Taurus

★ ★

January 1977
1st	7:43 pm	Gemini
4th	7:10 am	Cancer
6th	4:19 pm	Leo
8th	11:24 pm	Virgo
11th	4:47 am	Libra
13th	8:43 am	Scorpio
15th	11:18 am	Sagittarius
17th	1:04 pm	Capricorn
19th	3:17 pm	Aquarius
21st	7:35 pm	Pisces
24th	3:24 am	Aries
26th	2:43 pm	Taurus
29th	3:38 am	Gemini
31st	3:18 pm	Cancer

February 1977
3rd	0:13 am	Leo
5th	6:17 am	Virgo
7th	10:36 am	Libra
9th	2:04 pm	Scorpio
11th	5:12 pm	Sagittarius
13th	8:15 pm	Capricorn
15th	11:46 pm	Aquarius
18th	4:49 am	Pisces
20th	12:28 pm	Aries
22nd	11:06 pm	Taurus
25th	11:51 am	Gemini
28th	0:04 am	Cancer

March 1977
2nd	9:22 am	Leo
4th	3:16 pm	Virgo
6th	6:35 pm	Libra
8th	8:39 pm	Scorpio
10th	10:43 pm	Sagittarius
13th	1:42 am	Capricorn
15th	6:03 am	Aquarius
17th	12:09 pm	Pisces
19th	8:25 pm	Aries
22nd	7:08 am	Taurus
24th	7:40 pm	Gemini
27th	8:15 am	Cancer
29th	6:38 pm	Leo

April 1977
1st	1:25 am	Virgo
3rd	4:39 am	Libra
5th	5:41 am	Scorpio
7th	6:12 am	Sagittarius
9th	7:45 am	Capricorn
11th	11:28 am	Aquarius
13th	5:52 pm	Pisces
16th	2:54 am	Aries
18th	2:04 pm	Taurus
21st	2:38 am	Gemini
23rd	3:24 pm	Cancer
26th	2:43 am	Leo
28th	10:48 am	Virgo
30th	3:09 pm	Libra

May 1977
2nd	4:22 pm	Scorpio
4th	4:01 pm	Sagittarius
6th	3:59 pm	Capricorn
8th	6:05 pm	Aquarius
10th	11:29 pm	Pisces
13th	8:33 am	Aries
15th	8:05 pm	Taurus
18th	8:50 am	Gemini
20th	9:35 pm	Cancer
23rd	9:10 am	Leo
25th	6:27 pm	Virgo
28th	0:29 am	Libra
30th	2:55 am	Scorpio

June 1977
1st	2:54 am	Sagittarius
3rd	2:09 am	Capricorn
5th	2:47 am	Aquarius
7th	6:42 am	Pisces
9th	2:40 pm	Aries
12th	1:57 am	Taurus
14th	2:51 pm	Gemini
17th	3:28 am	Cancer
19th	2:50 pm	Leo
22nd	0:28 am	Virgo
24th	7:30 am	Libra
26th	11:36 am	Scorpio
28th	12:58 pm	Sagittarius
30th	12:48 pm	Capricorn

July 1977
2nd	1:01 pm	Aquarius
4th	3:38 pm	Pisces
6th	10:06 pm	Aries
9th	8:37 am	Taurus
11th	9:15 pm	Gemini
14th	9:48 am	Cancer
16th	8:51 pm	Leo
19th	5:56 am	Virgo
21st	1:06 pm	Libra
23rd	6:10 pm	Scorpio
25th	9:03 pm	Sagittarius
27th	10:14 pm	Capricorn
29th	11:04 pm	Aquarius

August 1977
1st	1:26 am	Pisces
3rd	6:59 am	Aries
5th	4:21 pm	Taurus
8th	4:30 am	Gemini
10th	5:03 pm	Cancer
13th	3:55 am	Leo
15th	12:24 pm	Virgo
17th	6:48 pm	Libra
19th	11:36 pm	Scorpio
22nd	3:03 am	Sagittarius
24th	5:29 am	Capricorn
26th	7:41 am	Aquarius
28th	10:50 am	Pisces
30th	4:15 pm	Aries

September 1977
2nd	0:51 am	Taurus
4th	12:28 pm	Gemini
7th	1:02 am	Cancer
9th	12:10 pm	Leo
11th	8:33 pm	Virgo
14th	2:07 am	Libra
16th	5:45 am	Scorpio
18th	8:29 am	Sagittarius
20th	11:05 am	Capricorn
22nd	2:14 pm	Aquarius
24th	6:32 pm	Pisces
27th	0:41 am	Aries
29th	9:24 am	Taurus

October 1977
1st	8:34 pm	Gemini
4th	9:09 am	Cancer
6th	8:57 pm	Leo
9th	5:55 am	Virgo
11th	11:25 am	Libra
13th	2:09 pm	Scorpio
15th	3:28 pm	Sagittarius
17th	4:53 pm	Capricorn
19th	7:38 pm	Aquarius
22nd	0:25 am	Pisces
24th	7:37 am	Aries
26th	4:54 pm	Taurus
29th	4:07 am	Gemini
31st	4:41 pm	Cancer

November 1977
3rd	5:01 am	Leo
5th	3:12 pm	Virgo
7th	9:50 pm	Libra
10th	0:42 am	Scorpio
12th	1:04 am	Sagittarius
14th	0:52 am	Capricorn
16th	2:02 am	Aquarius
18th	6:02 am	Pisces
20th	1:17 pm	Aries
22nd	11:09 pm	Taurus
25th	10:49 am	Gemini
27th	11:20 pm	Cancer
30th	11:51 am	Leo

December 1977
2nd	11:03 pm	Virgo
5th	7:13 am	Libra
7th	11:27 am	Scorpio
9th	12:18 pm	Sagittarius
11th	11:28 am	Capricorn
13th	11:06 am	Aquarius
15th	1:16 pm	Pisces
17th	7:16 pm	Aries
20th	4:57 am	Taurus
22nd	4:53 pm	Gemini
25th	5:29 am	Cancer
27th	5:51 pm	Leo
30th	5:11 am	Virgo

January 1978
1st	2:27 pm	Libra
3rd	8:32 pm	Scorpio
5th	11:02 pm	Sagittarius
7th	10:54 pm	Capricorn
9th	10:06 pm	Aquarius
11th	10:52 pm	Pisces
14th	3:09 am	Aries
16th	11:37 am	Taurus
18th	11:08 pm	Gemini
21st	11:51 am	Cancer
24th	0:04 am	Leo
26th	10:54 am	Virgo
28th	8:07 pm	Libra
31st	3:02 am	Scorpio

February 1978
2nd	7:11 am	Sagittarius
4th	8:48 am	Capricorn
6th	9:06 am	Aquarius
8th	9:52 am	Pisces
10th	1:03 pm	Aries
12th	7:54 pm	Taurus
15th	6:27 am	Gemini
17th	6:56 pm	Cancer
20th	7:09 am	Leo
22nd	5:39 pm	Virgo
25th	2:03 am	Libra
27th	8:27 am	Scorpio

March 1978
1st	1:00 pm	Sagittarius
3rd	3:57 pm	Capricorn
5th	5:51 pm	Aquarius
7th	7:47 pm	Pisces
9th	11:10 pm	Aries
12th	5:21 am	Taurus
14th	2:52 pm	Gemini
17th	2:50 am	Cancer
19th	3:11 pm	Leo
22nd	1:50 am	Virgo
24th	9:40 am	Libra
26th	3:00 pm	Scorpio
28th	6:38 pm	Sagittarius
30th	9:25 pm	Capricorn

April 1978
2nd	0:05 am	Aquarius
4th	3:21 am	Pisces
6th	7:55 am	Aries
8th	2:25 pm	Taurus
10th	11:29 pm	Gemini
13th	11:01 am	Cancer
15th	11:32 pm	Leo
18th	10:41 am	Virgo
20th	6:51 pm	Libra
22nd	11:41 pm	Scorpio
25th	2:01 am	Sagittarius
27th	3:30 am	Capricorn
29th	5:31 am	Aquarius

★ ★

May 1978
1st   9:03 am Pisces
3rd   2:29 pm Aries
5th   9:53 pm Taurus
8th   7:22 am Gemini
10th   6:44 pm Cancer
13th   7:16 am Leo
15th   7:14 pm Virgo
18th   4:22 am Libra
20th   9:35 am Scorpio
22nd 11:28 am Sagittarius
24th 11:43 am Capricorn
26th 12:15 pm Aquarius
28th   2:42 pm Pisces
30th   7:56 pm Aries

June 1978
2nd   3:52 am Taurus
4th   1:56 pm Gemini
7th   1:31 am Cancer
9th   2:08 pm Leo
12th   2:34 am Virgo
14th 12:51 pm Libra
16th   7:24 pm Scorpio
18th   9:50 pm Sagittarius
20th   9:52 pm Capricorn
22nd   9:11 pm Aquarius
24th   9:59 pm Pisces
27th   1:56 am Aries
29th   9:26 am Taurus

July 1978
1st   7:40 pm Gemini
4th   7:35 am Cancer
6th   8:13 pm Leo
9th   8:42 am Virgo
11th   7:46 pm Libra
14th   3:43 am Scorpio
16th   7:44 am Sagittarius
18th   8:30 am Capricorn
20th   7:44 am Aquarius
22nd   7:31 am Pisces
24th   9:52 am Aries
26th   3:56 pm Taurus
29th   1:33 am Gemini
31st   1:30 pm Cancer

August 1978
3rd   2:11 am Leo
5th   2:28 pm Virgo
8th   1:28 am Libra
10th 10:07 am Scorpio
12th   3:38 pm Sagittarius
14th   5:59 pm Capricorn
16th   6:14 pm Aquarius
18th   6:07 pm Pisces
20th   7:32 pm Aries
23rd   0:06 am Taurus
25th   8:36 am Gemini
27th   7:59 pm Cancer
30th   8:39 am Leo

September 1978
1st   8:47 pm Virgo
4th   7:14 am Libra
6th   3:36 pm Scorpio
8th   9:38 pm Sagittarius
11th   1:19 am Capricorn
13th   3:08 am Aquarius
15th   4:10 am Pisces
17th   5:52 am Aries
19th   9:47 am Taurus
21st   4:50 pm Gemini
24th   3:33 am Cancer
26th   4:01 pm Leo
29th   4:10 am Virgo

October 1978
1st   2:14 pm Libra
3rd   9:47 pm Scorpio
6th   3:06 am Sagittarius
8th   6:51 am Capricorn
10th   9:42 am Aquarius
12th 12:13 pm Pisces
14th   3:06 pm Aries
16th   7:23 pm Taurus
19th   2:05 am Gemini
21st 11:55 am Cancer
24th   0:04 am Leo
26th 12:29 pm Virgo
28th 10:51 pm Libra
31st   5:49 am Scorpio

November 1978
2nd   10:02 am Sagittarius
4th   12:40 pm Capricorn
6th   3:04 pm Aquarius
8th   6:07 pm Pisces
10th 10:12 pm Aries
13th   3:36 am Taurus
15th 10:48 am Gemini
17th   8:16 pm Cancer
20th   8:10 am Leo
22nd   8:56 pm Virgo
25th   8:03 am Libra
27th   3:33 pm Scorpio
29th   7:20 pm Sagittarius

December 1978
1st   8:44 pm Capricorn
3rd   9:36 pm Aquarius
5th   11:36 pm Pisces
8th   3:41 am Aries
10th   9:53 am Taurus
12th   5:57 pm Gemini
15th   3:51 am Cancer
17th   3:38 pm Leo
20th   4:32 am Virgo
22nd   4:35 pm Libra
25th   1:30 am Scorpio
27th   6:03 am Sagittarius
29th   7:13 am Capricorn
31st   6:55 am Aquarius

January 1979
2nd   7:12 am Pisces
4th   9:47 am Aries
6th   3:23 pm Taurus
8th   11:43 pm Gemini
11th 10:16 am Cancer
13th 10:17 pm Leo
16th 11:10 am Virgo
18th 11:40 pm Libra
21st   9:45 am Scorpio
23rd   4:02 pm Sagittarius
25th   6:23 pm Capricorn
27th   6:11 pm Aquarius
29th   5:27 pm Pisces
31st   6:15 pm Aries

February 1979
2nd   10:05 pm Taurus
5th   5:37 am Gemini
7th   4:08 pm Cancer
10th   4:28 am Leo
12th   5:18 pm Virgo
15th   5:35 am Libra
17th   4:09 pm Scorpio
19th 11:51 pm Sagittarius
22nd   3:58 am Capricorn
24th   5:10 am Aquarius
26th   4:53 am Pisces
28th   4:57 am Aries

March 1979
2nd   7:14 am Taurus
4th   1:04 pm Gemini
6th   10:36 pm Cancer
9th   10:49 am Leo
11th 11:44 pm Virgo
14th 11:40 am Libra
16th   9:50 pm Scorpio
19th   5:36 am Sagittarius
21st 10:53 am Capricorn
23rd   1:50 pm Aquarius
25th   3:04 pm Pisces
27th   3:49 pm Aries
29th   5:40 pm Taurus
31st 10:09 pm Gemini

April 1979
3rd   6:27 am Cancer
5th   5:59 pm Leo
8th   6:52 am Virgo
10th   6:45 pm Libra
13th   4:15 am Scorpio
15th 11:16 am Sagittarius
17th   4:22 pm Capricorn
19th   8:01 pm Aquarius
21st 10:41 pm Pisces
24th   0:52 am Aries
26th   3:30 am Taurus
28th   7:53 am Gemini
30th   3:16 pm Cancer

May 1979
3rd   1:57 am Leo
5th   2:41 pm Virgo
8th   2:48 am Libra
10th 12:07 pm Scorpio
12th   6:23 pm Sagittarius
14th 10:27 pm Capricorn
17th   1:26 am Aquarius
19th   4:19 am Pisces
21st   7:31 am Aries
23rd 11:22 am Taurus
25th   4:31 pm Gemini
27th 11:51 pm Cancer
30th 10:11 am Leo

June 1979
1st   10:41 pm Virgo
4th   11:08 am Libra
6th   9:03 pm Scorpio
9th   3:14 am Sagittarius
11th   6:23 am Capricorn
13th   8:08 am Aquarius
15th   9:39 am Pisces
17th 12:56 pm Aries
19th   5:21 pm Taurus
21st 11:24 pm Gemini
24th   7:27 am Cancer
26th   5:50 pm Leo
29th   6:15 am Virgo

July 1979
1st   7:06 pm Libra
4th   5:53 am Scorpio
6th   12:50 pm Sagittarius
8th   4:04 pm Capricorn
10th   4:59 pm Aquarius
12th   5:26 pm Pisces
14th   7:00 pm Aries
16th 10:45 pm Taurus
19th   5:03 am Gemini
21st   1:44 pm Cancer
24th   0:32 am Leo
26th   1:02 pm Virgo
29th   2:05 am Libra
31st   1:42 pm Scorpio

August 1979
2nd   10:03 pm Sagittarius
5th   2:21 am Capricorn
7th   3:27 am Aquarius
9th   3:06 am Pisces
11th   3:12 am Aries
13th   5:26 am Taurus
15th 10:47 am Gemini
17th   7:21 pm Cancer
20th   6:32 am Leo
22nd   7:13 pm Virgo
25th   8:13 am Libra
27th   8:11 pm Scorpio
30th   5:36 am Sagittarius

MOON CHARTS

September 1979
1st 11:28 am Capricorn
3rd 1:55 pm Aquarius
5th 2:02 pm Pisces
7th 1:31 pm Aries
9th 2:17 pm Taurus
11th 5:59 pm Gemini
14th 1:27 am Cancer
16th 12:28 pm Leo
19th 1:15 am Virgo
21st 2:10 pm Libra
24th 1:55 am Scorpio
26th 11:33 am Sagittarius
28th 6:36 pm Capricorn
30th 10:48 pm Aquarius

October 1979
3rd 0:23 am Pisces
5th 0:27 am Aries
7th 0:45 am Taurus
9th 3:09 am Gemini
11th 9:14 am Cancer
13th 7:13 pm Leo
16th 7:51 am Virgo
18th 8:44 pm Libra
21st 8:00 am Scorpio
23rd 5:07 pm Sagittarius
26th 0:11 am Capricorn
28th 5:15 am Aquarius
30th 8:26 am Pisces

November 1979
1st 10:08 am Aries
3rd 11:16 am Taurus
5th 1:30 pm Gemini
7th 6:27 pm Cancer
10th 3:16 am Leo
12th 3:21 pm Virgo
15th 4:15 am Libra
17th 3:26 pm Scorpio
19th 11:56 pm Sagittarius
22nd 6:00 am Capricorn
24th 10:35 am Aquarius
26th 2:16 pm Pisces
28th 5:16 pm Aries
30th 7:54 pm Taurus

December 1979
2nd 11:02 pm Gemini
5th 4:03 am Cancer
7th 12:13 pm Leo
9th 11:32 pm Virgo
12th 12:27 pm Libra
15th 0:08 am Scorpio
17th 8:32 am Sagittarius
19th 1:51 pm Capricorn
21st 5:12 pm Aquarius
23rd 7:50 pm Pisces
25th 10:40 pm Aries
28th 2:08 am Taurus
30th 6:34 am Gemini

January 1980
1st 12:33 pm Cancer
3rd 8:49 pm Leo
6th 7:50 am Virgo
8th 8:37 pm Libra
11th 8:50 am Scorpio
13th 6:12 pm Sagittarius
15th 11:51 pm Capricorn
18th 2:25 am Aquarius
20th 3:33 am Pisces
22nd 4:54 am Aries
24th 7:36 am Taurus
26th 12:14 pm Gemini
28th 7:05 pm Cancer
31st 4:11 am Leo

February 1980
2nd 3:23 pm Virgo
5th 4:04 am Libra
7th 4:43 pm Scorpio
10th 3:15 am Sagittarius
12th 10:06 am Capricorn
14th 1:14 pm Aquarius
16th 1:52 pm Pisces
18th 1:45 pm Aries
20th 2:39 pm Taurus
22nd 6:03 pm Gemini
25th 0:36 am Cancer
27th 10:14 am Leo
29th 9:54 pm Virgo

March 1980
3rd 10:40 am Libra
5th 11:24 pm Scorpio
8th 10:35 am Sagittarius
10th 6:59 pm Capricorn
12th 11:46 pm Aquarius
15th 1:10 am Pisces
17th 0:41 am Aries
19th 0:13 am Taurus
21st 1:49 am Gemini
23rd 7:00 am Cancer
25th 4:02 pm Leo
28th 3:53 am Virgo
30th 4:49 pm Libra

April 1980
2nd 5:21 am Scorpio
4th 4:34 pm Sagittarius
7th 1:41 am Capricorn
9th 7:56 am Aquarius
11th 11:03 am Pisces
13th 11:39 am Aries
15th 11:12 am Taurus
17th 11:47 am Gemini
19th 3:18 pm Cancer
21st 10:54 pm Leo
24th 10:14 am Virgo
26th 11:11 pm Libra
29th 11:34 am Scorpio

May 1980
1st 10:23 pm Sagittarius
4th 7:13 am Capricorn
6th 2:01 pm Aquarius
8th 6:31 pm Pisces
10th 8:44 pm Aries
12th 9:25 pm Taurus
14th 10:09 pm Gemini
17th 0:53 am Cancer
19th 7:19 am Leo
21st 5:35 pm Virgo
24th 6:12 am Libra
26th 6:37 pm Scorpio
29th 5:04 am Sagittarius
31st 1:13 pm Capricorn

June 1980
2nd 7:28 pm Aquarius
5th 0:10 am Pisces
7th 3:23 am Aries
9th 5:30 am Taurus
11th 7:25 am Gemini
13th 10:35 am Cancer
15th 4:26 pm Leo
18th 1:49 am Virgo
20th 1:56 pm Libra
23rd 2:27 am Scorpio
25th 12:58 pm Sagittarius
27th 8:45 pm Capricorn
30th 2:03 am Aquarius

July 1980
2nd 5:48 am Pisces
4th 8:48 am Aries
6th 11:32 am Taurus
8th 2:36 pm Gemini
10th 6:48 pm Cancer
13th 1:04 am Leo
15th 10:15 am Virgo
17th 9:55 pm Libra
20th 10:32 am Scorpio
22nd 9:40 pm Sagittarius
25th 5:42 am Capricorn
27th 10:32 am Aquarius
29th 1:10 pm Pisces
31st 2:55 pm Aries

August 1980
2nd 4:58 pm Taurus
4th 8:12 pm Gemini
7th 1:14 am Cancer
9th 8:28 am Leo
11th 5:58 pm Virgo
14th 5:33 am Libra
16th 6:14 pm Scorpio
19th 6:04 am Sagittarius
21st 3:06 pm Capricorn
23rd 8:30 pm Aquarius
25th 10:42 pm Pisces
27th 11:12 pm Aries
29th 11:42 pm Taurus

September 1980
1st 1:53 am Gemini
3rd 6:44 am Cancer
5th 2:26 pm Leo
8th 0:32 am Virgo
10th 12:24 pm Libra
13th 1:07 am Scorpio
15th 1:26 pm Sagittarius
17th 11:45 pm Capricorn
20th 6:26 am Aquarius
22nd 9:22 am Pisces
24th 9:36 am Aries
26th 8:55 am Taurus
28th 9:25 am Gemini
30th 12:51 pm Cancer

October 1980
2nd 7:59 pm Leo
5th 6:20 am Virgo
7th 6:31 pm Libra
10th 7:15 am Scorpio
12th 7:38 pm Sagittarius
15th 6:34 am Capricorn
17th 2:49 pm Aquarius
19th 7:28 pm Pisces
21st 8:40 pm Aries
23rd 7:55 pm Taurus
25th 7:19 pm Gemini
27th 9:02 pm Cancer
30th 2:40 am Leo

November 1980
1st 12:21 pm Virgo
4th 0:30 am Libra
6th 1:18 pm Scorpio
9th 1:25 am Sagittarius
11th 12:13 pm Capricorn
13th 9:08 pm Aquarius
16th 3:18 am Pisces
18th 6:18 am Aries
20th 6:48 am Taurus
22nd 6:29 am Gemini
24th 7:23 am Cancer
26th 11:28 am Leo
28th 7:40 pm Virgo

December 1980
1st 7:14 am Libra
3rd 7:59 pm Scorpio
6th 7:55 am Sagittarius
8th 6:09 pm Capricorn
11th 2:34 am Aquarius
13th 8:50 am Pisces
15th 1:18 pm Aries
17th 3:33 pm Taurus
19th 4:40 pm Gemini
21st 6:05 pm Cancer
23rd 9:35 pm Leo
26th 4:35 am Virgo
28th 3:06 pm Libra
31st 3:34 am Scorpio

January 1981
- 2nd 3:38 pm Sagittarius
- 5th 1:39 am Capricorn
- 7th 9:09 am Aquarius
- 9th 2:39 pm Pisces
- 11th 6:42 pm Aries
- 13th 9:45 pm Taurus
- 16th 0:17 am Gemini
- 18th 3:09 am Cancer
- 20th 7:24 am Leo
- 22nd 2:06 pm Virgo
- 24th 11:44 pm Libra
- 27th 11:48 am Scorpio
- 30th 0:10 am Sagittarius

February 1981
- 1st 10:31 am Capricorn
- 3rd 5:51 pm Aquarius
- 5th 10:20 pm Pisces
- 8th 1:02 am Aries
- 10th 3:12 am Taurus
- 12th 5:53 am Gemini
- 14th 9:46 am Cancer
- 16th 3:14 pm Leo
- 18th 10:34 pm Virgo
- 21st 8:14 am Libra
- 23rd 7:55 pm Scorpio
- 26th 8:26 am Sagittarius
- 28th 7:43 pm Capricorn

March 1981
- 3rd 3:47 am Aquarius
- 5th 8:07 am Pisces
- 7th 9:45 am Aries
- 9th 10:23 am Taurus
- 11th 11:46 am Gemini
- 13th 3:10 pm Cancer
- 15th 9:05 pm Leo
- 18th 5:22 am Virgo
- 20th 3:33 pm Libra
- 23rd 3:15 am Scorpio
- 25th 3:51 pm Sagittarius
- 28th 3:51 am Capricorn
- 30th 1:09 pm Aquarius

April 1981
- 1st 6:37 pm Pisces
- 3rd 8:22 pm Aries
- 5th 8:03 pm Taurus
- 7th 7:50 pm Gemini
- 9th 9:35 pm Cancer
- 12th 2:39 am Leo
- 14th 10:59 am Virgo
- 16th 9:38 pm Libra
- 19th 9:40 am Scorpio
- 21st 10:15 pm Sagittarius
- 24th 10:30 am Capricorn
- 26th 8:56 pm Aquarius
- 29th 3:54 am Pisces

May 1981
- 1st 6:53 am Aries
- 3rd 6:58 am Taurus
- 5th 6:03 am Gemini
- 7th 6:22 am Cancer
- 9th 9:46 am Leo
- 11th 4:59 pm Virgo
- 14th 3:25 am Libra
- 16th 3:39 pm Scorpio
- 19th 4:14 am Sagittarius
- 21st 4:19 pm Capricorn
- 24th 2:59 am Aquarius
- 26th 11:01 am Pisces
- 28th 3:39 pm Aries
- 30th 5:08 pm Taurus

June 1981
- 1st 4:49 pm Gemini
- 3rd 4:43 pm Cancer
- 5th 6:47 pm Leo
- 8th 0:26 am Virgo
- 10th 9:59 am Libra
- 12th 9:55 pm Scorpio
- 15th 10:32 am Sagittarius
- 17th 10:21 pm Capricorn
- 20th 8:34 am Aquarius
- 22nd 4:42 pm Pisces
- 24th 10:18 pm Aries
- 27th 1:16 am Taurus
- 29th 2:22 am Gemini

July 1981
- 1st 2:59 am Cancer
- 3rd 4:51 am Leo
- 5th 9:32 am Virgo
- 7th 5:45 pm Libra
- 10th 5:02 am Scorpio
- 12th 5:35 pm Sagittarius
- 15th 5:18 am Capricorn
- 17th 2:50 pm Aquarius
- 19th 10:25 pm Pisces
- 22nd 3:44 am Aries
- 24th 7:18 am Taurus
- 26th 9:42 am Gemini
- 28th 11:43 am Cancer
- 30th 2:25 pm Leo

August 1981
- 1st 6:58 pm Virgo
- 4th 2:26 am Libra
- 6th 1:01 pm Scorpio
- 9th 1:23 am Sagittarius
- 11th 1:17 pm Capricorn
- 13th 10:56 pm Aquarius
- 16th 5:32 am Pisces
- 18th 9:48 am Aries
- 20th 12:45 pm Taurus
- 22nd 3:20 pm Gemini
- 24th 6:18 pm Cancer
- 26th 10:12 pm Leo
- 29th 3:35 am Virgo
- 31st 11:07 am Libra

September 1981
- 2nd 9:13 pm Scorpio
- 5th 9:24 am Sagittarius
- 7th 9:48 pm Capricorn
- 10th 7:54 am Aquarius
- 12th 2:29 pm Pisces
- 14th 5:53 pm Aries
- 16th 7:30 pm Taurus
- 18th 9:01 pm Gemini
- 20th 11:40 pm Cancer
- 23rd 4:11 am Leo
- 25th 10:32 am Virgo
- 27th 6:43 pm Libra
- 30th 4:56 am Scorpio

October 1981
- 2nd 5:01 pm Sagittarius
- 5th 5:47 am Capricorn
- 7th 4:57 pm Aquarius
- 10th 0:32 am Pisces
- 12th 3:59 am Aries
- 14th 4:43 am Taurus
- 16th 4:43 am Gemini
- 18th 5:55 am Cancer
- 20th 9:39 am Leo
- 22nd 4:07 pm Virgo
- 25th 0:56 am Libra
- 27th 11:40 am Scorpio
- 29th 11:50 pm Sagittarius

November 1981
- 1st 12:46 pm Capricorn
- 4th 0:50 am Aquarius
- 6th 9:46 am Pisces
- 8th 2:33 pm Aries
- 10th 3:41 pm Taurus
- 12th 3:00 pm Gemini
- 14th 2:40 pm Cancer
- 16th 4:36 pm Leo
- 18th 9:55 pm Virgo
- 21st 6:34 am Libra
- 23rd 5:38 pm Scorpio
- 26th 6:01 am Sagittarius
- 28th 6:52 pm Capricorn

December 1981
- 1st 7:07 am Aquarius
- 3rd 5:13 pm Pisces
- 5th 11:49 pm Aries
- 8th 2:29 am Taurus
- 10th 2:29 am Gemini
- 12th 1:42 am Cancer
- 14th 2:09 am Leo
- 16th 5:41 am Virgo
- 18th 1:03 pm Libra
- 20th 11:38 pm Scorpio
- 23rd 12:11 pm Sagittarius
- 26th 0:58 am Capricorn
- 28th 12:51 pm Aquarius
- 30th 11:01 pm Pisces

January 1982
- 2nd 6:29 am Aries
- 4th 10:57 am Taurus
- 6th 12:46 pm Gemini
- 8th 1:01 pm Cancer
- 10th 1:24 pm Leo
- 12th 3:42 pm Virgo
- 14th 9:19 pm Libra
- 17th 6:48 am Scorpio
- 19th 6:50 pm Sagittarius
- 22nd 7:49 am Capricorn
- 24th 7:22 pm Aquarius
- 27th 4:47 am Pisces
- 29th 11:55 am Aries
- 31st 5:02 pm Taurus

February 1982
- 2nd 8:19 pm Gemini
- 4th 10:17 pm Cancer
- 6th 11:50 pm Leo
- 9th 2:16 am Virgo
- 11th 7:05 am Libra
- 13th 3:20 pm Scorpio
- 16th 2:44 am Sagittarius
- 18th 3:34 pm Capricorn
- 21st 3:11 am Aquarius
- 23rd 12:04 pm Pisces
- 25th 6:14 pm Aries
- 27th 10:32 pm Taurus

March 1982
- 2nd 1:49 am Gemini
- 4th 4:49 am Cancer
- 6th 7:51 am Leo
- 8th 11:29 am Virgo
- 10th 4:37 pm Libra
- 13th 0:17 am Scorpio
- 15th 11:05 am Sagittarius
- 17th 11:46 pm Capricorn
- 20th 11:48 am Aquarius
- 22nd 8:57 pm Pisces
- 25th 2:35 am Aries
- 27th 5:38 am Taurus
- 29th 7:44 am Gemini
- 31st 10:10 am Cancer

April 1982
- 2nd 1:39 pm Leo
- 4th 6:20 pm Virgo
- 7th 0:26 am Libra
- 9th 8:37 am Scorpio
- 11th 7:08 pm Sagittarius
- 14th 7:42 am Capricorn
- 16th 8:16 pm Aquarius
- 19th 6:15 am Pisces
- 21st 12:17 pm Aries
- 23rd 2:55 pm Taurus
- 25th 3:48 pm Gemini
- 27th 4:44 pm Cancer
- 29th 7:10 pm Leo

May 1982
1st 11:44 pm Virgo
4th 6:34 am Libra
6th 3:26 pm Scorpio
9th 2:18 am Sagittarius
11th 2:51 pm Capricorn
14th 3:44 am Aquarius
16th 2:42 pm Pisces
18th 10:03 pm Aries
21st 1:20 am Taurus
23rd 1:54 am Gemini
25th 1:38 am Cancer
27th 2:28 am Leo
29th 5:46 am Virgo
31st 12:06 pm Libra

June 1982
2nd 9:12 pm Scorpio
5th 8:33 am Sagittarius
7th 9:11 pm Capricorn
10th 10:06 am Aquarius
12th 9:43 pm Pisces
15th 6:16 am Aries
17th 11:01 am Taurus
19th 12:31 pm Gemini
21st 12:13 pm Cancer
23rd 11:50 am Leo
25th 1:41 pm Virgo
27th 6:34 pm Libra
30th 3:03 am Scorpio

July 1982
2nd 2:27 pm Sagittarius
5th 3:15 am Capricorn
7th 4:01 pm Aquarius
10th 3:33 am Pisces
12th 12:45 pm Aries
14th 6:56 pm Taurus
16th 10:03 pm Gemini
18th 10:46 pm Cancer
20th 10:36 pm Leo
22nd 11:21 pm Virgo
25th 2:47 am Libra
27th 10:04 am Scorpio
29th 8:49 pm Sagittarius

August 1982
1st 9:36 am Capricorn
3rd 10:17 pm Aquarius
6th 9:21 am Pisces
8th 6:20 pm Aries
11th 1:00 am Taurus
13th 5:21 am Gemini
15th 7:39 am Cancer
17th 8:42 am Leo
19th 9:44 am Virgo
21st 12:27 pm Libra
23rd 6:25 pm Scorpio
26th 4:13 am Sagittarius
28th 4:41 pm Capricorn
31st 5:22 am Aquarius

September 1982
2nd 4:07 pm Pisces
5th 0:24 am Aries
7th 6:26 am Taurus
9th 10:57 am Gemini
11th 2:18 pm Cancer
3th 4:46 pm Leo
15th 6:50 pm Virgo
17th 10:05 pm Libra
20th 3:36 am Scorpio
22nd 12:35 pm Sagittarius
25th 0:32 am Capricorn
27th 1:19 am Aquarius
30th 0:19 am Pisces

October 1982
2nd 8:02 am Aries
4th 1:07 pm Taurus
6th 4:38 pm Gemini
8th 7:40 pm Cancer
10th 10:45 pm Leo
13th 2:10 am Virgo
15th 6:26 am Libra
17th 12:26 pm Scorpio
19th 9:05 pm Sagittarius
22nd 8:41 am Capricorn
24th 9:36 am Aquarius
27th 9:08 am Pisces
29th 5:21 pm Aries
31st 10:03 pm Taurus

November 1982
3rd 0:23 am Gemini
5th 1:58 am Cancer
7th 4:12 am Leo
9th 7:43 am Virgo
11th 12:48 pm Libra
13th 7:44 pm Scorpio
16th 4:55 am Sagittarius
18th 4:23 pm Capricorn
21st 5:21 am Aquarius
23rd 5:41 pm Pisces
26th 3:04 am Aries
28th 8:28 am Taurus
30th 10:34 am Gemini

December 1982
2nd 10:58 am Cancer
4th 11:29 am Leo
6th 1:37 pm Virgo
8th 6:14 pm Libra
11th 1:35 am Scorpio
13th 11:30 am Sagittarius
15th 11:16 pm Capricorn
18th 12:13 pm Aquarius
21st 0:56 am Pisces
23rd 11:30 am Aries
25th 6:33 pm Taurus
27th 9:48 pm Gemini
29th 10:12 pm Cancer
31st 9:33 pm Leo

January 1983
2nd 9:51 pm Virgo
5th 0:45 am Libra
7th 7:20 am Scorpio
9th 5:16 pm Sagittarius
12th 5:27 am Capricorn
14th 6:26 pm Aquarius
17th 7:01 am Pisces
19th 6:05 pm Aries
22nd 2:34 am Taurus
24th 7:36 am Gemini
26th 9:24 am Cancer
28th 9:09 am Leo
30th 8:38 am Virgo

February 1983
1st 9:53 am Libra
3rd 2:37 pm Scorpio
5th 11:29 pm Sagittarius
8th 11:35 am Capricorn
11th 0:41 am Aquarius
13th 12:50 pm Pisces
15th 11:46 pm Aries
18th 8:28 am Taurus
20th 2:48 pm Gemini
22nd 6:29 pm Cancer
24th 7:46 pm Leo
26th 7:49 pm Virgo
28th 8:31 pm Libra

March 1983
2nd 11:51 pm Scorpio
5th 7:18 am Sagittarius
7th 6:30 pm Capricorn
10th 7:29 am Aquarius
12th 7:44 pm Pisces
15th 5:58 am Aries
17th 2:02 pm Taurus
19th 8:18 pm Gemini
22nd 0:53 am Cancer
24th 3:43 am Leo
26th 5:19 am Virgo
28th 6:50 am Libra
30th 10:02 am Scorpio

April 1983
1st 4:24 pm Sagittarius
4th 2:30 am Capricorn
6th 3:06 pm Aquarius
9th 3:29 am Pisces
11th 1:32 pm Aries
13th 8:56 pm Taurus
16th 2:12 am Gemini
18th 6:12 am Cancer
20th 9:25 am Leo
22nd 12:11 pm Virgo
24th 3:04 pm Libra
26th 7:07 pm Scorpio
29th 1:29 am Sagittarius

May 1983
1st 11:04 am Capricorn
3rd 11:09 pm Aquarius
6th 11:41 am Pisces
8th 10:14 pm Aries
11th 5:33 am Taurus
13th 9:59 am Gemini
15th 12:45 pm Cancer
17th 3:00 pm Leo
19th 5:37 pm Virgo
21st 9:12 pm Libra
24th 2:18 am Scorpio
26th 9:30 am Sagittarius
28th 7:09 pm Capricorn
31st 7:01 am Aquarius

June 1983
2nd 7:42 pm Pisces
5th 6:55 am Aries
7th 2:59 pm Taurus
9th 7:34 pm Gemini
11th 9:30 pm Cancer
13th 10:21 pm Leo
15th 11:37 pm Virgo
18th 2:38 am Libra
20th 8:02 am Scorpio
22nd 3:57 pm Sagittarius
25th 2:09 am Capricorn
27th 2:07 pm Aquarius
30th 2:51 am Pisces

July 1983
2nd 2:44 pm Aries
5th 0:05 am Taurus
7th 5:37 am Gemini
9th 7:47 am Cancer
11th 7:53 am Leo
13th 7:45 am Virgo
15th 9:15 am Libra
17th 1:43 pm Scorpio
19th 9:32 pm Sagittarius
22nd 8:12 am Capricorn
24th 8:26 pm Aquarius
27th 9:10 am Pisces
29th 9:21 pm Aries

August 1983
1st 7:33 am Taurus
3rd 2:38 pm Gemini
5th 6:06 pm Cancer
7th 6:35 pm Leo
9th 5:50 pm Virgo
11th 5:55 pm Libra
13th 8:46 pm Scorpio
16th 3:36 am Sagittarius
18th 2:01 pm Capricorn
21st 2:26 am Aquarius
23rd 3:09 pm Pisces
26th 3:07 am Aries
28th 1:35 pm Taurus
30th 9:47 pm Gemini

September 1983
2nd 2:51 am Cancer
4th 4:45 am Leo
6th 4:36 am Virgo
8th 4:16 am Libra
10th 5:54 am Scorpio
12th 11:14 am Sagittarius
14th 8:35 pm Capricorn
17th 8:45 am Aquarius
19th 9:29 pm Pisces
22nd 9:09 am Aries
24th 7:11 pm Taurus
27th 3:23 am Gemini
29th 9:21 am Cancer

October 1983
1st 12:52 pm Leo
3rd 2:14 pm Virgo
5th 2:44 pm Libra
7th 4:11 pm Scorpio
9th 8:24 pm Sagittarius
12th 4:33 am Capricorn
14th 4:03 pm Aquarius
17th 4:40 am Pisces
19th 4:16 pm Aries
22nd 1:46 am Taurus
24th 9:07 am Gemini
26th 2:45 pm Cancer
28th 6:49 pm Leo
30th 9:32 pm Virgo

November 1983
1st 11:32 pm Libra
4th 1:55 am Scorpio
6th 6:14 am Sagittarius
8th 1:37 pm Capricorn
11th 0:12 am Aquarius
13th 12:41 pm Pisces
16th 0:37 am Aries
18th 10:04 am Taurus
20th 4:42 pm Gemini
22nd 9:09 pm Cancer
25th 0:19 am Leo
27th 3:03 am Virgo
29th 5:57 am Libra

December 1983
1st 9:44 am Scorpio
3rd 2:50 pm Sagittarius
5th 10:30 pm Capricorn
8th 8:44 am Aquarius
10th 8:54 pm Pisces
13th 9:15 am Aries
15th 7:31 pm Taurus
18th 2:23 am Gemini
20th 6:00 am Cancer
22nd 7:43 am Leo
24th 9:03 am Virgo
26th 11:22 am Libra
28th 3:29 pm Scorpio
30th 9:44 pm Sagittarius

January 1984
2nd 6:11 am Capricorn
4th 4:32 pm Aquarius
7th 4:35 am Pisces
9th 5:15 pm Aries
12th 4:34 am Taurus
14th 12:35 pm Gemini
16th 4:43 pm Cancer
18th 5:48 pm Leo
20th 5:37 pm Virgo
22nd 6:11 pm Libra
24th 9:07 pm Scorpio
27th 3:14 am Sagittarius
29th 12:15 pm Capricorn
31st 11:10 pm Aquarius

February 1984
3rd 11:23 am Pisces
6th 0:04 am Aries
8th 12:03 pm Taurus
10th 9:37 pm Gemini
13th 3:19 am Cancer
15th 5:07 am Leo
17th 4:32 am Virgo
19th 3:42 am Libra
21st 4:48 am Scorpio
23rd 9:28 am Sagittarius
25th 5:52 pm Capricorn
28th 5:03 am Aquarius

March 1984
1st 5:30 pm Pisces
4th 6:07 am Aries
6th 6:08 pm Taurus
9th 4:28 am Gemini
11th 11:43 am Cancer
13th 3:17 pm Leo
15th 3:44 pm Virgo
17th 2:54 pm Libra
19th 2:54 pm Scorpio
21st 5:46 pm Sagittarius
24th 0:36 am Capricorn
26th 11:10 am Aquarius
28th 11:36 pm Pisces
31st 12:12 pm Aries

April 1984
2nd 11:54 pm Taurus
5th 10:01 am Gemini
7th 5:56 pm Cancer
9th 11:01 pm Leo
12th 1:10 am Virgo
14th 1:30 am Libra
16th 1:42 am Scorpio
18th 3:46 am Sagittarius
20th 9:16 am Capricorn
22nd 6:30 pm Aquarius
25th 6:26 am Pisces
27th 7:00 pm Aries
30th 6:27 am Taurus

May 1984
2nd 3:59 pm Gemini
4th 11:25 pm Cancer
7th 4:41 am Leo
9th 7:58 am Virgo
11th 9:52 am Libra
13th 11:24 am Scorpio
15th 1:54 pm Sagittarius
17th 6:46 pm Capricorn
20th 2:57 am Aquarius
22nd 2:10 pm Pisces
25th 2:38 am Aries
27th 2:10 pm Taurus
29th 11:21 pm Gemini

June 1984
1st 5:50 am Cancer
3rd 10:16 am Leo
5th 1:25 pm Virgo
7th 4:02 pm Libra
9th 6:48 pm Scorpio
11th 10:26 pm Sagittarius
14th 3:51 am Capricorn
16th 11:45 am Aquarius
18th 10:19 pm Pisces
21st 10:49 am Aries
23rd 10:37 pm Taurus
26th 7:59 am Gemini
28th 2:04 pm Cancer
30th 5:27 pm Leo

July 1984
2nd 7:26 pm Virgo
4th 9:26 pm Libra
7th 0:28 am Scorpio
9th 5:04 am Sagittarius
11th 11:25 am Capricorn
13th 7:43 pm Aquarius
16th 6:12 am Pisces
18th 6:26 pm Aries
21st 6:51 am Taurus
23rd 5:06 pm Gemini
25th 11:44 pm Cancer
28th 2:39 am Leo
30th 3:28 am Virgo

August 1984
1st 4:04 am Libra
3rd 6:07 am Scorpio
5th 10:33 am Sagittarius
7th 5:27 pm Capricorn
10th 2:26 am Aquarius
12th 1:14 pm Pisces
15th 1:27 am Aries
17th 2:11 pm Taurus
20th 1:30 am Gemini
22nd 9:14 am Cancer
24th 12:55 pm Leo
26th 1:31 pm Virgo
28th 12:59 pm Libra
30th 1:27 pm Scorpio

September 1984
1st 4:34 pm Sagittarius
3rd 10:55 pm Capricorn
6th 8:13 am Aquarius
8th 7:25 pm Pisces
11th 7:46 am Aries
13th 8:32 pm Taurus
16th 8:22 am Gemini
18th 5:32 pm Cancer
20th 10:47 pm Leo
23rd 0:19 am Virgo
24th 11:41 pm Libra
26th 11:04 pm Scorpio
29th 0:31 am Sagittarius

October 1984
1st 5:31 am Capricorn
3rd 2:07 pm Aquarius
6th 1:18 am Pisces
8th 1:50 pm Aries
11th 2:27 am Taurus
13th 2:12 pm Gemini
15th 12:00 pm Cancer
18th 6:38 am Leo
20th 9:52 am Virgo
22nd 10:31 am Libra
24th 10:11 am Scorpio
26th 10:49 am Sagittarius
28th 2:11 pm Capricorn
30th 9:16 pm Aquarius

November 1984
2nd 7:52 am Pisces
4th 8:21 pm Aries
7th 8:52 am Taurus
9th 8:09 pm Gemini
12th 5:28 am Cancer
14th 12:30 pm Leo
16th 5:04 pm Virgo
18th 7:28 pm Libra
20th 8:31 pm Scorpio
22nd 9:35 pm Sagittarius
25th 0:19 am Capricorn
27th 6:12 am Aquarius
29th 3:38 pm Pisces

December 1984
2nd 3:43 am Aries
4th 4:20 pm Taurus
7th 3:23 am Gemini
9th 11:53 am Cancer
11th 6:06 pm Leo
13th 10:35 pm Virgo
16th 1:52 am Libra
18th 4:27 am Scorpio
20th 7:00 am Sagittarius
22nd 10:24 am Capricorn
24th 3:52 pm Aquarius
27th 0:20 am Pisces
29th 11:52 am Aries

January 1985
1st 0:36 am Taurus
3rd 11:57 am Gemini
5th 8:16 pm Cancer
8th 1:28 am Leo
10th 4:40 am Virgo
12th 7:14 am Libra
14th 10:09 am Scorpio
16th 1:50 pm Sagittarius
18th 6:31 pm Capricorn
21st 0:39 am Aquarius
23rd 9:06 am Pisces
25th 8:06 pm Aries
28th 8:53 am Taurus
30th 9:00 pm Gemini

February 1985
2nd 5:56 am Cancer
4th 10:58 am Leo
6th 1:08 pm Virgo
8th 2:13 pm Libra
10th 3:52 pm Scorpio
12th 7:12 pm Sagittarius
15th 0:27 am Capricorn
17th 7:39 am Aquarius
19th 4:40 pm Pisces
22nd 3:45 am Aries
24th 4:28 pm Taurus
27th 5:09 am Gemini

March 1985
1st 3:19 pm Cancer
3rd 9:27 pm Leo
5th 11:44 pm Virgo
7th 11:49 pm Libra
9th 11:47 pm Scorpio
12th 1:31 am Sagittarius
14th 5:58 am Capricorn
16th 1:14 pm Aquarius
18th 10:50 pm Pisces
21st 10:21 am Aries
23rd 11:07 pm Taurus
26th 12:01 pm Gemini
28th 11:13 pm Cancer
31st 6:47 am Leo

April 1985
2nd 10:21 am Virgo
4th 10:53 am Libra
6th 10:13 am Scorpio
8th 10:22 am Sagittarius
10th 1:03 pm Capricorn
12th 7:06 pm Aquarius
15th 4:32 am Pisces
17th 4:19 pm Aries
20th 5:11 am Taurus
22nd 5:59 pm Gemini
25th 5:23 am Cancer
27th 2:06 pm Leo
29th 7:21 pm Virgo

May 1985
1st 9:21 pm Libra
3rd 9:17 pm Scorpio
5th 8:58 pm Sagittarius
7th 10:13 pm Capricorn
10th 2:41 am Aquarius
12th 10:50 am Pisces
14th 10:26 pm Aries
17th 11:23 am Taurus
19th 12:00 pm Gemini
22nd 11:01 am Cancer
24th 7:50 pm Leo
27th 2:04 am Virgo
29th 5:37 am Libra
31st 7:05 am Scorpio

June 1985
2nd 7:34 am Sagittarius
4th 8:37 am Capricorn
6th 11:58 am Aquarius
8th 6:51 pm Pisces
11th 5:26 am Aries
13th 6:12 pm Taurus
16th 6:43 am Gemini
18th 5:19 pm Cancer
21st 1:31 am Leo
23rd 7:29 am Virgo
25th 11:44 am Libra
27th 2:34 pm Scorpio
29th 4:29 pm Sagittarius

July 1985
1st 6:23 pm Capricorn
3rd 9:38 pm Aquarius
6th 3:44 am Pisces
8th 1:24 pm Aries
11th 1:44 am Taurus
13th 2:21 pm Gemini
16th 0:53 am Cancer
18th 8:22 am Leo
20th 1:26 pm Virgo
22nd 5:09 pm Libra
24th 8:16 pm Scorpio
26th 11:12 pm Sagittarius
29th 2:21 am Capricorn
31st 6:28 am Aquarius

August 1985
2nd 12:37 pm Pisces
4th 9:44 pm Aries
7th 9:42 am Taurus
9th 10:31 pm Gemini
12th 9:24 am Cancer
14th 4:53 pm Leo
16th 9:14 pm Virgo
18th 11:43 pm Libra
21st 1:51 am Scorpio
23rd 4:37 am Sagittarius
25th 8:26 am Capricorn
27th 1:33 pm Aquarius
29th 8:25 pm Pisces

September 1985
1st 5:43 am Aries
3rd 5:28 pm Taurus
6th 6:26 am Gemini
8th 6:07 pm Cancer
11th 2:25 am Leo
13th 6:49 am Virgo
15th 8:33 am Libra
17th 9:17 am Scorpio
19th 10:43 am Sagittarius
21st 1:52 pm Capricorn
23rd 7:13 pm Aquarius
26th 2:51 am Pisces
28th 12:44 pm Aries

October 1985
1st 0:34 am Taurus
3rd 1:35 pm Gemini
6th 1:58 am Cancer
8th 11:28 am Leo
10th 5:05 pm Virgo
12th 7:10 pm Libra
14th 7:12 pm Scorpio
16th 7:07 pm Sagittarius
18th 8:37 pm Capricorn
21st 0:55 am Aquarius
23rd 8:31 am Pisces
25th 6:48 pm Aries
28th 6:50 am Taurus
30th 7:58 pm Gemini

November 1985
2nd 8:29 am Cancer
4th 7:01 pm Leo
7th 2:17 am Virgo
9th 5:48 am Libra
11th 6:30 am Scorpio
13th 5:44 am Sagittarius
15th 5:57 am Capricorn
17th 8:32 am Aquarius
19th 2:48 pm Pisces
22nd 0:44 am Aries
24th 1:08 pm Taurus
27th 2:07 am Gemini
29th 2:20 pm Cancer

December 1985
2nd 0:59 am Leo
4th 9:09 am Virgo
6th 2:28 pm Libra
8th 4:54 pm Scorpio
10th 5:12 pm Sagittarius
12th 5:02 pm Capricorn
14th 6:20 pm Aquarius
16th 10:52 pm Pisces
19th 7:42 am Aries
21st 7:42 pm Taurus
24th 8:44 am Gemini
26th 8:42 pm Cancer
29th 6:42 am Leo
31st 2:40 pm Virgo

January 1986
2nd 8:43 pm Libra
5th 0:44 am Scorpio
7th 2:47 am Sagittarius
9th 3:43 am Capricorn
11th 5:05 am Aquarius
13th 8:45 am Pisces
15th 4:09 pm Aries
18th 3:16 am Taurus
20th 4:12 pm Gemini
23rd 4:14 am Cancer
25th 1:45 pm Leo
27th 8:51 pm Virgo
30th 2:09 am Libra

February 1986
1st 6:18 am Scorpio
3rd 9:31 am Sagittarius
5th 12:02 pm Capricorn
7th 2:38 pm Aquarius
9th 6:36 pm Pisces
12th 1:22 am Aries
14th 11:42 am Taurus
17th 0:18 am Gemini
19th 12:38 pm Cancer
21st 10:25 pm Leo
24th 4:58 am Virgo
26th 9:07 am Libra
28th 12:06 pm Scorpio

March 1986
2nd 2:53 pm Sagittarius
4th 5:57 pm Capricorn
6th 9:43 pm Aquarius
9th 2:50 am Pisces
11th 10:07 am Aries
13th 8:06 pm Taurus
16th 8:24 am Gemini
18th 9:05 pm Cancer
21st 7:35 am Leo
23rd 2:36 pm Virgo
25th 6:22 pm Libra
27th 8:06 pm Scorpio
29th 9:22 pm Sagittarius
31st 11:26 pm Capricorn

April 1986
3rd 3:13 am Aquarius
5th 9:06 am Pisces
7th 5:14 pm Aries
10th 3:37 am Taurus
12th 3:52 pm Gemini
15th 4:42 am Cancer
17th 4:06 pm Leo
20th 0:25 am Virgo
22nd 4:48 am Libra
24th 6:15 am Scorpio
26th 6:18 am Sagittarius
28th 6:45 am Capricorn
30th 9:11 am Aquarius

May 1986
2nd   2:35 pm Pisces
4th 11:01 pm Aries
7th 10:00 am Taurus
9th 10:25 pm Gemini
12th 11:17 am Cancer
14th 11:14 pm Leo
17th 8:41 am Virgo
19th 2:36 pm Libra
21st 4:59 pm Scorpio
23rd 4:55 pm Sagittarius
25th 4:15 pm Capricorn
27th 5:05 pm Aquarius
29th 8:58 pm Pisces

June 1986
1st   4:46 am Aries
3rd   3:48 am Taurus
6th   4:26 am Gemini
8th   5:14 pm Cancer
11th 5:09 am Leo
13th 3:14 pm Virgo
15th 10:37 pm Libra
18th 2:34 am Scorpio
20th 3:34 am Sagittarius
22nd 3:00 am Capricorn
24th 2:53 am Aquarius
26th 5:18 am Pisces
28th 11:41 am Aries
30th 9:55 pm Taurus

July 1986
3rd 10:33 am Gemini
5th 11:20 pm Cancer
8th 10:52 am Leo
10th 8:47 pm Virgo
13th 4:37 am Libra
15th 9:53 am Scorpio
17th 12:30 pm Sagittarius
19th 1:08 pm Capricorn
21st 1:20 pm Aquarius
23rd 3:03 pm Pisces
25th 8:06 pm Aries
28th 5:14 am Taurus
30th 5:20 pm Gemini

August 1986
2nd   6:03 am Cancer
4th   5:24 pm Leo
7th   2:44 am Virgo
9th 10:02 am Libra
11th 3:34 pm Scorpio
13th 7:14 pm Sagittarius
15th 9:21 pm Capricorn
17th 10:44 pm Aquarius
20th 0:52 am Pisces
22nd 5:30 am Aries
24th 1:40 pm Taurus
27th 1:01 am Gemini
29th 1:38 pm Cancer

September 1986
1st   1:07 am Leo
3rd 10:02 am Virgo
5th   4:32 pm Libra
7th   9:11 pm Scorpio
10th 0:41 am Sagittarius
12th 3:27 am Capricorn
14th 6:07 am Aquarius
16th 9:29 am Pisces
18th 2:36 pm Aries
20th 10:25 pm Taurus
23rd 9:15 am Gemini
25th 9:44 pm Cancer
28th 9:36 am Leo
30th 6:55 pm Virgo

October 1986
3rd   1:03 am Libra
5th   4:34 am Scorpio
7th   6:48 am Sagittarius
9th   8:54 am Capricorn
11th 11:47 am Aquarius
13th 4:05 pm Pisces
15th 10:14 pm Aries
18th 6:37 am Taurus
20th 5:15 pm Gemini
23rd 5:36 am Cancer
25th 6:00 pm Leo
28th 4:18 am Virgo
30th 11:00 am Libra

November 1986
1st   2:16 pm Scorpio
3rd   3:18 pm Sagittarius
5th   3:51 pm Capricorn
7th   5:31 pm Aquarius
9th   9:30 pm Pisces
12th 4:16 am Aries
14th 1:26 pm Taurus
17th 0:26 am Gemini
19th 12:46 pm Cancer
22nd 1:24 am Leo
24th 12:41 pm Virgo
26th 8:57 pm Libra
29th 1:13 am Scorpio

December 1986
1st   2:07 am Sagittarius
3rd   1:29 am Capricorn
5th   1:24 am Aquarius
7th   3:52 am Pisces
9th   9:55 am Aries
11th 7:12 pm Taurus
14th 6:42 am Gemini
16th 7:09 pm Cancer
19th 7:43 am Leo
21st 7:28 pm Virgo
24th 4:50 am Libra
26th 11:00 am Scorpio
28th 1:14 pm Sagittarius
30th 12:53 pm Capricorn

January 1987
1st 11:58 am Aquarius
3rd 12:43 pm Pisces
5th   4:57 pm Aries
8th   1:16 am Taurus
10th 12:42 pm Gemini
13th 1:19 am Cancer
15th 1:45 pm Leo
18th 1:14 am Virgo
20th 11:05 am Libra
22nd 6:28 pm Scorpio
24th 10:35 pm Sagittarius
26th 11:42 pm Capricorn
28th 11:17 pm Aquarius
30th 11:26 pm Pisces

February 1987
2nd   2:12 am Aries
4th   8:50 am Taurus
6th   7:26 pm Gemini
9th   7:56 am Cancer
11th 8:22 pm Leo
14th 7:25 am Virgo
16th 4:43 pm Libra
19th 0:05 am Scorpio
21st 5:08 am Sagittarius
23rd 7:55 am Capricorn
25th 9:08 am Aquarius
27th 10:09 am Pisces

March 1987
1st 12:41 pm Aries
3rd   6:16 pm Taurus
6th   3:28 am Gemini
8th   3:25 pm Cancer
11th 3:55 am Leo
13th 2:53 pm Virgo
15th 11:36 pm Libra
18th 5:56 am Scorpio
20th 10:30 am Sagittarius
22nd 1:47 pm Capricorn
24th 4:18 pm Aquarius
26th 6:47 pm Pisces
28th 10:13 pm Aries
31st 3:49 am Taurus

April 1987
2nd 12:20 pm Gemini
4th 11:34 pm Cancer
7th 12:02 pm Leo
9th 11:29 pm Virgo
12th 8:02 am Libra
14th 1:39 pm Scorpio
16th 5:01 pm Sagittarius
18th 7:22 pm Capricorn
20th 9:45 pm Aquarius
23rd 1:03 am Pisces
25th 5:42 am Aries
27th 12:08 pm Taurus
29th 8:45 pm Gemini

May 1987
2nd   7:41 am Cancer
4th   8:07 pm Leo
7th   8:05 am Virgo
9th   5:26 pm Libra
11th 11:09 pm Scorpio
14th 1:42 am Capricorn
16th 2:38 am Capricorn
18th 3:45 am Aquarius
20th 6:27 am Pisces
22nd 11:27 am Aries
24th 6:41 pm Taurus
27th 3:56 am Gemini
29th 3:01 pm Cancer

June 1987
1st   3:27 am Leo
3rd   3:54 pm Virgo
6th   2:22 am Libra
8th   9:01 am Scorpio
10th 11:49 am Sagittarius
12th 12:04 pm Capricorn
14th 11:49 am Aquarius
16th 1:00 pm Pisces
18th 5:02 pm Aries
21st 0:10 am Taurus
23rd 9:58 am Gemini
25th 9:22 pm Cancer
28th 9:52 am Leo
30th 10:33 pm Virgo

July 1987
3rd   9:50 am Libra
5th   5:58 pm Scorpio
7th 10:03 pm Sagittarius
9th 10:42 pm Capricorn
11th 9:50 pm Aquarius
13th 9:38 pm Pisces
16th 0:02 am Aries
18th 6:09 am Taurus
20th 3:36 pm Gemini
23rd 3:14 am Cancer
25th 3:50 pm Leo
28th 4:25 am Virgo
30th 3:56 pm Libra

August 1987
2nd   1:08 am Scorpio
4th   6:42 am Sagittarius
6th   8:47 am Capricorn
8th   8:36 am Aquarius
10th 8:04 am Pisces
12th 9:14 am Aries
14th 1:44 pm Taurus
16th 10:01 pm Gemini
19th 9:21 am Cancer
21st 9:58 pm Leo
24th 10:23 am Virgo
26th 9:35 pm Libra
29th 6:47 am Scorpio
31st 1:20 pm Sagittarius

September 1987
2nd 5:00 pm Capricorn
4th 6:19 pm Aquarius
6th 6:37 pm Pisces
8th 7:36 am Aries
10th 10:57 pm Taurus
13th 5:59 am Gemini
15th 4:25 pm Cancer
18th 4:50 am Leo
20th 5:13 pm Virgo
23rd 3:57 am Libra
25th 12:28 pm Scorpio
27th 6:48 pm Sagittarius
29th 11:08 pm Capricorn

October 1987
2nd 1:50 am Aquarius
4th 3:39 am Pisces
6th 5:36 am Aries
8th 8:50 am Taurus
10th 3:07 pm Gemini
13th 0:30 am Cancer
15th 12:34 pm Leo
18th 1:06 am Virgo
20th 11:47 am Libra
22nd 7:39 pm Scorpio
25th 0:57 am Sagittarius
27th 4:32 am Capricorn
29th 7:27 am Aquarius
31st 10:20 am Pisces

November 1987
2nd 1:41 pm Aries
4th 6:04 pm Taurus
7th 0:15 am Gemini
9th 9:12 am Cancer
11th 8:45 pm Leo
14th 9:28 am Virgo
16th 8:46 pm Libra
19th 4:43 am Scorpio
21st 9:13 am Sagittarius
23rd 11:31 am Capricorn
25th 1:13 pm Aquarius
27th 3:43 pm Pisces
29th 7:38 pm Aries

December 1987
2nd 1:06 am Taurus
4th 8:16 am Gemini
6th 5:22 pm Cancer
9th 4:40 am Leo
11th 5:29 pm Virgo
14th 5:36 am Libra
16th 2:35 pm Scorpio
18th 7:29 pm Sagittarius
20th 9:06 pm Capricorn
22nd 9:21 pm Aquarius
24th 10:12 pm Pisces
27th 1:07 am Aries
29th 6:40 am Taurus
31st 2:32 pm Gemini

January 1988
3rd 0:18 am Cancer
5th 11:49 am Leo
8th 0:35 am Virgo
10th 1:13 pm Libra
12th 11:39 pm Scorpio
15th 5:53 am Sagittarius
17th 8:10 am Capricorn
19th 8:02 am Aquarius
21st 7:31 am Pisces
23rd 8:37 am Aries
25th 12:43 pm Taurus
27th 8:06 pm Gemini
30th 6:14 am Cancer

February 1988
1st 6:08 pm Leo
4th 6:54 am Virgo
6th 7:35 pm Libra
9th 6:38 am Scorpio
11th 2:30 pm Sagittarius
13th 6:32 pm Capricorn
15th 7:23 pm Aquarius
17th 6:44 pm Pisces
19th 6:38 pm Aries
21st 8:54 pm Taurus
24th 2:45 am Gemini
26th 12:16 pm Cancer
29th 0:12 am Leo

March 1988
2nd 1:07 pm Virgo
5th 1:33 am Libra
7th 12:25 pm Scorpio
9th 8:58 pm Sagittarius
12th 2:29 am Capricorn
14th 5:06 am Aquarius
16th 5:42 am Pisces
18th 5:47 am Aries
20th 7:09 am Taurus
22nd 11:27 am Gemini
24th 7:30 pm Cancer
27th 6:55 am Leo
29th 7:50 pm Virgo

April 1988
1st 8:04 am Libra
3rd 6:25 pm Scorpio
6th 2:29 am Sagittarius
8th 8:17 am Capricorn
10th 12:08 pm Aquarius
12th 2:23 pm Pisces
14th 3:47 pm Aries
16th 5:33 pm Taurus
18th 9:12 pm Gemini
21st 4:08 am Cancer
23rd 2:38 pm Leo
26th 3:17 am Virgo
28th 3:36 pm Libra

May 1988
1st 1:39 am Scorpio
3rd 8:50 am Sagittarius
5th 1:53 pm Capricorn
7th 5:36 pm Aquarius
9th 8:40 pm Pisces
11th 11:24 pm Aries
14th 2:23 am Taurus
16th 6:35 am Gemini
18th 1:10 pm Cancer
20th 10:53 pm Leo
23rd 11:13 am Virgo
25th 11:50 pm Libra
28th 10:02 am Scorpio
30th 4:54 pm Sagittarius

June 1988
1st 8:59 pm Capricorn
3rd 11:35 pm Aquarius
6th 2:02 am Pisces
8th 5:06 am Aries
10th 9:05 am Taurus
12th 2:18 pm Gemini
14th 9:22 pm Cancer
17th 7:00 am Leo
19th 7:04 pm Virgo
22nd 7:56 am Libra
24th 6:56 pm Scorpio
27th 2:15 am Sagittarius
29th 5:57 am Capricorn

July 1988
1st 7:31 am Aquarius
3rd 8:36 am Pisces
5th 10:42 am Aries
7th 2:31 pm Taurus
9th 8:18 pm Gemini
12th 4:12 am Cancer
14th 2:15 pm Leo
17th 2:18 am Virgo
19th 3:20 pm Libra
22nd 3:11 am Scorpio
24th 11:36 am Sagittarius
26th 4:02 pm Capricorn
28th 5:22 pm Aquarius
30th 5:24 pm Pisces

August 1988
1st 5:57 pm Aries
3rd 8:28 pm Taurus
6th 1:45 am Gemini
8th 9:56 am Cancer
10th 8:29 pm Leo
13th 8:48 am Virgo
15th 9:52 pm Libra
18th 10:08 am Scorpio
20th 7:52 pm Sagittarius
23rd 1:47 am Capricorn
25th 4:02 am Aquarius
27th 4:01 am Pisces
29th 3:31 am Aries
31st 4:25 am Taurus

September 1988
2nd 8:17 am Gemini
4th 3:41 pm Cancer
7th 2:16 am Leo
9th 2:49 pm Virgo
12th 3:51 am Libra
14th 4:05 pm Scorpio
17th 2:25 am Sagittarius
19th 9:40 am Capricorn
21st 1:38 pm Aquarius
23rd 2:47 pm Pisces
25th 2:30 pm Aries
27th 2:32 pm Taurus
29th 4:47 pm Gemini

October 1988
1st 10:39 pm Cancer
4th 8:33 am Leo
6th 9:01 pm Virgo
9th 10:03 am Libra
11th 9:57 pm Scorpio
14th 7:57 am Sagittarius
16th 3:42 pm Capricorn
18th 9:03 pm Aquarius
20th 11:58 pm Pisces
23rd 0:58 am Aries
25th 1:22 am Taurus
27th 2:56 am Gemini
29th 7:33 am Cancer
31st 4:08 pm Leo

November 1988
3rd 4:02 am Virgo
5th 5:03 pm Libra
8th 4:44 am Scorpio
10th 2:03 pm Sagittarius
12th 9:11 pm Capricorn
15th 2:35 am Aquarius
17th 6:32 am Pisces
19th 9:11 am Aries
21st 11:02 am Taurus
23rd 1:15 pm Gemini
25th 5:24 pm Cancer
28th 0:52 am Leo
30th 12:02 pm Virgo

December 1988
3rd 0:57 am Libra
5th 12:47 pm Scorpio
7th 9:53 pm Sagittarius
10th 4:05 am Capricorn
12th 8:25 am Aquarius
14th 11:52 am Pisces
16th 3:03 pm Aries
18th 6:12 pm Taurus
20th 9:44 pm Gemini
23rd 2:36 am Cancer
25th 10:01 am Leo
27th 8:28 pm Virgo
30th 9:09 am Libra

★ ★

January 1989
1st   9:33 pm Scorpio
4th   7:07 am Sagittarius
6th   1:09 pm Capricorn
8th   4:29 pm Aquarius
10th 6:31 pm Pisces
12th 8:37 pm Aries
14th 11:38 pm Taurus
17th 3:59 am Gemini
19th 10:01 am Cancer
21st 6:05 pm Leo
24th 4:34 am Virgo
26th 5:02 pm Libra
29th 5:46 am Scorpio
31st 4:24 pm Sagittarius

February 1989
2nd   11:28 pm Capricorn
5th   2:48 am Aquarius
7th   3:52 am Pisces
9th   4:19 am Aries
11th 5:48 am Taurus
13th 9:28 am Gemini
15th 3:45 pm Cancer
18th 0:33 am Leo
20th 11:37 am Virgo
23rd 0:06 am Libra
25th 12:56 pm Scorpio
28th 0:29 am Sagittarius

March 1989
2nd   8:53 am Capricorn
4th   1:31 am Aquarius
6th   2:56 pm Pisces
8th   2:36 pm Aries
10th 2:29 pm Taurus
12th 4:22 pm Gemini
14th 9:29 pm Cancer
17th 6:17 am Leo
19th 5:42 pm Virgo
22nd 6:24 am Libra
24th 7:11 pm Scorpio
27th 6:52 am Sagittarius
29th 4:22 pm Capricorn
31st 10:45 pm Aquarius

April 1989
3rd   1:36 am Pisces
5th   1:50 am Aries
7th   1:07 am Taurus
9th   1:32 am Gemini
11th 5:02 am Cancer
13th 12:35 pm Leo
15th 11:40 pm Virgo
18th 12:33 pm Libra
21st 1:14 am Scorpio
23rd 12:38 pm Sagittarius
25th 10:16 pm Capricorn
28th 5:31 am Aquarius
30th 10:00 am Pisces

May 1989
2nd   11:49 am Aries
4th   11:55 am Taurus
6th   12:08 pm Gemini
8th   2:27 pm Cancer
10th 8:27 pm Leo
13th 6:33 am Virgo
15th 7:09 pm Libra
18th 7:47 am Scorpio
20th 6:51 pm Sagittarius
23rd 3:54 am Capricorn
25th 10:59 am Aquarius
27th 4:10 pm Pisces
29th 7:25 pm Aries
31st 8:50 pm Taurus

June 1989
2nd   10:04 pm Gemini
5th   0:19 am Cancer
7th   5:33 am Leo
9th   2:35 pm Virgo
12th 2:32 am Libra
14th 3:11 pm Scorpio
17th 2:12 am Sagittarius
19th 10:39 am Capricorn
21st 4:56 pm Aquarius
23rd 9:37 pm Pisces
26th 1:08 am Aries
28th 3:47 am Taurus
30th 6:10 am Gemini

July 1989
2nd   9:23 am Cancer
4th   2:43 pm Leo
6th   11:06 pm Virgo
9th   10:32 am Libra
11th 11:10 pm Scorpio
14th 10:28 am Sagittarius
16th 6:59 pm Capricorn
19th 0:36 am Aquarius
21st 4:07 am Pisces
23rd 6:42 am Aries
25th 9:13 am Taurus
27th 12:19 pm Gemini
29th 4:35 pm Cancer
31st 10:43 pm Leo

August 1989
3rd   7:22 am Virgo
5th   6:30 pm Libra
8th   7:04 am Scorpio
10th 7:00 pm Sagittarius
13th 4:13 am Capricorn
15th 9:54 am Aquarius
17th 12:43 pm Pisces
19th 1:59 pm Aries
21st 3:14 pm Taurus
23rd 5:43 pm Gemini
25th 10:15 pm Cancer
28th 5:16 am Leo
30th 2:33 pm Virgo

September 1989
2nd   1:49 am Libra
4th   2:24 pm Scorpio
7th   2:50 am Sagittarius
9th   1:08 pm Capricorn
11th 7:59 pm Aquarius
13th 11:06 pm Pisces
15th 11:38 pm Aries
17th 11:23 pm Taurus
20th 0:17 am Gemini
22nd 3:53 am Cancer
24th 10:48 am Leo
26th 8:35 pm Virgo
29th 8:17 am Libra

October 1989
1st   8:54 pm Scorpio
4th   9:29 am Sagittarius
6th   8:43 pm Capricorn
9th   5:02 am Aquarius
11th 9:32 am Pisces
13th 10:38 am Aries
15th 9:53 am Taurus
17th 9:23 am Gemini
19th 11:15 am Cancer
21st 4:52 pm Leo
24th 2:16 am Virgo
26th 2:12 pm Libra
29th 2:56 am Scorpio
31st 3:23 pm Sagittarius

November 1989
3rd   2:47 am Capricorn
5th   12:06 pm Aquarius
7th   6:21 pm Pisces
9th   9:06 pm Aries
11th 9:08 pm Taurus
13th 8:19 pm Gemini
15th 8:54 pm Cancer
18th 0:46 am Leo
20th 8:58 am Virgo
22nd 8:27 pm Libra
25th 9:12 am Scorpio
27th 9:30 pm Sagittarius
30th 8:25 am Capricorn

December 1989
2nd   5:40 pm Aquarius
5th   0:48 am Pisces
7th   5:09 am Aries
9th   6:56 am Taurus
11th 7:15 am Gemini
13th 7:53 am Cancer
15th 10:47 am Leo
17th 5:24 pm Virgo
20th 3:47 am Libra
22nd 4:18 pm Scorpio
25th 4:35 am Sagittarius
27th 3:08 pm Capricorn
29th 11:38 pm Aquarius

January 1990
1st   6:09 am Pisces
3rd   10:54 am Aries
5th   2:03 pm Taurus
7th   4:01 pm Gemini
9th   5:54 pm Cancer
11th 9:04 pm Leo
14th 2:50 am Virgo
16th 12:21 pm Libra
19th 0:16 am Scorpio
21st 12:41 pm Sagittarius
23rd 11:27 pm Capricorn
26th 7:22 am Aquarius
28th 12:48 pm Pisces
30th 4:32 pm Aries

February 1990
1st   7:28 pm Taurus
3rd   10:13 pm Gemini
6th   1:28 am Cancer
8th   5:55 am Leo
10th 12:17 pm Virgo
12th 9:10 pm Libra
15th 8:35 am Scorpio
17th 9:05 pm Sagittarius
20th 8:25 am Capricorn
22nd 4:48 pm Aquarius
24th 9:48 pm Pisces
27th 0:16 am Aries

March 1990
1st   1:44 am Taurus
3rd   3:39 am Gemini
5th   7:06 am Cancer
7th   12:28 pm Leo
9th   7:49 pm Virgo
12th 5:11 am Libra
14th 4:27 pm Scorpio
17th 4:56 am Sagittarius
19th 4:59 pm Capricorn
22nd 2:28 am Aquarius
24th 8:03 am Pisces
26th 10:11 am Aries
28th 10:27 am Taurus
30th 10:46 am Gemini

April 1990
1st   12:55 pm Cancer
3rd   5:53 pm Leo
6th   1:43 am Virgo
8th   11:46 am Libra
10th 11:18 pm Scorpio
13th 11:49 am Sagittarius
16th 0:16 am Capricorn
18th 10:48 am Aquarius
20th 5:53 pm Pisces
22nd 8:56 pm Aries
24th 9:01 pm Taurus
26th 8:13 pm Gemini
28th 8:42 pm Cancer

★ ★

May 1990
1st   0:09 am Leo
3rd   7:21 am Virgo
5th   5:30 pm Libra
8th   5:24 am Scorpio
10th 5:56 pm Sagittarius
13th 6:21 am Capricorn
15th 5:28 pm Aquarius
18th 1:53 am Pisces
20th 6:28 am Aries
22nd 7:40 am Taurus
24th 7:01 am Gemini
26th 6:38 am Cancer
28th 8:35 am Leo
30th 2:13 pm Virgo

June 1990
1st   11:31 pm Libra
4th   11:24 am Scorpio
6th   12:00 pm Sagittarius
9th   12:11 pm Capricorn
11th 11:09 pm Aquarius
14th 7:57 am Pisces
16th 1:51 pm Aries
18th 4:40 pm Taurus
20th 5:14 pm Gemini
22nd 5:12 pm Cancer
24th 6:29 pm Leo
26th 10:43 pm Virgo
29th 6:51 am Libra

July 1990
1st   6:02 pm Scorpio
4th   6:35 am Sagittarius
6th   6:39 pm Capricorn
9th   5:05 am Aquarius
11th 1:28 pm Pisces
13th 7:35 pm Aries
15th 11:29 pm Taurus
18th 1:32 am Gemini
20th 2:46 am Cancer
22nd 4:33 am Leo
24th 8:23 am Virgo
26th 3:24 pm Libra
29th 1:40 am Scorpio
31st 1:59 pm Sagittarius

August 1990
3rd   2:08 am Capricorn
5th   12:16 pm Aquarius
7th   7:54 pm Pisces
10th 1:15 am Aries
12th 4:56 am Taurus
14th 7:43 am Gemini
16th 10:14 am Cancer
18th 1:15 pm Leo
20th 5:37 pm Virgo
23rd 0:19 am Libra
25th 9:50 am Scorpio
27th 9:59 pm Sagittarius
30th 10:21 am Capricorn

September 1990
1st   8:49 pm Aquarius
4th   4:03 am Pisces
6th   8:21 am Aries
8th   10:56 am Taurus
10th 1:07 pm Gemini
12th 3:56 pm Cancer
14th 7:55 pm Leo
17th 1:20 am Virgo
19th 8:38 am Libra
21st 6:09 pm Scorpio
24th 5:54 am Sagittarius
26th 6:37 pm Capricorn
29th 5:51 am Aquarius

October 1990
1st   1:37 pm Pisces
3rd   5:38 pm Aries
5th   7:05 pm Taurus
7th   7:48 pm Gemini
9th   9:31 pm Cancer
12th 1:17 am Leo
14th 7:24 am Virgo
16th 3:30 pm Libra
19th 1:25 am Scorpio
21st 1:13 pm Sagittarius
24th 2:04 am Capricorn
26th 2:11 pm Aquarius
28th 11:23 pm Pisces
31st 4:11 am Aries

November 1990
2nd   5:30 am Taurus
4th   5:07 am Gemini
6th   5:10 am Cancer
8th   7:28 am Leo
10th 12:52 pm Virgo
12th 9:10 pm Libra
15th 7:42 am Scorpio
17th 7:40 pm Sagittarius
20th 8:33 am Capricorn
22nd 9:08 pm Aquarius
25th 7:27 am Pisces
27th 2:00 pm Aries
29th 4:33 pm Taurus

December 1990
1st   4:21 pm Gemini
3rd   3:30 pm Cancer
5th   4:05 pm Leo
7th   7:42 pm Virgo
10th 3:02 am Libra
12th 1:29 pm Scorpio
15th 1:43 am Sagittarius
17th 2:35 pm Capricorn
20th 2:59 am Aquarius
22nd 1:45 pm Pisces
24th 9:43 pm Aries
27th 2:07 am Taurus
29th 2:24 am Gemini
31st 3:04 am Cancer

January 1991
2nd   2:57 am Leo
4th   5:01 am Virgo
6th   10:39 am Libra
8th   8:01 pm Scorpio
11th 8:07 am Sagittarius
13th 8:59 pm Capricorn
16th 9:02 am Aquarius
18th 7:22 pm Pisces
21st 3:27 am Aries
23rd 8:57 am Taurus
25th 12:04 pm Gemini
27th 1:23 pm Cancer
29th 2:05 pm Leo
31st 3:48 pm Virgo

February 1991
2nd   8:05 pm Libra
5th   4:03 am Scorpio
7th   3:24 pm Sagittarius
10th 4:14 am Capricorn
12th 4:13 pm Aquarius
15th 1:58 am Pisces
17th 9:09 am Aries
19th 2:23 pm Taurus
21st 6:09 pm Gemini
23rd 8:56 pm Cancer
25th 11:13 pm Leo
28th 1:52 am Virgo

March 1991
2nd   6:06 am Libra
4th   1:13 pm Scorpio
6th   11:34 pm Sagittarius
9th   12:13 pm Capricorn
12th 0:29 am Aquarius
14th 10:05 am Pisces
16th 4:34 pm Aries
18th 8:39 pm Taurus
20th 11:36 pm Gemini
23rd 2:28 am Cancer
25th 5:44 am Leo
27th 9:43 am Virgo
29th 2:52 pm Libra
31st 10:02 pm Scorpio

April 1991
3rd   8:02 am Sagittarius
5th   8:21 pm Capricorn
8th   8:57 am Aquarius
10th 7:14 pm Pisces
13th 1:48 am Aries
15th 5:03 am Taurus
17th 6:42 am Gemini
19th 8:18 am Cancer
21st 11:06 am Leo
23rd 3:32 pm Virgo
25th 9:36 pm Libra
28th 5:36 am Scorpio
30th 3:46 pm Sagittarius

May 1991
3rd   3:56 am Capricorn
5th   4:50 pm Aquarius
8th   4:01 am Pisces
10th 11:29 am Aries
12th 3:03 pm Taurus
14th 3:50 pm Gemini
16th 4:16 pm Cancer
18th 5:33 pm Leo
20th 9:02 pm Virgo
23rd 3:10 am Libra
25th 11:44 am Scorpio
27th 10:21 pm Sagittarius
30th 10:42 am Capricorn

June 1991
1st   11:42 pm Aquarius
4th   11:34 am Pisces
6th   8:22 pm Aries
9th   1:12 am Taurus
11th 2:35 am Gemini
13th 2:16 am Cancer
15th 2:12 am Leo
17th 4:05 am Virgo
19th 9:06 am Libra
21st 5:21 pm Scorpio
24th 4:18 am Sagittarius
26th 4:50 pm Capricorn
29th 5:46 am Aquarius

July 1991
1st   5:48 pm Pisces
4th   3:31 am Aries
6th   9:48 am Taurus
8th   12:38 pm Gemini
10th 1:02 pm Cancer
12th 12:37 pm Leo
14th 1:17 pm Virgo
16th 4:39 pm Libra
18th 11:41 pm Scorpio
21st 10:19 am Sagittarius
23rd 10:57 pm Capricorn
26th 11:48 am Aquarius
28th 11:34 pm Pisces
31st 9:18 am Aries

August 1991
2nd   4:29 pm Taurus
4th   8:53 pm Gemini
6th   10:48 pm Cancer
8th   11:10 pm Leo
10th 11:36 pm Virgo
13th 1:54 am Libra
15th 7:39 am Scorpio
17th 5:14 pm Sagittarius
20th 5:34 am Capricorn
22nd 6:27 pm Aquarius
25th 5:49 am Pisces
27th 2:59 pm Aries
29th 10:00 pm Taurus

September 1991
1st	3:03 am	Gemini
3rd	6:19 am	Cancer
5th	8:14 am	Leo
7th	9:39 am	Virgo
9th	11:57 am	Libra
11th	4:48 pm	Scorpio
14th	1:17 am	Sagittarius
16th	1:05 pm	Capricorn
19th	1:56 am	Aquarius
21st	1:17 pm	Pisces
23rd	9:56 pm	Aries
26th	3:59 am	Taurus
28th	8:25 am	Gemini
30th	11:57 am	Cancer

October 1991
2nd	2:50 pm	Leo
4th	5:46 pm	Virgo
6th	9:03 pm	Libra
9th	2:03 am	Scorpio
11th	10:03 am	Sagittarius
13th	9:12 pm	Capricorn
16th	10:04 am	Aquarius
18th	9:52 pm	Pisces
21st	6:30 am	Aries
23rd	11:53 am	Taurus
25th	3:08 pm	Gemini
27th	5:37 pm	Cancer
29th	8:21 pm	Leo
31st	11:48 pm	Virgo

November 1991
3rd	4:14 am	Libra
5th	10:13 am	Scorpio
7th	6:26 pm	Sagittarius
10th	5:20 am	Capricorn
12th	6:08 pm	Aquarius
15th	6:31 am	Pisces
17th	4:04 pm	Aries
19th	9:49 pm	Taurus
22nd	0:23 am	Gemini
24th	1:26 am	Cancer
26th	2:38 am	Leo
28th	5:14 am	Virgo
30th	9:50 am	Libra

December 1991
2nd	4:36 pm	Scorpio
5th	1:34 am	Sagittarius
7th	12:45 pm	Capricorn
10th	1:28 am	Aquarius
12th	2:18 pm	Pisces
15th	1:06 am	Aries
17th	8:05 am	Taurus
19th	11:18 am	Gemini
21st	11:54 am	Cancer
23rd	11:41 am	Leo
25th	12:28 pm	Virgo
27th	3:42 pm	Libra
29th	10:05 pm	Scorpio

January 1992
1st	7:33 am	Sagittarius
3rd	7:11 pm	Capricorn
6th	8:00 am	Aquarius
8th	8:52 pm	Pisces
11th	8:19 am	Aries
13th	4:57 pm	Taurus
15th	9:54 pm	Gemini
17th	11:26 pm	Cancer
19th	10:57 pm	Leo
21st	10:23 pm	Virgo
23rd	11:43 pm	Libra
26th	4:35 am	Scorpio
28th	1:23 pm	Sagittarius
31st	1:07 am	Capricorn

February 1992
2nd	2:10 pm	Aquarius
5th	2:52 am	Pisces
7th	2:16 pm	Aries
9th	11:37 pm	Taurus
12th	6:09 am	Gemini
14th	9:32 am	Cancer
16th	10:16 am	Leo
18th	9:48 am	Virgo
20th	10:05 am	Libra
22nd	1:12 pm	Scorpio
24th	8:27 pm	Sagittarius
27th	7:34 am	Capricorn
29th	8:35 pm	Aquarius

March 1992
3rd	9:12 am	Pisces
5th	8:08 pm	Aries
8th	5:06 am	Taurus
10th	12:04 pm	Gemini
12th	4:51 pm	Cancer
14th	7:21 pm	Leo
16th	8:14 pm	Virgo
18th	8:56 pm	Libra
20th	11:21 pm	Scorpio
23rd	5:14 am	Sagittarius
25th	3:09 pm	Capricorn
28th	3:45 am	Aquarius
30th	4:24 pm	Pisces

April 1992
2nd	3:05 am	Aries
4th	11:19 am	Taurus
6th	5:34 pm	Gemini
8th	10:19 pm	Cancer
11th	1:47 am	Leo
13th	4:10 am	Virgo
15th	6:11 am	Libra
17th	9:11 am	Scorpio
19th	2:41 pm	Sagittarius
21st	11:41 pm	Capricorn
24th	11:39 am	Aquarius
27th	0:21 am	Pisces
29th	11:14 am	Aries

May 1992
1st	7:10 pm	Taurus
4th	0:29 am	Gemini
6th	4:10 am	Cancer
8th	7:08 am	Leo
10th	9:57 am	Virgo
12th	1:06 pm	Libra
14th	5:16 pm	Scorpio
16th	11:23 pm	Sagittarius
19th	8:14 am	Capricorn
21st	7:44 pm	Aquarius
24th	8:26 am	Pisces
26th	7:53 pm	Aries
29th	4:17 am	Taurus
31st	9:20 am	Gemini

June 1992
2nd	11:59 am	Cancer
4th	1:36 pm	Leo
6th	3:29 pm	Virgo
8th	6:34 pm	Libra
10th	11:28 pm	Scorpio
13th	6:30 am	Sagittarius
15th	3:51 pm	Capricorn
18th	3:20 am	Aquarius
20th	4:01 pm	Pisces
23rd	4:04 am	Aries
25th	1:29 pm	Taurus
27th	7:15 pm	Gemini
29th	9:43 pm	Cancer

July 1992
1st	10:16 pm	Leo
3rd	10:38 pm	Virgo
6th	0:28 am	Libra
8th	4:54 am	Scorpio
10th	12:18 pm	Sagittarius
12th	10:17 pm	Capricorn
15th	10:04 am	Aquarius
17th	10:45 pm	Pisces
20th	11:08 am	Aries
22nd	9:37 pm	Taurus
25th	4:45 am	Gemini
27th	8:09 am	Cancer
29th	8:40 am	Leo
31st	8:02 am	Virgo

August 1992
2nd	8:18 am	Libra
4th	11:17 am	Scorpio
6th	5:58 pm	Sagittarius
9th	4:01 am	Capricorn
11th	4:07 pm	Aquarius
14th	4:52 am	Pisces
16th	5:12 pm	Aries
19th	4:11 am	Taurus
21st	12:37 pm	Gemini
23rd	5:37 pm	Cancer
25th	7:16 pm	Leo
27th	6:47 pm	Virgo
29th	6:11 pm	Libra
31st	7:39 pm	Scorpio

September 1992
3rd	0:51 am	Sagittarius
5th	10:07 am	Capricorn
7th	10:09 am	Aquarius
10th	10:57 am	Pisces
12th	11:03 pm	Aries
15th	9:48 am	Taurus
17th	6:41 pm	Gemini
20th	1:00 am	Cancer
22nd	4:20 am	Leo
24th	5:09 am	Virgo
26th	4:56 am	Libra
28th	5:45 am	Scorpio
30th	9:34 am	Sagittarius

October 1992
2nd	5:30 pm	Capricorn
5th	4:54 am	Aquarius
7th	5:39 pm	Pisces
10th	5:37 am	Aries
12th	3:49 pm	Taurus
15th	0:09 am	Gemini
17th	6:37 am	Cancer
19th	11:02 am	Leo
21st	1:28 pm	Virgo
23rd	2:40 pm	Libra
25th	4:05 pm	Scorpio
27th	7:30 pm	Sagittarius
30th	2:19 am	Capricorn

November 1992
1st	12:44 pm	Aquarius
4th	1:14 am	Pisces
6th	1:20 pm	Aries
8th	11:20 pm	Taurus
11th	6:50 am	Gemini
13th	12:20 pm	Cancer
15th	4:24 pm	Leo
17th	7:29 pm	Virgo
19th	10:04 pm	Libra
22nd	0:53 am	Scorpio
24th	5:02 am	Sagittarius
26th	11:39 am	Capricorn
28th	9:20 pm	Aquarius

December 1992
1st	9:24 am	Pisces
3rd	9:50 pm	Aries
6th	8:17 am	Taurus
8th	3:38 pm	Gemini
10th	8:06 pm	Cancer
12th	10:48 pm	Leo
15th	0:57 am	Virgo
17th	3:34 am	Libra
19th	7:21 am	Scorpio
21st	12:43 pm	Sagittarius
23rd	8:05 pm	Capricorn
26th	5:44 am	Aquarius
28th	5:29 pm	Pisces
31st	6:08 am	Aries

★ ★

January 1993
2nd	5:31 pm	Taurus
5th	1:43 am	Gemini
7th	6:11 am	Cancer
9th	7:50 am	Leo
11th	8:21 am	Virgo
13th	9:31 am	Libra
15th	12:43 pm	Scorpio
17th	6:31 pm	Sagittarius
20th	2:47 am	Capricorn
22nd	1:01 pm	Aquarius
25th	0:48 am	Pisces
27th	1:29 am	Aries
30th	1:38 am	Taurus

February 1993
1st	11:16 am	Gemini
3rd	4:57 pm	Cancer
5th	6:52 pm	Leo
7th	6:30 pm	Virgo
9th	5:59 pm	Libra
11th	7:24 pm	Scorpio
14th	0:09 am	Sagittarius
16th	8:21 am	Capricorn
18th	7:06 pm	Aquarius
21st	7:13 am	Pisces
23rd	7:51 am	Aries
26th	8:12 am	Taurus
28th	6:53 pm	Gemini

March 1993
3rd	2:17 am	Cancer
5th	5:41 am	Leo
7th	5:53 am	Virgo
9th	4:47 am	Libra
11th	4:40 am	Scorpio
13th	7:34 am	Sagittarius
15th	2:29 pm	Capricorn
18th	0:53 am	Aquarius
20th	1:12 pm	Pisces
23rd	1:52 am	Aries
25th	2:00 pm	Taurus
28th	0:49 am	Gemini
30th	9:15 am	Cancer

April 1993
1st	2:22 pm	Leo
3rd	4:11 pm	Virgo
5th	3:55 pm	Libra
7th	3:33 pm	Scorpio
9th	5:11 pm	Sagittarius
11th	11:25 pm	Capricorn
14th	7:37 am	Aquarius
16th	7:33 pm	Pisces
19th	8:15 am	Aries
21st	8:09 pm	Taurus
24th	6:28 am	Gemini
26th	2:46 pm	Cancer
28th	8:40 pm	Leo

May 1993
1st	0:01 am	Virgo
3rd	1:21 am	Libra
5th	1:58 am	Scorpio
7th	3:35 am	Sagittarius
9th	7:52 am	Capricorn
11th	3:45 pm	Aquarius
14th	2:51 am	Pisces
16th	3:25 pm	Aries
19th	3:17 am	Taurus
21st	1:08 pm	Gemini
23rd	8:39 pm	Cancer
26th	2:04 am	Leo
28th	5:47 am	Virgo
30th	8:19 am	Libra

June 1993
1st	10:23 am	Scorpio
3rd	1:02 pm	Sagittarius
5th	5:27 pm	Capricorn
8th	0:40 am	Aquarius
10th	10:58 am	Pisces
12th	11:15 pm	Aries
15th	11:20 am	Taurus
17th	9:13 pm	Gemini
20th	4:06 am	Cancer
22nd	8:27 am	Leo
24th	11:19 am	Virgo
26th	1:46 pm	Libra
28th	4:38 pm	Scorpio
30th	8:29 pm	Sagittarius

July 1993
3rd	1:49 am	Capricorn
5th	9:15 am	Aquarius
7th	7:10 pm	Pisces
10th	7:12 am	Aries
12th	7:38 pm	Taurus
15th	6:08 am	Gemini
17th	1:09 pm	Cancer
19th	4:48 pm	Leo
21st	6:25 pm	Virgo
23rd	7:40 pm	Libra
25th	10:01 pm	Scorpio
28th	2:14 am	Sagittarius
30th	8:28 am	Capricorn

August 1993
1st	4:37 pm	Aquarius
4th	2:44 am	Pisces
6th	2:40 pm	Aries
9th	3:23 am	Taurus
11th	2:48 pm	Gemini
13th	10:47 pm	Cancer
16th	2:44 am	Leo
18th	3:42 am	Virgo
20th	3:36 am	Libra
22nd	4:28 am	Scorpio
24th	7:46 am	Sagittarius
26th	1:59 pm	Capricorn
28th	10:43 pm	Aquarius
31st	9:19 am	Pisces

September 1993
2nd	9:22 pm	Aries
5th	10:10 am	Taurus
7th	10:17 pm	Gemini
10th	7:38 am	Cancer
12th	12:52 pm	Leo
14th	2:21 pm	Virgo
16th	1:45 pm	Libra
18th	1:15 pm	Scorpio
20th	2:54 pm	Sagittarius
22nd	7:55 pm	Capricorn
25th	4:20 am	Aquarius
27th	3:14 pm	Pisces
30th	3:30 am	Aries

October 1993
2nd	4:14 pm	Taurus
5th	4:28 am	Gemini
7th	2:43 pm	Cancer
9th	9:35 pm	Leo
12th	0:37 am	Virgo
14th	0:48 am	Libra
16th	0:02 am	Scorpio
18th	0:24 am	Sagittarius
20th	3:43 am	Capricorn
22nd	10:50 am	Aquarius
24th	9:18 pm	Pisces
27th	9:40 am	Aries
29th	10:21 pm	Taurus

November 1993
1st	10:14 am	Gemini
3rd	8:26 pm	Cancer
6th	4:07 am	Leo
8th	8:48 am	Virgo
10th	10:43 am	Libra
12th	11:01 am	Scorpio
14th	11:21 am	Sagittarius
16th	1:35 pm	Capricorn
18th	7:09 pm	Aquarius
21st	4:28 am	Pisces
23rd	4:31 am	Aries
26th	5:15 am	Taurus
28th	4:49 pm	Gemini

December 1993
1st	2:18 am	Cancer
3rd	9:34 am	Leo
5th	2:44 pm	Virgo
7th	6:04 pm	Libra
9th	8:05 pm	Scorpio
11th	9:40 pm	Sagittarius
14th	0:07 am	Capricorn
16th	4:52 am	Aquarius
18th	1:00 pm	Pisces
21st	0:20 am	Aries
23rd	1:06 pm	Taurus
26th	0:47 am	Gemini
28th	9:47 am	Cancer
30th	4:00 pm	Leo

January 1994
1st	8:16 pm	Virgo
3rd	11:32 pm	Libra
6th	2:30 am	Scorpio
8th	5:35 am	Sagittarius
10th	9:17 am	Capricorn
12th	2:26 pm	Aquarius
14th	10:05 pm	Pisces
17th	8:43 am	Aries
19th	9:23 pm	Taurus
22nd	9:36 am	Gemini
24th	6:56 pm	Cancer
27th	0:39 am	Leo
29th	3:40 am	Virgo
31st	5:35 am	Libra

February 1994
2nd	7:50 am	Scorpio
4th	11:15 am	Sagittarius
6th	4:03 pm	Capricorn
8th	10:17 pm	Aquarius
11th	6:24 am	Pisces
13th	4:50 pm	Aries
16th	5:21 am	Taurus
18th	6:06 pm	Gemini
21st	4:28 am	Cancer
23rd	10:49 am	Leo
25th	1:28 pm	Virgo
27th	2:07 pm	Libra

March 1994
1st	2:44 pm	Scorpio
3rd	4:55 pm	Sagittarius
5th	9:25 pm	Capricorn
8th	4:16 am	Aquarius
10th	1:10 pm	Pisces
12th	12:00 am	Aries
15th	12:28 pm	Taurus
18th	1:30 am	Gemini
20th	12:55 pm	Cancer
22nd	8:40 pm	Leo
25th	0:15 am	Virgo
27th	0:47 am	Libra
29th	0:16 am	Scorpio
31st	0:42 am	Sagittarius

April 1994
2nd	3:38 am	Capricorn
4th	9:46 am	Aquarius
6th	6:52 pm	Pisces
9th	6:10 am	Aries
11th	6:49 pm	Taurus
14th	7:49 am	Gemini
16th	7:42 pm	Cancer
19th	4:46 am	Leo
21st	9:59 am	Virgo
23rd	11:41 am	Libra
25th	11:19 am	Scorpio
27th	10:49 am	Sagittarius
29th	12:06 pm	Capricorn

★ ★

★ ★

May 1994
1st	4:35 pm	Aquarius
4th	12:48 am	Pisces
6th	12:02 am	Aries
9th	0:51 am	Taurus
11th	1:44 pm	Gemini
14th	1:28 am	Cancer
16th	10:59 am	Leo
18th	5:32 pm	Virgo
20th	8:55 pm	Libra
22nd	9:52 pm	Scorpio
24th	9:44 pm	Sagittarius
26th	10:18 pm	Capricorn
29th	1:20 am	Aquarius
31st	8:04 am	Pisces

June 1994
2nd	6:32 pm	Aries
5th	7:15 am	Taurus
7th	8:04 pm	Gemini
10th	7:23 am	Cancer
12th	4:30 pm	Leo
14th	11:17 pm	Virgo
17th	3:49 am	Libra
19th	6:21 am	Scorpio
21st	7:33 am	Sagittarius
23rd	8:38 am	Capricorn
25th	11:11 am	Aquarius
27th	4:45 pm	Pisces
30th	2:08 am	Aries

July 1994
2nd	2:24 pm	Taurus
5th	3:13 am	Gemini
7th	2:18 pm	Cancer
9th	10:44 pm	Leo
12th	4:49 am	Virgo
14th	9:16 am	Libra
16th	12:36 pm	Scorpio
18th	3:10 pm	Sagittarius
20th	5:31 pm	Capricorn
22nd	8:39 pm	Aquarius
25th	1:57 am	Pisces
27th	10:32 am	Aries
29th	10:14 pm	Taurus

August 1994
1st	11:06 am	Gemini
3rd	10:23 pm	Cancer
6th	6:32 am	Leo
8th	11:43 am	Virgo
10th	3:08 pm	Libra
12th	5:57 pm	Scorpio
14th	8:54 pm	Sagittarius
17th	0:19 am	Capricorn
19th	4:35 am	Aquarius
21st	10:28 am	Pisces
23rd	6:56 pm	Aries
26th	6:14 am	Taurus
28th	7:08 pm	Gemini
31st	7:01 am	Cancer

September 1994
2nd	3:38 pm	Leo
4th	8:34 pm	Virgo
6th	10:58 pm	Libra
9th	0:27 am	Scorpio
11th	2:26 am	Sagittarius
13th	9:45 am	Capricorn
15th	10:43 am	Aquarius
17th	5:32 pm	Pisces
20th	2:31 am	Aries
22nd	1:48 pm	Taurus
25th	2:42 am	Gemini
27th	3:13 pm	Cancer
30th	0:56 am	Leo

October 1994
2nd	6:40 am	Virgo
4th	8:57 am	Libra
6th	9:23 am	Scorpio
8th	9:48 am	Sagittarius
10th	11:45 am	Capricorn
12th	4:10 pm	Aquarius
14th	11:19 pm	Pisces
17th	8:57 am	Aries
19th	8:35 pm	Taurus
22nd	9:29 am	Gemini
24th	10:16 pm	Cancer
27th	9:06 am	Leo
29th	4:22 pm	Virgo
31st	7:47 pm	Libra

November 1994
2nd	8:20 pm	Scorpio
4th	7:47 pm	Sagittarius
6th	8:03 pm	Capricorn
8th	10:49 pm	Aquarius
11th	5:05 am	Pisces
13th	2:45 pm	Aries
16th	2:45 am	Taurus
18th	3:42 pm	Gemini
21st	4:22 am	Cancer
23rd	3:34 pm	Leo
26th	0:10 am	Virgo
28th	9:23 am	Libra
30th	7:22 am	Scorpio

December 1994
2nd	7:14 am	Sagittarius
4th	6:43 am	Capricorn
6th	7:52 am	Aquarius
8th	12:25 pm	Pisces
10th	9:04 pm	Aries
13th	8:57 am	Taurus
15th	10:01 pm	Gemini
18th	10:26 am	Cancer
20th	9:14 pm	Leo
23rd	6:02 am	Virgo
25th	12:28 pm	Libra
27th	4:18 pm	Scorpio
29th	5:47 pm	Sagittarius
31st	5:58 pm	Capricorn

January 1995
2nd	6:40 pm	Aquarius
4th	9:50 pm	Pisces
7th	4:57 am	Aries
9th	3:59 pm	Taurus
12th	4:58 am	Gemini
14th	5:21 pm	Cancer
17th	3:37 am	Leo
19th	11:40 am	Virgo
21st	5:55 pm	Libra
23rd	10:33 pm	Scorpio
26th	1:38 am	Sagittarius
28th	3:27 am	Capricorn
30th	5:04 am	Aquarius

February 1995
1st	8:06 am	Pisces
3rd	2:13 pm	Aries
6th	0:10 am	Taurus
8th	12:45 pm	Gemini
11th	1:18 am	Cancer
13th	11:32 am	Leo
15th	6:53 pm	Virgo
18th	0:01 am	Libra
20th	3:56 am	Scorpio
22nd	7:14 am	Sagittarius
24th	10:12 am	Capricorn
26th	1,15 pm	Aquarius
28th	5:17 pm	Pisces

March 1995
2nd	11:31 pm	Aries
5th	8:51 am	Taurus
7th	8:56 pm	Gemini
10th	9:41 am	Cancer
12th	8:29 pm	Leo
15th	3:55 am	Virgo
17th	8:19 am	Libra
19th	10:53 am	Scorpio
21st	12:58 pm	Sagittarius
23rd	3:32 pm	Capricorn
25th	7:11 pm	Aquarius
28th	0:19 am	Pisces
30th	7:27 am	Aries

April 1995
1st	5:00 pm	Taurus
4th	4:50 am	Gemini
6th	5:41 pm	Cancer
9th	5:17 am	Leo
11th	1:40 pm	Virgo
13th	6:21 pm	Libra
15th	8:14 pm	Scorpio
17th	8:52 pm	Sagittarius
19th	9:55 pm	Capricorn
22nd	0:39 am	Aquarius
24th	5:52 am	Pisces
26th	1:42 pm	Aries
28th	11:54 pm	Taurus

May 1995
1st	11:54 am	Gemini
4th	0:46 am	Cancer
6th	12:56 pm	Leo
8th	10:34 pm	Virgo
11th	4:31 am	Libra
13th	6:54 am	Scorpio
15th	6:59 am	Sagittarius
17th	6:37 am	Capricorn
19th	7:40 am	Aquarius
21st	11:41 am	Pisces
23rd	7:14 pm	Aries
26th	5:47 am	Taurus
28th	6:08 pm	Gemini
31st	7:00 am	Cancer

June 1995
2nd	7:18 pm	Leo
5th	5:47 am	Virgo
7th	1:14 pm	Libra
9th	5:04 pm	Scorpio
11th	5:51 pm	Sagittarius
13th	5:06 pm	Capricorn
15th	4.53 pm	Aquarius
17th	7:14 pm	Pisces
20th	1:30 am	Aries
22nd	11:36 am	Taurus
25th	0:03 am	Gemini
27th	12:57 pm	Cancer
30th	1:03 am	Leo

July 1995
2nd	11:36 am	Virgo
4th	7:56 pm	Libra
7th	1:20 am	Scorpio
9th	3:39 am	Sagittarius
11th	3:44 am	Capricorn
13th	3:22 am	Aquarius
15th	4:38 am	Pisces
17th	9:24 am	Aries
19th	6:21 pm	Taurus
22nd	6:24 am	Gemini
24th	7:17 pm	Cancer
27th	7:08 am	Leo
29th	5:13 pm	Virgo

August 1995
1st	1:24 am	Libra
3rd	7:30 am	Scorpio
5th	11:15 am	Sagittarius
7th	12:53 pm	Capricorn
9th	1:29 pm	Aquarius
11th	2:47 pm	Pisces
13th	6:42 pm	Aries
16th	2:26 am	Taurus
18th	1:41 pm	Gemini
21st	2:25 am	Cancer
23rd	2:14 pm	Leo
25th	11:51 pm	Virgo
28th	7:16 am	Libra
30th	12:52 pm	Scorpio

★ ★

September 1995		
1st	4:58 pm	Sagittarius
3rd	7:46 pm	Capricorn
5th	9:48 pm	Aquarius
8th	0:09 am	Pisces
10th	4:15 am	Aries
12th	11:22 am	Taurus
14th	9:49 pm	Gemini
17th	10:17 am	Cancer
19th	10:20 pm	Leo
22nd	8:02 am	Virgo
24th	2:51 pm	Libra
26th	7:21 pm	Scorpio
28th	10:31 pm	Sagittarius

October 1995		
1st	1:11 am	Capricorn
3rd	4:00 am	Aquarius
5th	7:36 am	Pisces
7th	12:42 pm	Aries
9th	8:06 pm	Taurus
12th	6:11 am	Gemini
14th	6:21 pm	Cancer
17th	6:47 am	Leo
19th	5:12 pm	Virgo
22nd	0:16 am	Libra
24th	4:08 am	Scorpio
26th	5:57 am	Sagittarius
28th	7:16 am	Capricorn
30th	9:24 am	Aquarius

November 1995		
1st	1:18 pm	Pisces
3rd	7:22 pm	Aries
6th	3:36 am	Taurus
8th	1:56 pm	Gemini
11th	1:58 am	Cancer
13th	2:38 pm	Leo
16th	2:03 am	Virgo
18th	10:19 am	Libra
20th	2:41 pm	Scorpio
22nd	3:57 pm	Sagittarius
24th	3:49 pm	Capricorn
26th	4:16 pm	Aquarius
28th	7:00 pm	Pisces

December 1995		
1st	0:52 am	Aries
3rd	9:41 am	Taurus
5th	8:36 pm	Gemini
8th	8:45 am	Cancer
10th	9:25 pm	Leo
13th	9:27 am	Virgo
15th	7:10 pm	Libra
18th	1:08 am	Scorpio
20th	3:14 am	Sagittarius
22nd	2:47 am	Capricorn
24th	1:53 am	Aquarius
26th	2:46 am	Pisces
28th	7:07 am	Aries
30th	3:22 am	Taurus

January 1996		
2nd	2:30 am	Gemini
4th	2:57 pm	Cancer
7th	3:31 am	Leo
9th	3:30 pm	Virgo
12th	1:56 am	Libra
14th	9:31 am	Scorpio
16th	1:26 pm	Sagittarius
18th	2:08 pm	Capricorn
20th	1:16 pm	Aquarius
22nd	1:03 pm	Pisces
24th	3:39 pm	Aries
26th	10:17 pm	Taurus
29th	8:44 am	Gemini
31st	9:12 pm	Cancer

February 1996		
3rd	9:47 am	Leo
5th	9:23 pm	Virgo
8th	7:31 am	Libra
10th	3:36 pm	Scorpio
12th	8:59 pm	Sagittarius
14th	11:31 pm	Capricorn
17th	0:01 am	Aquarius
19th	0:10 am	Pisces
21st	1:59 am	Aries
23rd	7:09 am	Taurus
25th	4:15 pm	Gemini
28th	4:11 am	Cancer

March 1996		
1st	4:48 pm	Leo
4th	4:14 am	Virgo
6th	1:41 pm	Libra
8th	9:06 pm	Scorpio
11th	2:33 am	Sagittarius
13th	6:09 am	Capricorn
15th	8:16 am	Aquarius
17th	9:51 am	Pisces
19th	12:16 pm	Aries
21st	5:00 pm	Taurus
24th	1:00 am	Gemini
26th	12:07 pm	Cancer
29th	0:38 am	Leo
31st	12:16 pm	Virgo

April 1996		
2nd	9:27 pm	Libra
5th	3:58 am	Scorpio
7th	8:22 am	Sagittarius
9th	11:31 am	Capricorn
11th	2:10 pm	Aquarius
13th	5:01 pm	Pisces
15th	8:44 pm	Aries
18th	2:06 am	Taurus
20th	9:55 am	Gemini
22th	8:26 pm	Cancer
25th	8:45 am	Leo
27th	8:50 pm	Virgo
30th	6:28 am	Libra

May 1996		
2nd	12:44 pm	Scorpio
4th	4:06 pm	Sagittarius
6th	5:55 pm	Capricorn
8th	7:40 pm	Aquarius
10th	10:30 pm	Pisces
13th	3:01 am	Aries
15th	9:26 am	Taurus
17th	5:49 pm	Gemini
20th	4:17 am	Cancer
22nd	4:29 pm	Leo
25th	4:59 am	Virgo
27th	3:34 pm	Libra
29th	10:31 pm	Scorpio

June 1996		
1st	1:44 am	Sagittarius
3rd	2:30 am	Capricorn
5th	2:46 am	Aquarius
7th	4:20 am	Pisces
9th	8:24 am	Aries
11th	3:12 pm	Taurus
14th	0:17 am	Gemini
16th	11:09 am	Cancer
18th	11:23 pm	Leo
21st	0:08 pm	Virgo
23rd	11:38 pm	Libra
26th	7:55 am	Scorpio
28th	12:02 pm	Sagittarius
30th	12:48 pm	Capricorn

July 1996		
2nd	12:06 pm	Aquarius
4th	12:08 pm	Pisces
6th	2:43 pm	Aries
8th	8:44 pm	Taurus
11th	5:53 am	Gemini
13th	5:09 pm	Cancer
16th	5:32 am	Leo
18th	6:17 pm	Virgo
21st	6:15 am	Libra
23rd	3:44 pm	Scorpio
25th	9:25 pm	Sagittarius
27th	11:18 pm	Capricorn
29th	10:48 pm	Aquarius
31st	10:01 pm	Pisces

August 1996		
2nd	11:06 pm	Aries
5th	3:34 am	Taurus
7th	11:50 am	Gemini
9th	10:58 pm	Cancer
12th	11:30 am	Leo
15th	0:08 am	Virgo
17th	11:56 am	Libra
19th	9:51 pm	Scorpio
22nd	4:49 am	Sagittarius
24th	8:23 am	Capricorn
26th	9:11 am	Aquarius
28th	8:50 am	Pisces
30th	9:16 am	Aries

September 1996		
1st	12:20 pm	Taurus
3rd	7:09 pm	Gemini
6th	5:30 am	Cancer
8th	5:55 pm	Leo
11th	6:29 am	Virgo
13th	5:52 pm	Libra
16th	3:21 am	Scorpio
18th	10:32 am	Sagittarius
20th	3:13 pm	Capricorn
22nd	5:40 pm	Aquarius
24th	6:44 pm	Pisces
26th	7:47 pm	Aries
28th	10:25 pm	Taurus

October 1996		
1st	4:02 am	Gemini
3rd	1:15 pm	Cancer
6th	1:13 am	Leo
8th	1:50 pm	Virgo
11th	1:01 am	Libra
13th	9:47 am	Scorpio
15th	4:08 pm	Sagittarius
17th	8:38 pm	Capricorn
19th	11:52 pm	Aquarius
22nd	2:23 am	Pisces
24th	4:51 am	Aries
26th	8:12 am	Taurus
28th	1:35 pm	Gemini
30th	9:57 pm	Cancer

November 1996		
2nd	9:17 am	Leo
4th	9:58 pm	Virgo
7th	9:30 am	Libra
9th	6:03 pm	Scorpio
11th	11:27 pm	Sagittarius
14th	2:45 am	Capricorn
16th	5:15 am	Aquarius
18th	8:01 am	Pisces
20th	11:35 am	Aries
22nd	4:13 pm	Taurus
24th	10:21 pm	Gemini
27th	6:38 am	Cancer
29th	5:31 pm	Leo

December 1996		
2nd	6:12 am	Virgo
4th	6:24 pm	Libra
7th	3:40 am	Scorpio
9th	9:00 am	Sagittarius
11th	11:16 am	Capricorn
13th	12:15 pm	Aquarius
15th	1:45 pm	Pisces
17th	4:56 pm	Aries
19th	10:11 pm	Taurus
22nd	5:18 am	Gemini
24th	2:15 pm	Cancer
27th	1:10 am	Leo
29th	1:46 pm	Virgo

January 1997

1st	2:33 am	Libra
3rd	1:03 pm	Scorpio
5th	7:28 pm	Sagittarius
7th	9:56 pm	Capricorn
9th	10:01 pm	Aquarius
11th	9:52 pm	Pisces
13th	11:23 pm	Aries
16th	3:41 am	Taurus
18th	10:54 pm	Gemini
20th	8:30 pm	Cancer
23rd	7:51 am	Leo
25th	8:27 pm	Virgo
28th	9:22 am	Libra
30th	8:49 pm	Scorpio

February 1997

2nd	4:52 am	Sagittarius
4th	8:46 am	Capricorn
6th	9:22 am	Aquarius
8th	8:35 am	Pisces
10th	8:30 am	Aries
12th	10:57 am	Taurus
14th	4:54 pm	Gemini
17th	2:14 am	Cancer
19th	1:53 pm	Leo
22nd	2:39 am	Virgo
24th	3:24 pm	Libra
27th	2:58 am	Scorpio

March 1997

1st	12:02 pm	Sagittarius
3rd	5:40 pm	Capricorn
5th	7:56 pm	Aquarius
7th	7:58 pm	Pisces
9th	7:34 pm	Aries
11th	8:38 pm	Taurus
14th	0:49 am	Gemini
16th	8:52 am	Cancer
18th	8:09 pm	Leo
21st	9:00 am	Virgo
23rd	9:36 pm	Libra
26th	8:43 am	Scorpio
28th	5:41 pm	Sagittarius
31st	0:08 am	Capricorn

April 1997

2nd	4:00 am	Aquarius
4th	5:43 am	Pisces
6th	6:20 am	Aries
8th	7:21 am	Taurus
10th	10:29 am	Gemini
12th	5:04 pm	Cancer
15th	3:23 am	Leo
17th	4:01 pm	Virgo
20th	4:37 am	Libra
22nd	3:20 pm	Scorpio
24th	11:33 pm	Sagittarius
27th	5:33 am	Capricorn
29th	9:31 am	Aquarius

May 1997

1st	12:51 pm	Pisces
3rd	3:00 pm	Aries
5th	5:05 pm	Taurus
7th	8:22 pm	Gemini
10th	2:14 am	Cancer
12th	11:34 am	Leo
14th	11:44 pm	Virgo
17th	12:28 pm	Libra
19th	11:13 pm	Scorpio
22nd	6:52 am	Sagittarius
24th	11:52 am	Capricorn
26th	3:21 pm	Aquarius
28th	6:19 pm	Pisces
30th	9:19 pm	Aries

June 1997

2nd	0:40 am	Taurus
4th	4:56 am	Gemini
6th	11:03 am	Cancer
8th	7:59 pm	Leo
11th	7:44 am	Virgo
13th	8:36 pm	Libra
16th	7:52 am	Scorpio
18th	3:40 pm	Sagittarius
20th	8:03 pm	Capricorn
22nd	10:21 pm	Aquarius
25th	0:10 am	Pisces
27th	2:40 am	Aries
29th	6:24 am	Taurus

July 1997

1st	11:36 am	Gemini
3rd	6:34 pm	Cancer
6th	3:46 am	Leo
8th	3:23 pm	Virgo
11th	4:22 am	Libra
13th	4:21 pm	Scorpio
16th	1:03 am	Sagittarius
18th	5:46 am	Capricorn
20th	7:30 am	Aquarius
22nd	8:01 am	Pisces
24th	9:04 am	Aries
26th	11:54 am	Taurus
28th	5:05 pm	Gemini
31st	0:39 am	Cancer

August 1997

2nd	10:28 am	Leo
4th	10:16 pm	Virgo
7th	11:18 am	Libra
9th	11:51 pm	Scorpio
12th	9:46 am	Sagittarius
14th	3:43 pm	Capricorn
16th	5:59 pm	Aquarius
18th	6:02 pm	Pisces
20th	5:46 pm	Aries
22nd	6:58 pm	Taurus
24th	10:57 pm	Gemini
27th	6:12 am	Cancer
29th	4:20 pm	Leo

September 1997

1st	4:28 am	Virgo
3rd	5:31 pm	Libra
6th	6:11 am	Scorpio
8th	4:55 pm	Sagittarius
11th	0:24 am	Capricorn
13th	4:11 am	Aquarius
15th	5:00 am	Pisces
17th	4:26 am	Aries
19th	4:22 am	Taurus
21st	6:39 am	Gemini
23rd	12:34 pm	Cancer
25th	10:13 pm	Leo
28th	10:28 am	Virgo
30th	11:33 pm	Libra

October 1997

3rd	11:58 am	Scorpio
5th	10:44 pm	Sagittarius
8th	7:05 am	Capricorn
10th	12:30 pm	Aquarius
12th	3:00 pm	Pisces
14th	3:26 pm	Aries
16th	3:17 pm	Taurus
18th	4:27 pm	Gemini
20th	8:46 pm	Cancer
23rd	5:11 am	Leo
25th	5:00 pm	Virgo
28th	6:06 am	Libra
30th	6:16 pm	Scorpio

November 1997

2nd	4:28 am	Sagittarius
4th	12:32 pm	Capricorn
6th	6:34 pm	Aquarius
8th	10:36 pm	Pisces
11th	0:45 am	Aries
13th	1:46 am	Taurus
15th	3:06 am	Gemini
17th	6:33 am	Cancer
19th	1:39 pm	Leo
22nd	0:34 am	Virgo
24th	1:30 pm	Libra
27th	1:44 am	Scorpio
29th	11:29 am	Sagittarius

December 1997

1st	6:39 pm	Capricorn
3rd	11:59 pm	Aquarius
6th	4:08 am	Pisces
8th	7:25 am	Aries
10th	10:01 am	Taurus
12th	12:36 pm	Gemini
14th	4:26 pm	Cancer
16th	10:59 pm	Leo
19th	9:01 am	Virgo
21st	9:36 pm	Libra
24th	10:08 am	Scorpio
26th	8:08 pm	Sagittarius
29th	2:49 am	Capricorn
31st	6:59 am	Aquarius

January 1998

2nd	9:57 am	Pisces
4th	12:44 pm	Aries
6th	3:53 pm	Taurus
8th	7:43 pm	Gemini
11th	0:44 am	Cancer
13th	7:46 am	Leo
15th	5:32 pm	Virgo
18th	5:45 am	Libra
20th	6:35 pm	Scorpio
23rd	5:26 am	Sagittarius
25th	12:40 pm	Capricorn
27th	4:28 pm	Aquarius
29th	6:09 pm	Pisces
31st	7:22 pm	Aries

February 1998

2nd	9:26 pm	Taurus
5th	1:10 am	Gemini
7th	6:58 am	Cancer
9th	2:58 pm	Leo
12th	1:11 am	Virgo
14th	1:18 pm	Libra
17th	2:14 am	Scorpio
19th	1:57 pm	Sagittarius
21st	10:31 pm	Capricorn
24th	3:11 am	Aquarius
26th	4:43 am	Pisces
28th	4:43 am	Aries

March 1998

2nd	5:01 am	Taurus
4th	7:16 am	Gemini
6th	12:28 pm	Cancer
8th	8:47 pm	Leo
11th	7:36 am	Virgo
13th	7:59 pm	Libra
16th	8:52 am	Scorpio
18th	8:57 pm	Sagittarius
21st	6:45 am	Capricorn
23rd	1:03 pm	Aquarius
25th	3:44 pm	Pisces
27th	3:50 pm	Aries
29th	3:07 pm	Taurus
31st	3:38 pm	Gemini

April 1998

2nd	7:11 pm	Cancer
5th	2:37 am	Leo
7th	1:26 pm	Virgo
10th	2:05 am	Libra
12th	2:57 pm	Scorpio
15th	2:53 am	Sagittarius
17th	1:06 pm	Capricorn
19th	8:42 pm	Aquarius
22nd	1:07 am	Pisces
24th	2:32 am	Aries
26th	2:10 am	Taurus
28th	1:56 am	Gemini
30th	3:58 am	Cancer

May 1998

2nd	9:50 am	Leo
4th	7:48 pm	Virgo
7th	8:20 am	Libra
9th	9:11 pm	Scorpio
12th	8:49 am	Sagittarius
14th	6:40 pm	Capricorn
17th	2:31 am	Aquarius
19th	8:04 am	Pisces
21st	11:07 am	Aries
23rd	12:07 pm	Taurus
25th	12:26 pm	Gemini
27th	1:59 pm	Cancer
29th	6:39 pm	Leo

June 1998

1st	3:22 am	Virgo
3rd	3:18 pm	Libra
6th	4:07 am	Scorpio
8th	3:35 pm	Sagittarius
11th	0:51 am	Capricorn
13th	8:04 am	Aquarius
15th	1:32 pm	Pisces
17th	5:24 pm	Aries
19th	7:48 pm	Taurus
21st	9:27 pm	Gemini
23rd	11:40 pm	Cancer
26th	4:05 am	Leo
28th	11:55 am	Virgo
30th	11:06 pm	Libra

July 1998

3rd	11:46 am	Scorpio
5th	11:25 pm	Sagittarius
8th	8:28 am	Capricorn
10th	2:53 pm	Aquarius
12th	7:23 pm	Pisces
14th	10:46 pm	Aries
17th	1:34 am	Taurus
19th	4:19 am	Gemini
21st	7:44 am	Cancer
23rd	12:49 pm	Leo
25th	8:35 pm	Virgo
28th	7:15 am	Libra
30th	7:45 pm	Scorpio

August 1998

2nd	7:49 am	Sagittarius
4th	5:19 pm	Capricorn
6th	11:32 pm	Aquarius
9th	3:05 am	Pisces
11th	5:11 am	Aries
13th	7:05 am	Taurus
15th	9:47 am	Gemini
17th	1:56 pm	Cancer
19th	8:02 pm	Leo
22nd	4:22 am	Virgo
24th	3:03 pm	Libra
27th	3:26 am	Scorpio
29th	3:56 pm	Sagittarius

September 1998

1st	2:24 am	Capricorn
3rd	9:22 am	Aquarius
5th	12:49 pm	Pisces
7th	1:54 pm	Aries
9th	2:17 pm	Taurus
11th	3:41 pm	Gemini
13th	7:21 pm	Cancer
16th	1:49 am	Leo
18th	10:53 am	Virgo
20th	9:58 pm	Libra
23rd	10:23 am	Scorpio
25th	11:06 pm	Sagittarius
28th	10:31 am	Capricorn
30th	6:54 pm	Aquarius

October 1998

2nd	11:24 pm	Pisces
5th	0:33 am	Aries
6th	11:58 pm	Taurus
8th	11:45 pm	Gemini
11th	1:49 am	Cancer
13th	7:26 am	Leo
15th	4:33 pm	Virgo
18th	4:03 am	Libra
20th	4:37 pm	Scorpio
23rd	5:17 am	Sagittarius
25th	5:06 pm	Capricorn
28th	2:45 am	Aquarius
30th	8:59 am	Pisces

November 1998

1st	11:28 am	Aries
3rd	11:13 am	Taurus
5th	10:12 am	Gemini
7th	10:40 am	Cancer
9th	2:34 pm	Leo
11th	10:38 pm	Virgo
14th	9:59 am	Libra
16th	10:42 pm	Scorpio
19th	11:14 am	Sagittarius
21st	10:46 pm	Capricorn
24th	8:44 am	Aquarius
26th	4:15 pm	Pisces
28th	8:35 pm	Aries
30th	9:54 pm	Taurus

December 1998

2nd	9:31 pm	Gemini
4th	9:29 pm	Cancer
6th	11:56 pm	Leo
9th	6:22 am	Virgo
11th	4:44 pm	Libra
14th	5:17 am	Scorpio
16th	5:48 pm	Sagittarius
19th	4:56 am	Capricorn
21st	2:18 pm	Aquarius
23rd	9:46 pm	Pisces
26th	3:05 am	Aries
28th	6:06 am	Taurus
30th	7:23 am	Gemini

January 1999

1st	8:16 am	Cancer
3rd	10:32 am	Leo
5th	3:50 pm	Virgo
8th	0:54 am	Libra
10th	12:50 pm	Scorpio
13th	1:24 am	Sagittarius
15th	12:30 pm	Capricorn
17th	9:12 pm	Aquarius
20th	3:41 am	Pisces
22nd	8:26 am	Aries
24th	11:53 am	Taurus
26th	2:30 pm	Gemini
28th	4:58 pm	Cancer
30th	8:17 pm	Leo

February 1999

2nd	1:38 am	Virgo
4th	9:57 am	Libra
6th	9:07 pm	Scorpio
9th	9:39 am	Sagittarius
11th	9:11 pm	Capricorn
14th	5:58 am	Aquarius
16th	11:41 am	Pisces
18th	3:07 pm	Aries
20th	5:30 pm	Taurus
22nd	7:55 pm	Gemini
24th	11:10 pm	Cancer
27th	3:45 am	Leo

March 1999

1st	10:06 am	Virgo
3rd	6:35 pm	Libra
6th	5:23 am	Scorpio
8th	5:47 pm	Sagittarius
11th	5:55 am	Capricorn
13th	3:33 pm	Aquarius
15th	9:31 pm	Pisces
18th	0:14 am	Aries
20th	1:10 am	Taurus
22nd	2:06 am	Gemini
24th	4:34 am	Cancer
26th	9:23 am	Leo
28th	4:35 pm	Virgo
31st	1:50 am	Libra

April 1999

2nd	12:50 pm	Scorpio
5th	1:08 am	Sagittarius
7th	1:40 pm	Capricorn
10th	0:25 am	Aquarius
12th	7:36 am	Pisces
14th	10:47 am	Aries
16th	11:08 am	Taurus
18th	10:40 am	Gemini
20th	11:28 am	Cancer
22nd	3:07 pm	Leo
24th	10:05 pm	Virgo
27th	7:47 am	Libra
29th	7:14 pm	Scorpio

May 1999

2nd	7:37 am	Sagittarius
4th	8:13 pm	Capricorn
7th	7:41 am	Aquarius
9th	4:17 pm	Pisces
11th	8:54 pm	Aries
13th	9:57 pm	Taurus
15th	9:08 pm	Gemini
17th	8:40 pm	Cancer
19th	10:38 pm	Leo
22nd	4:16 am	Virgo
24th	1:30 pm	Libra
27th	1:06 am	Scorpio
29th	1:38 pm	Sagittarius

June 1999

1st	2:07 am	Capricorn
3rd	1:38 pm	Aquarius
5th	11:02 pm	Pisces
8th	5:09 am	Aries
10th	7:45 am	Taurus
12th	7:49 am	Gemini
14th	7:15 am	Cancer
16th	8:08 am	Leo
18th	12:13 pm	Virgo
20th	8:11 pm	Libra
23rd	7:19 am	Scorpio
25th	7:52 pm	Sagittarius
28th	8:13 am	Capricorn
30th	7:20 pm	Aquarius

July 1999

3rd	4:35 am	Pisces
5th	11:22 am	Aries
7th	3:23 pm	Taurus
9th	5:01 pm	Gemini
11th	5:28 pm	Cancer
13th	6:27 pm	Leo
15th	9:40 pm	Virgo
18th	4:20 am	Libra
20th	2:31 pm	Scorpio
23rd	2:49 am	Sagittarius
25th	3:09 pm	Capricorn
28th	1:55 am	Aquarius
30th	10:28 am	Pisces

August 1999

1st	4:48 pm	Aries
3rd	9:10 pm	Taurus
5th	11:58 pm	Gemini
8th	1:54 am	Cancer
10th	3:56 am	Leo
12th	7:23 am	Virgo
14th	1:25 pm	Libra
16th	10:41 pm	Scorpio
19th	10:33 am	Sagittarius
21st	11:00 pm	Capricorn
24th	9:50 am	Aquarius
26th	5:51 pm	Pisces
28th	11:10 pm	Aries
31st	2:42 am	Taurus

September 1999
2nd	5:26 am	Gemini
4th	8:11 am	Cancer
6th	11:30 am	Leo
8th	3:58 pm	Virgo
10th	10:17 pm	Libra
13th	7:09 am	Scorpio
15th	6:36 pm	Sagittarius
18th	7:15 am	Capricorn
20th	6:39 pm	Aquarius
23rd	2:52 am	Pisces
25th	7:35 am	Aries
27th	9:52 am	Taurus
29th	11:22 am	Gemini

October 1999
1st	1:32 pm	Cancer
3rd	5:14 pm	Leo
5th	10:41 pm	Virgo
8th	5:53 am	Libra
10th	3:02 pm	Scorpio
13th	2:19 am	Sagittarius
15th	3:05 pm	Capricorn
18th	3:18 am	Aquarius
20th	12:34 pm	Pisces
22nd	5:43 pm	Aries
24th	7:26 pm	Taurus
26th	7:34 pm	Gemini
28th	8:10 pm	Cancer
30th	10:48 pm	Leo

November 1999
2nd	4:08 am	Virgo
4th	11:58 am	Libra
6th	9:47 pm	Scorpio
9th	9:16 am	Sagittarius
11th	10:01 pm	Capricorn
14th	10:47 am	Aquarius
16th	9:22 pm	Pisces
19th	3:58 am	Aries
21st	6:27 am	Taurus
23rd	6:15 am	Gemini
25th	5:30 am	Cancer
27th	6:20 am	Leo
29th	10:12 am	Virgo

December 1999
1st	5:30 pm	Libra
4th	3:36 am	Scorpio
6th	3:28 pm	Sagittarius
9th	4:15 am	Capricorn
11th	5:00 pm	Aquarius
14th	4:19 am	Pisces
16th	12:31 pm	Aries
18th	4:46 pm	Taurus
20th	5:40 pm	Gemini
22nd	4:53 pm	Cancer
24th	4:33 pm	Leo
26th	6:35 pm	Virgo
29th	0:15 am	Libra
31st	9:37 am	Scorpio

January 2000
2nd	9:33 pm	Sagittarius
5th	10:25 am	Capricorn
7th	10:54 pm	Aquarius
10th	10:00 am	Pisces
12th	6:49 pm	Aries
15th	0:39 am	Taurus
17th	3:26 am	Gemini
19th	4:02 am	Cancer
21st	3:59 am	Leo
23rd	5:08 am	Virgo
25th	9:10 am	Libra
27th	5:02 pm	Scorpio
30th	4:19 am	Sagittarius

February 2000
1st	5:11 pm	Capricorn
4th	5:32 am	Aquarius
6th	4:03 pm	Pisces
9th	0:18 am	Aries
11th	6:22 am	Taurus
13th	10:24 am	Gemini
15th	12:46 pm	Cancer
17th	2:12 pm	Leo
19th	3:54 pm	Virgo
21st	7:22 pm	Libra
24th	1:59 am	Scorpio
26th	12:11 pm	Sagittarius
29th	0:46 am	Capricorn

March 2000
2nd	1:15 pm	Aquarius
4th	11:31 pm	Pisces
7th	6:55 am	Aries
9th	12:02 pm	Taurus
11th	3:47 pm	Gemini
13th	6:52 pm	Cancer
15th	9:44 pm	Leo
18th	0:50 am	Virgo
20th	4:58 am	Libra
22nd	11:19 am	Scorpio
24th	8:44 pm	Sagittarius
27th	8:52 am	Capricorn
29th	9:35 pm	Aquarius

April 2000
1st	8:13 am	Pisces
3rd	3:23 pm	Aries
5th	7:30 pm	Taurus
7th	9:59 pm	Gemini
10th	0:17 am	Cancer
12th	3:17 am	Leo
14th	7:20 am	Virgo
16th	12:37 pm	Libra
18th	7:36 pm	Scorpio
21st	4:59 am	Sagittarius
23rd	4:48 pm	Capricorn
26th	5:43 am	Aquarius
28th	5:07 pm	Pisces

May 2000
1st	0:56 am	Aries
3rd	4:55 am	Taurus
5th	6:24 am	Gemini
7th	7:15 am	Cancer
9th	9:02 am	Leo
11th	12:42 pm	Virgo
13th	6:28 pm	Libra
16th	2:17 am	Scorpio
18th	12:10 pm	Sagittarius
21st	0:02 am	Capricorn
23rd	1:01 pm	Aquarius
26th	1:08 am	Pisces
28th	10:09 am	Aries
30th	3:03 pm	Taurus

June 2000
1st	4:35 pm	Gemini
3rd	4:31 pm	Cancer
5th	4:46 pm	Leo
7th	6:58 pm	Virgo
9th	12:00 am	Libra
12th	7:56 am	Scorpio
14th	6:19 pm	Sagittarius
17th	6:28 am	Capricorn
19th	7:27 pm	Aquarius
22nd	7:53 am	Pisces
24th	5:57 pm	Aries
27th	0:20 am	Taurus
29th	3:00 am	Gemini

July 2000
1st	3:10 am	Cancer
3rd	2:39 am	Leo
5th	3:20 am	Virgo
7th	6:48 am	Libra
9th	1:49 pm	Scorpio
12th	0:07 am	Sagittarius
14th	12:29 pm	Capricorn
17th	1:28 am	Aquarius
19th	1:45 pm	Pisces
22nd	0:10 am	Aries
24th	7:45 am	Taurus
26th	12:03 pm	Gemini
28th	1:31 pm	Cancer
30th	1:25 pm	Leo

August 2000
1st	1:28 pm	Virgo
3rd	3:32 pm	Libra
5th	9:05 pm	Scorpio
8th	6:31 am	Sagittarius
10th	6:45 pm	Capricorn
13th	7:44 am	Aquarius
15th	7:42 pm	Pisces
18th	5:45 am	Aries
20th	1:32 pm	Taurus
22nd	6:56 pm	Gemini
24th	10:01 pm	Cancer
26th	11:18 pm	Leo
28th	11:56 pm	Virgo
31st	1:34 am	Libra

September 2000
2nd	5:56 am	Scorpio
4th	2:09 pm	Sagittarius
7th	1:48 am	Capricorn
9th	2:46 pm	Aquarius
12th	2:35 am	Pisces
14th	12:01 pm	Aries
16th	7:06 pm	Taurus
19th	0:23 am	Gemini
21st	4:17 am	Cancer
23rd	7:01 am	Leo
25th	9:03 am	Virgo
27th	11:23 am	Libra
29th	3:31 pm	Scorpio

October 2000
1st	10:51 pm	Sagittarius
4th	9:43 am	Capricorn
6th	10:34 pm	Aquarius
9th	10:37 am	Pisces
11th	7:52 pm	Aries
14th	2:07 am	Taurus
16th	6:20 am	Gemini
18th	9:38 am	Cancer
20th	12:43 pm	Leo
22nd	3:53 pm	Virgo
24th	7:31 pm	Libra
27th	0:24 am	Scorpio
29th	7:41 am	Sagittarius
31st	6:30 pm	Capricorn

November 2000
3rd	6:42 am	Aquarius
5th	7:14 pm	Pisces
8th	5:03 am	Aries
10th	11:13 am	Taurus
12th	2:28 pm	Gemini
14th	4:22 pm	Cancer
16th	6:20 pm	Leo
18th	9:16 pm	Virgo
21st	1:36 am	Libra
23rd	7:34 am	Scorpio
25th	3:34 pm	Sagittarius
28th	1:58 am	Capricorn
30th	2:27 pm	Aquarius

December 2000
3rd	3:24 am	Pisces
5th	2:18 pm	Aries
7th	9:28 pm	Taurus
10th	0:51 am	Gemini
12th	1:50 am	Cancer
14th	2:10 am	Leo
16th	3:31 am	Virgo
18th	7:02 am	Libra
20th	1:13 pm	Scorpio
22nd	9:58 pm	Sagittarius
25th	8:55 am	Capricorn
27th	9:26 pm	Aquarius
30th	10:28 am	Pisces

VENUS CHARTS

1925
15 Jan	Cp
8 Feb	Aq
5 Mar	Pi
29 Mar	Ar
22 Apr	Ta
16 May	Ge
10 Jun	Ca
4 Jul	Le
29 Jul	Vi
23 Aug	Li
17 Sep	Sc
12 Oct	Sa
7 Nov	Cp
6 Dec	Aq

1926
6 Apr	Pi
7 May	Ar
3 Jun	Ta
29 Jun	Ge
25 Jul	Ca
19 Aug	Le
12 Sep	Vi
6 Oct	Li
30 Oct	Sc
23 Nov	Sa
17 Dec	Cp

1927
9 Jan	Aq
2 Feb	Pi
27 Feb	Ar
23 Mar	Ta
17 Apr	Ge
12 May	Ca
8 Jun	Le
8 Jul	Vi
10 Nov	Li
9 Dec	Sc

1928
3 Jan	Sa
29 Jan	Cp
23 Feb	Aq
18 Mar	Pi
12 Apr	Ar
6 May	Ta
30 May	Ge
24 Jun	Ca
18 Jul	Le
12 Aug	Vi
5 Sep	Li
29 Sep	Sc
24 Oct	Sa
17 Nov	Cp
12 Dec	Aq

1929
7 Jan	Pi
3 Feb	Ar
7 Mar	Ta
2 May	Ar
31 May	Ta
8 Jul	Ge
6 Aug	Ca
1 Sep	Le
27 Sep	Vi
21 Oct	Li
14 Nov	Sc
8 Dec	Sa

1930
24 Jan	Aq
17 Feb	Pi
13 Mar	Ar
6 Apr	Ta
30 Apr	Ge
25 May	Ca
19 Jun	Le
14 Jul	Vi
10 Aug	Li
7 Sep	Sc
12 Oct	Sa
22 Nov	Sc

1931
4 Jan	Sa
6 Feb	Cp
6 Mar	Aq
1 Apr	Pi
26 Apr	Ar
21 May	Ta
15 Jun	Ge
10 Jul	Ca
3 Aug	Le
27 Aug	Vi
21 Sep	Li
15 Oct	Sc
8 Nov	Sa
2 Dec	Cp
26 Dec	Aq

1932
19 Jan	Pi
13 Feb	Ar
9 Mar	Ta
5 Apr	Ge
6 May	Ca
13 Jul	Ge
29 Jul	Ca
9 Sep	Le
7 Oct	Vi
2 Nov	Li
27 Nov	Sc
21 Dec	Sa

1933
14 Jan	Cp
7 Feb	Aq
3 Mar	Pi
28 Mar	Ar
21 Apr	Ta
15 May	Ge
9 Jun	Ca
3 Jul	Le
28 Jul	Vi
22 Aug	Li
16 Sep	Sc
11 Oct	Sa
7 Nov	Cp
6 Dec	Aq

1934
6 Apr	Pi
6 May	Ar
2 Jun	Ta
28 Jun	Ge
24 Jul	Ca
18 Aug	Le
11 Sep	Vi
5 Oct	Li
29 Oct	Sc
22 Nov	Sa
16 Dec	Cp

1935
9 Jan	Aq
2 Feb	Pi
27 Feb	Ar
23 Mar	Ta
17 Apr	Ge
12 May	Ca
8 Jun	Le
8 Jul	Vi
10 Nov	Li
9 Dec	Sc

1936
3 Jan	Sa
29 Jan	Cp
23 Feb	Aq
18 Mar	Pi
12 Apr	Ar
6 May	Ta
30 May	Ge
24 Jun	Ca
18 Jul	Le
12 Aug	Vi
5 Sep	Li
29 Sep	Sc
24 Oct	Sa
17 Nov	Cp
12 Dec	Aq

1937
6 Jan	Pi
2 Feb	Ar
10 Mar	Ta
14 Apr	Ar
4 Jun	Ta
8 Jul	Ge
5 Aug	Cn
31 Aug	Le
25 Sep	Vi
20 Oct	Li
13 Nov	Sc
7 Dec	Sa
31 Dec	Cp

1938
23 Jan	Aq
16 Feb	Pi
12 Mar	Ar
6 Apr	Ta
30 Apr	Ge
25 May	Cn
19 Jun	Le
14 Jul	Vi
10 Aug	Li
7 Sep	Sc
14 Oct	Sa
16 Nov	Sc

1939
5 Jan	Sa
6 Feb	Cp
6 Mar	Aq
31 Mar	Pi
26 Apr	Ar
21 May	Ta
14 Jun	Ge
9 Jul	Cn
3 Aug	Le
27 Aug	Vi
20 Sep	Li
14 Oct	Sc
7 Nov	Sa
1 Dec	Cp

25 Dec	Aq

1940
19 Jan	Pi
12 Feb	Ar
9 Mar	Ta
5 Apr	Ge
7 May	Cn
6 Jul	Ge
1 Aug	Cn
9 Sep	Le
7 Oct	Vi
2 Nov	Li
27 Nov	Sc
21 Dec	Sa

1941
14 Jan	Cp
7 Feb	Aq
3 Mar	Pi
28 Mar	Ar
21 Apr	Ta
15 May	Ge
9 Jun	Ca
3 Jul	Le
28 Jul	Vi
22 Aug	Li
16 Sep	Sc
11 Oct	Sa
7 Nov	Cp
6 Dec	Aq

1942		**1943**		**1944**		**1945**		**1946**	
6 Apr	Pi	8 Jan	Aq	3 Jan	Sa	6 Jan	Pi	23 Jan	Aq
6 May	Ar	1 Feb	Pi	28 Jan	Cp	2 Feb	Ar	16 Feb	Pi
2 Jun	Ta	25 Feb	Ar	22 Feb	Aq	10 Mar	Ta	12 Mar	Ar
28 Jun	Ge	22 Mar	Ta	17 Mar	Pi	14 Apr	Ar	5 Apr	Ta
24 Jul	Ca	16 Apr	Ge	11 Apr	Ar	4 Jun	Ta	29 Apr	Ge
18 Aug	Le	11 May	Cn	5 May	Ta	8 Jul	Ge	24 May	Ca
11 Sep	Vi	8 Jun	Le	29 May	Ge	5 Aug	Cn	18 Jun	Le
5 Oct	Li	8 Jul	Vi	23 Jun	Cn	31 Aug	Le	14 Jul	Vi
29 Oct	Sc	10 Nov	Li	17 Jul	Le	25 Sep	Vi	9 Aug	Li
22 Nov	Sa	8 Dec	Sc	11 Aug	Vi	20 Oct	Li	7 Sep	Sc
16 Dec	Cp			4 Sep	Li	13 Nov	Sc	16 Oct	Sa
				28 Sep	Sc	7 Dec	Sa	8 Nov	Sc
				23 Oct	Sa	31 Dec	Cp		
				16 Nov	Cp				
				11 Dec	Aq				

1947		**1948**		**1949**		**1950**		**1951**		**1952**	
5 Jan	Sa	18 Jan	Pi	13 Jan	Cp	7 Apr	Pi	8 Jan	Aq	3 Jan	Sa
6 Feb	Cp	12 Feb	Ar	6 Feb	Aq	6 May	Ar	1 Feb	Pi	28 Jan	Cp
6 Mar	Aq	8 Mar	Ta	2 Mar	Pi	2 Jun	Ta	25 Feb	Ar	22 Feb	Aq
31 Mar	Pi	5 Apr	Ge	26 Mar	Ar	27 Jun	Ge	22 Mar	Ta	17 Mar	Pi
26 Apr	Ar	7 May	Ca	20 Apr	Ta	23 Jul	Ca	16 Apr	Ge	11 Apr	Ar
21 May	Ta	29 Jun	Ge	14 May	Ge	17 Aug	Le	11 May	Cn	5 May	Ta
14 Jun	Ge	3 Aug	Ca	7 Jun	Ca	10 Sep	Vi	8 Jun	Le	29 May	Ge
9 Jul	Cn	9 Sep	Le	2 Jul	Le	4 Oct	Li	8 Jul	Vi	23 Jun	Cn
3 Aug	Le	7 Oct	Vi	27 Jul	Vi	28 Oct	Sc	10 Nov	Li	17 Jul	Le
27 Aug	Vi	1 Nov	Li	21 Aug	Li	21 Nov	Sa	8 Dec	Sc	11 Aug	Vi
20 Sep	Li	26 Nov	Sc	15 Sep	Sc	14 Dec	Cp			4 Sep	Li
14 Oct	Sc	20 Dec	Sa	10 Oct	Sa					28 Sep	Sc
7 Nov	Sa			6 Nov	Cp					23 Oct	Sa
1 Dec	Cp			6 Dec	Aq					16 Nov	Cp
25 Dec	Aq									11 Dec	Aq

1953		**1954**		**1955**		**1956**		**1957**		**1958**	
5 Jan	Pi	22 Jan	Aq	6 Jan	Sa	18 Jan	Pi	13 Jan	Cp	7 Apr	Pi
2 Feb	Ar	15 Feb	Pi	6 Feb	Cp	11 Feb	Ar	6 Feb	Aq	6 May	Ar
15 Mar	Ta	11 Mar	Ar	5 Mar	Aq	8 Mar	Ta	2 Mar	Pi	2 Jun	Ta
31 Mar	Ar	4 Apr	Ta	30 Mar	Pi	4 Apr	Ge	26 Mar	Ar	27 Jun	Ge
5 Jun	Ta	29 Apr	Ge	25 Apr	Ar	8 May	Ca	20 Apr	Ta	23 Jul	Ca
7 Jul	Ge	24 May	Ca	20 May	Ta	23 Jun	Ge	14 May	Ge	17 Aug	Le
4 Aug	Ca	18 Jun	Le	13 Jun	Ge	4 Aug	Ca	7 Jun	Ca	10 Sep	Vi
30 Aug	Le	13 Jul	Vi	8 Jul	Ca	8 Sep	Le	2 Jul	Le	4 Oct	Li
24 Aug	Vi	9 Aug	Li	1 Aug	Le	6 Oct	Vi	27 Jul	Vi	28 Oct	Sc
19 Oct	Li	7 Sep	Sc	26 Aug	Vi	1 Nov	Li	21 Aug	Li	21 Nov	Sa
12 Nov	Sc	24 Oct	Sa	19 Sep	Li	26 Nov	Sc	15 Sep	Sc	14 Dec	Cp
6 Dec	Sa	27 Oct	Sc	13 Oct	Sc	20 Dec	Sa	10 Oct	Sa		
30 Dec	Cp			6 Nov	Sa			6 Nov	Cp		
				30 Nov	Cp			6 Dec	Aq		
				24 Dec	Aq						

1959		**1960**		**1961**		**1962**		**1963**		**1964**	
7 Jan	Aq	2 Jan	Sa	5 Jan	Pi	22 Jan	Aq	6 Jan	Sa	17 Jan	Pi
31 Jan	Pi	27 Jan	Cp	2 Feb	Ar	15 Feb	Pi	6 Feb	Cp	11 Feb	Ar
24 Feb	Ar	21 Feb	Aq	6 Jun	Ta	11 Mar	Ar	5 Mar	Aq	8 Mar	Ta
21 Mar	Ta	16 Mar	Pi	7 Jul	Ge	4 Apr	Ta	30 Mar	Pi	4 Apr	Ge
15 Apr	Ge	9 Apr	Ar	4 Aug	Ca	28 Apr	Ge	25 Apr	Ar	9 May	Ca
11 May	Ca	4 May	Ta	30 Aug	Le	23 May	Ca	20 May	Ta	18 Jun	Ge
7 Jun	Le	28 May	Ge	24 Sep	Vi	17 Jun	Le	13 Jun	Ge	5 Aug	Ca
9 Jul	Vi	22 Jun	Ca	18 Oct	Li	13 Jul	Vi	8 Jul	Ca	8 Sep	Le
20 Sep	Le	16 Jul	Le	11 Nov	Sc	9 Aug	Li	1 Aug	Le	6 Oct	Vi
25 Sep	Vi	9 Aug	Vi	5 Dec	Sa	7 Sep	Sc	26 Aug	Vi	31 Oct	Li
10 Nov	Li	3 Sep	Li	29 Dec	Cp			19 Sep	Li	25 Nov	Sc
8 Dec	Sc	27 Sep	Sc					13 Oct	Sc	19 Dec	Sa
		22 Oct	Sa					6 Nov	Sa		
		15 Nov	Cp					30 Nov	Cp		
		10 Dec	Aq					24 Dec	Aq		

1965		1966		1967		1968		1969		1970	
12 Jan	Cp	6 Feb	Cp	7 Jan	Aq	2 Jan	Sa	5 Jan	Pi	22 Jan	Aq
5 Feb	Aq	25 Feb	Aq	31 Jan	Pi	27 Jan	Cp	2 Feb	Ar	15 Feb	Pi
1 Mar	Pi	7 Apr	Pi	24 Feb	Ar	21 Feb	Aq	6 Jun	Ta	11 Mar	Ar
25 Mar	Ar	5 May	Ar	20 Mar	Ta	16 Mar	Pi	7 Jul	Ge	4 Apr	Ta
19 Apr	Ta	1 Jun	Ta	14 Apr	Ge	9 Apr	Ar	4 Aug	Ca	28 Apr	Ge
13 May	Ge	26 Jun	Ge	10 May	Ca	4 May	Ta	30 Aug	Le	23 May	Ca
6 Jun	Ca	22 Jul	Ca	7 Jun	Le	28 May	Ge	24 Sep	Vi	17 Jun	Le
1 Jul	Le	16 Aug	Le	9 Jul	Vi	22 Jun	Ca	18 Oct	Li	13 Jul	Vi
26 Jul	Vi	9 Sep	Vi	9 Sep	Le	16 Jul	Le	11 Nov	Sc	9 Aug	Li
20 Aug	Li	3 Oct	Li	2 Oct	Vi	9 Aug	Vi	5 Dec	Sa	7 Sep	Sc
14 Sep	Sc	27 Oct	Sc	10 Nov	Li	3 Sep	Li	29 Dec	Cp		
10 Oct	Sa	20 Nov	Sa	7 Dec	Sc	27 Sep	Sc				
6 Nov	Cp	14 Dec	Cp			22 Oct	Sa				
7 Dec	Aq					15 Nov	Cp				
						10 Dec	Aq				

1971		1972		1973		1974		1975		1976	
7 Jan	Sa	17 Jan	Pi	12 Jan	Cp	30 Jan	Cp	6 Jan	Aq	2 Jan	Sa
6 Feb	Cp	10 Feb	Ar	5 Feb	Aq	1 Mar	Aq	30 Jan	Pi	27 Jan	Cp
4 Mar	Aq	7 Mar	Ta	1 Mar	Pi	7 Apr	Pi	23 Feb	Ar	21 Feb	Aq
30 Mar	Pi	4 Apr	Ge	25 Mar	Ar	5 May	Ar	20 Mar	Ta	16 Mar	Pi
24 Apr	Ar	11 May	Ca	19 Apr	Ta	31 May	Ta	14 Apr	Ge	9 Apr	Ar
19 May	Ta	12 Jun	Ge	13 May	Ge	26 Jun	Ge	10 May	Ca	4 May	Ta
12 Jun	Ge	6 Aug	Ca	6 Jun	Ca	21 Jul	Ca	6 Jun	Le	28 May	Ge
7 Jul	Ca	8 Sep	Le	1 Jul	Le	15 Aug	Le	9 Jul	Vi	22 Jun	Ca
31 Jul	Le	5 Oct	Vi	26 Jul	Vi	8 Sep	Vi	3 Sep	Le	16 Jul	Le
25 Aug	Vi	31 Oct	Li	20 Aug	Li	3 Oct	Li	4 Oct	Vi	9 Aug	Vi
18 Sep	Li	25 Nov	Sc	14 Sep	Sc	27 Oct	Sc	10 Nov	Li	3 Sep	Li
12 Oct	Sc	19 Dec	Sa	10 Oct	Sa	19 Nov	Sa	7 Dec	Sc	27 Sep	Sc
5 Nov	Sa			6 Nov	Cp	13 Dec	Cp			22 Oct	Sa
29 Nov	Cp			7 Dec	Aq					15 Nov	Cp
23 Dec	Aq									10 Dec	Aq

1977		1978		1979		1980		1981		1982	
5 Jan	Pi	22 Jan	Aq	7 Jan	Sa	16 Jan	Pi	11 Jan	Cp	23 Jan	Cp
2 Feb	Ar	15 Feb	Pi	6 Feb	Cp	10 Feb	Ar	4 Feb	Aq	2 Mar	Aq
6 Jun	Ta	11 Mar	Ar	4 Mar	Aq	7 Mar	Ta	28 Feb	Pi	7 Apr	Pi
7 Jul	Ge	4 Apr	Ta	30 Mar	Pi	4 Apr	Ge	24 Mar	Ar	5 May	Ar
4 Aug	Ca	28 Apr	Ge	24 Apr	Ar	13 May	Ca	18 Apr	Ta	31 May	Ta
30 Aug	Le	23 May	Ca	19 May	Ta	5 Jun	Ge	12 May	Ge	26 Jun	Ge
24 Sep	Vi	17 Jun	Le	12 Jun	Ge	7 Aug	Ca	5 Jun	Ca	21 Jul	Ca
18 Oct	Li	13 Jul	Vi	7 Jul	Ca	8 Sep	Le	30 Jun	Le	14 Aug	Le
11 Nov	Sc	9 Aug	Li	31 Jul	Le	5 Oct	Vi	25 Jul	Vi	8 Sep	Vi
5 Dec	Sa	7 Sep	Sc	25 Aug	Vi	30 Oct	Li	19 Aug	Li	2 Oct	Li
29 Dec	Cp			18 Sep	Li	24 Nov	Sc	13 Sep	Sc	26 Oct	Sc
				12 Oct	Sc	18 Dec	Sa	9 Oct	Sa	19 Nov	Sa
				5 Nov	Sa			6 Nov	Cp	13 Dec	Cp
				29 Nov	Cp			9 Dec	Aq		
				23 Dec	Aq						

1983		1984		1985		1986		1987		1988	
6 Jan	Aq	1 Jan	Sa	4 Jan	Pi	20 Jan	Aq	7 Jan	Sa	16 Jan	Pi
30 Jan	Pi	26 Jan	Cp	2 Feb	Ar	13 Feb	Pi	5 Feb	Cp	10 Feb	Ar
23 Feb	Ar	19 Feb	Aq	6 Jun	Ta	9 Mar	Ar	3 Mar	Aq	6 Mar	Ta
19 Mar	Ta	15 Mar	Pi	6 Jul	Ge	2 Apr	Ta	29 Mar	Pi	4 Apr	Ge
13 Apr	Ge	8 Apr	Ar	2 Aug	Ca	27 Apr	Ge	23 Apr	Ar	18 May	Ca
9 May	Ca	2 May	Ta	28 Aug	Le	22 May	Ca	17 May	Ta	27 May	Ge
6 Jun	Le	27 May	Ge	22 Sep	Vi	16 Jun	Le	11 Jun	Ge	7 Aug	Ca
10 Jul	Vi	20 Jun	Ca	17 Oct	Li	12 Jul	Vi	6 Jul	Ca	7 Sep	Le
27 Aug	Le	14 Jul	Le	10 Nov	Sc	8 Aug	Li	30 Jul	Le	5 Oct	Vi
6 Oct	Vi	8 Aug	Vi	4 Dec	Sa	7 Sep	Sc	24 Aug	Vi	30 Oct	Li
9 Nov	Li	1 Sep	Li	27 Dec	Cp			17 Sep	Li	24 Nov	Sc
7 Dec	Sc	25 Sep	Sc					11 Oct	Sc	18 Dec	Sa
		20 Oct	Sa					4 Nov	Sa		
		14 Nov	Cp					28 Nov	Cp		
		9 Dec	Aq					22 Dec	Aq		

1989		1990		1991		1992		1993		1994	
11 Jan	Cp	17 Jan	Cp	5 Jan	Aq	25 Jan	Cp	4 Jan	Pi	20 Jan	Aq
4 Feb	Aq	4 Mar	Aq	29 Jan	Pi	19 Feb	Aq	3 Feb	Ar	13 Feb	Pi
28 Feb	Pi	6 Apr	Pi	22 Feb	Ar	14 Mar	Pi	6 Jun	Ta	9 Mar	Ar
24 Mar	Ar	4 May	Ar	19 Mar	Ta	7 Apr	Ar	6 Jul	Ge	2 Apr	Ta
17 Apr	Ta	30 May	Ta	13 Apr	Ge	2 May	Ta	2 Aug	Ca	26 Apr	Ge
11 May	Ge	25 Jun	Ge	9 May	Ca	26 May	Ge	28 Aug	Le	21 May	Ca
5 Jun	Ca	20 Jul	Ca	6 Jun	Le	19 Jun	Ca	22 Sep	Vi	15 Jun	Le
29 Jun	Le	14 Aug	Le	11 Jul	Vi	14 Jul	Le	16 Oct	Li	11 Jul	Vi
24 Jul	Vi	7 Sep	Vi	22 Aug	Le	7 Aug	Vi	9 Nov	Sc	8 Aug	Li
18 Aug	Li	2 Oct	Li	7 Oct	Vi	1 Sep	Li	3 Dec	Sa	8 Sep	Sc
13 Sep	Sc	26 Oct	Sc	9 Nov	Li	25 Sep	Sc	27 Dec	Cp		
9 Oct	Sa	18 Nov	Sa	6 Dec	Sc	20 Oct	Sa				
5 Nov	Cp	12 Dec	Cp	1 Jan	Sa	14 Nov	Cp				
10 Dec	Aq					9 Dec	Aq				

1995		1996		1997		1998		1999		2000	
8 Jan	Sa	15 Jan	Pi	10 Jan	Cp	10 Jan	Cp	5 Jan	Aq	25 Jan	Cp
5 Feb	Cp	9 Feb	Ar	3 Feb	Aq	5 Mar	Aq	29 Jan	Pi	18 Feb	Aq
3 Mar	Aq	6 Mar	Ta	27 Feb	Pi	6 Apr	Pi	22 Feb	Ar	13 Mar	Pi
28 Mar	Pi	4 Apr	Ge	23 Mar	Ar	4 May	Ar	18 Mar	Ta	7 Apr	Ar
22 Apr	Ar	7 Aug	Ca	16 Apr	Ta	30 May	Ta	13 Apr	Ge	1 May	Ta
17 May	Ta	7 Sep	Le	11 May	Ge	25 Jun	Ge	8 May	Ca	26 May	Ge
11 Jun	Ge	4 Oct	Vi	4 Jun	Ca	20 Jul	Ca	6 Jun	Le	19 Jun	Ca
5 Jul	Ca	30 Oct	Li	29 Jun	Le	13 Aug	Le	13 Jul	Vi	13 Jul	Le
30 Jul	Le	23 Nov	Sc	24 Jul	Vi	7 Sep	Vi	16 Aug	Le	7 Aug	Vi
23 Aug	Vi	17 Dec	Sa	18 Aug	Li	1 Nov	Li	8 Oct	Vi	31 Aug	Li
16 Sep	Li			12 Sep	Sc	25 Oct	Sc	9 Nov	Li	25 Sep	Sc
10 Oct	Sc			8 Oct	Sa	18 Nov	Sa	6 Dec	Sc	19 Oct	Sa
3 Nov	Sa			5 Nov	Cp	12 Dec	Cp	31 Dec	Sa	13 Nov	Cp
28 Nov	Cp			12 Dec	Aq					8 Dec	Aq
22 Dec	Aq										

MARS CHARTS

1925
5 Feb Ta
24 Mar Ge
10 May Ca
26 Jun Le
13 Aug Vi
29 Sep Li
14 Nov Sc
28 Dec Sa

1926
9 Feb Cp
23 Mar Aq
4 May Pi
15 Jun Ar
1 Aug Ta

1927
22 Feb Ge
17 Apr Ca
6 Jun Le
25 Jul Vi
11 Sep Li
26 Oct Sc
8 Dec Sa

1928
19 Jan Ca
28 Feb Aq
8 Apr Pi
17 May Ar
26 Jun Ta
9 Aug Ge
3 Oct Ca
20 Dec Ge

1929
11 Mar Ca
13 May Le
4 Jul Vi
22 Aug Li
7 Oct Sc
19 Nov Sa
29 Dec Cp

1930
7 Feb Aq
17 Mar Pi
25 Apr Ar
3 Jun Ta
15 Jul Ge
28 Aug Ca
21 Oct Le

1931
17 Feb Ca
30 Mar Le
11 Jun Vi
2 Aug Li
17 Sep Sc
31 Oct Sa
10 Dec Cp

1932
18 Jan Aq
25 Feb Pi
3 Apr Ar
12 May Ta
22 Jun Ge
5 Aug Ca
21 Sep Le
14 Nov Vi

1933
7 Jul Li
26 Aug Sc
9 Oct Sa
19 Nov Cp
28 Dec Aq

1934
4 Feb Pi
14 Mar Ar
23 Apr Ta
3 Jun Ge
16 Jul Ca
31 Aug Le
18 Oct Vi
11 Dec Li

1935
30 Jul Sc
17 Sep Sa
29 Oct Cp
7 Dec Aq

1936
15 Jan Pi
22 Feb Ar
2 Apr Ta
13 May Ge
26 Jun Ca
10 Aug Le
27 Sep Vi
15 Nov Li

1937
6 Jan Sc
13 Mar Sa
15 May Sc
9 Aug Sa
30 Sep Cp
12 Nov Aq
22 Dec Pi

1938
31 Jan Ar
12 Mar Ta
24 Apr Ge
7 Jun Ca
23 Jul Le
8 Sep Vi
25 Oct Li
12 Dec Sc

1939
29 Jan Sa
21 Mar Cp
25 May Aq
22 Jul Cp
24 Sep Aq
20 Nov Pi

1940
4 Jan Ar
17 Feb Ta
2 Apr Ge
18 May Ca
3 Jul Le
20 Aug Vi
6 Oct Li
21 Nov Sc

1941
5 Jan Sa
18 Feb Cp
2 Apr Aq
16 May Pi
2 Jul Ar

1942
12 Jan Ta
7 Mar Ge
26 Apr Ca
14 Jun Le
1 Aug Vi
17 Sep Li
2 Nov Sc
16 Dec Sa

1943
27 Jan Cp
9 Mar Aq
17 Apr Pi
27 May Ar
8 Jul Ta
24 Aug Ge

1944
28 Mar Ca
23 May Le
12 Jul Vi
29 Aug Li
13 Oct Sc
26 Nov Sa

1945
6 Jan Cp
14 Feb Aq
25 Mar Pi
3 May Ar
11 Jun Ta
23 Jul Ge
8 Sep Ca
12 Nov Le
27 Dec Ca

1946
23 Apr Le
20 Jun Vi
10 Aug Li
25 Sep Sc
7 Nov Sa
17 Dec Cp

1947
25 Jan Aq
5 Mar Pi
12 Apr Ar
21 May Ta
1 Jul Ge
14 Aug Ca
1 Oct Le
1 Dec Vi

1948
12 Feb Le
19 May Vi
17 Jul Li
4 Sep Sc
17 Oct Sa
27 Nov Cp

1949
5 Jan Aq
12 Feb Pi
22 Mar Ar
30 Apr Ta
10 Jun Ge
23 Jul Ca
7 Sep Le
27 Oct Vi
26 Dec Li

1950
28 Mar Vi
12 Jun Li
11 Aug Sc
26 Sep Sa
6 Nov Cp
15 Dec Aq

1951
23 Jan Pi
2 Mar Ar
10 Apr Ta
22 May Ge
4 Jul Ca
18 Aug Le
5 Oct Vi
24 Nov Li

1952
20 Jan Sc
28 Aug Sa
12 Oct Cp
22 Nov Aq
31 Dec Pi

1953
8 Feb Ar
20 Mar Ta
1 May Ge
14 Jun Ca
30 Jul Le
15 Sep Vi
2 Nov Li
20 Dec Sc

1954
10 Feb Sa
13 Apr Cp
3 Jul Sa
25 Aug Cp
22 Oct Aq
4 Dec Pi

1955
15 Jan Ar
26 Feb Ta
11 Apr Ge
26 May Ca
11 Jul Le
27 Aug Vi
13 Oct Li
29 Nov Sc

1956
14 Jan Sa
29 Feb Cp
15 Apr Aq
3 Jun Pi
6 Dec Ar

1957
29 Jan Ta
18 Mar Ge
5 May Ca
22 Jun Le
8 Aug Vi
24 Sep Li
9 Nov Sc
23 Dec Sa

1958
4 Feb Cp
17 Mar Aq
27 Apr Pi
7 Jun Ar
21 Jul Ta
21 Sep Ge
29 Oct Ta

1959
11 Feb Ge
10 Apr Ca
1 Jun Le
20 Jul Vi
6 Sep Li
21 Oct Sc
4 Dec Sa

1960
14 Jan Cp
23 Feb Aq
2 Apr Pi
11 May Ar
20 Jun Ta
2 Aug Ge
21 Sep Ca

1961
6 May Le
29 Jun Vi
17 Aug Li
2 Oct Sc
14 Nov Sa
25 Dec Cp

1962		1963		1964		1965		1966		1967	
2 Feb	Aq	3 Jun	Vi	13 Jan	Aq	29 Jun	Li	30 Jan	Pi	12 Feb	Sc
12 Mar	Pi	27 Jul	Li	20 Feb	Pi	21 Aug	Sc	10 Mar	Ar	31 Mar	Li
20 Apr	Ar	12 Sep	Sc	29 Mar	Ar	4 Oct	Sa	18 Apr	Ta	20 Jul	Sc
29 May	Ta	26 Oct	Sa	8 May	Ta	14 Nov	Cp	29 May	Ge	10 Sep	Sa
9 Jul	Ge	5 Dec	Cp	17 Jun	Ge	23 Dec	Aq	11 Jul	Ca	23 Oct	Sc
22 Aug	Ca			31 Jul	Ca			26 Aug	Le	2 Dec	Aq
12 Oct	Le			15 Sep	Le			13 Oct	Vii		
				6 Nov	Vi			4 Dec	Li		

1968		1969		1970		1971		1972		1973	
9 Jan	Pi	25 Feb	Sa	25 Jan	Ar	23 Jan	Sa	11 Feb	Ta	12 Feb	Cp
17 Feb	Ar	21 Sep	Cp	7 Mar	Ta	12 Mar	Cp	27 Mar	Ge	27 Mar	Aq
28 Mar	Ta	5 Nov	Aq	19 Apr	Ge	4 May	Aq	13 May	Ca	8 May	Pi
9 May	Ge	16 Dec	Pi	2 Jun	Ca	7 Nov	Pi	29 Jun	Le	21 Jun	Ar
21 Jun	Ca			18 Jul	Le	27 Dec	Ar	15 Aug	Vi	13 Aug	Ta
6 Aug	Le			3 Sep	Vi			1 Oct	Li	30 Oct	Ar
22 Sep	Vi			20 Oct	Li			16 Nov	Sc	24 Dec	Ta
9 Nov	Li			7 Dec	Sc			31 Dec	Sa		
30 Dec	Sc										

1974		1975		1976		1977		1978		1979	
27 Feb	Ge	22 Jan	Ca	19 Mar	Ca	1 Jan	Cp	26 Jan	Ca	21 Jan	Aq
20 Apr	Ca	3 Mar	Aq	16 May	Le	10 Feb	Aq	11 Apr	Le	28 Feb	Pi
9 Jun	Le	12 Apr	Pi	7 Jul	Vi	20 Mar	Pi	14 Jun	Vi	7 Apr	Ar
28 Jul	Vi	21 May	Ar	24 Aug	Li	28 Apr	Ar	4 Aug	Li	16 May	Ta
13 Sep	Li	1 Jul	Ta	9 Oct	Sc	6 Jun	Ta	20 Sep	Sc	26 Jun	Ge
28 Oct	Sc	15 Aug	Ge	21 Nov	Sa	18 Jul	Ge	2 Nov	Sa	9 Aug	Ca
11 Dec	Sa	17 Oct	Ca			1 Sep	Ca	13 Dec	Cp	25 Sep	Le
		26 Nov	Ge			27 Oct	Le			20 Nov	Vi

1980		1981		1982		1983		1984		1985	
12 Mar	Le	7 Feb	Pi	3 Aug	Sc	18 Jan	Pi	11 Jan	Sc	3 Feb	Ar
4 May	Vi	17 Mar	Ar	20 Sep	Sa	25 Feb	Ar	18 Aug	Sa	15 Mar	Ta
11 Jul	Li	25 Apr	Ta	1 Nov	Cp	6 Apr	Ta	5 Oct	Cp	26 Apr	Ge
29 Aug	Sc	5 Jun	Ge	10 Dec	Aq	17 May	Ge	16 Nov	Aq	9 Jun	Ca
12 Oct	Sa	18 Jul	Ca			29 Jun	Ca	25 Dec	Pi	25 Jul	Le
22 Nov	Cp	2 Sep	Le			14 Aug	Le			10 Sep	Vi
31 Dec	Aq	21 Oct	Vi			30 Sep	Vi			28 Oct	Li
		16 Dec	Li			18 Nov	Li			15 Dec	Sc

1986		1987		1988		1989		1990		1991	
2 Feb	Sa	9 Jan	Ar	9 Jan	Sa	19 Jan	Ta	30 Jan	Cp	21 Jan	Ge
28 Mar	Cp	21 Feb	Ta	22 Feb	Cp	11 Mar	Ge	12 Mar	Aq	3 Apr	Ca
9 Oct	Aq	6 Apr	Ge	7 Apr	Aq	29 Apr	Ca	21 Apr	Pi	27 May	Le
26 Nov	Pi	21 May	Ca	22 May	Pi	17 Jun	Le	31 May	Ar	16 Jul	Vi
		7 Jul	Le	14 Jul	Ar	4 Aug	Vi	13 Jul	Ta	1 Sep	Li
		23 Aug	Vi	24 Oct	Pi	20 Sep	Li	31 Aug	Ge	17 Oct	Sc
		9 Oct	Li	2 Nov	Ar	4 Nov	Sc	14 Dec	Ta	29 Nov	Sa
		24 Nov	Sc			18 Dec	Sa				

1992		1993		1994		1995		1996		1997	
9 Jan	Cp	28 Apr	Le	28 Jan	Aq	23 Jan	Le	8 Jan	Aq	3 Jan	Li
18 Feb	Aq	23 Jun	Vi	7 Mar	Pi	26 May	Vi	15 Feb	Pi	9 Mar	Vi
28 Mar	Pi	12 Aug	Li	15 Apr	Ar	21 Jul	Li	25 Mar	Ar	19 Jun	Li
6 May	Ar	27 Sep	Sc	24 May	Ta	7 Sep	Sc	3 May	Ta	14 Aug	Sc
15 Jun	Ta	9 Nov	Sa	4 Jul	Ge	21 Oct	Sa	13 Jun	Ge	29 Sep	Sa
27 Jul	Ge	20 Dec	Cp	17 Aug	Ca	1 Dec	Cp	26 Jul	Ca	9 Nov	Cp
12 Sep	Ca			5 Oct	Le			10 Sep	Le	18 Dec	Aq
				12 Dec	Vi			30 Oct	Vi		

1998		1999		2000	
25 Jan	Pi	26 Jan	Sc	4 Jan	Pi
5 Mar	Ar	6 May	Li	12 Feb	Ar
13 Apr	Ta	5 Jul	Sc	23 Mar	Ta
24 May	Ge	3 Sep	Sa	4 May	Ge
6 Jul	Ca	17 Oct	Cp	17 Jun	Ca
21 Aug	Le	26 Nov	Aq	1 Aug	Le
8 Oct	Vi			17 Sep	Vi
27 Nov	Li			4 Nov	Li
				24 Dec	Sc

INDEX